Holiday Greetings

To: CALVIN

From: TOM

HONORABLE WARRIOR

HONORABLE WARRIOR

General Harold K. Johnson and the Ethics of Command

Lewis Sorley

University Press of Kansas

© 1998 by the University Press of Kansas
All rights reserved

Published by the University Press of Kansas (Lawrence, Kansas 66049),
which was organized by the Kansas Board of Regents and is operated
and funded by Emporia State University, Fort Hays State University,
Kansas State University, Pittsburg State University, the University of
Kansas, and Wichita State University

Library of Congress Cataloging-in-Publication Data

Sorley, Lewis, 1934–
Honorable warrior : General Harold K. Johnson and the ethics of
command / Lewis Sorley.
p.   cm.
Includes bibliographical references and index.
ISBN 0-7006-0886-9 (cloth : alk. paper)
1. Johnson, Harold K. (Harold Keith), 1912–1983. 2. Generals
—United States—Biography. 3. United States. Army—Biography.
I. Title.
E745.J65S67   1998
355′.0092—dc21
[B]   97-49708

British Library Cataloguing in Publication Data is available.

Printed in the United States of America

10 9 8 7 6 5 4 3 2 1

The paper used in this publication meets the minimum requirements
of the American National Standard for Permanence of Paper for
Printed Library Materials Z39.48-1984.

FOR KATHY, DOUG, TIM, AND SUSAN,
FOUR GOOD ARMY BRATS,
WITH LOVE AND ADMIRATION

CONTENTS

Photo insert follows page 138.

PROLOGUE

On a nondescript morning early in September 1945, elements of the 7th Infantry Division went ashore near Inchon, Korea, the first U.S. troops to arrive after Japan's surrender in August ended World War II. There they made contact with a handful of gaunt, ragged, bony survivors of the thousands of American prisoners of war the Japanese had, in manic determination to prevent their liberation, evacuated from the Philippine Islands nearly three years before. Among these few was Colonel Harold K. Johnson, Infantry, West Point Class of 1933, late of the 57th Infantry (Philippine Scouts).

Brought through the long ordeal of the Bataan death march, the hell ships, Japanese neglect and brutality, illness, and starvation by unusual stamina, faith, a tough pioneer spirit, luck, and—as he became absolutely convinced—the special favors of divine providence, Johnson was at the nadir of his military career—but he was alive. In the following years he fought his way back to professional prominence, commanding a regiment with conspicuous gallantry in the Korean War, then by reason of character, ability, and incredible industry rising rapidly to become Army Chief of Staff. There he encountered endless new crises and challenges, most related to the deepening American involvement in the Vietnam War.

Working feverishly to expand the force and deploy more and more of it to Vietnam, Johnson found himself in fundamental disagreement with the war policies of President Lyndon Johnson and Secretary of Defense Robert McNamara and with the strategy and battlefield tactics of General William C. Westmoreland. For four difficult years he struggled with a series of practical and ethical challenges, at times close to resignation, but was ultimately sustained by his sense of duty, religious convictions, devotion to the soldier, and a strong and loving wife.

Harold K. Johnson's struggles with President Johnson, with Secretary McNamara and his associates, and with Air Force Chiefs of Staff General Curtis LeMay and General John P. McConnell raged through the tumultuous years of deepening American involvement in Vietnam. Those years are filled with "what ifs?" and "might have beens," illuminating the fundamental decisions and blunders of policy, strategy, and tactics that determined the failed outcome of a long, sad war and the crucial role of personalities in bringing that about.

Harold K. Johnson was at the heart of it in a lonely struggle to turn things around. Rejecting the "search and destroy" tactics and "attrition" strategy being employed by Westmoreland in Vietnam, Johnson in effect lived a double life. Publicly he supported the field command and the American effort at every turn; in this he had no choice. Behind the scenes, though, he worked desperately to get the tactics changed and, failing that, to get the commander in Vietnam replaced. It was a long fight, but by the time he retired in July 1968, Johnson had finally succeeded on both counts. Westmoreland was replaced by General Creighton Abrams, previously Johnson's Vice Chief of Staff and then Westmoreland's Deputy, who immediately implemented fundamental changes in conduct of the war that were based on his and Johnson's shared convictions as to what had to be done if success were to be achieved.

Harold K. Johnson came to these climactic responsibilities over a long road of austerity, testing, and faith. He rose from pioneer stock on the North Dakota plains, came out of West Point into the small, scattered, and impoverished Army of the Great Depression; fought the Japanese in the Philippines, survived the long ordeal of captivity, demonstrated brilliant combat leadership in the Korean War, then found that his severest tests still lay ahead in the crucible that was Vietnam. This is his story.

CHAPTER ONE

EARLY LIFE

Harold Keith Johnson came from pioneer stock. When he entered this life in Bowesmont, North Dakota (population 152), on 22 February 1912, that state was less than a quarter of a century old. Both of his parents—Harold Cecil Johnson and Edna May Thomson Johnson—had been born in Dakota Territory, children of immigrants from Scotland and Ireland by way of Canada. A prominent soldierly ancestor on his mother's side was Myles Standish, leader of Plymouth Colony's military defenders.

Those early settlers proved quite entrepreneurial. One of Johnson's grandfathers ran a general store that provided an impressive array of goods and services. Along with sections for general merchandise, hardware, and farm machinery, there was a funeral parlor. The owner was also the postmaster and still found time to manage an auto dealership. Johnson's mother often presided over the Pioneer Daughters Club, and Johnson himself received North Dakota Pioneer Certificate No. 17 signifying that he was descended from Dakota Territory settlers.

In later years Johnson would observe that "since my very earliest days, I've been involved with a diversity of people, not just one single group." That was because in the farming region where Johnson grew up, there were concentrations of immigrants of many nationalities, including French, Swedish, Norwegian, Czech, and Polish. At one point, Johnson's parents both took lessons in Norwegian in order to better communicate with their neighbors.

Even as a small child, Johnson knew everyone in the community, in part because the rural mail carrier was a close friend of the family and often took the boy along on his rounds. In winter they traveled by sleigh, and when someone invited them in to get warm, Johnson would be given a splash of coffee with lots of hot milk, a treat he remembered with relish.

When Johnson was eight, the family settled in Grafton, North Dakota (population 3,000), where his father worked as manager of the local lumberyard. Located in the northeastern corner of the state, only about forty miles below the Canadian border, Grafton was a remote community in a region of very severe winter weather but productive for farming the lush, green Red River valley.[1]

Johnson had three younger siblings—Janet, Edna Ray, and Herbert. His sisters were four and six years younger than he, and by the time his brother came along, Johnson was a junior in high school. In the family, Johnson was called Keith, and Janet remembered that "he was the big brother—*period!*" He was also the oldest grandchild on both sides of the family, so he was always treated as something special—his much younger brother's recollection is that Keith was always "the fair-haired boy."

Life was somewhat spartan for Johnson and his family in those days. The first house they had in Grafton was primitive, with no indoor plumbing, and Johnson recalled that "when bath time came on Saturday nights, you hauled ice in to melt it for water, or if the snow was deep enough you used snow because it melted faster. We went through the bath water in reverse order of age, the youngest first and the largest and dirtiest last. With a bath once a week and a change of clothes at that time, we were pretty fragrant when bath time came around."

Family life was the centerpiece of Johnson's formative years, along with a close-knit community. For Christmas the family always assembled at Johnson's maternal grandmother's. The gathering was so large that there had to be two sittings for Christmas dinner, separated by an interval for washing the dishes. For Sunday dinners, with lots of family in attendance, Johnson often sat on the kitchen floor to help make hand-cranked ice cream, then helped some more as the entire eight-quart freezer was consumed at a single meal. They went to county fairs and the state fair, and on summer Sundays to baseball games in which their town team played teams from other nearby communities. "I had a very rich childhood in terms of family gatherings," said Johnson.

Johnson's father was a prominent Mason, Master of the Crescent Lodge in Grafton, an alderman for several years, and a longtime member of St. James' Episcopal Church, one of a congregation of three that kept the little mission church alive. Family members recall that on one occasion when a circuit rider visited Grafton, the elder Johnson was the only person in the congregation.

Religion was an important part of Johnson's early experience. As a boy and a young man, he regularly attended Sunday school and church. When he was seven, his grandmother gave him a book of Bible stories for children, one of the first books he learned to read and a volume he treasured over the years and eventually passed on to a grandson. In Sunday school, Johnson was required to memorize verses from the Bible, and later in life he would often quote the Bible to make a point. Sometimes, too, he would recite an adage he had been taught as a child: "There is so much good in the worst of us, and so much bad in the best of us, that it hardly behooves any of us to talk about the rest of us."

On Sundays his grandmother hitched a team of horses to her buggy and drove two miles to a little country community hall. There she lit a fire in the potbellied stove, swept the place out, and conducted Sunday school, then closed things up and drove herself home again. In the summers she sometimes found an evangelist to conduct services every day for two weeks and let the preacher stay at her home. Later Johnson would say of his grandmother that she practiced the biblical injunction to "love thy neighbor as thyself" better than anyone he had ever known. All in all it was, Johnson acknowledged, "a pretty religious family."

Although baptized an Episcopalian, young Keith eventually joined the larger and more active Methodist Church. There, Pastor P. Hewison Pollock was also the Scoutmaster. Johnson regarded him with admiration and affection: "He was a fine little man, a fine preacher, and a wonderful influence on the boys who were in the scout troop as well." Johnson reached only the rank of Star Scout, but Scouting nevertheless became a lifelong interest for him. He would later recall for young Scouts his pleasure in "evenings around the campfire, and the singing, and the stories." Sometimes he would even mention the bugling contest he entered at summer camp. He didn't have a bugle, and by the time his letter reached home, and a bugle had been located and sent to him, the day of the contest was at hand. Johnson was forever grateful to the wise and kind leaders who declared the contest a tie despite his raucous rendition of the prescribed bugle calls.

Along with the religious influences, there was a pioneer work ethic. Johnson's grandfather milked twenty-five cows morning and night, and his grandmother could handle more than that. The youngster tried to do his share. "I got along where I could keep up and maybe get four done while she was doing ten," he remembered.

Every spring they took out the "stone boat," loading it with rocks removed from the fields so they wouldn't break a plow or hurt a horse. But come autumn, more rocks would have made their appearance, and out would come the stone boat again. Johnson later used that experience as a metaphor for life, pointing out that even though current problems have been solved, more problems inevitably lie ahead. Knowing that, expecting that, he argued, makes it easier to cope.

Johnson remembered his mother as always working to make things better for her family, but at the same time being a "generous volunteer." She was the choir director for the Methodist Church, where she also played the piano and organ. And she loved dramatics, putting on the Christmas program at church, giving dramatic readings, and taking part in community plays. Johnson attributed his own interest in dramatics and oratory to his mother's influence and twice competed in state declamation contests at the University of North Dakota. As a schoolboy, he was on occasion also chosen to deliver the Gettysburg Address. In later life, he sometimes mentioned that experience when citing Lincoln as a model for military leadership, a man of initiative who was also forthright, honest, smart, modest, and humble.

Not all the influences struck home. "My grandmother used to tell me that if you didn't toot your own horn," Johnson wrote to a friend, "no one else would toot it for you. I have never really believed this viewpoint." His modest conduct in later life, even as he reached high levels in his profession, reflected Johnson's contrary outlook.

Johnson survived the usual childhood scrapes, some rather exciting. At age six, he was allowed to help a neighbor move from one farm to another. Johnson's job was to drive a team of horses pulling a wagon loaded with goods, while the farmer on horseback herded his dairy cattle and a couple of sheep. Somewhere along the way they passed a mechanical potato digger that spooked the team. The horses took off at a gallop, with their youthful driver barely able to stay aboard by clinging with all his strength to the high spring seat. The farmer gave chase on horseback, running the team down and bringing it under control in three-quarters of a mile or so. This drama was played out on the road that passed Johnson's house, where his mother looked out just in time to see her young son careening by atop a runaway wagon. When she learned that he was unharmed, though, she allowed him to continue the work.

Johnson was greatly relieved, since his primary motivation for helping with the move was the fried chicken dinner with mashed potatoes and a lot of good chicken gravy that the farmer's wife would serve when the work was done. "It was a great experience," he said. Johnson's family wasn't poor, and he never went hungry, but that good dinner was worth working for, and he remembered it for a long time.

Johnson also vividly recalled at the age of ten or eleven being picked out of a ditch by the town doctor after running into someone's horse and buggy with his grandfather's Ford pickup. Apparently, driver's licenses were in those days not a consideration, and the transition from driving a tractor or a team to driving a truck on the roadway was rather casual.

Many summers were spent with grandparents or uncles, which usually meant working on one farm or another. Johnson felt that he got "a good, practical education" from those sojourns. "I was the butt of a good many jokes," he recalled, "but on the other hand I picked up a lot of information as well."

His paternal grandparents had relocated to northwestern Minnesota, settling miles from the nearest railroad, just below the Canadian border. Their home was built mostly of logs, caulked with clay and cattle dung. When Johnson spent the summers there, he slept in an unheated outbuilding that was also used for storage. The family had no car, traveling everywhere by horse and buggy. Johnson would often ride Midget, a pony his grandfather had given him. The animal and Johnson had been born in the same year, so they sort of grew up together. But Johnson's father wouldn't let the pony live at home in Grafton, so only on visits to his grandparents did the boy get to ride. Those summertime days were strenuous and busy, but happy and productive all the same.

Other vacation days were spent with Johnson's Uncle Ross, his mother's brother, who had a large farm. There Johnson learned to drive a team, sometimes handling a plow pulled by horses, mules, or mixed teams of horses and mules. "I've always had a love of animals," he would later say, attributing it to his early days of working on farms.

GRAFTON HIGH SCHOOL was small but active, with only twenty-eight people in Johnson's graduating class. "A lot of kids didn't go to high school in those days," he said, because their help was needed in the fields. Keith became known as "Curly," in keeping with his shock of wavy sandy hair. Often he ran the fourteen blocks from home to school, then ran to one of his after-school jobs, his curly blond hair waving in the wind. He was, said the *Walsh County Press,* "an outstanding athlete," a judgment Johnson considered grossly exaggerated.

One early job was working at Roy's Teapot Dome Filling Station, where Johnson pumped gas. That was a long way from where he eventually ended up, a fact noted by a Grafton resident's letter to Johnson when he became Chief of Staff: "While never doubting your ability, I never dreamed that Uncle Roy's 'grease monkey' would head the United States Army." As for Johnson, he later recalled candidly that pumping gas in Grafton was where he "learned the value of a dollar—perhaps too much so."

Schooling was taken seriously in Johnson's community, and many of his teachers had been at it for decades. One who stood out was Miss Cora Lykken, who was also the principal. "When I think of discipline, I think of Miss Lykken," Johnson said. "When I think of understanding, a sympathetic understanding, I think of Miss Lykken." She brought to the classroom a "basic combination of steadfastness of purpose and kindness to others."

For Johnson, though, the "true gem" was his math teacher, Ellen Carlson, whom he described as "another old maid devoted to her profession." By this time, he had developed an interest in attending the United States Military Academy at West Point, and to gain admission, he needed some instruction in higher mathematics. Miss Carlson said that she would conduct the course if eight students enrolled. Johnson rounded up his friends to make the quota, and Miss Carlson kept her end of the bargain. "She came in for an entire year an hour early to teach this special class in trigonometry and spherical geometry, courses that weren't normally offered," Johnson recalled with gratitude.

By the end of his third year, Johnson had enough total credits to graduate from high school but lacked a few that were compulsory. In his senior year, he took only the courses he needed to fill those gaps plus an extra science course to prepare for West Point, spending most of his time on work and sports.

With all his courses clustered in the morning, he was able to take on three different jobs. He made thirty dollars a month as a janitor at the post office, building a fire to heat the place and sweeping out the lobby, plus shoveling the walkway when it snowed. Then he carried special-delivery letters, earning another ten or fifteen dollars a month at the rate of eight cents a letter. And finally he had his job at the filling station, where he worked the noon hour as a relief man and came back for the evening shift. That brought in another thirty dollars a month.

He was also taking part in the school's drama program and playing football and basketball as well. Johnson admitted that he was no star in the sports department, "not good at all as a matter of fact." In substantiation he recalled one basketball game in which the man he was guarding scored the winning basket by tossing the ball back over his head as he went away from the basket. The "shot" went in, and Johnson's team lost by the astounding score of 6–5.

The last summer at home, he drove the oil truck for Roy's, making deliveries around town. That was after he had gotten up at 5:00 A.M. to wash the windshields of all the cars around the local hotel, afterward putting cards under the wipers inviting the owners to come to the Teapot Dome to fill their tanks. "I was pretty busy," said Johnson, and nobody disagreed with him on that.

The respect for the value of money that Johnson had acquired through all this hard work manifested itself at graduation, when "he refused to purchase a new suit for the occasion on the grounds that he would have no use for it at West Point. Much to the chagrin of his parents, [he] graduated wearing 'high waters,' at least three inches above the prescribed level."[2] He barely took time out to do even that. On graduation day, he had a job unloading a carload of flour. When it was time for the ceremony, he left off that task just long enough to slip into his old suit, receive his diploma (graduating with honors), then rush back to finish unloading the flour. It is not recorded how much of the flour may have accompanied him to school. Recalling the events of that busy day, Johnson later admitted that he might have had "some streak of stubbornness."

Johnson was the first boy from Grafton to attend West Point. He learned about the Military Academy from Alice Holt, a seventh-grade teacher who knew a recent graduate. Johnson was able to get an appointment to the Academy from the local congressman.[3] The main attractions for him, he would later say, were the adventure and the educational opportunity. "It seemed like an exciting thing to do for a boy from North Dakota who had never been very far from home," he wrote. "Second, it answered the problem of how I could receive a higher education." Even before West Point, he had begun his military career by enlisting in Company C, 164th Infantry, North Dakota National Guard.

Johnson and his classmates graduated from Grafton High School in the spring of 1929, just as the Great Depression was about to descend on America, armed with a class motto that counseled "build for character, not for fame." Many years later, at the height of his professional achievement, Johnson received a letter from Grafton in which an old friend observed that he "could not help but think that this was all of a great pattern for you, Keith, your Boy Scout training . . . your Christian home—nothing would be the same without that good boyhood start." Johnson agreed. "I look back on those days as great days," he wrote in response.

CHAPTER TWO

CADET DAYS

The United States Military Academy at West Point, New York, is situated on the Hudson River about fifty miles north of New York City. When it was time for Johnson to enter, he made his way to New York and was greeted by his uncle, an engineer who was building a subway tunnel, and his aunt. They showed him a bit of the city and then, on the last Sunday in June, accompanied him up the river aboard one of the Hudson River Day Liners then plying that route, depositing him at the Hotel Thayer. Johnson and his new classmates reported in the following day, 1 July 1929. Each entering cadet was required to deposit three hundred dollars to establish an account for uniform purchases and the like. "My folks didn't put up a nickel when I went in," said Johnson. All that hard work had paid off, and he covered travel expenses and the initial deposit from his earnings.

Johnson's career as a West Point cadet had almost been derailed before it began. The nearest place where he could take the entrance examination was Fort Snelling, Minnesota, near Minneapolis. When Johnson had traveled there by train the previous spring, a distance of some 375 miles, that was the farthest he had ever been from home. He hadn't felt very well on the trip, and when he reported in for his physical examination, he found out why. The first doctor who saw him immediately isolated him in a remote corner, then admitted him to the post hospital with a case of scarlet fever. There he languished for four weeks before recovering. Fortunately, he also passed all the examinations and, after appearing before a board of officers, was qualified for admission.

When Johnson's class entered West Point that summer of 1929, the Military Academy was small, insular, and austere. All cadets followed the same curriculum, the only variation being in the foreign language they elected to study. Not until the second Christmas of the four-year program were cadets authorized leave; until then, they remained at West Point. The barracks were spartan; the discipline firm, bordering on harsh; and the daily routine demanding, beginning with reveille at dawn. Not everyone completed the difficult course. Of the 470 who entered with the Class of 1933, only 347 would graduate four years later.

There had been only one other cadet from North Dakota in the Class of 1933, Leo Skeim from Minot. Skeim, along with classmate Alan Light, drowned while canoeing on the Hudson River in the spring of their third year. Also entering with the class was Alonzo Parham, remembered by Johnson as one of the first black cadets in many years. "He tried very hard to do what was expected of him," said Johnson, "but no one at all was friendly with him and no one helped him." The cadet cadre had issued instructions "to be scrupulously fair in our dealings with him, but the implication also was that our contacts with him would be limited to those that were necessary." "Both Johnny [Johnson's nickname] and I made some attempts to talk to him before we learned that wasn't allowed," said another classmate, Oren Hurlbut. Eventually Parham dropped out.

When Johnson reported to West Point to begin Beast Barracks, the rugged summer session of orientation training for new cadets, he carried a mere 132 pounds on his five foot ten inch frame. He had been working hard physically during his last year of high school, then suffered the bout of scarlet fever, so he was a bit runty at the time. Most people lost weight during that strenuous first summer as a cadet, especially since any infraction at the dining table could result in a plebe's being told to "sit up," to brace at attention instead of eating, but Johnson gained an astounding fifteen pounds. "We came, we saw, we were conquered," said a class publication of the Beast Barracks experience, but Johnson thrived on it.

Johnson at this point considered himself a "country boy," one who had not grown up in distressed circumstances but who had worked hard at a number of jobs. His academic preparation in rural schools had not equipped him to compete very effectively at first, so he ranked near the bottom of his class in the early going. Eventually, though, he worked his way up to a more secure position, standing at graduation 232d among the 347 receiving diplomas.

The Corps of Cadets was in those days organized into one regiment of twelve companies, arranged by height.[1] After Beast Barracks, Johnson was assigned to Company C. He and four classmates shared a room so cavernous that it was referred to as the "riding hall." The furnishings were austere, with an iron washstand and a bucket for water. The bath and toilet facilities were in the basement, four flights down. "I got used to it," said Johnson, who had not previously been much accustomed to luxury anyway.

He got along well with his peers. "Johnny was eminently sound and likable," said Edson Schull, one of his roommates. "He had a sense of humor, and readily saw the joke on himself." Neil Wallace, another roommate, agreed, remembering that Johnson "had a magnificent sense of humor."

In Johnson's cadet company all his classmates had nicknames, issued arbitrarily by Jimmy Skinner. Johnson, known earlier as Keith and Curly, now became "Olaf," by virtue of his skill in using a fake Scandinavian accent for humorous purposes. He was also called "Swede," that is, when he wasn't being hailed as "GOP," a reference to the Republican Party's symbolic elephant's resemblance, some claimed, to Johnson's prominent ears. Some in the group were even less lucky. Neil Wallace, for example, became known as "Droopy Drawers," while others were dubbed "The Duck," "Hoodlum," "Cowboy," and "The Brooklyn Doughboy." Some of these labels stuck for life.

Johnson was also now called "Johnny" by many, and that is how he referred to himself informally for the rest of his life—except, of course, with family and early friends, to whom he remained Keith. Those who did not know him personally often referred to him in speaking to others as "Harold K.," with the middle initial almost invariably a part of it.

As a plebe, Johnson accumulated the usual number of demerits, and for the usual things—shoulder belts too short at parade, one demerit; belts too long at Saturday inspection, one demerit. (Once while an upperclassman he missed his assigned train for the return from an Army-Pittsburgh football game, was reported by his tactical officer, Lieutenant Sorley, and received a quite merciful five demerits.)

The class spent yearling (sophomore) summer in encampment at West Point, following a crowded schedule of daily drill and parades, riding, weapons training, swimming classes, and dancing instruction under the tutelage of the legendary M. Vizay. In later years, they treasured the memory of a day on the rifle range when a fierce thunderstorm interrupted firing and sent all hands running for shelter. Once the storm had passed, the officer in charge reassembled his pupils and ordered: "All those who have completed the 500-yard range will move to the pits; those who have not will go to the firing line; those who have done neither, report to me!"

In Johnson's day, chapel attendance at West Point was compulsory, but he lapsed a bit from his pious upbringing, claiming that he was adept at "getting up on the balcony where you could stretch out on the floor and sleep during service." During these same years, the Methodist Church, which Johnson had joined as a young man, was much involved in the pacifist movement, or so it seemed to Johnson. During a summer-long furlough at home after yearling year, he took the certificate of church membership off the wall of his room and returned it to the pastor. "If the Methodist Church is preaching pacifism," he declared, "I don't want any part of you."

Later he would write that, although he had made many far-reaching tactical and strategic decisions in his military career, perhaps the most compelling involved his personal relationship with the church. When his denomination joined the pacifist movement, said Johnson, "I could not accept that decision because I have never believed that God intended that force in the hands of those who would use it wrongly should go unchallenged." For the rest of his life, although he was widely, and accurately, viewed as a very religious man, Johnson steered clear of affiliation with any particular denomination.

During that same summer leave, Johnson returned temporarily to his old job at the Teapot Dome, where, he said, he "wrestled oil drums" as a matter of necessity. "I had to earn enough money to get back to school and to support myself during the summer," he later told a nephew.

Johnson described his own achievements as a cadet in modest terms. "I was not prominent in the class," he told an interviewer, "and I suppose to a degree maybe [I was] a modest part of the Mafia of the class. Maybe not Mafia, but the structure that would have been voted least likely to succeed if votes were taken at the time." In an admission that seems surprising, given his background, he added: "I did an awful lot of gambling as a cadet. I was a pretty fair crapshooter." In addition to that, "in my second class year, several of us organized a football pool, which was strictly illegal." Nevertheless, Johnson's entry in the *Howitzer,* the cadet yearbook, listed "the crowning achievement of his four years—a success in the form of the golden chevrons of Sergeant."

As an upperclassman, Johnson did not take a harsh and aggressive approach to training the plebes, as many others did. One man recalled Johnson's "gentle, fatherly voice advising Ryder [a classmate] and me to follow the paths of righteousness." That was definitely not the norm.

Throughout his cadet years, Johnson seems to have been almost antisocial when it came to off-duty activities. "He liked to read," said Hurlbut, "and spent a lot of time doing that." There is no evidence that he dated anyone in particular, a circumstance that Hurlbut attributed to Johnson's being bashful. In fact, before Christmas of plebe year, Johnson made a bet with his roommate Jim Skinner that he would never attend a hop (a dance) as a cadet.

One of the big events of a cadet's first class year is the Ring Hop, when everyone invites his best girl and the highly prized class rings are distributed and worn for the first time. Johnson and his roommate went over during intermission and collected their rings, then promptly departed. "I did go to Graduation Hop," said Johnson, "but I did not dance." So if he didn't win his bet, he came mighty close. "I really took no part in mixed social life at West Point at all," he added, something that he was unable to explain. "Just plain zero, and I guess this comes back to . . . that streak of something. I don't know how to identify it, whether it's a streak of stubbornness or rebelliousness or just what."

There was one memorable "double date" in New York City when his classmate Patrick Guiney invited Johnson to join him for dinner and the theater in the company of his two maiden aunts. Dinner was at the Fifth Avenue apartment of one of them, who told her nephew that she found Johnson quite charming. Then it was on to the theater, where Johnson recalled "squirming during the course of the show, which did not seem entirely suitable for relatively elderly single ladies accompanied by two wet-eared cadets."

Johnson worked on the *Howitzer* and was its sports editor his senior year. He also took part in putting on the 100th Night Show, an annual musical revue written and performed by cadets in celebration of there being only a hundred days left until graduation. A decidedly amateur production, it provided a vehicle for some satire at the expense of the establishment and typically played to a full house. That year's show was entitled "As You Were," and Johnson edited the program, showing a special talent for the task. "We used the football pool sales structure to sell programs for the 100th Night Show," he explained with some satisfaction. That generated enough profit so that they could use color printing for the program, which described an opening scene featuring "a conclave of dry-throated future generals sitting in the tavern of Benny Havens and engaging in pleasant banter with Lizzie, his daughter, and the barmaid Fanny, a lovely thing." Since Lizzie, Fanny, and all the other parts were played by cadets, the descriptions must be viewed as notional.

Johnson thought that the finished program was an attractive product, especially since they had had "some young ladies with cadet attachments draw sketches for the program that were on the edge of being risqué, at least in 1933, and not entirely in keeping with the image of the United States Military Academy and . . . we sort of slid this by the Officer in Charge, and we had some spoofs on some of the officers in the articles in the program, and particularly on the Commandant of Cadets." When the program made its appearance, the Commandant was predictably not amused, "but it was too late." Johnson and his collaborators got off with a verbal admonishment.

Not an athlete of varsity caliber, Johnson nevertheless became assistant manager of the West Point football team. He once said that he considered typing to be the most valuable course he had taken in high school, because it opened up many opportunities that he would not otherwise have had, one of which was the chance to compete successfully for the job of assistant manager of the football team at the end of his plebe year (apparently, there was some administrative work involved). Thus, as a yearling—a "proud but rather blushful cadet," said the *Grafton News and Times*—he was chosen to provide commentary on an Army football game to the visiting Secretary of War. "Keith Johnson Explains Football to Secretary of War P. J. Hurley," headlined Johnson's hometown paper, concluding that the assignment must have gone well, because "the cadet seemed highly elated when he joined his companions."[2]

In his junior year ("cow" year in cadet parlance, because it follows yearling year), Johnson became assistant equipment manager. This put him in close contact with J. P. McConnell, the first classman who was football manager that year and who had something of a mixed reputation. One scheme came to light in which McConnell benefited from a confidential deal with a supplier who sold automobiles to graduating cadets, and he wound up having to write a letter of apology to the Corps of Cadets. Even though McConnell was also the First Captain, the highest ranking cadet officer, he "was not a perfect example of a West Point cadet," according to James Woolnough, a classmate who had known McConnell since they were Beast Barracks roommates. Johnson had further close involvement with McConnell as assistant sports editor of *The Howitzer* when McConnell was sports editor, a post that Johnson took over the following year.

In Johnson's senior year, his classmate and close friend "Pete" Carroll became football manager, a position that had been held in the past by such luminaries as Douglas MacArthur and Matthew B. Ridgway. Johnson became the team's equipment manager, an appointment that involved him in a controversial situation that almost ended his Army career before it had fairly begun.

Continuing a practice inherited from his predecessor, Johnson collected a large number of football tickets, including eighty for the Army-Navy game, from members of the team and other cadets. He sold these tickets to a civilian, who predictably scalped them. Investigators for the Army Athletic Association identified some of the tickets in the hands of scalpers and traced them back to the cadets who had originally purchased them, exposing the matter to Academy authorities.[3]

Johnson was placed on report for "accumulating from other cadets a large number of tickets to the Army-Navy football game by leading these cadets to believe that tickets were for use of his personal friends." In his required response, Johnson stated that "the report is believed to be partially incorrect." He had gathered the tickets, he admitted, "but I did not intend to mislead cadets into believing that the tickets were for personal friends."

Johnson was required to submit a handwritten spreadsheet detailing his football ticket activities for the season. This demonstrated that, if his own complimentary tickets were included at face value, he had made no profit on the transactions. "I received the face value of the tickets I sold and paid the face value for those I sold," Johnson certified. "I have acted as an intermediary between cadets in ticket transactions, but with no remuneration or gain." He also observed that "this practice has been established by precedent, and has been in vogue as long as I have been connected with the football squad."

Major R. L. Eichelberger, Adjutant of the Tactical Department, analyzed Johnson's report of this matter and in a memorandum to the Commandant of Cadets observed that a number of "unethical practices have sprung up in the Corps of Cadets," including the selling of personal-use tickets to strangers and the selling of complimentary tickets by members of the football squad. Soon thereafter, the Superintendent directed that the Commandant, in cooperation with the Graduate Manager of Athletics, provide him with recommendations as to "how these unethical practices may be avoided in future years."

Johnson was severely punished for his involvement in this scheme, being awarded twelve demerits, two months' confinement, and forty-four punishment tours (each consisting of an hour marching back and forth across the paved inner courtyard of the cadet area while shouldering a rifle). He escaped dismissal only because it was accepted that he had not personally profited from the arrangement. He had, however, demonstrated a degree of naïveté that he never entirely overcame. This was particularly apparent in his overly trusting attitude toward some people who later let him down, a trait that would cause him much heartache in years to come.

Following a summer furlough remembered by some of Johnson's classmates as featuring "plenty of snares but no delusions," it was back to West Point for the final year. Radio was then in its early days, but cadets were not authorized to have radios in their rooms. Besides, the electricity in the barracks was direct current, whereas the radios needed alternating current to function. But, wonder of wonders, the new cadet mess hall was wired for alternating current, some of which was siphoned off by enterprising cadets who ran lines from the mess hall through the steam tunnels to the barracks. Leads were then laid to the attic and dropped down fireplace flues, there to be hooked to the clandestine radios. Johnson and his roommate took advantage of this arrangement, which for a while proved quite satisfactory. "Our room had very good luck until just before graduation," Johnson recalled, "when we lost three radios in three weeks. Very bad luck at the end."

Somewhere along the line, the Class of 1933 adopted "Lucky Stars" as a sobriquet. One reason was that the cadet curriculum included a difficult course in descriptive geometry. Quite a few people in the class ahead of them had been "found" (dismissed for academic deficiency) in that course. But the next year the course was transferred to the Drawing Department, transforming it into a much easier drill, and nobody in 1933 was found in that course. "The Class of 1932 really resented that," said Johnson's classmate and close friend Hurlbut, "but we took it as an example of our class's lucky stars at work."

The Class of 1933 graduated on 13 June, receiving their diplomas from Secretary of War George Dern. The principal speaker was Army Chief of Staff General Douglas MacArthur. "The security of the United States is imperiled by politics, pacifists and retrenchment in the national defense program," he told the young graduates. Furthermore, MacArthur predicted, if the "unabashed and unsound propaganda" of the "peace cranks" were not curbed, there would be another world war, "with a score of nations ready for the sack of America." He commended to them the qualities of "tolerance, balance, intelligence, courage—these four will carry you on; for you must go on, or you will go under." And he reminded them that "any nation that would keep its self-respect must keep alive its martial ardor and be prepared to defend itself."[4]

Armed with that counsel, the young officers marched off to take their places in the small, scattered, and impoverished Army of the Great Depression. Soon, like every class that had gone before them, they would face great challenges, and they would do well. Fully a quarter of the class were destined to become general officers, and five—Johnson among them—would reach the highest rank of four stars. They were, said a class publication, a "West Point class whose members entered the Military Academy at the end of the 'Roaring Twenties,' graduated in the midst of the Great Depression, and thereafter served their country in three wars." As they began that long journey, Johnson set out to be a foot soldier, on orders to one of the great old outfits, the historic 3d Infantry. "I left the Military Academy," he said, "never wanting to go back."

CHAPTER THREE

DEPRESSION ARMY

At Fort Snelling, Minnesota, during four years in the 3d Infantry, Johnson learned to be an officer, determined that he liked the Army and was good at it, and met and married his life's partner. It turned out to be a fine assignment all the way around.

Johnson and his classmates were joining an Army that, in the depths of the depression, was small, scattered, antiquated, ill-equipped, and seriously impoverished. Said one analysis, "in 1933 the Army was at the lowest effectiveness that it had touched since World War I, standing seventeenth among the world's armies by the estimate of the current chief of staff."[1] One of Johnson's classmates called it "a shoestring army." Congress had limited the active Army to a strength of 12,000 commissioned officers and 125,000 enlisted men, and even those units that existed on paper were often not filled. Instead of the nine infantry divisions authorized, for example, only three were actually in being. Those units that did exist were, in a legacy from the Indian Wars, located in penny packets at many small and widely dispersed posts. The twenty-four regiments available for field service in the United States in 1932 were spread among forty-five posts, most garrisoning a battalion or less. As a result, training above company or battalion level was seldom possible.

Beginning in 1933, the Army was required to provide many officers and noncommissioned officers to lead the Civilian Conservation Corps, an enterprise designed to put large numbers of unemployed young men to work on reforestation and other reclamation projects. Although worthwhile for its own sake, the CCC took these leaders away from their regular units, further undermining the training and combat readiness of an already inadequate force. Nevertheless there were compensating advantages, especially for Johnson.

Fort Snelling, located near Minneapolis, had been established in 1825 as part of a chain of forts designed to tame what was then the wild northwest frontier.[2] When Johnson reported there after a three-month graduation furlough in North Dakota, he was sent immediately to Bina, Minnesota, for temporary duty with Company 707 at the Deer River CCC Camp. "We brand new 2nd Lieutenants, full of P&V, reported in the first week of September 1933 and within three days were on our way to remote areas of Minnesota, miles from civilization," recalled his classmate Fred Zierath, who got a similar assignment.

Johnson found himself at a camp located in the Chippewa National Forest, where he came under the tutelage of Captain John H. Rodman, an experienced officer who had entered the Army during World War I. Johnson soon came to admire him as a fine man who devoted a lot of time to his development and training. Along with coaching Johnson on his assigned duties, Rodman taught the younger man how to administer a company fund, maintain supply records, and perform other necessary details of administration. During this three-month assignment, they covered many basics that a new lieutenant has to master.

Leadership in the CCC was different from that in the Army and was a beneficial experience for a young officer just learning his profession. There were essentially no sanctions except discharge for a man who didn't do his job. If too many were discharged, there wouldn't be enough manpower to get the job done, and the program's purpose of providing useful work for the unemployed would be undermined. Therefore, said Johnson, you had to figure out how to operate without the sort of sanctions relied on by military leaders. "Personal leadership was the only way that you got things done," he recalled.

Early on, he had a chance to prove his leadership abilities. Most of the young men in the camp were from Finnish immigrant families out of the iron-mining range of northeastern Minnesota. "And," said Johnson, "they were *tough*." Most of them carried knives, and they were "*wicked* in a fight." Replacements were sent to the camps at six-month intervals, and the next batch was drawn mostly from the streets of Minneapolis. Johnson saw them as "street-wise young men—and very, very smartie."

One of the new men, returning from work in the back of a truck, took to yelling at Johnson, "Hi, Sarge!" Johnson, novice second lieutenant that he was and quite conscious of his newly issued gold bars, took the young man aside. "Murphy," he said, "I'm a lieutenant, and I expect to be called lieutenant." Murphy nodded wordlessly, but the next day it was "Hi, Sarge!" again. When Murphy got off the truck, Johnson caught up with him. "Murphy," he explained, "if you do that again I'm going to knock your head clear off your shoulders." From then on, there was no problem. Johnson admitted that it probably wasn't the right way to handle the problem, but it had been effective. "I don't think I could have taken Murphy," said Johnson, essentially a gentle man for all his soldierly qualities, "but *he* didn't know that."

Other problems he handled in other ways. For example, he had to go into town every Sunday morning and pay five dollars to get his truck driver out of jail, where he had been incarcerated for public drunkenness. The money was always paid back to him eventually, said Johnson, who concluded from these and other experiences that "you had to look after these young men, and you had to be sympathetic—not in a maudlin way, not in a weak way, but work with them in order to get their support and to get response from them in their work forces."

Just as the Class of 1933 was graduating from West Point, President Franklin Roosevelt ordered a 15 percent depression-induced pay cut for the Army, so duty at the CCC camp also had certain fiscal advantages. Second lieutenants were then drawing all of $106.25 a month in basic pay, plus an $18 ration allowance. But, said Johnson, up in the woods it cost only fifteen or twenty dollars a month to live, plus "we were drinking up World War I alcohol in cans, good grain alcohol, and mixing that with some kind of a spirit of the day, and we got icicles up in northern Minnesota" for nothing. "It was a fine life for a gay blade bachelor."

During this time, Johnson also went along on a hunting party, but he didn't like the experience. "I vowed at that time," he said more than thirty years later, "that I would never shoot another bird or animal. I haven't, except for taking aim a couple of times at the two-legged kind."

AFTER THREE MONTHS in the woods, Johnson was reassigned to Fort Snelling. Captain Rodman rated his performance as excellent, saying that he had "unusual common sense and judgment for an officer just commissioned." As for Johnson, he concluded that the CCC was "the finest leadership laboratory" he had ever seen. "It was just great duty."

Johnson was next assigned to Company C, 3d Infantry, where he again came under Captain Rodman. He spent a lot of time with horses, qualified as expert on the bayonet, and learned the business of garrison duty in an undermanned troop unit. In those days, four afternoons a week were devoted to company officers school, covering such topics as mess management, conduct of a court-martial, and horseshoeing. "You learned the duties of the officer in the company from somebody who had been through the mill," said Johnson, "and you were doing it in the environment where it was performed, in contrast to the somewhat sterile environment of a school." He viewed that as the best way of passing on the Army's lore, at least at that level. In his spare time, Johnson tutored enlisted men who were preparing for the West Point entrance examinations.

Fort Snelling was a harsh place to be in the depths of winter. "Many times," said Louis Delmonico, "we had to wear both gloves and mittens. Our headpiece unfolded down to our shoulders. It had slits for our eyes and mouth. A flap could be buttoned to cover the mouth slit." In contrast, "in summer it was so hot many slept on their lawn."

Once a year, the regiment would spend about three weeks on temporary duty at Camp Ripley, Minnesota, a National Guard facility. Or rather they would spend that amount of time getting to and from Ripley, with a brief stay in between, since the point of the exercise was to accomplish the required annual hundred-mile march on foot. The staff made the journey on horseback.

Horses were still an important part of Army life, both on duty and in such recreational pursuits as horse shows, hunts, and polo matches. The Army's transport, wrote Johnson's classmate Herbert Sparrow, "included trucks, horses and mules of World War I vintage."[3] Horse shows were popular events, as were races across the parade ground of mules pulling machine-gun carts. During the caisson drill, the horses pulling the caissons "galloped at such a fast speed in the intricate maneuvering of crisscrossing, the caissons and horses passed in front of each other by inches." It was a memorable and nostalgic day when a column of trucks arrived to replace the horses and mules.

Johnson became an excellent polo player, although he had not played polo at West Point. (He had, of course, taken the required equitation course and gone on long mounted hikes during summer training.) A fellow officer praised "the way the Army ponies acquitted themselves on the polo field. They were no great beauties," said Howard La Pray, "but they performed nobly against some pretty high-priced civilian stock." "Sometimes we retired to General Scott's quarters for beer and sandwiches after our Sunday games," said Ralph Waltz, another teammate. Johnson valued the experience. "There is nothing like knowing animals to understand the necessity for compassion on the part of a human," he observed, "and I think that the people who don't have that opportunity with an animal miss something in terms of developing compassion. I've always felt that an understanding of animals is important."

Social life centered around horses and horse events and around Stone

Lodge, a newly constructed officers' club. The Fort Snelling band played for monthly dinner dances, and there was a family feeling to life in the regiment. Some of the friendships formed there lasted a lifetime.

Johnson was one of six members of his West Point class assigned to the 3d Infantry upon graduation. Two of them got married early on and were given their own quarters. The four bachelors were quartered in a building consisting of four apartments, and Johnson was soon put in charge. "I have many fond memories of Fort Snelling myself," he responded to a correspondent. "I must say that trying to run that four-bachelor apartment is not among the happier ones!" It had some happy consequences, though.

One summer evening, a man from Minneapolis and his date came to call on one of the other officers, but he was not at home. They stopped by to see Johnson instead, and that was when he met Dorothy Rennix. A month or so later, the same man, accompanied by the same girl, attended a party at Fort Snelling. Johnson was there with a date of his own, but when Dorothy publicly announced her telephone number, he alertly made a note of it. Soon she was the girl he was taking out.

Dorothy was from North Dakota, Johnson's home state, and was visiting an aunt and uncle in Minneapolis. Her father was an insurance man who had moved his family to Aberdeen, South Dakota, when his wife contracted tuberculosis. Dorothy attended a teachers college there, then a business school, then what is now known as North Dakota State University, where she was a member of Kappa Kappa Gamma sorority and studied home economics.[4]

Her visit to Minneapolis just seemed to keep being extended, and eventually Dorothy went home to tell her family that she and Johnson were planning to be married the following June. As it turned out, they did not wait that long. Their first date was in September, and they were married the following April, so it had not taken them long to decide that they were right for each other.

The marriage ceremony, which Dorothy described as "very strange," took place on 13 April 1935 in Cavalier, North Dakota. She explained that after the June wedding date had been decided on, her prospective husband called and said that he was driving up for the weekend. "I think we'd better get married," he told her. "I have to go on maneuvers, and if we get married we'll get quarters on post." So they got married on a single day's notice in Cavalier, because Johnson had an uncle who was a county judge there. The judge performed the ceremony, Johnson's aunt and uncle stood up for the couple, and after the ceremony he took the bride home to meet his parents.

As for her own parents, recalled Dorothy, "my mother and father almost had a heart attack."[5]

After the weekend marriage, Dorothy said that her new husband "took me back home (to my parents' home) and dumped me." But the ploy worked. After the maneuvers were over, Johnson and his bride returned to Fort Snelling. "And we did get quarters on post," said Dorothy, "just as Johnny had said we would." Many of his classmates were also getting married, but they had waited until after the big maneuvers and wound up having to find places to live off post. Meanwhile, the Johnsons luxuriated in a three-bedroom brick apartment surrounded by screen porches. In short order, all the bachelors who had been sharing the apartment building got married, dividing their meager furniture as they moved out. "I remember we got a couch out of it," said Dorothy.

During these early years in the Army, religion was not a major factor in Johnson's life. While he was at home on graduation leave in the summer of 1933, he and his father had gone to a Protestant church. "On this Sunday," said Johnson, "the Sacrament of the Holy Communion was observed. As my father arose to proceed to the altar rail and looked expectantly at me, I shook my head and said, 'I cannot.' He never questioned me." Now Johnson's church attendance was confined to an annual event with his soldiers, when the unit was designated to sponsor a service at the post chapel. "This was," he said, "in the days when you were permitted to march your company to church once a year and help the chaplain on his attendance."

In the autumn of 1934, Johnson was appointed adjutant of the 1st Battalion for the period of maneuvers. "He is conscientious, sensible, and tactful, and has displayed initiative and capability normally only expected of officers of considerably more experience and service," read his efficiency report for that period. That judgment may have led to an early opportunity to command that soon followed.

Near the end of 1934, Captain Rodman was reassigned. He recommended that Johnson succeed him in command of Company C, and this was approved by the regimental commander. So Johnson, still a second lieutenant with only a year and a half of commissioned service, became a company commander. It was a great opportunity for a young officer, but not without its problems. "Right next door," said Johnson, "were lieutenants in companies with fifteen or sixteen years' service, and there was a modest amount of hostility about this."

Johnson kept his first command for nearly five months, until a more senior officer arrived to take his place. It had been a good experience for him.

"I suppose I made every mistake in the book with that rifle company," he later said, but that judgment was influenced by his customary modesty. His efficiency report for the period rated his performance as superior and noted in particular that he had "an excellent manner toward enlisted men."

The soldiers who served under him viewed Johnson with respect and admiration, even affection. One man later described it this way: "At that time a young and very promising officer joined our Company, I and the others of the enlisted men's barracks agreed that 2nd Lt. Harold K. Johnson had the qualities to go far in his chosen profession." Reuben Everson, once Johnson's company clerk, later wrote to congratulate him on becoming Chief of Staff of the Army: "I am pleased that you made it, Sir!" He also recalled that one of his duties had been "to mail those Special-Delivery letters you sent to the one who later became your wife."

There were no illusions on Johnson's part about the soldiers entrusted to his command. "We didn't have an educated enlisted force in the '30's, I'll tell you that," he acknowledged. "We had 28-day soldiers. Every payday they were gone for several days while they slept off their hangover." But, when the situation demanded, many of these soldiers demonstrated their inherent worth, and a number who served under Johnson in C Company took on far greater responsibility when World War II came along. Arthur Leonard, who had been a private first class in that outfit, wrote to Johnson to tell him that he had reached the rank of master sergeant and on D day in Europe had parachuted in with General Maxwell Taylor, both landing in the same cow pasture. He reported that Corporal Rosenthal of C Company had become a lieutenant colonel, and that after the war he met former Private First Class Olson, by then a first lieutenant and Army pilot. Leonard was living in retirement near Dodger Stadium in Los Angeles. There, he told Johnson, "they have a ball team about half as good as the one we had in C Company."

In the summer of 1935, Johnson was appointed mess officer for the Summer Training Camps program. It was a job that involved many details, and the potential for letting something fall through the cracks was great. Johnson kept it all together, even getting many compliments on the quality of the food from those upon whom it was inflicted. Afterward, his efficiency report said something quite significant: Johnson, still a second lieutenant, was evaluated as qualified to take command of a company in peacetime—something he had already successfully demonstrated—and a battalion if war came.

In May 1936, Johnson took command of Company M, a machine-gun company equipped with machine-gun carts and mules. He held that post for fourteen months. During these early years, he was coming into contact with some of the Army's most experienced old-line noncommissioned officers, developing a respect and admiration for them that carried through the rest of his service. "There was a relationship in those days," he said of the interaction between officers and noncoms, "that was a very warm and rich one."

One of the most memorable old soldiers in his experience was Frank Cumiskey, M Company's 1st Sergeant. He took Johnson under his experienced tutelage in a graceful and effective way. Cumiskey had previously served in the 19th Infantry in Hawaii under Captain Charles H. Coates, a much-admired company commander. Now on many afternoons, Cumiskey would sit down in the company orderly room and explain to Johnson concerning some matter of current interest, "Lieutenant, in D Company of the 19th, Captain Coates would do this." And most mornings about 11:30, Cumiskey would knock on the orderly room door and say something like, "Sir, Private So-and-So would like to see you." Johnson would ask, "What does he want to see me about, Sergeant Cumiskey?" And the 1st Sergeant would reply, "Well, he wants to explain why he had dust on his shoes at reveille inspection this morning." Then, as he withdrew to fetch the offender, Cumiskey might add, "And I think that maybe two days on KP would be an adequate punishment for his lack of explanation." The man would be brought in, Lieutenant Johnson would listen to his predictably inadequate explanation, and a couple of days on KP would be duly imposed. "It didn't take me long to learn that what Captain Coates did in D Company was what was expected of M Company of the 3rd," said Johnson.[6] As a result, things went very smoothly in that outfit.

According to Johnson, Cumiskey had gone only as far as the fourth grade in formal schooling, but he was wise and understanding, a very impressive man. "He wore steel-rim glasses," remembered Johnson, "and his eyes were steely blue behind them." Cumiskey had learned the ways of the Army to perfection. In the front of the company fund book was an illustration of how the records should be maintained. Naturally it was a model of neatness and accuracy. "That's the way our company fund book looked," said Johnson, and it was because 1st Sergeant Cumiskey maintained it that way.

After a while, it began to dawn on Johnson that maybe Captain Coates, paragon though he might be, hadn't really demonstrated a solution to every single problem that came up in M Company, that maybe 1st Sergeant Cumiskey was coming up with a great deal of it himself. But Johnson was grateful for the schooling, whatever its source. "He gave me a lot of lessons in human relations," Johnson said of Cumiskey, who became a lieutenant colonel during World War II and subsequently retired as a full colonel. Later, after Johnson had become Army Chief of Staff, he wrote to his old 1st Sergeant to say, "I look back upon that period as one of my most profitable learning periods and regard Frank Cumiskey as one of my great teachers." On the eve of retirement, he wrote to Cumiskey again, thanking him for providing "the grounding that gave me a solid base for moving through the fierce competitive system in the Army."

Cumiskey for his part felt that he had good material to work with in young Lieutenant Johnson. "I'll tell you what he's like," said Cumiskey a long while later. "He was a great inspiration to me. He never lost his temper. He always had a smile. And he always had a solution for whatever problem bothered us."[7]

Johnson thought that he was a better company commander the second time around, applying things he had learned earlier in his brief service. "In two years as a company commander," he said, "I signed one set of charges — one. I don't believe in court-martialing people except as a last resort. Where did I learn this? I learned it because in my first three months of service I was on CCC duty." In that assignment, he said, Captain Rodman had taught him a lot about how to deal with people, and as a result, Johnson did a lot of counseling. Whereas Johnson thought that he was lucky to have good teachers, and that he was learning a lot from them, his efficiency report credited his skill with soldiers as being built-in, calling him "a natural leader of men."

In an amazing coincidence, one of the members of Company M was a man named Peter Gourde, an eighth-grade classmate of Johnson's back in Grafton, North Dakota. "We first began to realize that Johnny might be something special," said his sister Janet, "when a soldier from our hometown who was stationed at Fort Snelling came home and said to his aunt about Johnny, 'He's going to be a general some day.' "[8] Not everyone figured that out so early on. A fellow officer who later reached the level of brigadier general wrote to Johnson to say, "if I had had any idea when we were Second Lieutenants together at Fort Snelling that I was associating with the future Chief of Staff . . . certainly I would have treated you with considerably more respect."

In a surprising admission, Johnson revealed that while all this was going on, he was ambivalent about remaining in the Army. "Every year after I graduated," he said, "and this was true up until almost the end of my service, I debated about leaving the service at some time during each year." This he attributed to "a belief that there were opportunities somewhere that were somewhat greater than the service offered. Now, what kept me in I don't know." (On another occasion, though, he wrote that "my natural curiosity with respect to what the next assignment and next challenge would be kept me in the military service.") Johnson added that he "came very close to resigning one time at Fort Snelling" in 1936. The man who owned the oil company where he had worked while in high school became ill and offered Johnson a half interest at no cost if he would come back and take over the operation. "I came very close to doing it," said Johnson.

Instead, he soldiered on, gaining a sound fundamental grounding in the profession. It was the people who made up for the serious shortages of just about every other kind of wherewithal that plagued the Army then. And the lessons they taught were sound. "We learned that after a hard day in the field we should care first for the animals, then the men, last ourselves," observed a classmate. "And we learned to respect and know our soldiers: what they thought, how they felt, to what they would respond." Even the austerity had its uses. "It [the Army] was poor and small," said Johnson's classmate David Gray, "but everything was simple and direct."[9]

While Johnson was commanding M Company, another event took place that gave meaning to the Class of 1933's "Lucky Stars" nickname. While they were cadets, one member of the class had calculated that, the way things were progressing, they would come up for promotion to lieutenant colonel at the age of 124. They were stuck behind what was referred to as the World War I "hump." But only a year after they graduated, a new promotion bill was enacted, and as a result, the entire class was promoted to 1st Lieutenant after only three years' service. "Before that," said Herbert Sparrow, "there were officers who had spent a decade or more as 2nd Lieutenants. Again our lucky stars had come through."

Finally, after four years with the 3d Infantry, it was time to move on. But those years had been, said Johnson a long while after, "one of the richest experiences of my service."

JOHNSON'S NEXT ASSIGNMENT was as a student officer at the Infantry School at Fort Benning, Georgia. Enrolled in the Regular Course, he was there for the academic year that began in late August 1937 and ended the following June. Early on, he got some insight into his new status when a woman who came to his quarters to be interviewed for a maid's job asked Johnson, "Is you an officer, or is you a student?"

The Infantry School in those days was still much influenced by Colonel George C. Marshall, soon to be the Army's World War II Chief of Staff. Marshall had spent five years (1927–1932) as Assistant Commandant, completely revamping the curriculum and methods of instruction to make them more practical and dynamic. Among his innovations was a new type of field order, geared to a map overlay, that greatly reduced the time required to get the word out and permitted much more rapid reaction to developing battlefield situations. Johnson and others were the beneficiaries of much that Marshall had introduced.

Johnson later spoke of Marshall as the World War II commander he admired the most, and his reasons are reflective of Johnson's own values. He viewed Marshall's service, both during the war and afterward, as "the epitome of the kind of selflessness that I think is the hallmark of a really great commander." Others, including MacArthur, Eisenhower, Bradley, and Patton, he didn't see as that selfless, although he considered Lucian Truscott another great soldier. But Marshall he admired most of all: "I think Marshall put it all together and had the iron will to hold it all together."

There were 112 student officers in the 1937–1938 class, all with the same curriculum, except for ten who substituted advanced equitation for communications. Thanks to a letter written by Mike Halloran, a polo teammate of Johnson's at Fort Snelling who had previously served with the regiment that provided the horses for the Infantry School, Johnson was given a slot in advanced equitation. This suited him just fine. He loved horses and liked to be around them, and he treasured the friendships he had made playing polo.

At the beginning of the school year, each officer in advanced equitation was issued a remount, a horse that had been broken, but had absolutely no other training. The task was to school that horse by the end of the course. When it was time for this class to meet, the officers took a little train from the main post out to the maneuver area, about a half hour's ride sitting on hard little seats, and there all the horses would be waiting. Each officer worked with his assigned horse, and progress was demonstrated at a Saturday evening show in the autumn and a three-day test in the spring, the latter involving cross-country riding, ring jumping, and dressage. "Johnny was a good horseman," said his classmate Royal Reynolds. He worked at it. Training that horse was time-consuming, noted Johnson, and as a consequence, "you devoted a whole lot of hours to this in comparison to the hours that you avoided in communications." Nevertheless, he considered it "a wonderful experience."

As it had been in the regiment, social life at Benning was close-knit and fun, centered around the Officers' Club, where most people congregated on Friday and Saturday nights. Everybody had quarters on post, and sometimes friends gathered in the Johnsons' kitchen for a few beers. On occasion,

Johnson would entertain by reciting, in his best imitation Scandinavian accent, a little ditty at the expense of his wife Dorothy: "Little Emmy Yahnson is my little pearl, God never made a nicer girl." After that, Dorothy went through a period of being called "Emmy" by all their friends.

The Army's school system is often credited with being what enabled it to survive the long lean years of the interwar period and come up with the leadership needed by the massively expanded force that fought World War II. At the branch schools, wrote Johnson's classmate Herbert Sparrow, the young officers "discovered what the Army in its wisdom had carefully hoarded, the wherewithal to support professional standards of instruction: ammunition for service practice, gasoline for motor marches, supplies and equipment for field training, younger animals—and instructors, including Leavenworth graduates, who were real pros."[10]

Johnson later described the time spent at Fort Benning as "one of the major influences on my life, because somehow, and I don't know why this was, it gave me a confidence that I really hadn't had before in a professional way. It was just a superb course."

When the school year ended, Johnson was designated a superior graduate, "convincing, dignified, quiet, firm, discerning, well informed, thorough and efficient," according to the efficiency report rendered by the assistant commandant. He was headed back to troops.

JOHNSON'S NEW POST was with the 28th Infantry, stationed at Fort Niagara, New York. Having missed out on the communications course at Fort Benning, it was perhaps inevitable what his next assignment would be. When he reported in, said Johnson, "the Adjutant announced very proudly that they were rid of their horses—and here I had had advanced equitation. They had just received a complement of trucks. I would be the communications officer, and I had skipped communications in order to take advanced equitation!"

That job lasted for two months. Then a new regimental commander moved Johnson to the inglorious job of post exchange officer, with orders to straighten the place out and make it profitable. At the same time, he was given additional duties as recreation officer, signal officer, and librarian. In those tasks he was rated superior, except for librarian, at which he was only excellent. After six weeks—having shaped the PX up as ordered—he escaped to company command, his third stint in that key post and the third time as a lieutenant that he had filled a billet authorized a captain. This time he took over the regimental Headquarters Company, further diversifying the experience he had previously gained in command of a rifle company and then a machine-gun company.

This turned out to be quite a job. The somewhat aged regimental commander, who had not been with troops for a long time, took a liking to Johnson, putting more and more tasks on his plate. Thus he became simultaneously regimental adjutant, commander of the regimental service company, and commander of the regimental band. And, said Johnson, "when the Inspector General made his annual inspection of Fort Niagara, I turned over eight funds for him to audit," funds for which Johnson had been given responsibility. It was hard work, but also a compliment. "I was the second most junior officer on the post" at the time, Johnson recalled. The regimental commander "didn't trust many people. Somehow he liked me."

During this assignment, the Johnsons had their first child, a son who was named after his father. "I was still itchy-footed," said Johnson of this period. Perhaps because of this, he applied to attend a civilian business school. He was told that if he transferred to the Quartermaster Corps, then spent a year as a commissary officer, that—depending on his performance—his application might then be considered. Johnson declined to take that path. "It seemed to me," he said, "that if I had to count beans for a year to qualify myself for business school that that was a strange way of getting there."

By 1939, it was belatedly becoming apparent that the United States ought to be improving its long-neglected defense capability. Thus, when a reorganization was instituted in September of that year, the 1st Infantry Division was restructured, becoming a "triangular" division of three infantry regiments rather than a "square" one with four, and the 28th Infantry was dropped from that division's complement. "This was a blow to unit pride," remembered Johnson, "because the 28th Infantry had been the first unit ashore in France in World War I and they had done a lot of fighting for the 1st Division in France. To be dropped from the 1st Division was really a rather shattering blow and shattering experience."

The 28th Infantry, with only two active battalions, became caretaker for four posts in northern New York—Fort Niagara, Fort Ontario, Plattsburgh Barracks, and Madison Barracks. One or two companies were also customarily maintained at Pine Camp to conduct winter exercises and experiments. Johnson and his unit were in overnight bivouac at Pine Camp, returning from maneuvers at Schuyler Falls Military Reservation west of Plattsburgh, when the German invasion of Poland was announced. "That was a pretty tense period," he remembered.

By the summer of 1940, it was time to move on again, and to an assignment that Johnson had specifically requested. He, Dorothy, and young Johnny traveled across the country, visiting their families in the Dakotas en route to San Francisco. One stop was at the home of Johnson's uncle, where the pony Midget, by then twenty-eight years old, still lived. It was the last time he would ever see his old pet, who died during the war, but Johnson photographed his son perched atop the animal at just about the same age he had been when the pony had first been given to him.

Soon thereafter, aboard the U.S. Army Transport *Grant* (widely regarded as an "old tub"), the young family set sail for the Philippine Islands and an assignment with another famous outfit, the 57th Infantry (Philippine Scouts). "I had been asking for it for a long time," said Johnson. "Which was the first and last time he ever asked for an assignment," added Dorothy.

CHAPTER FOUR

PHILIPPINE SCOUTS

Johnson and his family boarded ship at Fort Mason, the port of embarkation near San Francisco. They were assigned a very nice cabin—perhaps a surprisingly nice cabin—and right away there was a problem. Another officer making the voyage was Chester L. Johnson, an artilleryman who had been four years behind Harold K. Johnson at West Point. He had just been married, and a quartermaster officer who had taken a liking to him had promised, "I'm going to get you the best suite on the ship." The happy recipient mentioned this favor to his bride, but when they were escorted to their cabin, they proceeded down a ladder, then down four more levels into the bowels of the ship, to a tiny cramped cabin. The reaction was not favorable. "Well, Mr. Johnson," inquired Lieutenant Chester Johnson's new bride, "and this is the marvelous accommodation you promised me?" (He had married the colonel's daughter, who had probably become used to somewhat more privileged treatment.)

As the voyage proceeded, various groups congregated in the evenings, and especially among the captains and majors, the conversation would turn to a certain Lieutenant Johnson, who apparently had the best accommodations on the ship. Chester Johnson gathered from the tone of their remarks that the unfortunate officer so billeted, this other Johnson, this *Harold K. Johnson*, was ruined, absolutely ruined. "He swiped my cabin, and I considered him an upstart," said Chester Johnson with some asperity.

Soon, though, events conspired to bring about a dramatic change. "The next thing I knew we were at war. I was tossing artillery shells over his shoulder, and Harold K. Johnson turned out to be anything but ruined. Indeed I came to view him as by far the most honorable man I ever knew, and also one of the bravest," said Chester Johnson.

It took three weeks for the venerable *Grant* to make the long voyage to the Philippines. Fighting was by then raging in Europe, and the scare had spread to the Pacific as well. Large American flags were painted on the sides of the ship, and at night these were brilliantly illuminated. The transit ended safely, with "a very happy Johnson family" arriving in Manila on 20 July 1940. "War clouds were gathering even at that time," said Johnson. The preceding week, British families had been evacuated from Hong Kong.

Duty in the Philippines was in those days considered a choice assignment. The regiment Johnson was joining was stationed at Fort William McKinley, the largest U.S. Army installation in the Islands. It was located on high ground on the main island of Luzon, where reliable breezes not only cooled the tropic temperatures but also kept away the malarial mosquitoes that plagued those living at lower elevations around nearby Manila.[1]

Servants were part of the way of life, and even lieutenants had several. The Johnsons hired an amah for young Johnny, plus a laundress, a cook who also supervised the staff, and a houseboy who doubled as a table waiter at meals. Ah Ho, the amah, and the cook, Ng Sen, both Chinese, became not only trusted members of the family but also friends, as they later proved at some personal risk. By September, an increment of the Johnsons' furniture had arrived, or at least somewhat. It had been sent up to Fort Stotsenburg with the effects of some major who had come from ROTC duty in Missouri, so a little internal rerouting was necessary before the Johnsons actually got to use it themselves.

Social life in the close community of the Philippines was robust, although perhaps not so carefree as in years gone by. The regiment was the focus of activity, with much socializing at the Officers' Club, and also at the famous Army-Navy Club in Manila. There they would gather to listen on the radio to the Army-Navy football game, broadcast about three in the morning their time, watching the progress of play on a big display board. John Olson, who got to know Johnson intimately during these years, viewed him as "not antisocial, but just not particularly socially minded." Johnson liked watching jai alai, and sometimes three or four of the officers would go together and place some bets, and he liked basketball and often served as a referee. He played more polo on the regimental team and was a member of the Manila Polo Club and Los Tamaraos Club, the big civilian clubs, so there was a lot going on.

Johnson, still a lieutenant, was assigned to command Company L, 3d Battalion, 57th Infantry (Philippine Scouts), the fourth time that he had had the privilege of company command. By then he was getting a little tired of that particular duty. "I don't like it very well," he wrote to his mother soon after taking on the new assignment, "but I guess I can't have a good job all the time."

The Scouts had American officers and Filipino soldiers and noncommissioned officers. Lieutenant General John M. Wright, Jr., who served with them as a young officer, reflected the views of many: "In my view, the Philippine Scouts were probably—at that time—as fine a group of professional soldiers as you could find anywhere in the world. I was proud to serve with them." The regiment that Johnson was joining was small, at an authorized 1,110 men about a third the size of a U.S. regiment of the day, and good men were standing in line to join. In fact, every company had a half dozen or so supernumeraries who worked at odd jobs for room and board, hoping thereby to gain consideration when a rare vacancy occurred. "Most losses resulted from retirement," Johnson observed. "A man didn't get to be private first class in that outfit until he had over twenty years' service. It was a very prestigious outfit as far as the Filipinos were concerned." Alva Fitch, who served there with Johnson, agreed: "Philippine Scouts were something else. They were professional soldiers in every sense of the word."

Even so, Johnson found what he called "a pretty lax atmosphere" prevalent in the regiment, with not a lot of hard work under way at the time. "I go to work at 7:00 and quit at 12:30," he wrote, "with no afternoon work usually. Two days a week, I ride from 6:00–7:00 and then go to work at 8:00. It's too hot to sleep after 7:00 anyhow." By the turn of the year, though, things had begun to change dramatically. For one thing, the size of the Scouts was doubled, and in January 1941, they began recruiting to meet the new authorization. "We set up criteria that an individual to be enlisted had to be a college graduate," said Johnson. "That's a pretty high goal."

"We're a long way from home," Johnson told his mother in an early letter, "and we are very conscious of it." As war loomed, the Class of 1933, seven years out of West Point, was on 9 September 1940 promoted to captain. It was a grade that most of them would pass through rapidly as war-driven expansion moved them quickly into positions of increasing responsibility. Johnson welcomed the advancement. A few weeks earlier, responding to speculation on the impending promotions in the service journals, he had written to his mother that he hoped it would come through "if they give us the pay. I've been doing a captain's job for five years on a lieutenant's pay and it would be a welcome break."

Meanwhile, a group of classmates stationed at West Point started putting out a newsletter under the class nickname "Lucky Stars." Reacting to that, another group of classmates in Hawaii, less securely situated and with perhaps a more realistic appreciation of what lay ahead, began a rival publication called "Dull Thud." Seventeen members of the Class of 1933 were stationed in the Philippines at that juncture. "We feel," wrote one of them, "that we're sitting on a powder keg over here." When the keg blew, eleven lost their lives, four survived as prisoners of war, and only two escaped or evaded capture.[2] The famous lucky stars were getting a bit dim for those way out on the end of the vine.

Those on duty in the Islands, at least at the working (and fighting) level, had few illusions as war loomed. "We had an inadequate force for the defense of the Philippines, as was demonstrated," observed Johnson. "I don't think that this country should, in all good conscience, expect its people in the armed forces to stand out at the end of a line that is inadequate for the task that has been given them."[3]

"The sparkle went out of Manila in the spring of 1941," said General Jonathan Wainwright. "War was coming and we all knew it."[4] There came a day, "Boat Day" it was called, when the last families were sent home from the Philippines. Only ten months after a joyful arrival, Dorothy was on her way back with little Johnny and a new daughter, Ellen Kay, just four months old. Many people had gone earlier, some of those who had come out with them on the *Grant* the previous July heading back as early as January. "Quite a few people are volunteering" to leave, Dorothy wrote home, "but we aren't. I'm not a bit afraid." Now there was no choice; it was the last boat scheduled. They went aboard the U.S. Army Transport *Washington*, another veteran of the American President Lines that had been taken over by the government, sailing for San Francisco on 14 May 1941. Dorothy thought that her husband looked haggard and tired as he stood on the dock to see them off, dressed in a civilian suit that seemed to hang on him because he had already lost so much weight.[5] When that last vessel pulled out from Manila, recalled Wainwright, "there were sudden tears along the rails of the ship and all of us on the dock, waving with frozen smiles, felt mighty bad."[6]

There were a few minor adventures on the long trip back. "We were told the ship was chased by submarines on the way home," said Dorothy, and during one set of evasive maneuvers in the middle of the night, little Ellen Kay was pitched out of her berth. Then young Johnny, perhaps deciding to liven things up a bit, took it upon his two-and-a-half-year-old self to go across the way, knock on the door of another cabin, and tell the surprised occupants, "My Momma wants you to come over for a drink with my baby and me." And they did.

When they reached San Francisco, things got more difficult, a lot more difficult. "Our country wasn't ready for us—at all," said Dorothy. No place had been arranged for the arriving passengers to stay, and they were made to stand in line at customs for an entire day. Dorothy was nursing, and she had to pay people to hold her place in line while she went back to the ship periodically to feed the baby. The family car had also made the trip, lashed to the deck of the ship, so by the time they arrived, the salt spray had scoured off most of the paint. That was minor compared with other problems. Young Johnny had been so completely spoiled by his amah that he was impossible. "Ah Ho, come!" he would demand, but of course Ah Ho was not there, left behind in the Philippines. The car proved up to the trip to Dorothy's parents' home in South Dakota, but just barely. "When we got to Aberdeen and stopped the car outside my parents' house, every tire went down," Dorothy remembered. "My father couldn't believe it."

JOHNSON KEPT HIS QUARTERS after the families departed, and Lieutenant John Olson, the Adjutant, and Major George Fisher, the Supply Officer, came to share them with him. Other officers took their meals there, including Lieutenant Alexander Nininger, who had graduated from West Point only the preceding June and would, before he had served a year, be killed in action on Bataan while earning a Medal of Honor. Ng Sen stayed as the cook, so they were well looked after. "For me personally," said Johnson, "this period was a very rich professional experience in the months before war broke out."

After a stint as Adjutant, Johnson had become Regimental S-3 while still a captain. This was the key staff position and gave him responsibility for plans, training, and operations. The 57th Infantry was then commanded by Colonel William E. Brougher, much admired within the regiment despite his requirement that officers attend 6:00 A.M. horseback riding classes several mornings a week.[7] Brougher later wrote an account of an event that captured much of the atmosphere of prewar service in the Philippines. Early one evening, he recalled, his wife and daughters called for him to look outside their quarters at Fort McKinley. Going to the front door, he saw advancing across the parade ground the officers and ladies of the regiment dressed in their best party clothes, "all laughing, talking, skipping, and singing: 'Happy birthday to you! Happy birthday to you! Happy birthday, dear Colonel! Happy birthday to you!' " In the meantime, a truck had arrived at the kitchen door, where orderlies were busy unloading its cargo of festive food and beverages brought from the Officers' Club.

"Then followed," wrote Brougher, "what I shall always recall as one of the most memorable occasions in my lifetime—an occasion when that most charming and exciting of all military families, the officers and ladies of a peace-time regiment, foregathered as a surprise party to do honor to and express affection for their Colonel—me!"[8]

It was well that General Brougher was able to retain that charming tableau in his mind's eye, for harsh reality was about to sweep away forever the way of life it represented. Three months later, those wives and their children had been shipped home, and within a year, the officers—those left alive—and the soldiers they led were locked in the final stages of a bloody battle for survival.

It was the spring of 1941 when Johnson became Regimental S-3, and he soon put his imprint on the outfit. "Johnny Johnson continues in inimitable manner to dictate training memos, solve problems, answer any and all foolish questions, and grin at the same moment," reported a regimental newsletter. Colonel Brougher said in rating Johnson's performance that "he was priceless to me as regimental commander. His energy, initiative, and ambition are unlimited. He will be at the top in any group." General Wainwright concurred.

In July 1941, the Philippine Division, commanded by Wainwright, was the best trained and equipped military force in the Islands. It consisted of the U.S. 31st Infantry, three regiments of Philippine Scouts—the 26th Cavalry, 45th Infantry, and 57th Infantry—and supporting elements, although it "rarely functioned as a division, for its elements were scattered."[9]

In August 1941, the Philippine Army mobilized and was inducted into the Armed Forces of the United States. At one swoop, the 57th Infantry lost two-thirds of its officers, sent to be instructors for the units called up, and large numbers of noncommissioned officers who were also reassigned. Other elements of the Scouts suffered similar decrements. It was not a good way to get ready to go to war, at least not for the regiment, and besides, it was too late to do much for the woefully neglected Philippine Army. In the 21st Division, for example, "the divisional artillery had not fired a shot in training, and one regiment of infantry had not even been issued rifles."[10]

General Wainwright confirmed this alarming state of affairs. There had been no field training, he acknowledged, nor much training in the use of weapons, and in fact it was not until the summer of 1941 that any unit training was even attempted by Philippine Army units.[11] In the Philippine Scouts, of course, the situation was much different.

Even before hostilities commenced, many in the regiment looked up to Johnson, especially after his assignment as regimental operations officer gave him a central role in war preparations. "In the 57th Johnny was highly regarded as being a real dynamo, a comer," said John Olson. "I learned from his quick and agile mind, his keen wit, his positiveness, his impatience with inefficiency and sloth, his knowledge of tactics and techniques, his ability to stimulate those who worked for him and those he worked for (with a few exceptions), and his dedication to his job," said Olson.

A principal activity during this period of frantic preparation was the planning and conduct of field exercises, and here Johnson had the lead role. Generally, these exercises went well, but Johnson remembered one marked exception. General MacArthur and some members of his staff came to visit the unit as the exercise was under way. Johnson was asked by MacArthur's chief of staff, General Sutherland, why the regiment hadn't conducted a double envelopment. Since they were at the time involved in a meeting engagement, feeling the opposing force out, Johnson didn't think that was the time to be trying to sweep around flanks that hadn't yet been identified. "I was somewhat indignant that the type of maneuver we were conducting would be questioned," he said. "General MacArthur simply stood off to one side and drew silently on his pipe and had no observations to make. He let the discussion go on between General Sutherland and me, then Captain Johnson. It was an encounter that I never have quite forgotten, nor have I quite forgiven, either, in some respects." Those comments were made more than three decades later, indicating the depth of Johnson's resentment.

Captain Thomas Trapnell, commanding F Troop, 26th Cavalry (Philippine Scouts), had a similarly uninspiring experience during a visit by MacArthur. His troop was the aggressor force maneuvering against the Philippine Division when MacArthur stopped to talk with him. "He spent two minutes on the exercise," recalled Trapnell, "and forty-three on Army football. This was a week before the war began."

In late November 1941, General MacArthur sent General Wainwright to Fort Stotsenburg, about sixty-five miles north of Manila, to take command of what was called the North Luzon Force. An indication of Wainwright's outlook at the time was the fact that he had Sergeant Carroll, his orderly, take along his three horses.[12] Wainwright was known as an enthusiastic horseman, as well as an enthusiastic consumer of Scotch. "I've seen him ride from McKinley to Nichols Field and take a tumbler full of clear Scotch and down it virtually at a gulp before he'd dismounted," recalled Johnson, who nevertheless viewed Wainwright as a fine person.

Despite the intensified tempo of training, Johnson continued to pursue his interest in basketball. For a while, he coached teams in the 57th Infantry. Then he and another officer, Dick Jones, decided to see whether they could break into the Filipino Officials Association and referee college basketball games. The Filipino members of the association were not in favor of this, Johnson found out, but "some American priests with the universities were favorably inclined because some of the officials had been known to change their decisions in the face of pressure from the audience." Johnson and Jones were accepted as officials and began to work games together. Later Jones was reassigned to work with the Philippine Army and had to give up refereeing, but Johnson continued, sometimes working alone during the first and third games of a three-game set, in the process shedding as much as a dozen pounds in the tropical heat.

Johnson was a no-nonsense official who called them as he saw them. His younger son remembers hearing about the time his father cleared the gym because the crowd was too rowdy. The teams played the rest of the game with only the reserve players on the bench watching. Only a couple of months before the war began, Johnson was chosen to accompany a champion college basketball team on a tour of the southern islands, where it played a series of exhibition games. General Wainwright approved the assignment.

Before long, Wainwright received a remarkable letter from Rev. Anthony V. Keane, S.J., the dean of discipline at Ateneo de Manila, the college whose basketball team had made the tour. Father Keane had accompanied the team and had watched Johnson's work as a referee. "So deeply impressed was I (to say nothing of the civilians in these various places visited) by the superb conduct of Captain Johnson that I felt it my duty to write and acquaint you with the facts." Commenting on how well Johnson "acted the part of a gentleman, official, soldier and man," the priest reported that "his simplicity, directness, fearlessness and unquestioned honesty won him the respect of everyone. It is common knowledge that, in the Provinces, not infrequently the people take the situation in their own hands at games if they do not like the way things are going. In all the eight games Captain Johnson officiated there was not so much as a murmur of complaint. He truly reflected glory on the American Army, and I must confess I was indeed proud of him and went out of my way on every occasion to show him off." Soon there would be no more basketball, with more serious matters crowding the agenda, but that was a good way for Johnson to wrap up his brief career as a member of the Filipino Officials Association.

WAR CAME, courtesy of the international date line, a day later in the Philippines. When the Japanese bombed Pearl Harbor in Hawaii on 7 December 1941, it was already 8 December in the Philippines. The Japanese also attacked military installations in the Philippines, but the real blow was the one struck at Pearl Harbor, for destruction of the American battle fleet meant that there was no possibility that the Philippines could be reinforced, even if troops and materiel had been made available. "The Philippines were isolated, cut off from the nearest base 5,000 miles away," observed Army historian Louis Morton, "even before they had felt the first blow of war."[13]

Johnson had largely fallen away from the Protestant religious practices of his youth. Now he found himself in a regiment composed almost entirely of Filipinos, who were all Catholics. As a consequence, so were all the chaplains. That made no difference. When the bombs began to drop in Manila in December 1941, said Johnson, "that chaplain was good enough for me." This marked the beginning of his return to a deep and lasting religious commitment that would sustain him for the rest of his days.

Even though it had become increasingly apparent that hostilities were inevitable, realistic preparations were in some cases overlooked. "I don't think we began to appreciate what we were coping with until pretty late in the game," said Johnson. "We had very good intelligence on the Japanese, on their organization, on their tactics, on their methods, on their psychology. The documents . . . were confidential, and they were religiously kept locked up in a safe and were not often looked at. It wasn't until we were back in Bataan that we began to haul some of these things out." And the custom of having a duty officer at regimental headquarters during off-duty hours had only been instituted in late November, less than two weeks before the Japanese began hostilities.[14]

War planners had for decades been studying how best to defend the Philippines in the event of a Japanese invasion. They had settled on WPO-3, short for War Plan Orange No. 3, which prescribed that in the event of a Japanese landing on Luzon the defending forces would, if they were unable to repel the invaders, fight a delaying action as they withdrew into the Bataan Peninsula. It was calculated that this plan would result in a six-month stand on Bataan, sufficient time for assistance to arrive from the United States.[15]

When General Douglas MacArthur was recalled to active duty in July 1941 and placed in command of American forces in the Philippines, he rejected this approach. Rather he insisted that the defending forces make their stand on the beaches, fighting to a finish there. This proved to be a recipe for disaster. Furthermore, a public argument over the matter developed in the press, with MacArthur's view that the Philippine Army could defend on the beaches being hotly disputed by Philippine president Manuel Quezon. This disgusted Johnson. "To me this always seemed to be a rather shameful kind of argument to be carried on publicly between two figures of the stature of General MacArthur and President Quezon," he said. "Neither was going to be able to prove his point in the absence of overt attack."

When the enemy attacks came, it became clear that MacArthur had been wrong and Quezon correct. Unfortunately, MacArthur had also ordered supplies and munitions moved forward to the beach area. These were soon lost as the initial attacks swept quickly inland, driving ten miles by nightfall of the first day and thus depriving the defenders of vital stores when they had to fall back in an attempt to defend Bataan in accordance with the original plan. Likewise, the stockpiling of food and medicines in rear areas had been neglected because of MacArthur's insistence on defense on the beaches, with predictably devastating consequences. The defending forces were forced to go on half rations as early as 7 January 1942. Said Johnson, "it was the lack of food that contributed materially to the fall of the force there" and later increased the number of deaths in prison camp due to the soldiers' already debilitated condition when they entered captivity. Olson agreed. "MacArthur forced us to be forward," he recalled. "As a consequence we lost the food."[16] Johnson estimated that when surrender was ordered, the defenders had approximately 79,000 in their force, whereas Japanese general Homma had invaded with some 43,000. Johnson recognized that even if there had been more robust supplies of food and medicine, the eventual outcome was never in doubt. But he maintained that, as things played out, "it wasn't the enemy that licked us. It was disease and an absence of food."[17]

There were some last-minute efforts to upgrade the antiquated equipment in the final months before war erupted. The regiment had been equipped with Springfield .03 rifles, 3-inch trench mortars, and water-cooled machine guns—relics of World War I not just in design but also in being the actual equipment used, which was now decades old.[18] Just before the war, they received the new M1 rifle and some 81mm mortars. The new mortars were good weapons, but since no ammunition was sent along with them, it was necessary to use the old 3-inch ammo intended for the Stokes mortars. This not only reduced the range but also produced a lot of duds. In fact, said Johnson, "when we fired on Bataan, we were suffering something better than sixty percent duds."

During the period of intensive preparation just before war broke out, there had been concern in the 57th Infantry that some of the older men might not be up to the physical rigors of combat, and a number of them were transferred out of the regiment. "In retrospect," said Johnson, "that was a mistake." When the regiment got to Bataan, and those men were back with them by necessity, they turned out to be some of the best soldiers of all. "They were best in terms of physical staying power," said Johnson, "best in terms of native cunning, best in terms of demonstrating initiative, and I think best in terms of just plain courage. In contrast, too many of the younger soldiers that we felt should have been good just didn't seem to have a heart for the tough going."

In September 1941, Colonel Brougher had given up command of the 57th Infantry, headed for promotion to brigadier general and duty with the Philippine Army. The unit had given him a review, and then at the Officers' Club put on a Regimental Despedida and Bienvenida to wish Brougher farewell and welcome his successor, Lieutenant Colonel George S. Clarke. Clarke was not an unknown entity, having previously served with the 57th as regimental executive officer, but no one could have imagined what lay ahead under his uncertain command.

CHAPTER FIVE

JAPANESE INVASION

When the first word came of the Japanese attacks on the Philippines, Johnson was in his bathrobe having breakfast at his quarters. Captain Van Oosten, a friend who was staying with the regimental commander, called and said, "Colonel Clarke wants you to alert the regiment and move it out of the barracks."

"Well, I'll tell you," Johnson responded, "I think that with an order like that I probably ought to talk to Colonel Clarke. I wonder if you would put him on the line?" Clarke came on and repeated the order in person, so Johnson immediately got things moving. That early-morning interruption caused him much regret in the days to come. "I could see," said Johnson, "all during Bataan and the prison camp days, those two fried eggs that were never consumed sitting there staring up at me from the breakfast plate."

As the troops vacated their barracks, they took up positions on a hillside within the boundaries of Fort McKinley, and there they remained for a couple of days until being ordered to central Luzon on what turned out to be a wild-goose chase in search of paratroopers reported to have landed in the vicinity of Mount Arayat. Things soon got worse.

When they got into San Fernando, Pampanga, it was after dark, and someone was in the streets paging "Colonel Clarke, Colonel Clarke." Johnson heard the page and responded for him. It was a telephone call from the chief of staff of the Philippine Division, who asked, "Where are you?" Johnson told him that they were in San Fernando en route to search for the reported paratroop invasion. "Well," said that officer, "your instructions are you are to go to Bataan and hide."

"Where?" Johnson asked.

"Just go to Bataan and hide," the colonel repeated.

Johnson didn't see that as tactically sound, so he selected a position partway into the Bataan Peninsula that could serve as a blocking position to cover the withdrawal of other forces. Reflecting the logistical state of affairs even before combat began, the move was made using "a motley collection of Army sedans, command & reconnaissance cars, weapons carriers, cargo trucks, civilian buses, trucks, taxis and passenger cars."[1] It turned out that

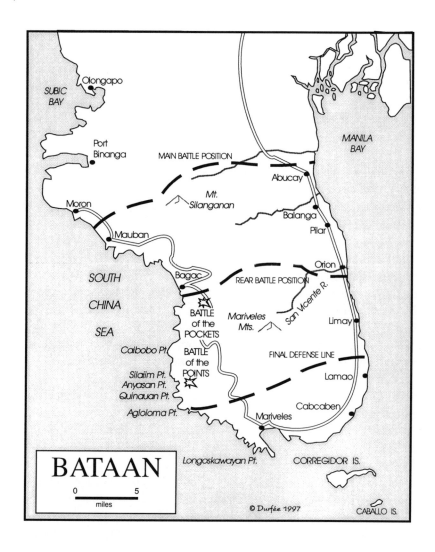

SUBIC BAY

Olongapo

Port Binanga

MAIN BATTLE POSITION

MANILA BAY

Abucay

Moron

Mt. Silanganan

Balanga

Mauban

Pilar

SOUTH

Bagac

Orion

CHINA

REAR BATTLE POSITION

San Vicente R.

SEA

BATTLE of the POCKETS

Mariveles Mts.

Limay

Caibobo Pt.

BATTLE of the POINTS

FINAL DEFENSE LINE

Silaiim Pt.
Anyasan Pt.
Quinauan Pt.

Lamao

Agloloma Pt.

Cabcaben

Mariveles

BATAAN

0   5

miles

Longoskawayan Pt.

CORREGIDOR IS.

© Durfée 1997

CABALLO IS.

the dispositions ordered by Johnson were what division headquarters had really wanted all along.

When first light came, it was apparent that tall fields of green sugarcane restricted the fields of fire in front of many positions. Captain Johnson recommended to the regimental commander, Lieutenant Colonel Clarke, that details be sent out to clear the cane. Clarke disapproved on the grounds that clearing the cane would disclose the regiment's position to the enemy. "To try to compensate, Johnson ordered that all defensive works be strongly outposted and that frequent night patrols be sent out."[2]

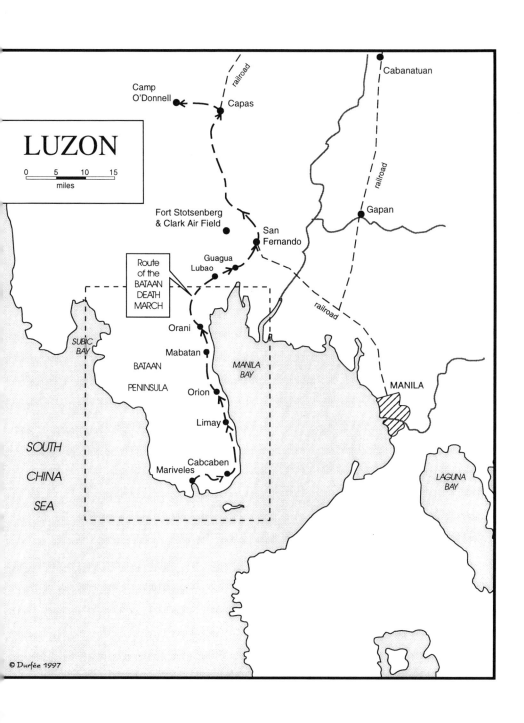

LUZON

0   5   10   15
miles

Cabanatuan

Camp
O'Donnell   Capas

railroad

railroad

Fort Stotsenberg
& Clark Air Field

Gapan

San
Fernando

Route
of the
BATAAN
DEATH
MARCH

Guagua
Lubao

railroad

SUBIC
BAY

Orani

Mabatan

MANILA
BAY

BATAAN

PENINSULA

Orion

MANILA

Limay

SOUTH

CHINA

SEA

Cabcaben
Mariveles

LAGUNA
BAY

© Durfée 1997

At Clark Field, nine hours after Pearl Harbor had been struck, the Japanese demolished MacArthur's air forces. Why they had been left there is inexplicable, as Douglas Brinkley noted nearly half a century later. "MacArthur's decision to leave his planes resting wing-to-wing like sitting ducks," he wrote, "has long baffled scholars of the Pacific War."[3] The consequences were severe. On 27 December, MacArthur cabled the War Department that "the enemy has had utter freedom of naval and air movements."[4]

Soon after the initial aerial bombardment of the Philippines, troops of the Japanese Fourteenth Army under Lieutenant General Masaharu Homma commenced assault landings on the northern coast of Luzon. They quickly overwhelmed the defending forces on the beaches, driving south toward Manila and, in the process, causing the retreating elements to abandon large amounts of stores.

There is a famous West Point song known as "Benny Havens," which includes the lyrics "may the Army be augmented, promotions be less slow." That plea was finally being answered. In the middle of this mess, late on the morning of Christmas Eve, a pouch arrived from division headquarters containing a special order announcing promotions. Clarke, the regimental commander, became a full colonel, and almost all the other officers were also promoted one grade. Thus Johnson became a major as of 19 December 1941. Things were moving fast, young officers were stepping up to greater responsibility, and the long stagnation of promotions had finally given way. In Johnson's case, because of special circumstances soon to be disclosed, he had been running a regiment as a captain, so at least he was now doing that as a field grade officer.

On 20 December, a regiment of the Philippine Army's 2d Division, mobilized for active duty three days earlier, was attached to the 57th Infantry for operational control. This unfortunate unit proved to be entirely disorganized, with an untrained staff, no functioning supply operation, and a single vehicle—a station wagon. Lieutenant Anders, the 57th's intelligence officer, was sent to establish contact with the attached regiment. He returned with a grim report: "No kitchens. No entrenching tools. Pressed cardboard helmets well varnished against rainy weather. 90% in low cut tennis shoes." And, to cap it off: "Less than 15% have ever fired a rifle."[5] The next morning, Clarke, Johnson, and Olson went over to see what could be done, but in four or five days, the attached regiment was reassigned to meet its eventual fate in other company. That brief encounter did, however, raise questions about what General MacArthur had been doing during his five years as chief military advisor to the Philippine Army.[6]

The main Japanese invasion by a force of two divisions, under cover of total air and naval superiority, began 22 December 1941. The following day, MacArthur ordered a general withdrawal of the defending forces into the Bataan Peninsula. Manila was declared an open city and fell with no resistance.[7] Colonel Olson remembered that everyone in the regiment had his own idea about how long the war would last, with the guesses ranging from two months to two years. "Captain Harold K. 'Johnny' Johnson, Operations Officer," said Olson, "who held out for the latter period, was regarded as an unqualified pessimist."[8]

The 57th Infantry remained where it had been positioned for more than three weeks, on Christmas Day drinking cranberry juice toasts to an early and victorious termination of the war.[9] They got the "early" part. On 4 January 1942, orders came to withdraw further into Bataan to what became known as the Abucay Line, a series of positions aligned east-west across the width of the peninsula. They reached that position on about 7 January, the same day they were put on half rations.[10] For them, no fighting had yet taken place, and already they were short of that most necessary commodity, food. A letter written to Johnson by his mother only a week later was returned to her stamped RETURNED TO SENDER SERVICE SUSPENDED. Things were closing in.

"The action during that [first] month was a mixture of gallant stands and heroic actions by small groups and individuals mixed with hasty withdrawals and unbecoming actions by other units," said Johnson. Part of the problem at this stage, at least for the 57th Infantry, was their regimental commander, Colonel Clarke. Known informally as "Spoony" Clarke, he was in his late forties and had been in World War I. "Clarke had a phobia about airplanes," explained Johnson. "Any time one could even be seen he tended to throw himself in a hole to escape the sight of it, and he insisted — to the extent he could do this with his face turned to the earth — that the people near him and close to him do the same thing, on the theory that there would be no disclosure of positions to the enemy."[11]

During January, Colonel Clarke had a visit from General Charles A. Willoughby, MacArthur's G-2, who apparently came over for the purpose of shoring up his old friend. The visit seemed to have the opposite effect. By this time, the situation had become untenable with respect to both the command situation in the regiment and on the larger scene. Clarke, said Johnson, "was so deathly afraid of aircraft in Bataan that he spent virtually all of his daylight hours in a dugout, away from any association with aircraft." And Johnson viewed Willoughby's trip as "one of the most demoralizing performances that I've seen. He said that there was little probability of any reinforcements, that we could not withstand even the first sign of an attack by the Japanese, that the Philippine Army had demonstrated that it wouldn't fight because it had come back into Bataan in a shambles, and that the Philippine Scouts were unlikely to fight." When Willoughby left, said Johnson, "the spirits of my regimental commander were no higher than in the beginning when he arrived. I doubt that they were lower, because spirits were at rock bottom when the visitor arrived."

Willoughby's comments were in complete contradiction to what his commander, MacArthur, had been predicting before hostilities began, but they were in most respects accurate. Two divisions of the Philippine Army were supposed to have counterattacked the invading Japanese forces, with the 26th Cavalry (Philippine Scouts) moving into position behind them. But when the 26th moved north to get into position, noted an officer, "we were passed by the 11th Infantry Division (Philippine Army) and the other division that was supposed to be attacking the Japanese. Instead, they were headed south in buses." Where Willoughby was wrong was in his estimate of the Philippine Scouts. When the time came, they fought hard and well.

The problems with Colonel Clarke became ridiculous as the regiment moved further back into Bataan, making it difficult for Johnson to carry on with his duties, which now included de facto command of the regiment. Every time Johnson started off to attend to some task, Clarke summoned him. "Johnny, come back. I've got to talk to you," he would say. When Johnson returned, his comment would be, "I don't think that you should be away from the phone." That had its effect. "Once you spend some time like that," Johnson conceded, "it's very easy to spend more time. You could get a case of 'dugoutitis' very, very quickly. I'm afraid that I suffered from it for a period of time." This was typical—Johnson being harder on himself than anyone else would ever be. Other officers in the regiment knew that under very difficult circumstances he was holding things together. "When Clarke was in command," confirmed Royal Reynolds, who commanded one of the battalions, "H. K. Johnson ran the regiment. Johnny Johnson had to run the regiment, and he *did!*"[12]

It didn't take long for the Japanese to begin an attack against the positions at Abucay, and for a while it was touch and go.[13] The 57th Infantry had been positioned on the right of the line in what was considered the critical sector, covering the coastal plain and a main road that was expected to carry the principal enemy attack. On the regiment's left were the 41st Philippine Army Division and, farther west, the 51st.

The enemy's initial onslaught, as expected, hit the 57th's lines, late on the afternoon of 10 January. The heaviest assaults banged into the 3d Battalion, where Major Paul D. Wood, then the battalion executive officer, requested artillery fire from the regiment. Colonel Clarke denied the request, fearing that such fire "would trigger retaliatory counterbattery from the enemy, which might fall on the 57th command post." Lieutenant Colonel Philip T. Fry, fearing that his position was about to be overrun, demanded that the battalion be given artillery support. This time Major Johnson, ignoring Clarke, authorized direct communication with the artillery fire direction center. Soon supporting fire was on the way.[14]

Despite fierce resistance by the 3d Battalion, an early penetration was made in the regimental sector. Johnson directed the 2d Battalion to dispatch a company to help restore the main line of resistance. At the regimental CP, said Olson, Johnson was handicapped by having little help, a consequence of Colonel Clarke's insistence on dispersing the staff into multiple locations to make less of an aerial target, but Johnson "was doing a superhuman job of trying to keep up with the situation on the front, placate Lt. Col. Fry, secure the much-needed ammunition and additional artillery support, and appraise II Corps of what was going on." He made it through with the help of two experienced staff NCOs, Master Sergeant Leonardo Versola and Sergeant Francisco Alvarado, dedicated soldiers who were "personally devoted to Johnson."[15]

In the midst of this, a critical shortage of artillery ammunition developed. How this crisis was resolved revealed a lot about Johnson's inner steel. At 6:00 P.M. on 11 January, every battery had on hand what was calculated to be sufficient ammunition for three days' fire. By 9:00 the next morning, they were down to one *hour's* fire. A request to corps for resupply was turned down on the grounds that they should have two days' supply left, ignoring the combat realities in favor of arbitrary calculations of expenditure rates. Getting no satisfaction from the corps ordnance officer, Johnson took the matter up with Major General George M. Parker, Jr., the corps commander. Parker, too, was unyielding, saying that the policy had been set by higher headquarters. Johnson, undeterred, contacted that next level, back on Corregidor, speaking to Brigadier General Richard K. Sutherland, MacArthur's autocratic chief of staff, and persuading him to break loose the needed ammunition.[16] At this time, Johnson was a major with about three weeks' time in grade, acting as commander in place of the prostrate Colonel Clarke, and in the midst of a desperate battle with the attacking Japanese.

The following night, the enemy mounted a moonlight banzai attack in which "wave after wave of screaming Japanese troops hurled themselves forward in the face of intense fire."[17] Counterattacks were able to restore the line after several days of very heavy fighting, and the Japanese, thwarted in their efforts to roll over the 57th Infantry, shifted their main effort to the west.

Nevertheless, pockets of Japanese snipers remained behind friendly lines, causing substantial problems. Lieutenant Nininger volunteered to lead a small force that would attempt to clear the snipers. So heroically did he perform this task, operating almost single-handedly until he was fatally wounded, that he earned the Medal of Honor, the first awarded in World War II. Johnson assisted in preparing the citation for his brother officer with whom he had shared many meals in the days of Quarters 5 at Fort McKinley.

"It was during this time," said Johnson, "that Colonel Clarke was relieved, pretty much a broken man because he was the victim of his fears. He was evacuated by submarine prior to the fall of Bataan." The relief took place on 15 January 1942.

Next it fell to Colonel Arnold J. Funk to lead the regiment, but he had the job only six days before being promoted to brigadier general and reassigned. Colonel Philip T. Fry was next, and his tenure lasted somewhat longer—eight days altogether, before he became ill and had to be replaced. "He was a drunk," said Royal Reynolds. Finally—on 29 January 1942—came Colonel Edmund J. Lilly, Jr., a man greatly respected and admired by the officers of the 57th. He would lead until there was no more regiment left to command.

Lilly had endured all the previous changes of command while serving as regimental executive officer, so he knew the regiment inside and out when he took over. He did a fine job with what he had to work with, and the eventual outcome was in any event inevitable, but it certainly hadn't helped that since shortly before the outbreak of hostilities the 57th Infantry had gone through five regimental commanders in just over seven months.

The left flank of the Abucay Line had been anchored on Mount Natib on the west, supposedly impassable to enemy forces. That judgment turned out to be wrong—disastrously so—as the persistent Japanese just kept sliding across the front until they came to the end of the friendly lines and then made their way through the undefended mountain area, outflanking defenders at Abucay. After that experience, Johnson later told a group of student officers, "I am not one who takes too much for granted any more."

Once the positions had been rendered untenable, orders were issued to withdraw to a line deeper into Bataan south of the Pilar–Bagac road, essentially the last lateral route above the southern tip of the peninsula. MacArthur wrote to General Marshall that on this position "I intend to fight it out to complete destruction."[18] Meanwhile, the Japanese commenced further flanking operations by amphibious means.

No sooner had the 57th Infantry reached its position on the Pilar–Bagac line than new orders were received, occasioned by Japanese landings behind friendly lines. The regiment was rushed to the west coast to repel this new incursion, and what came to be known as the Battle of the Points was under way. Johnson played a key role in bringing about that tasking.

To this point, Johnson, as the regimental operations officer, had been directing the regiment's defensive operations. Then, without warning, he was summarily relieved by Colonel Fry, who had just taken command from Colonel Funk. The reasons for this abrupt and surprising action remain uncertain. "I never really knew why," admitted Johnson. "I presume it was because he felt that I had been somewhat preemptory in my relationships with him when he was serving as a battalion commander and I was serving as the operations officer and taking actions in the name of Clarke, who gave me a rather substantial latitude in the things that I could do as the operations officer in the regiment." That seems a likely explanation, as well as an exquisitely phrased description of Johnson's relationship with Colonel Clarke, but it is difficult to fathom why Fry would not have understood and appreciated Johnson's situation under those circumstances. Given his own brief tenure and apparent relief for cause, perhaps Fry was just too absorbed with his own problems to know or care. The relief was shocking to other officers who had worked closely with Johnson, said Olson, who remembered how Johnson had "slaved so diligently and effectively" as the S-3, only to be thrown into limbo.[19]

For a period of twenty-four hours, Johnson had no assigned duties. Then a call came asking the regiment to provide a volunteer to conduct a survey of the developing situation on behalf of Brigadier General Clinton A. Pierce, the sector commander. Johnson at once volunteered for the duty. Pierce was an aggressive officer who had commanded the 26th Cavalry during the initial delaying actions, then been promoted to a larger role. He had asked for an experienced infantry field grade officer, and Johnson filled the bill as well as anyone could under the circumstances.

The enemy initially made landings at a place known as Longoskawayan Point. The 2d Battalion, 57th Infantry, was committed against this attack and, in very hard fighting, cleaned things out in about three days. The Japanese followed with landings at Anyasan, Silaiim, and Quinauan Points. As these were in the rear of the established line of resistance, they were highly threatening to the main body of friendly forces.

On the night of 29 January, Johnson arrived at Pierce's command post, where he was briefed on the situation. The news was not good. Some three miles of beach were open, efforts to deal with the attack in this sector were not coordinated, and not much was being done about it. Early the next morning, Johnson set out on a personal reconnaissance of the sector. He quickly concluded that the forces at hand were insufficient to drive out the enemy's landing forces and, in fact, "were not inclined to take offensive action." Johnson recommended that General Pierce ask for the 57th Infantry from the reserve. After approval from Wainwright's headquarters, and with the concurrence of MacArthur's staff, the regiment was released to Pierce.[20]

Meanwhile, Johnson set about doing what he could with the troops already deployed. The forces he had found in place during his reconnaissance were motley indeed, including "one constabulary regiment and some odd elements activated after the outbreak of war consisting principally of ROTC cadets and some Philippine Army Air Corps, without planes."[21] He took one rifle company of the 57th Infantry that was patrolling the road and dispatched it to Anyasan Point to establish contact with the enemy. A Philippine Army battalion was instructed to sweep the beach in its sector. He put a battalion of the 45th Infantry (Philippine Scouts) on the move along the Silaiim River toward the beach in the center of the sector, and the constabulary battalion did likewise along the Anyasan River. The 17th Pursuit Squadron, which had already been blooded when it stumbled into a Japanese machine-gun nest, he ordered to hold in place.[22] This at least introduced a little energy into the situation while the 57th Infantry made its way to the scene.

On the same day that Johnson conducted his initial reconnaissance, 29 January, Colonel Fry was relieved of command of the 57th Infantry and replaced by Colonel Lilly, so it was Lilly who reported to Pierce when the regiment was released to him. Lilly immediately reinstated Johnson in his former position as regimental operations officer,[23] and together they fought the Battle of the Points. For that purpose they were given, besides major elements of their own regiment, a battalion of the 45th Infantry, two battalions of the 1st Constabulary, and a company of tanks.[24]

By the morning of 2 February, things were ready, and an attack was launched with three battalions abreast (two from the 57th Infantry and one from the 45th Infantry, all Philippine Scouts). So thick was the jungle that it took one battalion four days to establish contact with the enemy. Johnson brought tanks along the trails, using them essentially as moving pillboxes. The enemy succeeded in disabling one and killing its crew, then filled the tank with dirt. (Once the advance moved beyond that point, friendly forces were able to scoop it out and restore the tank to action.) The thick jungle also made employment of indirect fire, including artillery and mortars, almost impossible.

After the first five days, it became necessary to rotate battalions in the assault, for the simple reason that the troops had been on half rations for a solid month and lacked the energy to sustain offensive action without some relief. Johnson found the situation sadly instructive. "A prolonged period on reduced rations destroys the will to fight almost entirely," he observed, "and as subsequent events proved, may even destroy the will to survive."[25] Nevertheless, the defenders stuck with it, and eventually prevailed.

"At the Battle of the Points," exulted Royal Reynolds, "we drove the Japanese into the sea." It took two weeks of hard fighting to do it, but the enemy's landings at all three points were decisively defeated. The 57th Infantry, and Johnson personally, played key roles in the victory. As usual, Johnson was restrained in his reaction. Japanese failure to move aggressively out of the landing areas was a major factor in their defeat, he concluded. "Bataan would have fallen not later than 7 February if such action had been taken on the part of the attacker." He was at a loss to explain this desultory behavior, except that it was "just another instance of the Japanese outfumbling us, not for the first time, and certainly not the last."[26]

Since early January, the Japanese had suffered some 7,000 battle casualties and an astounding 10,000 to 12,000 more dead of disease. On 8 February, they withdrew from forward positions and called for reinforcements.[27]

An extended lull followed, and the 57th Infantry saw little activity until the hectic last ten days of the war. Instead, they battled another enemy, one they could not overcome. "So serious was the shortage of food after the first few weeks on Bataan," noted the official history, "that the search for food assumed more importance than the presence of the enemy to the front." Foraging parties from the Philippine Scouts went hunting for carabao, and when those were mostly gone, for iguanas, monkeys, and wild pigs. The 26th Cavalry sorrowfully sacrificed its horses one by one, and the faithful mules of the 57th Infantry's Quartermaster Pack Train were slain. "It was a great outfit," said Johnson, "and we ate it all." By this time, lack of essential medicines, especially quinine, had become an equally serious problem.[28]

Placed in a reserve position in the vicinity of Signal Hill, the outfit occupied itself with reconnaissance and preparation of counterattack plans. Mostly, though, they simply tried to conserve their waning energies. Along the trail, said Johnson, there were clusters of soldiers squatting around a small fire, boiling a piece of mule hide or carabao hide in a tomato can, then chewing the thing in an effort to extract some nourishment. "The soldiers never complained," he recalled with regret, "but all the time you could just see the question in their eyes, 'What in the world have you done to us?' It was a sad, sad circumstance in which to find yourself."

During the lull, General Wainwright visited the bivouac area, where he presented his sporting rifle to Colonel Lilly, along with a letter addressed to the officers and men of the regiment. "I particularly wish to emphasize the magnificent conduct of the 57th Infantry on Bataan," Wainwright told them. "They have been staunch, loyal and brave and they overcame the enemy on every occasion while serving in the I Philippine Corps."[29] At that juncture, Wainwright had little left to give, but he gave them what he had, including his respect and gratitude, and it meant a lot.

On 1 April, the Bataan Force surgeon made a survey of the health of the command, concluding that 60 percent were incapacitated due to malaria, dysentery, or diarrhea. It was a requirement that a man have a temperature of at least 102 degrees to be so categorized.

Meanwhile, the Japanese were bringing in fresh troops, restocking logistically, and preparing to resume the offensive. On 3 April—Good Friday—they were ready. After nearly two months of preparation, the Japanese launched a large attack in the Mount Samat area and by nightfall of Easter Sunday had broken through on a broad front. The 57th Infantry, the last remaining reserve in Bataan, was moved up to the San Vicente River line on the east side of the peninsula. Johnson had just been reassigned from his post as regimental operations officer to take command of the 3d Battalion. Several times earlier he had resisted this move because the incumbent commander, Paul D. Wood, was a classmate and good friend. But now the regimental commander insisted that the change be made, and it was, with Wood remaining as executive officer.[30]

Johnson and his new command were sent to help close the gap created by the enemy attack, in the process being attached to the 31st Infantry, the regiment of the Philippine Division composed entirely of Americans. Johnson reported to the sector commander, Brigadier General Clifford Bluemel, and was told where to put his battalion into the line on the east side of the gap. It was after dark, and they were moving into a position they had not reconnoitered. Although successful in reaching the assigned sector, they were never able to identify the extent of the gap the Japanese had ripped in friendly lines.

Johnson gathered his company commanders and issued their orders, then went to confer with the regimental commander of the 31st Infantry. To his shock, he found that "they had withdrawn without informing us. We were sitting in splendid isolation from friendly forces."[31] Meanwhile, the rest of their parent outfit, the 57th Infantry, had been committed on the west side of the gap. There they made contact with the enemy but were never really able to get into their assigned positions before being forced to fall back.

Faced with this situation, Johnson again assembled his company commanders, this time issuing instructions to withdraw. The plan was to fall back to Trail 46 and go into position on the left of the 31st Infantry. He gave each of them an azimuth to follow and a rendezvous point, which was how it had been taught at Fort Benning. "That was a mistake," he later concluded, because he never saw his battalion again. It just melted into the jungle night and was swallowed up without a trace. So did everything else in the way of organized resistance. By early afternoon on 7 April 1942, said the official history, "the San Vicente line had evaporated," and the next day all was "chaos." As though to underscore the disaster, that night a major earthquake shook the peninsula.[32]

Johnson formed his command group and moved to the designated point, where he waited in vain for his companies. "I never saw any of my company commanders again," said Johnson, "until we all reached prison camp." He speculated that he had learned the wrong lesson from the Infantry School. "I probably would have kept the battalion together if I had said 'Follow me' and moved out."

Later analysis revealed that the companies had been unable to move on jungle trails because those routes were interdicted by Japanese forces. At night, in mountainous terrain with heavy undergrowth, trying to maintain a sense of direction while navigating overland was just too tough a task.[33]

"He gave us coordinates, gave us good instructions, gave us an azimuth," recalled Harry J. Stempin, who had been commanding K Company of Johnson's battalion. "But almost at once we found ourselves behind enemy lines, coming across foxholes, mess kits, rice that was still warm. We tried to follow the azimuth we'd been given, but had to deviate from it because we encountered fire, then were ambushed. Soon night fell, and we were in deep jungle. The battalion just completely disintegrated."

"I had it long enough to lose it," Johnson said ruefully, and accurately, of his brief tenure in battalion command.[34] He had a technique, Johnson once told a friend at Fort Snelling, of being able to take a quick nap and become refreshed in a short time. He was able, he said, to remove disturbing thoughts from his mind in order to do this. Now, his command lost in the jungle, he lay down in a ditch and went to sleep.

A couple of hours later, Johnson and his small group began to explore the situation around their position. They found Japanese on first one side and then the other. To their rear, a Japanese air attack struck the position they had moved out from the previous day. "It looked like things were in a state of absolute collapse at that time," said Johnson. "And they were." By now it was the night of 8–9 April, and the end was very near. For Johnson, the saddest thing was the Filipinos who came to him and asked, "But, sir, what do we do now?" In the dark, he and the others tried to link up with some friendly elements. All they encountered was one truck, about midnight, that was trying to bring rations forward. They didn't locate the regimental commander until two weeks later in prison camp.

Johnson hooked up with Major Elbridge R. Fendall, the regimental supply officer, who had been with the ration truck. By now, it was early on the morning of 9 April, and word reached them that the defending forces had been surrendered, along with instructions that everyone was to remain in place and await contact by the Japanese. The two men debated whether to try to reach the beach and maybe swim to Corregidor or paddle there with the help of a log. That seemed feasible, and they decided to try it. Fifty yards down the trail, they had second thoughts. That would just be delaying the inevitable, they concluded. Instead, they decided to return to Signal Hill, where the regiment had previously been held in reserve, and see what the situation was there. Others had had the same idea, and a number of soldiers eventually congregated at that location.

The senior officer present was Colonel Harrison Browne, chief of staff of the Philippine Division. People just sort of hung around. Some meager rations were located, and Johnson afterward remembered that someone put together "a strange kind of pie" made of grape jam. Johnson and Fendall again debated taking off. "But," Johnson said, "I think the unfortunate part was that we had been in the Philippines a little bit too long. We had been there long enough to believe that, while we trusted 97½ to 98 percent of the Filipinos, there were about two percent that we knew you couldn't trust and that would sell you for a penny to the Japanese, so you could expect to be a hunted animal if you avoided capture. This proved to be true for many of the people who avoided capture initially and who stayed near the more populated areas."[35] The Japanese came in on the afternoon of 11 April.

"The first one that saw me took my fountain pen and reached for my ring," said Johnson, referring to his West Point class ring. "I said 'no.' He made a pass at me, but I drew out of the way."[36]

The Japanese were convinced that there was a tunnel between Bataan and Corregidor. They insisted on it. "You will help us look for it," they said. Colonel Browne designated Johnson to stay and guide the Japanese and said that he could choose someone to stay with him. "Sut" Fendall volunteered to be that man. The Japanese put them in something like "an elevated playpen," a cagelike structure covered in netting, and gave them a single can of C rations. Japanese soldiers crowded around, viewing the captives like animals in a zoo. It was, said Johnson, the end of life as he had known it.

The next day, Johnson and Fendall took their captors to the top of Signal Hill and finally convinced them that there was no tunnel. The Japanese gave the two Americans a truck and instructed them to catch up with the other prisoners. The truck was a captured American engineer vehicle that was missing its radiator and front springs, but it was good for a few miles. Johnson and Fendall reached a point where the Japanese were assembling prisoners at Mariveles airfield and quickly decided to take a bypass road and see what lay ahead. Of course, there was no way that they could avoid the inevitable for long, and they soon found themselves in the midst of a Japanese convoy moving through heavy dust. By this time, they had acquired a group of about twenty-five Air Force enlisted men who had hailed the truck and asked for a ride. Johnson and Fendall put them in the back and tagged along in the convoy. They got nearly to Balanga when a Japanese standing in the middle of the road flagged them down and ordered them to dismount and join another large group of Americans being herded into a dry rice paddy. There they remained overnight, miserable and apprehensive. Perhaps, too, Johnson was having second thoughts, for later he would acknowledge that he had spent World War II as "a guest of the Japanese—not of my own volition—except in part, because I really had the chance to have taken off and didn't do it."

The next morning, the Japanese divided their captives into groups of 100 and put them on the road headed north. The Bataan Death March was under way.[37]

CHAPTER SIX

DEATH MARCH

Some analysts have suggested that the Japanese were surprised by and unprepared for the tens of thousands of prisoners they took in the Philippines and that much of the hardship experienced by those prisoners was the inevitable consequence. Yet no rationale has been offered for the brutality with which sick, starving, exhausted men were beaten, clubbed, and bayoneted as they desperately sought water or rest during the forced trek that has come to be known as the Bataan Death March.

Johnson was among some 72,000 prisoners (about 12,000 of them Americans) rounded up by the Japanese and sent north, mostly on foot, sixty or more miles to Camp O'Donnell. More than 650 Americans, along with untold numbers of Filipinos, died along the way from exhaustion, starvation, disease, wounds, or execution by their captors.

"I saw my first Jap atrocity that [first] morning," said Johnson. "Not far off, in a field, a Filipino was on his knees pleading with a Jap officer. You could see the man's arms in the air, imploring the soldiers to spare his life. The Jap laughed and shot him through the chest."[1]

Johnson also saw people bayoneted and was pushed aside at a water spigot by two Japanese who wanted to wash the blood off their bayonets. Later, as he observed the Japanese over long months of captivity, he came to realize that the Japanese handled their own soldiers in equally brutal ways. "Looking back," he concluded, "we were treated about the same way that they treated their own people, including civilians and soldiers."[2] Even so, there were also instances of kindness and compassion on the part of some guards. Prisoners never knew what to expect, and in some ways that made life even more difficult.

As the march continued, guards on bicycles prodded the prisoners to keep moving, to go faster. These were men who had been on half rations for four months and on quarter rations near the end of the fighting. Some 60 percent of them were suffering from malaria and dysentery and had received little medication.[3] Few people survived on their own, recalled Chester Johnson. Friends helped one another, and that was what got them through.

This "sadistic ordeal" stretched essentially from the village of Mariveles northward to San Fernando, Pampanga. Groups of prisoners were strung out along the route. Johnson and others departed Balanga late one afternoon after having spent the day lined up in the broiling sun. "We were forbidden to get out of line to get water," he said. "More than one American lost his life in his efforts to get to an artesian well."[4]

But even here, the anomalies of Japanese captivity surfaced. "Everybody had a different pace that he followed during the march," said Johnson, "because there were plenty of opportunities to hide out. You didn't know what the result would be if you got caught," of course. "Some people were bayoneted. Other people were helped into a little *caratella* or *calesa*, the little cart that is pulled by a pony, and sent on to the next stopping point. It all depended on the whim or the mood of the guard that saw you as to what happened to you."

Johnson cited his service in the Philippine Scouts as an important advantage. The Scouts who had not been captured were moving around relatively freely and would search out their officers and try to help. They might produce a can filled with porridge rice, called *lugao,* or some sugar. "They would give you a section of sugar cane so that you could suck it," remembered Johnson gratefully. "The fact that you could get a meal or two made just a whale of a lot of difference. I suspect that the psychological boost was even more favorable."

At a place called Orani, on Manila Bay, they stopped for the night and were confined in a pigpen. They had been given no food, and the next day made one of their longest marches, still without food. During a midday halt, the guards required them to sit on hot pavement. "That day," remembered Johnson, "several Americans wandered off, out of their minds, insulting the guards in an effort to be shot." As they plodded along, mile after mile, with no food and very little water, "all that kept most of us alive was the fact that maybe somehow we would be able to communicate with our families and relieve them of the awful anguish of not knowing what had become of us."[5]

AT HOME, Dorothy Johnson had gone to Grafton, North Dakota, to visit her husband's mother. Johnson's father had died a year earlier, so when Dorothy went up in September 1941, she wound up staying for a year. It was there that she heard on the radio about Pearl Harbor and learned somehow that the 57th Infantry was withdrawing into Bataan. After that, there was nothing. "For one year I didn't even hear that he was a prisoner," she said. "I didn't know whether he was alive or not."

ARRIVING AT LUBAO the following night, the prisoners were herded into a huge tin warehouse, perhaps 3,000 of them crammed into a space that might comfortably have accommodated 500. They managed to sit, but there was no room to lie down, and few got much rest. The American and Filipino captives had quickly been separated by the Japanese. Now "a Filipino staggered into the building, with a Jap soldier directly behind him. There was the thud of a large club, and the skull of the Filipino was split. The body was carried outside and thrown into the brush."[6]

The marchers arrived at their destination piecemeal over a period of about ten days in mid-April. For Johnson and his group, the second-longest march was from Lubao to San Fernando. Several Americans dropped out, some never to be seen again. Johnson reached the end of the line on 22 April, estimating that he had covered a distance of 80 to 100 kilometers since setting out on 12 April. Along the way, he had managed to lie low for a couple of days. "I just hid out and rested," he said, "and Philippine Scout soldiers would provide a couple of meals."[7]

At San Fernando, the survivors were herded into cramped holding areas, first in a cock-fighting pit for several days and then in a schoolyard so crowded that there was barely room to sit.[8] Many Filipinos took risks to help the unfortunate captives. When prisoners began arriving, women from the Philippine Red Cross and other women's clubs cared for the sick and wounded to the extent the Japanese permitted. They also attempted to prepare and serve food, but the guards would not allow it.

Food for Johnson's group was a rice ball about the size of a baseball, issued the following morning. Then the prisoners were marched to the railroad station and loaded into undersized boxcars, perhaps 100 men to a car, standing close together. The heat was extreme, there was no water, and even air became scarce. Many collapsed, and some died, while the train was en route to Capas, a town about forty kilometers farther north—four hours or more on the rickety railroad. There still remained to be endured "the Last Kilometers."[9]

Unloaded from the boxcars, the prisoners were formed up and marched west through the streets of the barrio. Despite stern warnings and blows from the guards, local Filipinos darted in among the prisoners and thrust into their hands small gifts of rice, sugarcane, and water. Others hovered at a distance, tossing food to the marching men; when bits fell to the ground, guards went out of their way to trample it. Some Filipinos took off their hats and handed them to prisoners who had no protection from the intense sun.[10]

From Capas, the captives were marched six kilometers to what would be for many their last stop. It was known as Camp O'Donnell, but Colonel Olson called it the Andersonville of the Pacific.[11]

AN UNFINISHED CAMP intended for mobilization use by a Philippine Army division, Camp O'Donnell was wholly inadequate to house the 90,000 prisoners crammed into it by the Japanese. Spread out on a flat, treeless plain and completely exposed to the brutal tropical sun, it provided only bamboo-framed huts with thatched grass roofs for shelter. It stank, and the stink got worse every day.[12]

New arrivals at the camp were given a "welcome" ceremony conducted by Captain Yoshio Tsuneyoshi, called disdainfully by Olson "an insignificant, overage-in-grade junior officer." He started his new charges out with a shakedown of every man.[13]

The Adjutant of the prisoners' organization established a "Journal" in which he recorded, among other things, the rules laid down by the camp commander. The first was that the Japanese Army did not recognize ranks of prisoners of war. The second was a curfew confining all prisoners to their barracks from 7:00 P.M. until 6:40 A.M., a particularly cruel restriction to impose on men suffering from dysentery; fortunately, this provision was rescinded the following day. (Prisoners developed the term "a rice brain act" to describe such inanities.) The third rule was that "anyone disobeying orders or trying to escape will be shot to death."[14]

Johnson, like the other prisoners, was assigned to a nipa-roofed barracks, where he slept on the upper deck of a bamboo rack. Each man had about two feet of space, so no one could even turn over without disturbing those on either side. At O'Donnell, there was generally a substantial ration of rice, but water was in desperately short supply. Sometimes only one tap was available for use by thousands of thirsty prisoners, and getting enough water to stay alive became "the prime concern" of every man in camp. The long line to reach the tap inched slowly forward, and men frequently had to stand for half a day to fill one canteen, sometimes leaving behind someone who had quietly expired while waiting his turn. Then the pump would break down, and for an agonizing time there would be no water for anyone. Eventually, the Japanese allowed water-carrying parties to go to a nearby river, and those men always took raincoats under which they could smuggle back small quantities of food obtained from local Filipinos.[15]

Decades later, Johnson wrote of "the first meal at which salt was available for the rice. I can also recall the first meal when a tiny quantity of meat was available for gravy for the rice."[16] Such small things assumed enormous significance in the prison camp environment. "The first ten days I was a prisoner . . . our rice was unsalted," Johnson would later say. "On the eleventh day we got salt and a new life began." Olson recorded a common saying of the day: "Perhaps the greatest virtue of rice is that *anything* will improve it."[17]

The prisoners established their own set of guards, stationed ten yards inside the fence. Their purpose, according to the Journal, was "to prevent other prisoners from violating standing orders and to put out fires."[18] The key incentive for this self-policing was what the Japanese called the "ten man rule": if anyone escaped, all the others in his ten-man squad would be executed. Olson reports that although this draconian measure was never enforced at O'Donnell proper, it was applied to work details sent out from there.[19]

At the end of May, Captain Olson was hospitalized with dengue fever, and Johnson briefly took over his responsibility for preparing daily strength reports. This was potentially hazardous duty, since the Japanese had decreed that, should any discrepancies turn up between the strength report and the head count at periodic unscheduled musters, "the American Personnel Officer would be suitably punished." According to Olson, "suitably punished" meant death before a firing squad.[20] Fortunately, neither man was caught in any discrepancies.

Virtually everyone was ill with one or more ailments—malaria, amoebic and bacillary dysentery, wet and dry beriberi—on top of endemic malnutrition. In late April, Johnson was afflicted with severe diarrhea, in one twenty-four-hour period making thirty-six visits to a slit trench. "Each visit to the latrine took a lot of energy," he said, "and sometimes the reservoir of energy and determination was close to empty."

Finally Johnson was moved to the prison hospital—in reality, no more than a separate holding area. Transfer there was a virtual death sentence, especially to the feared "Zero Ward," described by Olson as "the miserable little room where the terminal dysentery cases spent their final hours."[21] A friend managed to get three sulfathiozol tablets from somewhere and passed them to Johnson. Maybe that made the difference in pulling him through. "I was one of the very few that came out of that place," said Johnson, "and again I don't know why. I just know that I came out." Clearly this was the beginning of a growing feeling on Johnson's part that he was being watched over, and spared, for some purpose he could not yet divine. Later he would say that the closest he ever came to dying while in the Philippines was during those first two weeks at O'Donnell.[22]

Under conditions like these, every man sought some source of inner strength. Johnson returned with renewed intensity to the religious teachings of his youth. "There were a lot of times when you just wondered whether God up there in the sky was going to pull you through," he recalled. "God was close and very real in those hours."

In later years, every man in the Army knew of Johnson's abiding religious faith, and those who served closely with him saw daily evidence of it. Most, like Harris Hollis, also thought they knew its origins. "The Bataan experience and the long years of incarceration by the Japanese, with incredible suffering, gave this man a religious faith and resolution which sustained him mightily in adversity," he wrote of Johnson. "If he had a flaw it lay perhaps in according to others that probity and sense of duty that he, himself, had in abundance."[23]

In later life, Johnson would often refer to the prison camp experience when discussing his religious convictions. "I don't think you can get by without a faith in God," he told a group of student officers as he described his ordeal. He recalled his early religious training and how he had developed "a faith in God and that God will take care of you. And then a faith in family, and you're just determined that you're going to get back to them."

In prison camp, "I couldn't remember the Lord's Prayer to save me," he recalled. "Boy, I wanted to. Some people carried small New Testaments. They were pretty treasured pieces." Under these circumstances, his religious convictions were reawakened and strengthened: "You've got a real consciousness that you had to have an anchor to hold to in the prison camp— this just came to you."

When Johnson recovered from his illness, he was assigned as work detail officer for the camp. This was the start of a desperate game for survival. Work details were sent out of camp to cut wood or haul supplies. Some men had concealed money, despite the frequent inspections and shakedowns by the Japanese; others acquired it by selling watches and rings to their guards. With this money, those on the outside might surreptitiously acquire small amounts of food or medicine. Johnson quickly observed that work detail assignments "were very eagerly sought, and the system quickly got to a point where favors were exchanged between prisoners to see that the right persons got to go outside. I was assigned as work detail officer to stop that kind of exchange and put it on an honest basis, with no fees attached, which I did."

These duties brought Johnson into close daily contact with the Japanese camp administration, something he found frustrating, aggravating, and fascinating. "I carried on a steady confrontation at a very low-key level on the matter of bowing and saluting," he said. He decided that he would bow when he went into the Japanese headquarters because that was their practice as a courtesy to officers. Then the interpreters told him that he must also bow to noncommissioned officers when he spoke to them. "No," he replied, "Americans do not bow. Americans salute, but an American officer doesn't salute a noncommissioned officer."

That logic didn't satisfy the Japanese. "Oh," they would protest, "but you must do this, too. You are now with the Japanese."

"But I am an American," Johnson insisted. This dialogue continued throughout his imprisonment in the Philippines, said Johnson, but the Japanese "never got very insistent about it. They never said, 'You will bow.' It was an interesting experience."

"I have looked upon the period as a prisoner of war as a great laboratory of human behavior," Johnson said in later years. He was referring to the behavior of people under stress—his fellow prisoners—and to dealings with their captors. In some sense, Johnson viewed his relations with the Japanese as his "salvation, because we were always trying to figure ways to outwit them without them losing face among themselves or overtly to us."

The matter of how to behave in this new status as prisoner of war was a troubling one. The Japanese had, from the beginning, separated Americans and Filipinos, and soon they took the senior American officers to separate confinement facilities. They next adopted practices that, if not specifically designed to undermine any semblance of a functioning chain of command among the prisoners, in practice had that effect. They assigned prisoners supervisory responsibilities without regard to their rank or authority as American soldiers. Likewise, in billeting prisoners, the Japanese broke down unit integrity by assigning men to barracks according to their civilian skills—clerks, drivers, carpenters, and so forth. "Later," wrote Olson, "when the move was made to Cabanatuan, all semblance of the former organizations was lost and never regained."[24]

Johnson was candid in assessing what happened. "The standard of the officer deteriorated very, very badly," he testified, "through a whole variety of circumstances. With the passage of time some standards were restored, but the ethic and the aura of officer integrity simply could not be recaptured fully." The consequences for the prisoners were devastating. "There was just a complete disregard, in most instances, and virtually all instances, for the welfare of anyone," he emphasized. "It was just sort of every man for himself and the devil take the hindmost."

Johnson and some others did what they could to get things back on track. Among the prisoners, rank was restored (despite Japanese dictates that there would be none), an internal prisoner structure for administering the camp was established, and some semblance of responsibility and accountability was regained. According to Johnson, the results were tangible, reflected especially in reduction of the very high death rate, which had, to a substantial degree, resulted "from just not caring. People just didn't care. The people that died didn't care any more—they just gave up—and the people who were near the people who died didn't care if they died, so it was a combination of a number of attitudes."

The outlook of the Japanese reinforced such attitudes. "I was asked many times by the Japanese," said Johnson, " 'Why you no suicide?' I said, 'Americans don't suicide.' 'Oh, but you should suicide,' they would say." In the Japanese soldier's code, as Johnson came to understand it, a soldier who surrendered to the enemy dishonored himself and his nation. The only honorable course of action when one could no longer fight was to commit suicide. Thus the Japanese had only disdain for these Americans who rejected that outlook. "Of course," added Johnson practically, "it would have taken a burden from their shoulders if we had committed suicide."[25]

After the war, Johnson wrote a thoughtful paper in which he analyzed the breakdown of discipline and leadership among the American prisoners, developments that troubled him greatly. The critique was too hard-hitting for *Military Review.* Its editor, Colonel Nadal, expressed the conviction that it was better that "some of the break-down in our national system be left *unsaid."*

"Greed and self-aggrandizement were rampant on the route of the Death March as men of all ranks fought for the pitifully small tokens of food offered by friendly Filipinos along the road," Johnson had written. As evidence of the widespread failure of leadership, he reported that "there was no mutual confidence, no obedience, no respect for the individual or his rights, and certainly there was no cooperation on a large scale." That was too stiff for *Military Review,* which advised Johnson to select another topic.

Later, after yet another war had revealed the vulnerabilities of prisoners of war and the need for some standards of behavior for those unfortunate enough to find themselves incarcerated, American authorities developed and promulgated what was called a "Code of Conduct" for prisoners of war. Johnson approved. "I don't expect that many people will abide by [it,]" he acknowledged, because most people would find its standards hard to meet, especially under duress, "but it's important to have, because it gives you a yardstick against which to measure conduct. It tells you what's expected of you." In the absence of such standards, observed Johnson, many prisoners of the Japanese were overcome by despondency, caught in a situation that they were not equipped to cope with.

Clearly, too, Johnson's views on the Code of Conduct revealed his own second thoughts about what had happened on Bataan. "One of the very vivid things in my memory was . . . the surrender . . . when we had no Code of Conduct and people could only sort of guess generally what was expected of them. And the Filipino soldier, Philippine Scout, with whom I was associated would come to his American officer and say, 'Sir, what do we do now?' Well, we were ordered to surrender. That was what we had to tell them. This is the order that came from our commanders, our chain of command. But the practical thing was to hide out, evade, not turn ourselves in, and, I guess, nothing struck me quite as hard as did this total reliance of the Philippine Scout on his American officer. 'Sir, what do we do now?' " That regret, if regret is the right word, stayed with Johnson for the rest of his life.

"My most vivid memory of Camp O'Donnell," wrote Johnson, "is the rate at which prisoners died from lack of medicines and from malnutrition."[26] Olson confirmed that O'Donnell was, "in terms of death and suffering, . . . by far the worst."[27] By this time, it was possible for the prisoners to keep some sort of track of their numbers and what happened to people, and of course their Japanese captors kept tabs on the prisoners as well. By Johnson's recollection, about 1,800 Americans died and were buried at Camp O'Donnell, mostly in the six weeks before the camp was largely closed and the bulk of the inmates moved elsewhere. That represented nearly 20 percent of the American prisoners incarcerated there.[28]

On 4 June 1942, most of the Americans left O'Donnell, bound for new prison quarters at a place called Cabanatuan. They were, as things turned out, going to be there for a long, long time.

CHAPTER SEVEN

CABANATUAN

Cabanatuan was another Philippine Army camp, named for a nearby town. When the prisoners were moved there the camp was still incomplete, lacking even a fence. Whereas all the captives at O'Donnell had been taken on Bataan, here they were joined by men seized on Corregidor and elsewhere in the Philippines.[1] The site housing the Americans was designated Camp No. 1.

Once they had been moved to Cabanatuan, Johnson began what was to become a very significant document, both for him personally and for what it preserved of the prisoner of war experience, a prison camp diary. The project was not without risk, for the Japanese would confiscate any such materials they discovered, so both preparation and retention of the diary had to be clandestine. For this purpose he somehow acquired a small school notebook, four by six inches in size. On the cover was printed "Lecture Note Book," and underneath that Johnson wrote "Personal I, Lt. Col. Harold K. Johnson, Cabanatuan Prisoner of War Camp." (Later there would be a second nearly identical notebook, designated "Personal II.")

The first entry is dated 1 October 1942, almost six months after Johnson entered captivity, and begins like a letter, addressed "Dearest Dorothy." "I hope during the course of the next few weeks," Johnson wrote, "to bring the whole war up to date as far as I can remember." Sadly, and tellingly, the subject then turns immediately to food. Recalling the morning of 8 December 1941, when Colonel Clarke called to have Johnson alert the regiment, Johnson tells his wife that "the remainder of my breakfast remains uneaten, much to my regret. I know I left two fried eggs, turned over to a turn."

Over succeeding months and years, the diary reflects Johnson's analysis of the defensive campaign they had waged against the Japanese, details of prison life, philosophical reflections, and aspirations for the future. The last entry, made in mid-October 1944, anticipates evacuation of the surviving prisoners to Japan. Clearly Johnson does not think that he will be able to carry the diary with him when they are shipped out, so he is closing it and apparently making provisions to secure it somewhere.

Many of the early entries recount the weeks of combat. Johnson is uncompromising in assessing his own performance, a trait that appears deeply ingrained. "As I look back," he wrote, "I am dreadfully ashamed of my conduct during the first month of the war. Col. Clarke was a craven coward, nothing more. I attempt to excuse myself by saying that I had come to believe in him almost implicitly." This self-evaluation is contrary to that of other officers in the regiment, who perceived that Johnson, as operations officer, was all that was holding things together. He is also very clear in his evaluation of the Scouts: "In retrospect I think that the work of the Filipinos, taken as a whole, was excellent," he wrote. "We let them down, horribly so, and at a tremendous cost to them."

The Japanese divided the prison population into three groups of presumably healthy prisoners and a hospital group for those who were ill. Early on, Johnson was appointed adjutant for one of the three groups, numbering about 2,000 men. It was frustrating duty. Every morning, and again in the late afternoon, Johnson would have to report to the Japanese the results of head counts taken at roll call formations. Almost invariably, the count he reported did not agree with the number carried by the Japanese. Sometimes Johnson would be tied up for as long as two hours trying to reconcile the figures or would be sent back to take another head count and report again. Since there was no fence, Johnson didn't know whether someone had walked off or not. "It was a pretty dreary job," said Johnson. Eventually he got out of it the hard way by coming down with jaundice.

Following on the severe diarrhea that had afflicted him at Camp O'Donnell, this was one of a series of ailments that Johnson contracted while a prisoner, including malaria, wet beriberi and then dry beriberi, and finally dysentery, all the while losing more and more weight.

After recovering somewhat, Johnson was designated commissary officer for the new camp, a position he elevated to an art form. The guards permitted local Filipino vendors to deliver bulk foodstuffs to the camp for resale to the prisoners. The prisoners were being paid by the Japanese at a prescribed rate for their equivalent grade, as required by the Geneva Convention. Although the Japanese retained most of these amounts for mandatory deposit to postal savings accounts, the prisoners did receive the small residual.

Prisoners placed orders for the goods they wanted and deposited the funds required to pay for them. Johnson then negotiated the purchases, paid for them, and oversaw distribution of the groceries. The Japanese told Johnson that he could not spend more money than the prisoners earned— that is, the amount he received officially from them. But the food they were buying on the outside was all that was keeping many men alive, and Johnson was determined to get all that he could. The task, then, was to deceive the Japanese as to the amount of goods being acquired and the sources of the funds to pay for them. Under these circumstances, Johnson, a man of impressive integrity, proved to have impressive deceptive skills as well. Creative bookkeeping was part of the strategy. "I have had my books audited twice by the Japanese with no faults to date," he wrote in his diary in late August 1943. "My biggest difficulty is explaining our distribution of profits." Meanwhile, a prisoner committee carefully audited the scrupulously maintained real books.

The prisoners viewed the position of commissary officer as extremely powerful. Food, after all, represented the difference between life and death. It was no accident that Johnson was chosen for the job. "They needed the most honest man in the camp to handle the food," said a fellow prisoner. "There was only one choice—Johnny Johnson."[2] Johnson found the distraction of the work a blessing. "I think it is as interesting a job as there is in camp," he wrote to Dorothy in the diary. "It is also subject to the most criticism, so the two factors are compensatory." On one occasion, he recorded that there had been "a big wrangle" in the Camp Council of Administration regarding his operation. "As our food supply grows shorter," he wrote, "more suspicious eyes are cast on the commissary and the methods of distribution." Johnson was philosophical: "I feel that I have been fair all the way through and more I cannot do."

"My commissary business is booming," wrote Johnson in early January 1943. "Our pay and the increased number of items available has helped tremendously. Eggs and fresh fruits are the only commodities that don't show with enough volume. There are enough for a taste around, however." Again, his duties put him in frequent contact with the Japanese, and he made a study of how to deal with them. "They have to be pushed a great deal to grant even small concessions," he noted, "and my one fear, due to repeated warnings from them, is that all buying privileges will be revoked." He walked a line between pushing hard and getting results and pushing too hard and getting cut off, with only his own judgment and intuition to guide him in handling the volatile and often unpredictable Japanese. The effort cost him something, Johnson acknowledged. "The constant pounding is bearing fruit, but at no little cost to my own self-respect, what with the incessant bowing, scraping, and kowtowing to these very stupid people," he wrote in his diary. Sometimes Johnson even sold a few items to the *Japanese*, once being rewarded with a cup of warm beer from a guard he allowed to buy two bars of soap.

On one occasion, Johnson showed that he wasn't afraid to take risks if he thought it would advance the cause. Going into the supply section of Japanese headquarters, he sat down at the typewriter and began banging out a note. In the presence of the Japanese officer in charge, the noncommissioned officers who supervised the operation, and two English-speaking interpreters, he typed "To Whom It May Concern," followed by a request for free passage through roadblocks on routes leading into nearby Cagayan Valley for the purpose of procuring materials for the American prisoners at Cabanatuan. The Japanese paid no attention, and Johnson walked out with his official-looking pass in hand.

So successful was Johnson that on one occasion he even persuaded his captors to let him go into Cabanatuan (escorted, of course) to see what he could purchase there. To his surprise, he was able to arrange a rice allotment. Ratcheting the Japanese up, he next lobbied successfully for a trip to Manila. He was taken by train, spending about three hours in the city. As Johnson walked down the platform of the railroad station, with a Japanese guard on either side of him, he caught the sound of a tune being whistled by someone and recognized it as "God Bless America." Turning his head slowly, so as not to attract the attention of his guards, he saw a small Filipino boy, maybe nine or ten years old, wagging a "V" sign at him as he whistled the tune. The encounter boosted Johnson for weeks.

During his eighteen months as commissary officer, Johnson spent a million and a half pesos. Only a third of the total, half a million pesos, came from "legitimate" prisoner pay. The rest was money the men had concealed, money they had obtained by selling watches and rings to their guards, and especially money smuggled in from outside.[3] With these funds, he procured fruits and vegetables, sugar, oil, lard, rice, and eggs to supplement the prison diet, and soap, lime, matches, and cigarettes to provide some comfort. He also persuaded the Japanese to sell him leftovers from their canteen.

In later years, Johnson said that this was the toughest job he ever had, and also the job in which he took the greatest pride, "because I think that I was helpful and I endeavored to be honest to the extent that I understand the word." During the time he held the job, some 2,500 or more American prisoners met their deaths. It seems certain that, but for Johnson's commissary operation, that figure would have been much higher.

One reason is that Johnson used the power of his position to insist that those prisoners who were able to work and earn money donate some of it to help those who were too ill to work. When the hospital's ration was cut to two sacks of rice a day, he replaced the shortfall with purchases made from the commissary fund's profits. This undoubtedly saved more lives, and it was only at Johnson's insistence that it was done. A few people took the initiative to "socialize the distribution of commissaries," Johnson wrote, with limited success "due to opposition from almost all hands." Another charitable mechanism in which Johnson had a hand was a group of fifty officers who arranged to donate a portion of their meager pay to buy supplemental food for men who were too sick to work.

On one occasion, implausibly, Johnson received a turkey at some holiday season, perhaps sent by his family. Instead of keeping it for himself, Johnson conducted a drawing for the whole camp. The winner received this "invaluable prize," as it was described by one man. Later, Johnson explained that the raffle was "simply the way I chose to avoid taking advantage of the position" of commissary officer. "I should say that it was somewhat hard to do," he admitted. Johnson's character and integrity were remembered with respect by those who benefited from this scrupulous honesty. "It doesn't matter that he was an officer," said a fellow prisoner, "or that he got to be a four-star general. He was just a good *man.*"

"Life in prison camp was almost a sine curve of ups and downs," wrote Johnson,[4] and it was an emotional roller coaster as well. Rumors abounded, often majestic in their plausibility and inventiveness, and they had their uses. They were "all fantastic," said Johnson, "but, in large measure, responsible for the hope that everyone holds that it won't be too long." One of the most fantastic was a September 1943 report (somewhat premature) that Germany was out of the war. "We grasp at all straws," said Johnson.[5]

Much of the variation in camp life revolved around the availability of food. On New Year's Eve in 1942, Johnson and his friend Jack acquired a couple of bottles of gin, and Jack baked some type of small cakes. "Zero" Wilson directed the production of a melodrama for entertainment, and at midnight, cocoa and cookies were served. "Little did we think that the New Year would treat us so well," wrote Johnson in his diary.[6] It wasn't always that easy, and by August 1944 Johnson called their food problems "most acute." Every day, at least five men were admitted to the hospital, most suffering from severe malnutrition. Johnson referred to these as the "black days" at Cabanatuan.

The tedium and boredom were also difficult to endure. Sometimes they played cribbage or bridge or poker with a couple of decks of well-worn and carefully handled plastic cards. Poker wasn't exactly Johnson's forte. Back home after the war, he had to write a check for $1,078 to another man to settle his poker debt. He didn't regret that at all, Johnson maintained, "because I figured if I came out of there broke, but I came out alive, I was ahead of the game." The agreement was that if you survived you paid your debts, but if you didn't make it, those debts were forgiven. "The living paid and the dead didn't. It was just that simple."[7]

Food, rumors, and word from home were the great morale builders, but there was little of the latter. When Johnson received a package from Dorothy in March 1944, it was the first mail he had had from her in a year. (Of course, she was writing frantically, but the Japanese did not allow the mail to get through.) Johnson was ravenous for the image of his loved ones and was bitterly disappointed that the package contained no photographs. Communication the other way was equally spotty. The Japanese sometimes provided their prisoners with postcards bearing preprinted blocks that could be checked to indicate their state of health and the like, and once in a while Dorothy would receive one of those in Aberdeen, South Dakota, where she was waiting out the war.[8] "Everybody in town knew," she said. "It would be in the paper before I even knew about it."

Contemplation of spiritual questions occupied Johnson as well. "I have been reading some books on religion the last two weeks," he wrote in his diary in February 1944. "I would like very much to come to an understanding with myself regarding religious matters." He felt the need for some new approach: "I am certain that Methodism as I understand and was taught it is definitely not the answer. . . . I have done so much thinking, and I am so uncertain." His outlook on religion was influenced by some of the chaplains who were his fellow prisoners, especially a Catholic priest he came to know well. This man constantly circulated among the prisoners, day after day, encouraging them, helping with physical and emotional problems, with depression. His credo was "God will protect, God will provide." Johnson came to admire him greatly, calling him a "fabulous individual who brought a deep conviction and reverence to many," including himself.[9] He later wrote, "during the years of my time in Japanese prison camps I turned to the Bible and derived a great deal of comfort from it."

Johnson was also impressed by the Masons he observed in prison camp, by the way they cared for one another and banded together to get through the ordeal. This was a factor in his decision after the war to join the Masonic order.

September 1944 brought the most exciting event of their long captivity—American planes in the sky over the Philippines. "You can have no idea of the mixed feeling that swept us when the first large flight came into view over the mountains to the southeast," Johnson wrote in his diary. "A short while later another flight of about sixty passed almost overhead." Johnson wanted to believe that they were American but was unsure until the nearby airport was strafed and a Japanese plane shot down practically in their own backyard. "That convinced me," he said with obvious satisfaction.

Johnson was at Cabanatuan for twenty-eight months. There he survived some serious illnesses, maintained his mental health and optimism, provided moral leadership and practical help to his fellow prisoners in his role as commissary officer, and—in common with them all—longed for freedom, family, and home. "Somehow I have an abiding faith that I will be with you again in the not too distant future," he wrote to Dorothy in his prison diary a year into the ordeal. But that was still years away, and in the meantime, things were going to get worse, much worse.

As EARLY AS the spring of 1943, there had been disquieting reports that the Japanese were preparing to evacuate their prisoners to Japan to prevent their being liberated by advancing Allied forces. "If there is any chance of the Philippines being retaken it would be heartbreaking to climb aboard a ship bound for Japan," wrote Johnson in his diary. But that was exactly what was about to happen. In October 1944, the prisoners at Cabanatuan were moved to Bilibid Prison in Manila, in preparation for their transport to Japan. Johnson was in the last of three groups that made the move on successive days, being transferred on 21 October.

The prisoners had a clandestine radio in camp, built into a canteen for concealment. Johnson was aware of it because he had helped procure batteries and parts, but he had avoided knowing the radio's location so that, if he were interrogated, he would be unable to give it away. On the night before they were to be moved to Bilibid, Johnson listened to the radio for the first time. What he heard was a rebroadcast of MacArthur's return to the Philippines, the famous landing on Leyte that had taken place earlier that day. "This is the Voice of Freedom, General MacArthur speaking," he heard. "People of the Philippines, I have returned." There the prisoners were, scheduled to be moved the next day, just as their liberators were at hand. "You just hoped against hope," said Johnson, "that something would interfere with that movement." Nothing did.

Johnson had one last important task before departing Cabanatuan: completing and securing his prison diaries. "This will be my last entry," he wrote on 16 October. "I only hope that we can read this together, and I feel certain that we will." The diaries had been kept, on and off, for just over two years. Written in the form of an extended letter to Dorothy, the entries had nevertheless been austere in terms of personal expression. Now, at the end, he said what was in his heart: "I love you, my darling, with all of my being, and I never did realize how much until this was started. You are all I ever want. Johnny." Then he went to a carefully chosen spot where he dug a hole, deposited a tin containing the precious diaries, covered it up, and walked away.

CHAPTER EIGHT

HELL SHIPS

Even before leaving Cabanatuan, Johnson had begun thinking about how he was going to handle the prisoner of war experience after the fact. "I have about come to the conclusion," he wrote in his diary, "that the sooner I forget everything that happens in here the better off I will be." A few weeks later, he added that "despite the monotony and routine, this confinement has been rich in experiences. I cannot feel too much regret except for the separation." Adoption of this outlook must have represented an enormous effort of will, and the experiences that still lay ahead were going to make it even more difficult.

Johnson was a brave spirit, and his example had sustained many another man during the long years of confinement. But as one milestone after another passed with no release in sight—one more birthday for Dorothy or the children, another Christmas, another anniversary, another year since his family had sailed home from Manila—the ordeal became more difficult to endure. If he were not home by the time little Ellen Kay went off to school, three years hence, wrote Johnson in his diary, "I doubt much that my own resiliency of spirit will stand it. I am aware each day of certain minute changes in my own mental attitude and am powerless to stop them. They are hard to analyze. I wish so desperately to go home and can see no quick end to our present condition." That had been his outlook in January 1944.

During the long wait in Bilibid Prison, Johnson often thought about what made the difference between those who survived and those who did not. He concluded that participation in the Boy Scouts may have been a factor. In the primitive and deprived circumstances of prison camp, he said, "the ability to care for one's self that had been instilled during Scouting days came to the fore, and you could almost identify on a case-by-case basis those people who had had Scout training, and those people who had not." Johnson observed that those who live through prison camp "do so because they have a strong spiritual foundation, an ability to care for material needs under conditions of the greatest austerity, and an abiding faith in their ability to survive, coupled with a determination to survive."

The two months in Bilibid had been filled with foreboding, and now the worst fears were realized. Instead of rescue and an end to the ordeal, it was evacuation to Japan and a most uncertain future.

ON THE APPOINTED DATE, the prisoners were taken from Bilibid and, carrying their few belongings on their backs, marched through Manila to Pier 7. The streets were lined with Filipinos, who regarded the unfortunate captives with sympathy. That reaction, said Johnson, seemed to puzzle the Japanese, who thought that they would be exposing their charges to scorn and humiliation.[1]

Late in the afternoon, after a large number of Japanese women, children, and merchant mariners had boarded the ship, loading of the prisoners began. Johnson later learned that the famed guerrilla leader Colonel Russell Volckmann had some of his men positioned on the bluff above San Fernando as the prisoners were being loaded. They had debated a rescue attempt, Volckmann later told Johnson, but decided that it was too risky.[2]

The ship they boarded, soon to become infamous, was the *Oryoku Maru,* a Japanese passenger liner. Johnson was in Group 2, consigned to the forward baggage hold. Some 588 men were crammed into that space, where temporary platforms had been constructed to hold more people. No water had been available during the long wait at the docks, and there was none on the ship, although some rice and fish and a little tea were issued on board. The crowded conditions meant that the men had to sit with their knees drawn up in order to have any space at all. If someone stood up, he lost his place to sit, and there was constant jockeying for position.

That first night gave a foretaste of what lay ahead. Crowded in, the heat nearly unbearable, without water or latrine facilities, the conditions were unspeakable. Johnson remembered that after it got dark, people took turns getting up on the first steps of the ladder and just talking soothingly, "reminiscent of talking to a herd of cattle in a lightning storm or thunderstorm." Even so, many men literally went out of their minds, driven mad by unbearable thirst. Some undetermined number in the hold where Johnson was—later he put the figure at forty-three—suffocated, and this before they had even sailed. It was quickly becoming apparent why this and other vessels used to evacuate prisoners would soon become known as "hell ships."[3]

Under way the next morning, the ship—which was not marked in any way to show that it was carrying American prisoners—was attacked by a small flight of U.S. planes and driven aground. The Japanese women and children on the upper decks suffered tremendously; in the holds, a few prisoners were wounded by ricocheting bullets. During the day, the aircraft returned again and again, making a dozen or more attacks altogether. "During the worst of the bombings Father Cummings stood and in a slow loud voice led the Lord's Prayer," wrote Roy Bodine in his diary.[4] Deep in the hold, Johnson confessed, "I bowed my head and prayed, and in the course of my prayer said: 'Lord, I am ready if you want me.' And I knew a great peace." When the stranded ship could be refloated, it was run into Subic Bay, where the civilians were evacuated during the night.

The next morning, about an hour after daylight, American planes off the U.S.S. *Hornet* returned and resumed the attack. A Japanese guard leaned down into the hatch and, pointing to the sky, shouted excitedly: "Many! Many! Many!" This time the attackers scored a direct hit on the after hold, killing about half of the 500 prisoners there. Among those killed that day was "Sut" Fendall, Johnson's companion when they first fell into Japanese hands.[5] The survivors were ordered to abandon ship and swim ashore. "All go home! Speedo!" screamed the guard. The shore was 500 yards away, a daunting challenge for men in such sorry physical condition.[6]

As Johnson and the others left the ship, on the upper decks they could see evidence of American Red Cross supplies—precious canned meat, powdered milk, butter, and chocolate meant for them—that had been looted by the Japanese. Most men made it to shore, some clinging to pieces of driftwood or life vests snatched up as they jumped overboard. Guards on shore fired warning shots at those who drifted too far to the flanks. When the sodden and exhausted prisoners reached shore, the Japanese rounded them up and herded them into a single tennis court, with a single water faucet, to begin a new ordeal. A roll call taken a day or so later showed 1,308 survivors of the 1,619 originally put aboard the *Oryoku Maru*. In the harbor, that ship burned, turned over, and sank to the bottom.

They spent five long days on the tennis court—terribly hot in the daytime and cold at night. Most had few articles of clothing to protect them from either extreme. Food consisted of raw rice, issued by the teaspoonful into the palm of one's hand, once a day. Johnson's group was then moved by truck to San Fernando and housed in a provincial jail. There they received a rice ball, the first decent food in five days, and subsequently some other food—rice and camotes (yam-like vegetables), with some kelp—to prepare themselves. And there was water.

By now, it was Christmas Eve 1944. The prisoners were loaded into railroad boxcars for travel to San Fernando, La Union. As many as 187 men were crammed into each small car for a fourteen-hour trip. The only water available was what each man had in his canteen when he went aboard. Given the dysentery and severe diarrhea afflicting many of the men, and the fact that no one was allowed to disembark before reaching their destination, the journey was a ghastly ordeal. Johnson remembered a few feeble voices raised in a croaking attempt at a carol.

On Christmas, the prisoners were herded into a schoolyard. Two meals were provided, but the water shortage was now so acute that it had to be issued by the spoonful. That night they were marched to the dock area near Miramonte, where they were kept in the broiling sun throughout the next day. Each man received about fifteen spoonfuls of water during the day and some raw rice in the late afternoon. Early the next morning—now some twelve days after abandoning the *Oryoku Maru*—they were marched to a pier and prodded to jump twenty or more feet down into various tugs and lighters to be ferried out to waiting ships. The Japanese evidently feared renewed aerial attack, for this operation was carried out in extreme haste. Most prisoners were put aboard a single large ship, but Johnson found himself among a group of 236 men taken to a smaller ship that hurriedly set sail from Lingayen Gulf. "This was the 27th of December," recalled Johnson, "and the Americans landed there on the 9th of January. It was just that close."[7]

WHEN THE PRISONER DETAILS left Bilibid to board ship, a few men judged too ill to make the move had been left behind. One of them was Major Frank Anders, formerly assigned to the regimental staff of the 57th Infantry and Johnson's close friend. Before long, advancing U.S. forces overran Luzon, and Anders was freed. Immediately he penned a letter to Dorothy Johnson, whom he had last seen when she and the children were evacuated from the Philippines. "I am writing to you at Johnny's request," he told her, "and on my own behalf." He had been with her husband in Bilibid Prison, he explained, until Johnson had been moved for transport to Japan. "I have had no word concerning him since that time," Anders added, but Johnson had been in excellent health and spirits when he departed the Philippines. "He's the same old Johnny, still stacks way above the crowd."

Then Anders revealed some thrilling news. "I have two letters which Johnny left with me and which are buried for safe keeping. As soon as possible I shall get to them and forward them to you." The "letters" were Johnson's prison diaries, and they were about to be safely reclaimed and sent to her. Whatever his fate, some part of her husband would live on.

That fate was very much in doubt by the time Dorothy received this word. By then, she knew "the grim thing" that the ship carrying her husband had been sunk, that many prisoners had been lost, and that those who survived had been recaptured by the Japanese. "I've hit rock bottom," she said in a letter to Johnson's mother, passing along the news from Anders, "and I hate to write. But I do still have so much hope."

FROM THE TIME they boarded the ship in Lingayen Gulf until the afternoon of 6 January 1945, when the ship arrived in Takao harbor, Formosa,[8] there were three days that the prisoners received no water and five days without food. On the days they were fed, they typically received one canteen cup of rice for every two people. "I personally appealed to the Formosan guards with us for both food and water," Johnson recalled, "but was generally refused and told on several occasions that 'it is better if you all die.' Pleading to persons with that attitude is little better than useless."

At Formosa, Johnson's small group was consolidated with the group aboard the larger ship, the *Enoura Maru*. Three days later, they were bombed again, taking two direct hits, one of which killed about half the 500 men housed in the forward hold. Although many more were seriously injured, no medical attention was provided. Four more days passed—days of terrible suffering for the untreated wounded—and then the survivors were transferred to yet a third ship, the *Brazil Maru*. By this time, it was turning cold, so the usual crowded conditions seemed a bit more tolerable as men huddled together for warmth. The last leg of the long journey to Japan was uneventful, at least in that there were no more attacks, but adequate water continued to be a problem. Johnson became convinced that there was nothing wrong with the condensers, that the paucity of water resulted from "a deliberate attempt on the part of the officer in charge to kill everyone aboard the ship."

Every day more prisoners died, and every evening after dark, deep in the ship's hold amidst the dwindling survivors, "a strong voice was raised in a corner of the hold, and a Catholic priest asked for God's mercy and God's blessing for that group of men," Johnson later recounted reverently. "As the voyage neared its end, two weeks later, that voice, having grown more feeble with each passing night, was finally stilled in death. God had taken one of His children."

What saved the handful who survived was a cargo of brown sugar in the hold below the one occupied by the prisoners. "Without the sugar there was little hope for anyone," concluded Johnson, even though eating it raw and in quantity led many to develop serious diarrhea. The sugar had to be obtained surreptitiously, of course, since the guards had threatened to execute anyone caught stealing it, but men were able to slide down between the ribs of the ship, rip open the sacks, and fill socks or mess kits with the precious sugar. Johnson thought that they were helped in getting away with this by the guards' fear of communicable disease, which meant that for the most part they steered clear of the lower holds.

Johnson's sense of destiny, or perhaps mission, deepened during this voyage. "I didn't get wounded myself," he later told an interviewer. "Somebody was looking after me." The sugar episode was a part of it. Even though they were afraid to go down and mingle with their diseased prisoners, the guards would peer into the holds from the upper decks to see whether their orders about leaving the sugar alone were being obeyed. "We tried to cover up the broken sacks," said Johnson, "but were not always successful. Some people were physically weak, and others just did not care."

At one point, Johnson made his way over to another lieutenant colonel, intending to ask that man to take a detail into the hold to ensure that evidence of sugar theft was covered up. Just as he finished that conversation and was returning to his original position, an aerial attack struck the ship. The results made a powerful impression on Johnson. The two people between whom he had originally been sitting only minutes before were both hit—one struck dead instantly with the top of his head sheared off, and the other painfully injured, his throat cut by flying shrapnel. Where Johnson had been sitting, with his back against the hull, there was now a gaping hole. Meanwhile, the man he had gone to see, and whose side he had just left, was wounded in the arm so severely that he died within a few days. "Somebody was giving me a very real protection about this stage," Johnson concluded.[9] Later, asking himself why he had been spared when others were taken, he answered: "I can only conclude that God had some purpose for me."

Even with the sugar, people died every day, especially those who had been wounded, those with dysentery, and others who succumbed to exposure. As winter advanced, there was often snow and ice on the decks, and many men had only bits and pieces of clothing—little more than rags—to provide protection. The day before the trip ended, Johnson conducted a roll call, which revealed that only 550 persons were left alive of the 1,619 who had sailed from the Philippines. It was probably the nadir of the whole ghastly ordeal.

On 30 January 1945, these pathetic fragments were put ashore at Moji in the northern part of Kyushu, then taken to Fukuoka, where other prisoners were already housed. Some winter clothing was issued, and some men got shoes. There were not enough to go around, though, so others remained barefoot. Three prisoner doctors—an American and two Dutchmen—were able to help the new arrivals, although many still died of pneumonia or of what Johnson called "general inanition," one definition of which is simply "emptiness." That seemed about right.

Fukuoka, although austere, represented a major improvement. Even so, fifty-three more men died during the three months the prisoners were held there, and every one of the 110 men who were taken to a hospital in Moji died. The survivors benefited from food parcels that were distributed—one eleven-pound assortment for every three men. On his birthday, 22 February, Johnson weighed himself. He was coming down with pneumonia and lacked the strength even to raise his leg to cross an obstacle. "I would let myself down to my hands and knees, crawl across, and then pull myself erect again," he said. He weighed ninety-two pounds.

"There was," said a physician who attended Johnson at the time, "no medical reason why he should have been alive." That was Captain Walter Kostecki, an Army doctor and survivor of the Death March who had arrived at Fukuoka earlier and did much good work there. When the group including Johnson arrived at Fukuoka, said Kostecki, "they were the most horribly exposed Americans I had seen yet. I was shocked, and I'm not ashamed to say I wept." Kostecki managed to get from the Japanese twenty-four units of intravenous feedings. One of the guards had gone to Tufts University with him, so perhaps that helped. There were so many men who needed help that, to determine who would get these life-saving fluids, Kostecki decided on a raffle. In a drawing from a Japanese soldier's fatigue cap, Johnson won one of the infusions. He also shared with four other men a can of meat from a Red Cross package that Kostecki had kept hidden for eight months.[10] Before long, he was gaining strength. Always thereafter, Johnson credited Dr. Kostecki with saving his life, and the two became close friends. "I attribute to him, and to him alone, the fact that I am alive today," Johnson often stated.

Another close friend, Bruce Palmer, Jr., drew this conclusion: "That's the true measure of Johnny Johnson. He could have died any time he felt like it. He decided not to die." He was unwilling to let others die, either, according to another Army doctor who wrote to Johnson when he became Chief of Staff. He recalled their shared experience on the three hell ships, "where you exercised what I considered to be great leadership under the most abysmal of adverse conditions, and again at Fukuoka where you saved my life by forcing me to eat when I had neither the will nor the energy to do so."[11]

Earlier, Johnson had traded his West Point class ring to a guard for a tin of salmon, which he then tried to feed to a fellow prisoner. The man refused to eat. "It doesn't matter," he said. "I'm going to die tomorrow." And so he did. Chester Johnson was there and saw what Johnson had done. "He carefully brought this food and water down and, in view of all these men in that hold, he meted out what he had been given. In his lifetime many honors were accorded him, but never to equal how he was regarded by these men in this instance. It was a small amount of food and a small amount of water, but it was distributed with perfect integrity on his part."

(When Johnson got home from the war, he bought a new class ring. Then he got his wife Dorothy a new miniature, the petite version of the class ring that West Pointers give their prospective brides as engagement rings. "Put away the old one," he told her. "We are starting anew.")

The Japanese persisted to the end of the war in efforts to avoid giving up their prisoners. Thus in late April, Johnson and others were moved a final time, to Inchon, Korea, where they were when the war ended. In the new camp, meals were provided three times a day, and there was adequate water. Even so, two more officers died there—the last casualties—tragically near the end of the long incarceration.

"When we were informed of the surrender" by the Japanese, said Johnson, "we were told that the Emperor and Roosevelt had agreed to get together." The prisoners did not know that Roosevelt had already been dead for a number of months.

As a final act, his captors tried to cheat Johnson. He was the finance officer and paymaster for the camp, so it was up to him to receive the postal savings on behalf of all the surviving inmates. "I sat this night and counted the savings," he said, "and I was 100,000 kwan short. So they said, 'Well, you take it, and we'll give you 100,000 kwan in the morning.' I said, 'No. You give it all to me.' They said, 'Maybe it was a mistake. Count again.' " So he counted and recounted the money until four o'clock in the morning. Finally the Japanese gave up. They rolled out the safe, counted out another 100,000 kwan, and handed it over. Johnson took the money back to the barracks and paid off every man the full amount he was due. "It was just a case of we had to stand, and stand, and stand, and stand," he observed.

About the middle of August, the guards announced that the war was over, and they stopped guarding the camp. Alva Fitch set up a requisitioning system in town. By his estimate, there were by then about 168 men in camp. "We ate about 2,000 eggs a day and one bull every three days," he exulted.

Before long, a B-29 flew over and dropped food and supplies by parachute. This was not altogether a blessing, since one bundle broke loose from its canopy and smashed through the roof of the kitchen, another flattened the dispensary, and a third plummeted into a supply room attached to the prisoner barracks. On the positive side, another drop broke a high tension line and electrocuted five guards.

The newly freed prisoners gorged themselves until they were sick on the gifts from the sky and Fitch's take from town. And, using silk from the different colored parachutes that had brought their supplies, they stitched together an American flag. Soon, at what John Wright remembered as "the most impressive flag-raising ceremony any of us had ever witnessed," they were once again under the Star Spangled Banner.

Two days later, on 7 September 1945, forty-one months after his capture by the Japanese, Johnson stood with other survivors on a dock in Inchon, Korea, and greeted the 7th Infantry Division as it came ashore.[12] He had survived. What is more, he had maintained intact his spirit and self-respect. He had also, although he didn't know it at the time, become a full colonel. Orders published five days earlier had elevated him to that rank.

Johnson came away from his wartime experience with no self-pity, nor would he tolerate it in others, then or later. And he would never look back, declining even to associate himself with the various organizations of former prisoners formed after the war. "My basic premise is that a man's future lies ahead of him and not behind him," he said by way of explanation.

That was very much in keeping with his sister Janet's assessment of what had pulled her brother through: "Just plain determination," she said, "and a work ethic that we were all imbued with from that time. 'Just do the best you could with what you had, and keep going.' "

Clearly, too, Johnson's love for his family and his fierce desire to be reunited with them were important factors. "Dorothy," said a friend who had known her for many years, "is a very, very wholesome and decent woman, and she was always very supportive of Johnny." He remembered a conversation with her, after the war, when she said that, during all the time of her husband's absence and captivity, she "had faith that God would watch over him and bring him home to me."

Many did not survive. Of those who had been in the horrible hell ships, far more died than made it through. And in all the camps, there had been a steady procession to the grave. Gavan Daws devoted a decade to studying those who underwent this ordeal. While granting that the Japanese did not take direct action to exterminate their prisoners, he argued that "they drove them toward mass death just the same. They beat them until they fell, then beat them for falling, beat them until they bled, then beat them for bleeding. They denied them medical treatment. They starved them. When the International Red Cross sent food and medicine, the Japanese looted the shipments. They sacrificed prisoners in medical experiments. They watched them die by the tens of thousands from diseases of malnutrition like beri-beri, pellagra, and scurvy, and from epidemic tropical diseases: malaria, dysentery, tropical ulcers, cholera. Those who survived could only look ahead to being worked to death." Daws reached a final stark conclusion: "If the war had lasted another year, there would not have been a POW left alive."[13]

The 7th Division put the surviving men from Inchon, now *former* prisoners, on board a transport and took them to Manila. Johnson, though, was in a lucky group of four who were offered air transportation. He gratefully accepted and soon found himself in Okinawa, expecting to go from there to Guam and then home. But at Okinawa, the travelers were informed of General MacArthur's decree that anyone who had been a prisoner in the Philippines would be returned to the United States by way of the Philippines, so they detoured south instead of east and were soon in Manila, where they got stuck. Air priorities were hard to get, and Johnson waited fifteen days to get on a flight. During that time, the others from Inchon who had proceeded by ship also arrived in Manila.

While Johnson was waiting it out in Manila, his classmate Oren Hurlbut looked him up. Alongside Red Cross headquarters was a huge board where each day, the names of returning former prisoners were posted. Naturally it drew a lot of attention. One day when "Hurley" Hurlbut stopped by to have a look, he saw the name "Lt. Col. H. Johnson." He figured that had to be his close friend and classmate Johnny, so he went out to have a look in the repatriation camp. There Johnson was, wispy but intact. Hurlbut had access to steak, and he made sure that Johnson got all he wanted. He also lent him a jeep and a driver—after Johnson had looked at Hurlbut's jeep and asked, "what's that?"—and Johnson spent ten days trying to find Ah Ho and Ng Sen, the former servants who had helped him while he was in prison camp. To his regret, he couldn't locate either of them.

Johnson finally got on a flight, and when they stopped to refuel in Hawaii, he called Dorothy to tell her that he was on the way. She was out with some friends, so he left a message: "Colonel Johnson has just left for the mainland."

Some weeks earlier, Dorothy had gotten a call or a wire from someone saying "Colonel Johnson is in Korea." That was magnificent news. It had been a year since there had been any word, and she hadn't even known whether her husband was alive or dead. "I was so relieved!" she said. Some cousins had been visiting from Minneapolis, and they had all gone out to lunch at a local hotel. In the middle of it, the reality sank in and Dorothy, simply overcome, had to be taken home.

A week after Johnson was liberated, his mother received a Western Union telegram from the Army Adjutant General. "THE SECRETARY OF WAR
HAS ASKED ME TO INFORM YOU THAT YOUR SON LT/COL JOHNSON HAROLD
K. RETURNED TO MILITARY CONTROL 7 SEPT 45 AND IS BEING RETURNED TO
THE UNITED STATES WITHIN THE NEAR FUTURE."[14] Dorothy found out about
that two days later when someone saw a notice in a Minneapolis newspaper
and called her. Dorothy telephoned Johnson's mother. "Yes, I heard about
that the day before yesterday," she acknowledged, but she hadn't let Dorothy
know. That incredible omission foreshadowed a certain distance in familial
relationships between Johnson and his extended family.

With her husband on his way home, Dorothy decided to meet him in San
Francisco. Making connections in that war-swollen city turned out to be a
challenge. Dorothy made her way to the elegant St. Francis Hotel, where
they had never heard of her or any reservations for a Colonel Johnson. But,
being uncommonly understanding and sympathetic, and to their everlasting
credit, they gave her the bridal suite. There she waited for her husband to
join her—and waited, and waited.

Returning ex-prisoners were required to process through a clinic at Let-
terman Army Hospital. Hospital officials, eager to demonstrate the fine care
they were giving returnees, had scheduled a visit by some Washington dig-
nitary to observe the processing. When that worthy was somehow delayed,
everything was put on hold, pending his arrival. By the time things finally
got under way, it was 5:30 in the evening. Johnson eventually made his escape and rushed to the St. Francis. It was 8:30 by that time. Out of breath
and no doubt nearly delirious with anticipation, he presented himself at his
wife's apartment. At his knock, the door flew open and Dorothy snapped
out a question: "Where have *you* been?!!" Thanks to the bureaucracy, that
was his welcome home.

They had an idyllic week in that beautiful city before boarding a train
for the trip to South Dakota. To Johnson's delight, when they reached
Aberdeen, little Ellen Kay, a baby of four months when the families were
evacuated from the Philippines and now nearly five years old, acted as
though he had always been around the house. And his bulldog Happy was
still there. "She was getting old," said Dorothy, "but she seemed to be waiting for something. Three days after Johnny got back to South Dakota, the
dog died."

After settling in at home, Johnson went for treatment at Denver's Fitzsi-
mons Army Hospital—"getting dewormed and getting my teeth taken care
of," he said—followed by four months' leave.

Remembering how the Masons in prison camp had looked after one another, Johnson took steps to join the Masonic order. Dorothy's father, George Rennix, put him through the work, and he affiliated in December with Crescent Lodge Number 11 in Grafton, North Dakota, where his father had been a longtime member and Worshipful Master. Both his grandfathers had been Master Masons, and among his treasured possessions were Masonic aprons that had belonged to his father and to his father's father. He also had fond memories of his father's riding a freight train ten miles to attend lodge meetings and then returning by railroad handcar.

To build up his stamina, Johnson began refereeing basketball games again. He figured he had achieved his objective when in February he officiated thirteen games in three days, by himself, in "a little country tournament." It was time to go back to work.

CHAPTER NINE

ADRIFT

Homecoming, joyous though it was, had some negative aspects. Johnson had long been out of touch with his own country and had no sense of public attitudes at home. He was thus unprepared for what he encountered. "The most vivid impression and, I might add, the greatest shock I felt on my return," he later recalled, "was a national attitude of 'what's in it for me?' Money under the counter if you expected to rent an apartment. Must know a friend to get nylons for your wife—or even a white bath towel. Must know someone on the Ration Board to get tires for your car. 'What's in it for me?' "

He was dismayed by all this—so starkly at odds with the desperate austerity of his own life, and with the pioneer values of his early life—and never quite got over it. The military ethic, with its emphasis on selflessness and service, became even more admirable and appealing to him, and he became one of its most effective advocates and exemplars.

He also had some reflections on what he had just gone through. "The only time I ever volunteered for an assignment was in the years before 1940 when I attempted to get to the Philippines, finally made it, and you can recall what happened," he later wrote to a friend. After the collapse of the Allied effort there, said Johnson, "I felt that I'd been let down by a country that could have afforded adequate defenses prior to World War II. There was no reason for them to put me out at the end of the line with an inability to get there to relieve me should the need arise."

That was definitely not, however, an excuse for self-pity. "When we sign up in the United States Army," he responded to a soldier who had written to him, "we sign up with the basic knowledge that we may be called upon to defend the interests of our country wherever it might be." He added that the service they both had rendered on Bataan was simply the price they had paid to defend their own country. "I expect to go wherever I am called. I expect each soldier in the United States Army to do no less. The Army is not a welfare institution."

*   *   *

"THE FIRST REQUIREMENT was to survive prison camp with a whole mind," Johnson told a friend. He had done that. Regaining fitness was Johnson's second task, and he had accomplished that as well. The third, regaining his bearings in the Army, would be more difficult.

"We worried . . . that the lack of a combat record—desirably, command in combat—might penalize us after the war," wrote Bert Sparrow in a history of the Class of 1933.[1] Johnson had commanded a battalion for four days, not counting his surrogate regimental command time as a stand-in for Colonel Clarke. That wasn't much, and besides, like all his fellow prisoners, he was essentially several years out of date with respect to what was going on in the Army. They didn't know the equipment, didn't know the organization, didn't know the battle history, and in many cases—and perhaps most importantly—didn't know the personalities. "They were," suggested Gavan Daws, "Rip Van Winkles in their twenties, waking up."[2]

The Army in its wisdom and compassion set about to compensate for this, at least to the extent possible. It developed a series of short courses at the principal service schools for classes composed entirely of former prisoners of war, then organized those returnees into groups and sent them on the rounds. In early March 1946, they started at Fort Knox, home of the Armored School. Next came Fort Benning, familiar ground for an infantryman like Johnson, in what was straightforwardly termed Officers' Prisoner of War Orientation Course No. 2. All told, they made stops at five different schools, adding Forts Sill, Bliss, and Riley before they were through. Dorothy stayed home in South Dakota. She was pregnant and had two little children, and that seemed a better base than the peripatetic academic circuit. Still, she regretted that she missed out on some good times as a consequence.

Johnson, like the other repatriated officers, was doing some soul-searching as to what he should do next. One idea was an ROTC assignment, somewhere he could get his bearings after the long absence. He applied to a number of colleges, all of which turned him down. "I am not sure, in looking back," Johnson said about the quest for such an assignment, "that it wasn't a sort of foxhole in which to hide." Whatever it was, it didn't work. "This was a bit discouraging," he admitted.

After the school tour, the repatriated officers were asked to submit preference statements, indicating the assignments they desired next. Johnson had lined up a couple of good jobs on the staff and faculty of the Infantry School back at Fort Benning, so he submitted that as his preference. Unfortunately, the Commandant of the Infantry School was Major General John W. O'Daniel, whose policy was not to accept on the faculty anyone who had been a prisoner of war in the Pacific. Higher headquarters soon overruled him on that, but not before Johnson had been ordered to the Command & General Staff College at Fort Leavenworth, Kansas, where he would be a student officer. "Nobody wanted him," remembered Dorothy.

Fort Leavenworth was a great post out of the Old Army, first established during the opening up of the American West. Just about every officer who was going to get ahead in the Army passed through it, and in normal times, those sent there for schooling were mostly captains and majors. The war had interfered with the normal progression of classes, however, so senior officers such as Johnson were just now getting around to attending. He was part of the first regular class after the war, commencing in September 1946, and took with him an expanded family. A second son, Robert (called Bobby), had just been born in Aberdeen.

After the war, there was a dramatic reduction in the size of the Army, and many officers who had been promoted during the wartime expansion were reduced a grade. Johnson thus reverted to lieutenant colonel. Even so, he was a fairly senior officer to be going to Leavenworth, and many of his contemporaries (who had seen extensive combat during the war) were given constructive credit for the course and excused from attending. This was just more tangible evidence of the handicaps Johnson would have to overcome to regain professional competitiveness. Fort Leavenworth, though, turned out to be just what he needed.

THE JOHNSONS LIVED in "The Beehive," a block-long apartment house full of children and dogs and old friends and fun—the perfect place to get the family back together. The school year was filled with map exercises and maneuvers, terrain studies, lectures, and problems on things such as logistics, doctrine, and intelligence. Every time they caught their breath, the student officers had another examination—something like forty-one during the nine-month course. Johnson wrote his student research paper on the Battle of the Points, in which he had played such an important part, and it was hugely successful. People worked hard and played hard at the school, and it was a good professional and social atmosphere.

When the year ended, Johnson's results were spectacular. He graduated fourteenth in a class of 308, earning an academic rating of "superior." His efficiency report listed as his special aptitude "infantry division commander," a job calling for a major general. What is more, he had regained his professional confidence.

When he first reported to Leavenworth to begin the course, Johnson "still had quite a feeling of having missed the war." But as he listened to his classmates talk about their experiences, he realized that he had had as much combat experience—brief though it was—as many others, and more than some. Then he began to perceive that each man knew about a small part of the war, but nobody knew it all. He set out to know more than most of them, and with hard work and intense study was a conspicuous success.

JOHNSON WAS KEPT ON at Fort Leavenworth and assigned to the faculty of the School of Combined Arms. He was placed in the Department of Operations & Training, working for a colonel named Paul D. Adams. Adams was one of the Army's legendary hardnoses, destined to become a full general. If you could satisfy him, you could satisfy anyone, and Johnson did.[3]

In the next class at Leavenworth was Royal Reynolds, Johnson's West Point classmate and close friend from their days in the Philippines. He remembers Johnson up on the platform in Gruber Hall, a converted old riding hall, standing up there with no notes, nothing to read. He "just stood up there and laid it out, one man teaching 500 officers. Johnny was good at that."

In later years, Johnson recalled a class supervisor who had had an interesting sign on his desk that read: "Think. There must be a harder way to do it."[4] And he remembered an old man with silver hair standing in the center of the stage, arm raised almost in benediction, telling the young students in solemn tones, "You stand at the dawn of a new era." It was the first time Johnson had ever heard Douglas Southall Freeman, and those words had sent shivers running down his spine.

Bill Rosson was on the faculty with Johnson and came to know him well. Rosson was a bachelor, and sometimes when they walked home together, Johnson would invite him in for a drink or to stay for supper. Other than that, Rosson remembered, the Johnsons did little entertaining. "Johnny was not a socialite," he said. "I think it was a reflection of his priorities. He felt he was there to catch up professionally."

Rosson also remembered how often Johnson spoke of Dorothy, saying how much he depended on her, how she had never lost faith while he was away, how well she had raised the children, how much he admired her. It was clear that he derived great strength from his family.

Two years on the faculty was long enough, according to the Army, so in the summer of 1949, Johnson was given an interim assignment: more schooling at the Armed Forces Staff College in Norfolk, Virginia. The course, which included students from all the services, lasted about five months. "I look back upon the Armed Forces Staff College as a place where

I probably got two months of education and spent about three months imparting to the other services what I had learned at Leavenworth," Johnson said.

Much later, when he had become a very senior officer, he had this observation for his colleagues: "You'll find in your discussions with me that I tend to talk harder and harder as the argument gets more heated. I don't know where I picked up this habit. I think probably at the Armed Forces Staff College, where the fellow that talked the loudest and the fastest prevailed in an argument."

When the course ended, Johnson's student evaluation described him as "a sound, thorough, intelligent, level-headed officer." New orders in hand, he was headed back to the real Army, service with troops. And soon he was going to need all those qualities and more.

CHAPTER TEN

KOREA

Johnson was headed for Fort Devens, Massachusetts, with orders to the 7th Infantry. That should, he wrote to his family, "give me troop duty of some sort. I hope that it will be a battalion, at least for awhile. I need the contact with troops." On 2 February 1950, he took command of the 3d Battalion, 7th Infantry.

The drawdown of America's military establishment following World War II had been dramatic, leaving a residual force minimally capable of responding to any renewed threat. The Army was down to 591,000 soldiers, yielding ten understrength divisions, half of them stationed overseas. Of those, four infantry divisions were on occupation duty in Japan, operating with truncated structures that provided only two of the normal three infantry regiments, two of the usual three battalions in each of those regiments, and so on. Their equipment was left over from World War II, and much of it was obsolete, unserviceable, or both. The usual support forces were largely absent, replaced by more than 150,000 hired Japanese civilians.[1] All this would soon become relevant to Harold K. Johnson.

Six days into his new command, Johnson was sent on temporary duty to Fort Bragg, North Carolina, where he was assigned as an umpire for something called Exercise Swarmer. Brigadier Gerald J. Higgins, the Chief Umpire, later reminded Johnson how he had "swarmer-umpired two opposing regiments into executing a simultaneous withdrawal into each other's rears—obviously another Napoleon on the way." That maneuver kept Johnson away from his command until mid-May.

Back with his unit, he promptly moved it to Pine Camp, New York, to provide demonstrations during summer training for reserve forces. He found a cottage on a nearby lake for his family to rent and brought them from Massachusetts for the summer. They were there when, on 25 June 1950, war erupted in Korea.

Two weeks went by. Then, one evening, Johnson received a telephone call instructing him to be back at Fort Devens at eight o'clock the next morning for a meeting with his regimental commander, Colonel John Guthrie. That was 300 miles away. Sensing what might be in the offing,

Johnson alerted his family to get ready to travel, saying that he would pick them up at midnight.

At nine that evening, Johnson held an officers' call. The moment war had broken out, their unit began being milked for individual replacements, and they were down to only about seventy-five riflemen in the entire battalion. Johnson directed that they all be transferred to the weapons company. Everyone was told to get ready to return to Fort Devens.

Johnson and his family drove all night to get back to Devens by early the next morning. Johnson reported as ordered to Colonel Guthrie, who told him that he was to form a provisional battalion and be prepared to move it to some as yet unspecified location in the Far East. Of course, everyone knew that meant Korea. The remnants of Johnson's own battalion were to provide the nucleus of the provisional unit and were promptly brought back from Pine Camp. Over the next ten days, they scrambled to scrape up replacements from wherever they could find them, prepare and ship a trainload of equipment to the West Coast, and process the troops for movement overseas.

During that time, an officer came up from 1st Army Headquarters, then located at Governor's Island in New York, to get an assessment of the combat capability of the provisional unit. "It is zero," Johnson informed him. "It can't be," protested the staffer. "Well, it is," maintained Johnson, refusing to pretend that things were better than they were, "because this is a thrown-together unit that hasn't done anything together." The staff officer was a friend of Johnson's, and he gave him what was intended to be some friendly advice. "You had better get some other assessment than that," he urged. Johnson was adamant. "Well, *you* can make it," he said, "but mine is zero." He stuck with that.

Johnson's regimental commander was fully aware of what he was asking of Johnson by selecting him to command the provisional battalion. Colonel Guthrie had been awarded two Silver Stars during European duty in World War II, and soon he too would be headed for Korea, where he would add two more Silver Stars and a Purple Heart before eventually retiring as a major general. He was a good soldier and a compassionate commander. "Since in my opinion Johnny was far and away my strongest battalion commander," explained Guthrie, "I felt constrained to send him and his battalion to Korea, despite the horrendous experience he had just undergone as a POW in World War II. As it turned out, I believe I acted in the best interests of Johnny, as well as the interests of the U.S. Army." Indeed he had.

Johnson's newly constituted unit, now designated the 1st Provisional Infantry Battalion, headed for San Francisco by rail on 4 August. A week later, they were aboard a troop transport—itself just ten days out of mothballs—

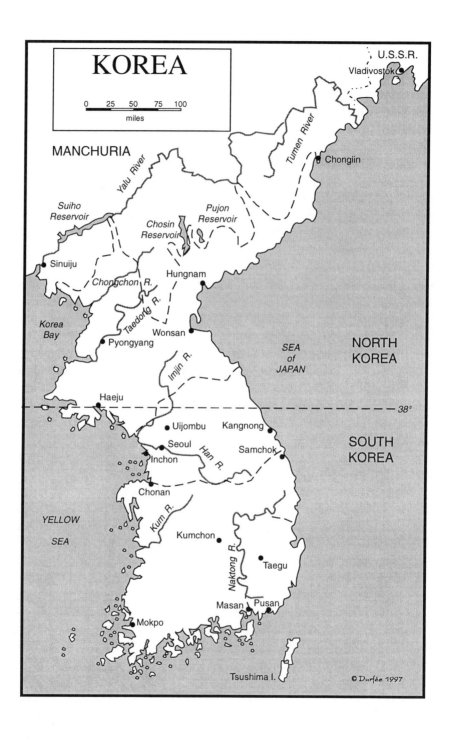

headed for Pusan, Korea. The ship departed a day later than planned, because Johnson discovered that the dispensary had not been stocked—there was literally no medicine on board. Johnson summoned the Inspector General from nearby Sixth Army Headquarters, meanwhile refusing to allow the ship to sail until some medicine was issued. As it turned out, that was a prudent move, because en route they had two emergency appendectomies.

Two weeks afloat was all the training time Johnson had with his new unit. He didn't let it go to waste. Back at Fort Devens, they had been almost totally occupied with shipping their equipment and getting through the necessary predeployment processing. As one means of improving their physical conditioning, Johnson insisted that they run wherever they went. He also managed to get everyone through an infiltration course under live fire and to move them close to a fixed artillery concentration fired overhead, to give them "the sound and sensation of artillery helping and not hurting." But they had absolutely no unit training before going to war. There simply wasn't time.

On the train, Johnson started them working on things like weapons disassembly and cleaning. Once on board ship, they trained constantly. Fortunately, the officers and noncommissioned officers were experienced and capable. They used chalkboards to take the men through some of the squad and platoon tactics they would be using. That was not much of a substitute for actual field training, but it was all they could do under the circumstances. It probably contributed in one important respect, however. "I think that much of the readiness of a unit is actually dependent upon its state of mind," Johnson maintained, and the intense concentration on getting the men ready for battle must have helped develop a positive state of mind.

The initial onslaught of North Korean forces had rapidly pushed South Korean and U.S. forces southward, driving them into a defensive enclave that came to be known as the Pusan Perimeter. The choice was hang on there or get pushed into the sea, and hanging on was what it amounted to at that point. The troop ship carrying Johnson and his troops docked in Pusan on 25 August. There Johnson's unit was redesignated the 3d Battalion, 8th Cavalry, and assigned to the 1st Cavalry Division.[2] Four days later, they were in a shooting war in a sector of the Pusan Perimeter.

Those four days were occupied with unloading equipment and traveling 100 miles by rail to the defensive perimeter. Despite supposedly having been "filled" with replacements before departure, the battalion's rifle companies, authorized 205 men at full strength, went into combat with only 160. During the Korean War, said a later Army Chief of Staff, "we sent poorly equipped and untrained soldiers into combat to buy time while we rebuilt the Army."[3] Johnson and his men were part of that.

The 1st Cavalry Division was commanded by Major General Hobart Gay, who had been General George S. Patton's chief of staff during World War II. The division had come over from Japan in mid-July and was immediately engaged in defensive operations, with responsibility for blocking the advance of a North Korean division along the Taegon–Taegu corridor, where it had relieved the hard-pressed 24th Infantry Division. In late July, General Gay ordered "withdrawal to new positions covering Kumchon, an important rail center thirty miles northwest of Taegu." Soon thereafter, Lieutenant General Walton Walker, commanding the Eighth Army, visited the division's headquarters and issued some clear orders: "There will be no more retreating, withdrawal or readjustment of the lines or any other term you choose."[4] They were going to fight it out right there, and the augmentation by Johnson's unit and other provisional battalions—the first reinforcing units shipped from the United States—must have been welcome indeed.

When Johnson arrived, it was determined that he was the senior lieutenant colonel in the regiment, so he was offered the position of regimental executive officer. He declined, preferring to stay with his battalion, believing that someone who knew the outfit should lead it until it had engaged in battle.

Johnson's battalion was first positioned as a reserve unit on the Naktong River west of Taegu, but the next day, front-line units were overrun, and the reserve was committed. "We were trying to plug up a breakthrough," Johnson said, where the 2d Battalion had given way. "We were spread out all over." He went forward personally to put one company into position at night. As he was threading his way back to the command post, an enemy tank came through and fired right over his head as Johnson made for the nearest ditch.

Subsequently the unit was cut off. During daylight hours, when the enemy could observe the road and bring in mortar and artillery fire, Johnson's men couldn't resupply or evacuate casualties. All that had to be done at night. Along the way, Johnson had one command post destroyed by mortar fire and another that was severely damaged. They were getting a pretty warm welcome, and taking substantial casualties as well.

"We sort of played yo-yo for about five days at a place called Tabudong," said Johnson. Actually, it was a lot more than that. After elements of his battalion had been driven from a critical piece of high ground by fierce enemy attacks, Johnson personally led a counterattack to regain the lost position. Placing himself with the forwardmost elements, he rallied the men and led them forward. Apparently unconcerned about being exposed to enemy artillery, mortar, and small arms fire, Johnson set an example that kept the attack moving. When devastating enemy fire threatened to bring it to a halt, he moved close to the enemy, where he set up and personally operated a forward observation post. From that exposed position he directed mortar counterfire against the enemy positions.

Ultimately, however, the weight of the opposing forces prevailed. When Johnson's mortars were disabled and his unit's casualties continued to mount, it became necessary to withdraw. He remained in his exposed position until the last unit had cleared, ensuring that weapons and equipment were salvaged as the troops moved out, then reorganized the survivors. Two days later, coming at it from another direction, they seized their objective. By the time nightfall came on 4 September, Johnson's battalion had been in combat for just one week, and he had earned for "extraordinary heroism" the Distinguished Service Cross.[5]

One of his platoon leaders later recalled the situation for *Time* magazine: "The world was coming apart. Our company commander had been killed. There was heavy firing 100 yards away. Colonel Johnson said we could handle it. He parceled out firepower and called in air strikes. He hadn't slept for three days, but he never used a profane word."[6]

Afterward, Johnson was critical of his own performance. "We didn't use artillery effectively," he said, "and I attribute that to me. That was a personal failure." But part of it was also severe difficulties with communications, beginning with the fact that they didn't have the proper crystals for their radios and couldn't communicate over the fire control channels assigned to them. They had to double up on use of the command nets, which clogged them and only made things more difficult. But Johnson, brushing aside those realities, took the blame on himself.

A few days later, Johnson was ordered to begin a new attack to seize a piece of high ground known as Hill 570, a three-pronged peak from which the enemy was interdicting the road to their rear. Johnson had one rifle company that was down to only nineteen men. The mission required a withdrawal followed by an attack in another direction—"a very unusual maneuver," Johnson observed.

The attacks proceeded without benefit of artillery, mortar, or air support, since the mountain peaks held by the enemy were obscured by clouds. Johnson put all three of his line companies into the attack, one for each peak. Two succeeded, but one of those was subsequently driven off by enemy counterattacks. The third, directed against the highest peak where the bulk of the enemy force was concentrated, got nowhere. The commander of one company was killed, as was the executive officer of another, along with a number of noncommissioned officers.

Meanwhile, Eighth Army intelligence estimated that there were 1,000 enemy soldiers on the objectives[7]—an insuperable force, given its defensive positions on the high ground, the depleted units of the attacking force, and the absence of supporting fires. Amazingly, after two or three tries over the next two days, the objective was finally seized. "While we were not successful in taking the whole objective [the first time]," said Johnson, "we were successful a couple of days later by going at it from another direction." When they were then pulled out for an overnight rest, the battalion had been in continuous combat for eleven days since its initial entry into battle.[8]

Having successfully taken a difficult objective after hard fighting, Johnson received word from his regimental commander that he was to bypass enemy resistance and go to "Boston." No maps or overlays that Johnson had portrayed any such position. He radioed back, "Where's Boston?" No reply. Johnson decided to stay where he was.

The next day, encountering the division commander, Johnson said, "I have been told to leave this high ground, but I haven't left it. I do not intend to leave it until somebody replaces the battalion, because the position cost too much to take." The division commander's response was gratifying: "I want you to stay right where you are." Johnson perceived that there was a little difference of opinion between the regimental commander and the division commander.

On 15 September 1950, the U.S. X Corps (composed of the 7th Infantry Division and the 1st Marine Division) launched an amphibious landing at Inchon, on the west coast of the Korean peninsula (the same Inchon where Johnson had been released from captivity by elements of that same 7th Division almost five years earlier). At the same time, Eighth Army forces that had been defending the Pusan Perimeter launched a breakout operation. The 1st Cavalry Division secured a bridgehead over the Naktong River, then headed north. In the breakout, said a citation accompanying another decoration awarded to Johnson, "during the rapid advance northward he fearlessly led his troops in a spearhead drive through 123 miles of enemy territory."

By 27 September, elements of the 1st Cavalry and the 7th Infantry had linked up. "The jaws of the trap had been closed," wrote General Matthew Ridgway. "Now the NKPA [North Korean People's Army] began to disintegrate."[9] Elements of the 1st Cavalry Division crossed the Han River and made their way up to the Imjin, nearly all the way to Kaesong. They ran into resistance just beyond there, at the 38th parallel, and there was some initial uncertainty as to whether they should cross that political demarcation line.

On 9 October, they pushed northward again. Johnson's battalion was in reserve when the advance stalled. He suggested to the regimental commander that they weren't going to make it in trucks on the road, and that gaining control of the high ground was the only way they could proceed. After two days of dogged fighting, they finally broke through. One tank of a sister battalion, advancing through heavy fog, banged head-on into an enemy tank coming south on the same road. Reacting quickly, it backed off and fired the first round, settling the issue of right-of-way.

The British 27th Brigade was attached to the 1st Cavalry Division and moved up to take the point, with Johnson's battalion following. Things got a bit sticky when, unbeknownst to Johnson, the Brits pulled off the road to have tea and he pushed on, thinking that he was moving along a road that had already been cleared by friendly forces. "The British brigadier gave me a real lesson in invective for having usurped his prerogative of leading the attack," Johnson reported. Even with these little interruptions, by 18 or 19 October they had reached the outskirts of Pyongyang, with the 5th Cavalry leading the advance.

THE KOREAN WAR was primarily one of infantry, and it was a tough, hard-slogging, bitter war besides. "I remember vividly the faces of many of your stalwarts along the Naktong and the bloodletting at such places as Hill 314," wrote an officer who had been with Johnson on the ship to Korea. "I remember seeing Colonel Johnson below Hill 314 when we were getting ready to attack," he said later. "He looked very weary. He had just been in a tough battle." Another officer later told Johnson that he remembered a talk they had had in an apple orchard north of Taegu at a place called the "Bowling Alley." "Things were very grim," he recalled. "Your concern then was for your men and in taking objectives with minimum loss of life." Even with that concern, three weeks after entering combat Johnson had taken 400 casualties in his battalion of 703 men. It is not surprising that he remembered these as "dark, bitter days." The cost had been high, but they had done what was asked of them. "It was," he thought, "a superb effort on the part of a green unit. My pride in that unit has never diminished."

A long time later he wrote to his mother about the experience: "During my first week in combat I didn't see any generals unless I went to the rear a couple of miles. Our generals weren't any cowards, either, but it was really hot. I feel in my own heart that the third day we were in [action] my outfit held the Pusan perimeter and the main road leading to Taegu. There just wasn't anything behind us. We paid dearly but we held pretty well."

Johnson had a rather free hand with his battalion, his regimental commander visiting his command post only once during the two months Johnson was in command. On that occasion, the man showed up with a map, beautifully colored the way students did it back at Fort Leavenworth. "I want you to take these two hills," he told Johnson, pointing to the map. "Will you just take a couple of steps out here?" Johnson asked. They stepped from behind a rock formation and Johnson, pointing, asked, "Do you mean those two hills there?" The colonel jabbed his map again: "I mean these right here." Johnson was stunned. "I have never forgotten that," he said a long time later, talking to the Army Staff about responsibility and competence and candor—all the things that meant the most to him professionally.

About mid-September, that regimental commander was going to Japan on leave, and there were rumors that he would not be coming back. Pretty soon an individual wearing dark glasses showed up and introduced himself as the new regimental commander. He had been a year behind Johnson at West Point, and Johnson knew him. They chatted for a few minutes, then the fellow moved along on his "get acquainted" tour of the regiment.

Later that day, the assistant division commander showed up at Johnson's CP. "What gives with the new regimental commander?" Johnson asked him. "I am senior to him by something like about eight months in date of rank, and I am a year ahead of him at the Military Academy. If I am not qualified to command this regiment, you should fire me as a battalion commander and get someone else. As far as I am concerned, since my battalion has been here, we have been doing most of the fighting for this regiment." Johnson suggested that the 1st Battalion had been sitting on some hill for about two weeks with hardly a shot fired in anger, and that the 2d Battalion had essentially disintegrated.

The brigadier acknowledged that there was some merit in what Johnson had to say, but nothing much came of the conversation at the time. In fact, the original regimental commander came back from Japan and resumed his post, so the fellow with the sunglasses didn't take over after all. But a month later, Johnson was reassigned to command a different regiment of the division, the 5th Cavalry. "A great combat leader who should progress to general officer grade" was the send-off in his efficiency report covering the period of battalion command.

Before he left, though, Johnson had one last duty to perform. In mid-October, on the outskirts of Pyongyang, he personally conducted a memorial service for the 400 killed and wounded the battalion had lost since arriving in Korea in late August. Along with him, he recalled, "a pitifully small remainder" from the original contingent paid tribute to their fallen comrades. Then he bade them all farewell.

JOHNSON WAS A COMPASSIONATE LEADER who took very seriously the heavy burden of asking men to risk their lives in combat. "I spent a great many nights on my knees" in prayer, Johnson said of his days in command in Korea. "I didn't expect any voice to answer me, but we operate so much of the time in the gray area, where it is hard to tell the difference between right and wrong. It is important to have some kind of star that can take you through troubled times."

During the two months that he commanded the 5th Cavalry, that unit continued the drive north to the Yalu River, recoiled in the face of the Chinese onslaught, and participated in delaying actions all the way back to Seoul. There was very little glory and considerable heartache involved in those operations.

AT ONE POINT, Johnson confronted the problem of what to do about a lieutenant leading an infantry platoon who reportedly ran away during a firefight, leaving his men to fend for themselves. Somewhere in the far north of Korea, the two men sat in a little room and went over the matter. The young officer said that he couldn't remember running, that when he got to the top of the hill something happened, and the next thing he knew, he was back down at the bottom of the hill.

Johnson knew that the man had been commissioned in the Adjutant General's Corps and was only in the Infantry while he served the mandatory two-year detail in a combat arm. He also knew that the lieutenant had already taken part in a lot of assaults and had received three Purple Hearts. "So he had been lucky, on the one hand," concluded Johnson, "but he had certainly been up where the action was on the other." They talked for a long time.

"I believe that everybody has a breaking point," said Johnson, "and there is no one standard or hard line. You have got to . . . walk through all the circumstances and see what caused this particular incident." After he had heard everything there was to say about it, Johnson decided not to court-martial the young officer, but he did have him take off his Combat Infantryman's Badge—"You can't wear that anymore," he instructed—and arranged for him to be reassigned to his basic branch, where he would no longer be exposed to combat. "There comes a breaking point for every man," Johnson repeated, and he dealt compassionately with this man when that point came for him.

ON THE DRIVE NORTH, the sorry state of the unit's equipment came into sharp focus. "We were at 75 percent strength and 75 percent equipment and 75 percent vehicles, and no backup," said Johnson. "My regiment went to Pyongyang, across the Chongchon, and back on about 60 percent broken front springs." He added on another occasion, "Now this doesn't mean that it's good, but it does mean that you can get along with a whole lot less than you think you ought to have."

In the autumn of 1950, Chinese Communist forces entered the war, and the 1st Cavalry Division was the first U.S. division to engage them.[10] Johnson had been in command of the 5th Cavalry for a week when the initial contacts were made. They involved, among other forces, the battalion of the 8th Cavalry he had recently commanded.

General Gay, commanding the 1st Cavalry Division, was quick to recognize the threat to some of his dispersed and exposed units, and on 1 November he asked I Corps commander Major General Frank W. Milburn for permission to withdraw the 8th Cavalry from Unsan. Milburn refused to authorize that. Apparently, concluded General J. Lawton Collins in his study of the war, "Milburn and the I Corps staff did not accept fully the reports of strong Chinese forces on the Corps front" at that point.

During the afternoon of the same day, the Chinese cut the road south of Unsan (a road Johnson had negotiated round-trip by jeep without interference only the day before, although he said that it had made the back of his neck prickle) and attacked adjacent forces, both U.S. and ROK. That night, Milburn issued orders for the corps to pass to the defensive, the first time it had done so since the breakout from the Pusan Perimeter. He also directed that the 8th Cavalry be withdrawn from Unsan to positions further south.

That decision came too late. By dawn the next day, the regiment was almost completely surrounded. Although some portions of the 1st and 2d Battalions were able to break through Chinese roadblocks, suffering heavy losses in the process, most of the 3d Battalion was trapped.[11]

Johnson was ordered to attack with his regiment to pierce the enemy encirclement and rescue his old battalion. As things turned out, he lacked sufficient combat power to accomplish this mission. Attacking from the south with his 1st and 2d Battalions abreast, he sought to seize an enemy-held ridge to the front that blocked the main road so that he could pass through his 3d Battalion—which was being returned to his control and en route with an accompanying tank company—to go to the relief of the 3d Battalion, 8th Cavalry. Johnson's own 3d Battalion was expected to join by the afternoon.

He was also given operational control of the 1st Battalion, 7th Cavalry, but it "really contributed nothing to the effort," according to Roy Appleman's analysis, "as it merely moved off into rough country and never entered the fight." Johnson's attack proceeded virtually without artillery support, and air strikes were limited in their accuracy by a dense smoke haze—the result of forest fires set by the enemy—hanging over the objective area. In valiant efforts to seize the commanding ridge, Johnson's 1st and 2d Battalions suffered some 350 casualties, with nothing to show for them.

The battle was still in progress when the corps commander decided that it was time to call a halt.[12] The opposing forces were just too overwhelming in numbers to be thrown back at that juncture. Meanwhile, defeated South Korean forces were streaming south, heads down, not knowing or caring where they were going. "To me it was very reminiscent of the last days of Bataan," said Johnson.

General Milburn, determining that rescue of the trapped unit was not possible with the forces available, ordered the entire 1st Cavalry Division to withdraw south of the Chongchon River. "The abandonment to the enemy of any unit runs counter to the traditions of the United States Army," wrote General Collins. "Sadly, and with bitter gall, Hap Gay, scion of General George Patton, ordered Colonel Johnson to break off his attack." Johnson watched helplessly as his former battalion was decimated. Most of its soldiers were killed or captured, and Johnson's successor as battalion commander died of wounds. "The 3d Battalion, 8th Cavalry, ceased to exist as a unit," said General Collins. "It died gallantly."[13]

Johnson had visited his former battalion only the day before. As he prepared to depart, he offered an observation to its new commander: "You had better get out of this low ground and get yourself up on a slope where you can provide some protection from the position." Unfortunately, he sadly recalled, "that advice was ignored."

Not long before this disaster, Johnson had typed a letter to his mother and brother at home in North Dakota. "The worst job is the letter to the family of my officers [killed in action], and I've lost so many, many of them close friends," he wrote. "This is a terribly grim game. It is bad enough behind a rifle platoon, but the toll in the rifle platoon is high."

Entry of the Chinese forces into the war was the nastiest kind of shock.

General MacArthur had assured President Truman that it could not happen, and now seemingly unlimited masses of Chinese soldiers were swarming everywhere. In fact, by mid-November there were some 300,000 Chinese troops in the field, 180,000 of them confronting the Eighth Army. "About all there is to do is hang on and pray each day," Johnson wrote to his mother. "I've done a lot of it and it has brought a certain peace of mind and spiritual comfort."

Meanwhile, the weather was turning cold. A harsh winter was beginning early, with frigid winds and plummeting temperatures. Incredibly, the troops lacked proper winter clothing. In mid-October, said Johnson, "a choice had to be made as to the type of clothing that would be requisitioned with winter coming on. . . . Are you going to have winter clothing for combat in the field, or are you going to have clothing that will be suitable for the return to Tokyo? And the choice was for the return to Tokyo. They were going to win the war, and there was going to be a victory parade in Tokyo by Thanksgiving," according to the view of higher headquarters. So the troops went into the harsh Korean winter without the proper clothing. "Maintaining troop morale under that circumstance," said Johnson, "was a monumental task."[14]

The troops also thought that the war was almost over, and they weren't the only ones. "We see issues of *Time* and *Newsweek*," wrote one of Johnson's company commanders in a letter to his mother, "stating 'War over—only mopping up—troops in Japan for Thanksgiving—home by Christmas.' " But now the Chinese had come in, and the harsh reality was a sharply discouraging contrast. "It's a nasty realization, with the casualties returning on jeeps and tanks, that the war is still on and we are still in it."[15]

By Thanksgiving, they were back near Pyongyang at a place called Kunuri. It was a painful change from the situation there only a month earlier, when Johnson took command of the 5th Cavalry. The last time through, remembered a soldier in one of Johnson's companies, "General MacArthur announced that we would be home by Thanksgiving. We believed him. Life seemed good in P'yongyang. Morale was sky-high."[16]

At about that same time Johnson wrote to his mother and brother to offer an optimistic viewpoint: "This shouldn't last too much longer. I imagine that we will have another tough scrap for the capital, but there shouldn't be too much between here and there, at least that is my fervent hope." The Bob Hope Show entertained the regiment, complete with Marilyn Maxwell wearing a memorable sweater, and I Company captured some warehouses belonging to the abandoned Russian Embassy that were filled with good Russian booze.

MacArthur also came to visit, his optimistic predictions of early autumn turned to ashes by the Chinese intervention. Unchastened, MacArthur "announced the launching of an attack intended to recover all of Korea that would be completed in time to permit some units to return to Japan by Christmastime," recalled Johnson. On Thanksgiving Day, Johnson attended chapel services and took his first communion since cadet days.

The regiment was designated Army reserve, but almost immediately the Chinese onslaught recommenced, and Johnson was ordered to set up a blocking position at the south end of what came to be known as "The Gauntlet." A badly battered 2d Division passed through, and then elements of a disintegrated Turkish brigade. By 15 December, the entire allied line had been driven back by the advancing Chinese masses, and the 5th Cavalry wound up in the vicinity of Seoul. On that date, Johnson gave up command of that regiment and immediately assumed command of the 8th Cavalry, the regiment that had been so badly mauled by the initial Chinese assault and in which he had only recently commanded a battalion.

Johnson later spoke candidly of his doubts in the midst of those dark days. "On a lonely road just southeast of Pyongyang," he recalled, "a lonely commander was deeply troubled by the threat to the men he was charged with safeguarding. Could he do the job that was his to do and still give his men a fighting chance to survive? And out of the still of the night, as if from a great distance, came God's voice saying, 'Be strong, have no fear, I am with you.'"

At some point during these difficult times, Johnson passed near another troubled soul—one of his men who was trying to scrape out a foxhole in the frozen earth. In later years, Johnson often spoke of this youngster, who made a great impression on him. "On a bitterly cold and gusty day," he recounted, "following a harsh and galling retreat from North to South Korea, a soldier from my regiment—dog-dirty, bone-weary, discouraged, obviously frightened, and probably a little hungry—came up to me and asked, 'Sir, why am I here?'" The man argued that he would be better off in jail, said Johnson, where he would at least be warm, well fed, and clean and have a bed to sleep in.

The query shook Johnson. It had not occurred to him that it was necessary to explain to young Americans what the defense of freedom was all about. "I replied to him that he was there as an alternative between two choices. He could defend his home, his family, his sweetheart on that cold, snowy hill in Korea, or someday he could expect to defend his home from a foxhole in his own front yard." Johnson pointed to the long line of Korean refugees streaming south to get out of the line of fire as evidence of what he meant. But it hit him hard that he should have to explain something he viewed as so obvious.

"The basic point is," he later explained, "why should I have to tell any young American why he has an obligation to defend his freedoms when those freedoms are challenged?" But it also seems clear that Johnson was not entirely satisfied with the answer he gave, and that the young soldier was not entirely convinced by it. "These kinds of questions are terribly difficult to answer," Johnson confessed to an audience more than a decade later.

WHEN JOHNSON TOOK COMMAND, the 8th Cavalry needed some substantial rebuilding. In the fighting at Unsan, it had lost more than half its people and much of its equipment, including howitzers, tanks, trucks, and recoilless rifles.[17] There may have been some attitudinal problems, too, as became clear to Johnson very shortly. On Christmas Eve, they established the regimental command post in an abandoned Korean house. There was a lot of snow on the ground, and the temperature was near zero. To try to stay warm, they installed a gasoline heater and ran the stovepipe out a window.

About one o'clock in the morning, Johnson was awakened by a tremendous commotion. Somebody hadn't run the stovepipe out far enough from the eaves, and the layer of straw insulating the roof had caught fire. It was smoking and smoldering, and people were running around trying to put it out.

When Johnson looked into the matter after things quieted down a bit, he learned an interesting thing. The duty officer, in awakening the man who was to relieve him, had said, "You had better hurry up and get over to the CP, because if you don't it is going to burn to the ground." And then he had gone off to bed. Johnson concluded that he had his work cut out for him.

The first order of business was integrating into the outfit the replacements that soon came streaming in. Many of them, noted Johnson, were men who had made enlisted reserve commitments following World War II, "probably without any real expectation of ever having to serve again." Now they had been called to active duty and had been given limited orientation—in some cases only eight days—no training, and only partial issues of old equipment. They formed the bulk of the reconstituted 3d Battalion. "Understandably," said Johnson, "their attitude left a great deal to be desired. They were vocally dissident and highly skeptical about promises. Perhaps cynical might be a better word than skeptical."

Johnson felt that, given these realities, the 3d Battalion needed to achieve an early success. Thus he put it in the lead as the Eighth Army turned around and headed north. And as a confidence builder, he put his own regimental command post out in front of the line of departure for the attack. Then he preceded the attack with a robust reconnaissance operation, so that no major surprises would be encountered.

With these precautions, he launched the 3d Battalion, which immediately got into a pretty heavy fight. To Johnson's gratification, they conducted themselves very well. "And from that point on," he said proudly, "they were once again a good battalion."

WHEN JOHNSON WAS A BATTALION COMMANDER, he had his first encounter with an impressive Korean officer, General Paik Sun Yup, then commanding general of the 1st ROK Division. That unit was on the right flank of Johnson's battalion at Tabu-dong. Later, as a regimental commander, Johnson saw more of Paik as their units fought side by side north of the Chongchon River. Johnson often visited Paik's command post and knew his American senior advisor.

One night about nine o'clock, while Johnson was in his regimental command post at Yong Dong Po, he got a call from that advisor saying that General Paik would like to see him in private. Paik arrived about ten o'clock, and the two men sat down to talk. Paik said that he had orders to take a position along the Imjin River and that he didn't think he would be able to carry out those orders because he didn't believe that his division was capable of holding the position.

Johnson listened quietly while Paik recalled how his division had been on the 38th parallel, north of Kaesong, when the war began. His troops had given way, leaving him to make his way out cross-country, eventually to be evacuated by boat. And he spoke of how the enemy had launched an attack on New Year's Eve and outflanked his division by crossing a river and approaching the rear of his position. His reserve had been engaged almost at once, leaving him with no way to influence the battle.

Paik said that he had contemplated suicide both times. Now he feared that once again they had a mission beyond their means and that suicide was the only honorable course of action.

Johnson and Paik talked until almost three o'clock in the morning, going over every aspect of the assignment, reviewing all the principles of defense of a river line. When he left, Paik was satisfied that he could in fact perform the assigned mission, and he did. The 1st ROK Division stubbornly held its position in the ensuing battle. "He was a capable man, very capable," Johnson said of Paik, gratified that an officer he held in such high regard would consult him professionally. When Paik went on to become a corps commander, and later Chief of Staff of the Korean Army, Johnson felt deep satisfaction.

TWO WEEKS after taking command of the 8th Cavalry, Johnson was again promoted to full colonel. Four and a half years after losing that rank in the great postwar reduction, he had won his eagles back in battle.

Meanwhile, General Matthew Ridgway had taken command of the Eighth Army. This was welcome news to Johnson, who developed great respect and affection for Ridgway.

Desiring to consolidate his forces in anticipation of resuming offensive action, in early January 1951 Ridgway ordered withdrawals from the Seoul area to positions south of the Han River. Johnson was convinced that there was still lots of hard fighting to be done. "As a regimental commander," he said, "I had bets with my assistant division commander and division commander—I was betting candy against booze—that we would be in Korea at the end of February of 1951, and they were betting we'd be back in Japan. Now, when you get your top leadership in your unit thinking that, you see, you've got somebody with bug-out-itis."

In mid-January, Johnson wrote to his mother that "the soldier still wants to know what we expect to gain in Korea and no answer has been forthcoming as yet. Makes the job of instilling a fighting spirit or killing attitude more than hard. That will change, though," he assured her. He was right about that. Four days later, General Ridgway "sent a personal message to all of his troops, laying out the reasons US forces were fighting in Korea." Four days after that, Eighth Army went on the attack.[18]

Johnson remembered that General Ridgway visited units throughout his command, holding conferences with division commanders and their principal subordinates. In the 1st Cavalry Division, leaders down through company commanders attended. "General Ridgway talked forcefully and encouragingly," Johnson said. "The sheer force of his own personality turned the situation in Korea. A retreating, despondent, defeated army was turned around by the power of the personality of its commander. That is quite a lesson."

Once Ridgway had realigned his forces, stiffened the spines of his senior subordinates, and explained the mission to his troops, he was ready to move, and he never gave up the initiative. He knew what he wanted to accomplish, and he was determined to find men who could help him achieve it. Operating in this vein, General Ridgway "sent a shock wave through his staff when, at his very first staff meeting, he called for the relief of the I Corps G-3, who made the mistake of presenting a briefing on contingency plans for withdrawing. There were no plans for attacking."[19] That relief directly affected Johnson, who was chosen to fill the abruptly vacated G-3 billet.

First, though, Ridgway put the Eighth Army back on the offensive with combat operations unambiguously entitled Thunderbolt, Killer, Ripper, Rugged, and Courageous.[20] Johnson and his regiment took part in Operation Rat Killer.

Johnson first sent a patrol out with the mission of reestablishing contact with the enemy. Advancing some twelve miles in a day, they found not only the enemy but some fierce fighting as well, so Johnson moved the rest of his regiment forward. During a night engagement, he had three different companies cut off at one point or another. "But they stuck where they were supposed to and didn't get hurt," Johnson noted in a letter to his mother. "One reason so many units have suffered," he added, "is because they were running when they should have been fighting. We can take these Chinks any day in the week, only I don't quite see what we gain or prove."

In early February, with his regiment on the attack and performing well, Johnson moved to the new assignment, formally designated Assistant Chief of Staff for Operations (G-3) of I Corps. His division commander, General Gay, sent him off with a rating as "the most outstanding officer I know" as a "regimental commander in combat."

LIEUTENANT GENERAL FRANK W. MILBURN was commanding I Corps when Johnson joined. "One of the first things I ran into at I Corps in early February," said Johnson, "was that we were out of plans." His view was that at the corps level they should have plans drafted for what they anticipated during the next week or so, and preferably two weeks. Those plans could of course be modified based on the evolving tactical situation. But so short-sighted was the planning horizon when Johnson joined I Corps that on one occasion the corps commander had to get General Ridgway out of bed to get his concept on how the corps should cross the Han River and continue the attack to the 38th parallel. Johnson cut his teeth in the new assignment by getting that situation straightened out.

When he had settled into the routine of the staff job, Johnson wrote to his mother with some reflections on the command assignments he had just completed. "This job is radically different from what I've been doing over here," he told her. "Command is a terrible strain. There is never a moment when you aren't conscious of the responsibility for the lives of the men in your command. My regiment had over 3,000 most of the time, and that is a lot of responsibility. You had to be in touch with moods of the moment, and there was always the fear that the constant running would continue when we were supposed to be going the other way. There was a lot of satisfaction to doing a job, too, and I left my outfit when it was at its peak."

Later, Johnson reinforced his conclusions about General Ridgway and his actions when he took command of Eighth Army. "It was a disintegrating army," Johnson said. "It was an army really not in retreat—in flight! It was something that was bordering on disgrace. In a matter of about six weeks General Ridgway had turned a defeated army around." By the latter part of March, Ridgway had five corps advancing north in the pursuit.[21] Johnson was by then deeply engrossed in his new job as operations officer of one of those corps.

That job involved planning corps tactical operations, writing and issuing the written orders and map overlays, and providing staff support to the commander in supervising the implementation of those orders. When Johnson had the job, it also entailed coping with a renewed Chinese offensive that began in late April 1951; then, when that had been contained, it involved shaping the corps counteroffensive that drove north again.

A YOUNG OFFICER serving as reconnaissance platoon leader of the 70th Tank Battalion had a memorable encounter with Johnson as corps G-3 at Uijombu. Around the middle of April, with his unit in support of the 7th Cavalry, Lieutenant William Ward was called to that unit's regimental CP to receive instructions. While being briefed by the S-3, he noticed the regimental commander sitting at a map and talking with Johnson. The S-3 told Ward to take his platoon, which included tanks, and establish a blocking position where enemy troops were moving down the Uijombu corridor. That understood, Ward turned to his platoon sergeant and said, "All right, let's go out and kill those sons of bitches." Recalled Ward many years later, "Colonel Johnson turned from his map and spoke to me, quietly but forcefully: 'Son, those are enemy soldiers.' 'Yes, sir,' I replied, then quickly moved out."

HIS CORPS COMMANDER described Johnson as "a complete master of the situation at all times." He cited Johnson's planning of the crossing of the Han River in March and the subsequent drive that carried the corps across the 38th parallel; then a classic withdrawal when overwhelming enemy force drove the corps back almost to Seoul; and finally his coordination of the defense along that line, where the enemy suffered such heavy casualties and disorganization that the corps was able to resume the offensive and again drive north to Pyongyang. Then, said his commander, Johnson "devised the brilliant [and] eminently successful plan 'Commando' executed in early October [1951] which drove the enemy out of heavily fortified positions and seized critical terrain features which dominate avenues of approach and deny important assembly areas to the enemy." By then, it was time to move on.

As HIS CAREER EVOLVED in succeeding years, Johnson surprisingly never commanded again. He would serve as an assistant division commander, head up a major Army school, run the most important Army staff element, and ultimately head the entire Army as its chief of staff, but never again would he command an Army unit. Nevertheless, it is certain that in those later assignments he applied the lessons he learned from his battle commands in the Korean War.

Johnson described three major insights gained from his experience as a commander. One was that if you could command successfully at the battalion level, you could also successfully command substantially larger elements. What that boiled down to, he maintained, was "being a man of integrity as the commander of a unit. That is, your relationships with subordinate and superior alike are open and frank, and you stand up and take the consequences of your actions."

Second, he held that "a foremost consideration of any commander has to be the welfare of the men under him, and that he does not abuse his subordinates for personal gain under any circumstances. That is," he insisted, "just something that cannot be condoned under any circumstances."

And third, he stressed the commander's obligation to do everything possible to improve his technical and tactical competence, by which he meant those aspects of the job that are outside the area of human relations. "Command to me," he explained, "is a series of continuing problems in human relations, and a good commander is a fellow who solves them and the bad commander is the fellow who pushes them aside or ignores them. I believe that any reasonable person can solve most problems in human relations."

These were not, the record makes clear, simply theoretical constructs that Johnson developed. Rather, they embody his own style and values as demonstrated in command. The way he was regarded by his fellow soldiers reflects that, as expressed, for example, by Major James Huey, an assistant regimental S-3 in the 8th Cavalry when Johnson had command. " 'Duty, honor, country,' yes; but courage, morality and fortitude must follow those words to truly and honestly describe this outstanding soldier," he wrote of his former commander. "At times, I felt General Johnson was a very lonely man, but later I was to discover this was not true. He was merely so deep in thought about the outcome of the next day's fighting, and the welfare of his troops and their families, that he just had to be alone to work out those difficult problems that face a commander in combat. I say, 'Thank you, God,' for providing this nation such an outstanding leader."[22]

DURING THE G-3 ASSIGNMENT, Johnson tried to intersect with his brother Herb. Sixteen years younger than Johnson, Herb had enlisted in the Army at the end of World War II, served a three-year hitch, and then left the service to go to school. But he had also enlisted in the National Guard and was called up with the 47th Infantry Division during the Korean War. He was a sergeant at the battle of Heartbreak Ridge and eventually became sergeant major of a battalion of the 9th Infantry. Johnson was proud of his younger brother and wanted to have a look at him.

That took some doing. Johnson learned that his brother was stationed near Pusan, so he flew there one day to look him up. Unfortunately, Herb had left for the 2d Division ten days earlier. Time was running out, because Johnson was about to rotate home. Two days before his flight departed, he made the connection.

Herb was in his bunker near the 38th parallel, looking over the Yalu Valley, when he got word to report to his commanding officer right away. He hustled back to the command post, where he was told, "Sergeant Johnson, the general wants to have lunch with you."

Sergeant Johnson found that pretty astounding. "Why me?" he asked.

"I don't know," said his commander. "Get your stuff and get in the jeep."

Herb was driven down the mountain and taken to a compound where he was treated to a hot shower, clean fatigues and socks, and the use of a razor. This was beginning to look like a good thing after all.

Suitably spruced up, Herb was driven the rest of the way to division headquarters, where a lieutenant colonel came dashing out. "Are you Sergeant Johnson?" Herb admitted that he was, and finally all was explained to him. "Your brother is flying in to see you," said the colonel.

Herb was unabashed. "That must be something when the Army stands perfectly still because a fellow's brother is flying in to see him," he blurted out.

"In this case it is," the colonel admitted good-naturedly.

Soon a helicopter whirled in, depositing Colonel Johnson in the midst of a welcoming crowd of assembled officers. After pleasantries were exchanged, he and Herb were shown to a tent where they could visit in private. "What's this all about?" Herb asked.

"Mom wants to know how you are," his older brother explained.

BY MID-OCTOBER 1951, Johnson had been in Korea for fourteen months. During that time he had commanded one battalion and two regiments, served as a corps operations officer, earned promotion to colonel, and been decorated four times, including award of the Distinguished Service Cross for extraordinary heroism in action. He was solidly back in business as a soldier, and it was time to go home.

He was then working for his second corps commander, Major General John W. O'Daniel. Near the end of Johnson's tour of duty, O'Daniel called him in for a talk. He was very pleased with the job Johnson was doing as the corps G-3, O'Daniel said, and would like him to extend his tour for six months to continue in the job. "I don't see how I could possibly get along without you," said the corps commander.

"No, sir, I think it's time for me to go home," Johnson replied. Then he reminded his commander of an earlier time, when Johnson was just back from prison camp after World War II and seeking to reestablish himself, only to have the Commandant veto his assignment to the Infantry School because he refused to have any former POWs on his staff. "Sir, you could have had me working for you then," Johnson told him. Then: "Good afternoon, General! I have some packing to do."

CHAPTER ELEVEN

MOVING UP

Although Johnson's tour of duty there was over, the war in Korea dragged on for two more years, bogged down in inconclusive local actions pending conclusion of the seemingly endless peace negotiations. Johnson was sent to Fort Monroe, Virginia, where he spent eight months in the G-3 element of the Office, Chief of Army Field Forces. It was his first high-level staff experience and a useful assignment for him. When he left in late summer to attend the National War College, his efficiency report included a gratifying statement: "This officer is a real soldier."

The Army, Navy, and Air Force all operate separate War Colleges, the final level of schooling for a carefully screened group of professional officers thought to have the most potential for future high-level responsibilities. In addition, there is the National War College at Fort McNair in Washington, D.C., a joint institution whose student body is drawn in proportional parts from all the services, with a sprinkling of civilians from some of the major defense and intelligence agencies. Although it is officially maintained that all the war colleges are equivalent, the National War College is considered the most prestigious, and selection as a student there is a harbinger of exciting career prospects ahead.

Late in the academic year, Johnson and a handful of other students were assigned to something called Project Solarium, headed by George Kennan, former ambassador to the Soviet Union and architect of the policy of containment. This study, intended to provide useful input to the National Security Council, was commissioned by President Dwight Eisenhower. Its purpose was to look at possible redirection of strategic policy, which was then focused primarily on global confrontation with the Soviet Union. To that end, three panels were organized: one to study containment; a second to look at "drawing a line," which related to massive retaliation; and the third, on which Johnson served, to consider rollback. "The rollback option," recalled General Andrew J. Goodpaster, who had also been on that panel, "sank without a trace except for propaganda and covert operations." Johnson later concluded that—"manipulated very smoothly" by Ike—Solarium provided the basis for the "New Look," a strategic approach defined primarily by reliance on massive retaliation.

Work on Solarium continued for about six weeks, culminating with a presentation at the White House. Afterward, President Eisenhower wrote to Johnson (as he undoubtedly did to the others involved) to thank him for his part. "When we worked out the idea of the project in May," said the President, "we hoped that it could . . . be a real help to the [National Security] Council in its considerations. The actual performance of the Task Forces lived up to our best hopes. I realize how much time and thought and earnest purpose went into your share of Solarium." Johnson, for his part, described how he had "suffered through" Solarium, then through a follow-on exercise called the Everest Committee that, in his judgment, "provided the military blessing for the New Look, although the Army fought every step of the way."

WITH SOLARIUM BEHIND HIM, Johnson reported to the Office of the Assistant Chief of Staff G-3, an element of the Army Staff in the Pentagon. G-3 was the busiest, and probably the most important, staff section. Certainly it had the most interaction with the other services and with the Joint Chiefs of Staff, for it supported the Army Chief of Staff in his role as a member of the JCS. The prospective commanders at senior levels, those whose aspirations are to be warriors rather than specialists or staff officers, tend to gravitate there or are brought in by more senior officers of the same stripe to learn the business and help them carry the load. The load is heavy and the schedule demanding—one officer recalled Johnson's being called back to the Pentagon to work on some crisis just as he began carving his family's Thanksgiving turkey. At any given time, much of the cream of the Army's leadership, current and prospective, is assigned to G-3. In this atmosphere, Harold K. Johnson prospered.

Johnson's first billet was Chief of the Joint War Plans Branch of the Plans Division. A few weeks after he took up this new assignment, General Matthew B. Ridgway, so admired by Johnson for his command of Eighth Army during the Korean War, became the Army Chief of Staff. The G-3 was by turns the versatile Lieutenant General Clyde D. Eddleman, the famous and charismatic Lieutenant General James M. Gavin, and the hard-driving Major General Paul D. Harkins, with a brilliant young brigadier named Paul Caraway heading up War Plans. Most of the colonels were people who later became general officers. As "massive retaliation" became the Eisenhower administration's dominant strategic concept, said Johnson, "the Army found itself in a position of steady and continuing deterioration. Army ideas of restraint, of the requirement to impose control, of the notion that force and necessity had some kind of relationship, simply were not accepted." Observed Charles Corcoran, "we started evolving the view that the task of Army War Plans and Joint War Plans was to keep the Army alive."

To that end, they began developing scenarios calling for possible deployment of Army forces, including Far Eastern and Middle Eastern versions set in Okinawa and Libya. They recommended contingency deployments of Army forces to deal with these theoretical situations, and real-life forward storage of brigade-size equipment packages to support such deployments should they become necessary. Like others, said Corcoran, "Johnny felt that massive retaliation as the only choice you had was suicide."

Eventually they got permission to present one of these scenarios to General Ridgway, who in turn arranged for them to brief Secretary of Defense Charles Wilson. That turned out to be a disappointing exercise. Recalled Corcoran, "a big ugly fellow who was the deputy to Wilson" was also present, and the two men continually whispered back and forth during the presentation. When the briefer paused to let them deal with whatever was distracting them, Wilson protested and ordered him to continue. The same thing happened when the telephone rang—Wilson had the briefer continue while he talked to somebody on the phone. Somehow they got through the presentation, and at the end Wilson had only one question: "What does all this have to do with our policy of massive retaliation?"

"Sir, it's an alternative," they told him, then packed up their briefing materials and slunk away.

A dedicated and talented civilian, Maxine Clark, was assigned as Johnson's secretary. "About him," she remembered, "was an aura of honesty, dignity, honor, dedication, loyalty, perseverance, determination, conviction, strength, stamina, courage, and good humor. He was unique— he had a sort of magnetism. Right away those of us fortunate enough to work for him wanted to do our very best for him." That would have been an impressive assessment coming from any professional colleague, but from an old hand who had seen lots of colonels come and go, it was especially so.

The officers who served with Johnson, contemporaries and subordinates alike, sought and valued his views. "Of all the senior officers I've known," Elmer "Hook" Almquist said of Johnson, "he represented about the highest level of integrity. He addressed *everything* at the highest ethical plane." Michael Greene still remembers what Johnson told him when he left Plans to take command of a tank battalion in Europe. "They're always watching what you do," Johnson said. "Set a good example."[1]

Six months into the assignment, Johnson moved up and became assistant chief of the Plans Division, working directly for Caraway. These duties occupied him for the next year and a half. "Caraway was feisty and difficult," said John Sitterson, another veteran of the operation, "but he recognized the talent in Johnson." Johnson seemed to have a natural affinity for the work, and Corcoran recalled a frequent Johnson observation: "Ninety percent of all the planning you do is not going to result in a plan, but planning for planning's sake is something we must always do. We must always be asking and thinking and questioning." Corcoran also remembered that "Johnny in G-3 looked at things very broadly. He never got locked in on just one approach. He was always looking for alternatives."

Johnson admired Caraway and felt that he learned much from his association with him. "He had a special way of doing things," Johnson said, "and he had one of the keenest minds that I've ever encountered in all of my service in the Army. He was a very, very skillful planner and maneuverer, and also a hard worker. His attention was directed solely to his job and, of course, I was sympathetic to that sort of approach."

In the late spring of 1955, Johnson got a special assignment. General Maxwell Taylor had been designated the next Army Chief of Staff, and Johnson was sent to accompany him on an around-the-world orientation tour. Johnson flew out to the Far East, joining General Taylor there, and together they traveled through Southeast Asia, the Middle East, and Europe en route back to Washington. Johnson's job was to advise General Taylor, who had been in Korea and Japan for the past two years, on current policies and plans as seen from the Pentagon.

Taylor was coming home to replace the much revered General Ridgway. "The big, inarticulate mass of the Army is tired of being kicked around and wants fighting leadership," wrote Johnson's War Plans boss, Paul Caraway. "Everyone speaks of the fight Ridgway made and all approve," he said, referring to the Army's struggle to preserve its equities in the face of the doctrine of massive retaliation. "General Taylor is still a question in their minds."

After the trip with Taylor, Johnson became Executive Officer to the G-3, a high-profile—and high-risk—job that resembled being ringmaster of a three- (or maybe five-) ring circus. Basically, his task was to manage the flow of actions in the fast-paced G-3 portfolio, ensuring that they were completed in time to be of use to the G-3 and the Chief of Staff, that they met quality standards, and that the people who needed to know were briefed about them in a timely way.

Everything going to or from the G-3 passed through Johnson's hands, an incomparable learning experience. It could be an enormously satisfying and even fun job for someone who had the capacity to handle it, and Johnson had a lot of fun, indulging his natural proclivities as a workaholic.

In the midst of all this, Johnson gave some thought to his career prospects, and his outlook was surprisingly gloomy. Apparently he had gotten informal word of his impending reassignment to a division, where he would again fill a billet calling for a colonel. One evening when he and Colonel Laurence Legere were working late together, Johnson confided his misgivings to his friend. Some members of his class were beginning to receive first stars, Johnson observed. He spoke "openly, but not at all bitterly," recalled Legere, about the end of his chances in the Army: he had missed most of World War II, had twenty-three years' service, and was now facing three more years of colonel-level duty. Perhaps, Johnson mused, he ought to retire "before the barnacles ate away both his eagles and himself."

Not long after that morose evening, things changed dramatically for the better. In December 1955, a list of selectees for brigadier general was published, and Johnson's name was on it. On 1 January 1956, he was promoted, and later that month he departed the Pentagon for a new post at Fort Carson, Colorado. With his new star firmly in place, he would take up duties as assistant division commander of the 8th Infantry Division.

As significant as Johnson's selection for promotion was the way it was regarded by others. A contemporary of Johnson's, a man who also became a general officer but not until later, explained why he did not resent Johnson's good fortune. "That was the one case, the only time in my career, when I cheerfully admitted that someone deserved to be promoted ahead of me," he said. "Why? Because he is the ablest soldier I ever had the privilege of serving with."[2]

COMMANDING THE 8TH INFANTRY DIVISION when Johnson arrived was Major General Thomas M. Watlington. Some people viewed him as pompous, and most of his subordinates found him unapproachable. All were wary of his temper. But those who were close to him also saw another side. "What a splendid character!" said Colonel William Whitesel. General Watlington had an aide who wore glasses, but the general wouldn't let him wear his glasses outside the office, because he thought that it didn't look soldierly. Since Watlington was himself severely myopic, the two of them were forced to more or less feel their way along through the division area.

Johnson's leadership style, approved by Watlington, was to spend most of his time out with the troops. "He was *always* out," said Ellis Williamson, a regimental commander in the division. One time, as Johnson approached an area where Williamson had some training under way, a sentry stopped his jeep. "I'm sorry, sir," he informed the assistant division commander, "nobody comes in without Colonel Williamson's permission." Johnson asked, in a reasonable tone: "I'm a general and he's a colonel, and he says I can't come in?" The guard pondered that for a moment. "Makes sense to me," he responded, and Johnson didn't get past the diligent soldier until he had contacted Williamson and gotten his clearance.

Watlington liked what he saw in his new assistant. "He is extremely intense," he wrote, "but counsels junior commanders rather than drives them." The subordinate commanders in the division appreciated Johnson too, especially for his help in dealing with General Watlington. The division commander, himself configured like "a string bean," had become fixated on a "fat man program" designed to get rid of protruding waistlines. His methods appeared overly draconian to some, and they were even written about in *Life* magazine. General Watlington wanted to court-martial those who failed to meet prescribed weight standards for disobedience to orders. Johnson and the regimental commanders thought that there had to be a better way to deal with the problem, favoring the use of established board procedures.

Watlington had on his side directives issued by the Secretary of the Army, however, which made the issue a bit complicated. The press got involved when a lawsuit was brought against Watlington by a sergeant in the division, and a captain commanding one of the regimental headquarters companies joined in the suit. Things simmered down quite a bit, however, when that overweight captain assembled his company one morning, ordered "right face," and left them standing there. The men waited, then waited some more. Finally, some of them looked around, and there was the captain, felled by a heart attack, lying dead on the ground.

Somewhere in the midst of all this commotion, the Secretary of the Army telephoned General Watlington to discuss his implementation of the fat man program. "Are you rescinding your order to me?" asked Watlington. "That pretty much routed the Secretary," remembered Williamson. In cases where Johnson was not able to dissuade him, Watlington, pressing on, still insisted on courts-martial. Later, some of the cases were thrown out on review by the Court of Military Appeals.

At about this time, Johnson was invited to volunteer for what was referred to as the Army antiaircraft program. In his West Point class's twentieth reunion book, Johnson had been described as "a doughboy all the way," so his reaction was predictable. "I am reluctant to leave the combat elements who enjoy the opportunity of offensive action on the battlefield," Johnson said in his letter of declination. "I dislike the idea of assuming a role that requires the force under your command to wait for the enemy to strike." That outlook was probably shared by a lot of his former colleagues from the Philippine Scouts.

Not long after Johnson joined the division, General Watlington underwent lung surgery, taking him away from his duties for an extended period. During that time, Johnson served as acting division commander. It was a busy time, what with preparation for reorganization and an upcoming move of the division overseas. In the late summer of 1956, the entire 8th Infantry Division was ordered on a permanent change of station to Germany, exchanging places with another U.S. division in what was known as Operation Gyroscope. Johnson went over with the first increment and oversaw the arrival of succeeding echelons.

With the division in Europe, Johnson continued to spend a lot of time in the field, especially at the great maneuver areas of the day at Grafenwöhr and Hohenfels. William Odom was a lieutenant in one of the battalions at Hohenfels, getting ready for a battalion test, when Johnson visited his unit. "Instead of just screwing around," as a lot of other senior visitors might do, "he checked to see whether the machine guns could fire their final protective line," getting down on his belly and looking through the sights to be sure. "He was very calm," said Odom, "and I was impressed."

These tests were major events in the training year, closely monitored by higher headquarters, and they constituted "make or break" events for battalion commanders. Wesley Curtis commanded one of those battalions and noted how ubiquitous General Johnson was during preparation for the tests. "I don't remember ever seeing him in other than a field uniform," he said. "His visits were low-key, walking-around, watching-listening visits." Johnson seemed to know the names and jobs of all the officers and noncommissioned officers, and his comments were constructive and low-key. "He spoke soldier talk and stressed the fundamentals," said Curtis.

All nine of the division's infantry battalions passed the tests with scores above the U.S. Army, Europe, average, one achieving a new record high score and another coming in second. Curtis thought that Johnson deserved much of the credit. "He was the one who checked every item on the umpire checklist," he said. "He was tenacious, hard-working, and thorough." Some sense of the pace is provided by a letter Johnson wrote to his mother when, just back from a division field exercise in mid-December 1956, he took a few days of leave. "I was trying to remember the last time I had such a lazy day," he wrote. "I guess it was in June 1953."

Busy as he was, Johnson and his family enjoyed being in Germany. Young Johnny enrolled in the University of Maryland's overseas program, and Ellen Kay played the role of Mary in a Christmas Eve church pageant. Bobby took up the harmonica, a gift from his grandmother. And as usual, there were dogs, three of them by now. One, inherited from another family, was a shepherd named Dorothy. The lead role, though, was played by a dachshund. Johnson loved candy, as did his wife, and this dog made three. "He gets in front of you every time you have a piece of candy," Johnson apprised his mother, "and sits up until you have to produce for him."

Things got a little sticky when the Watlingtons arrived with *their* dog, who turned out to be a chicken killer, nailing three before they'd fairly gotten unpacked. The Germans were not amused.

AN OCEAN AWAY FROM HOME, it became increasingly apparent that Johnson was not very close to his mother or to his siblings. His letters to them are pedestrian, lacking in warmth, with no real sparkle or enthusiasm. He generally gives the impression that writing to them is a burdensome chore. Sometimes the letters border on the boastful in describing his activities, and clearly it matters to him that the recipients understand the importance of what he is doing and how hard he is working at it.

Seldom does he write to one of his siblings individually; rather, he sends out multiple copies of an all-purpose "Dear Family" letter. During the years in Germany, he responds, but only in answer to queries, that Christmas gifts have indeed been received, but includes no word of thanks for them. In one case, in fact, he ungraciously informs his mother (who had written to ask) that while Bobby has received the harmonica she sent him, he already had one.

In a letter to his ill mother, he writes that since he had gotten a report on her condition from one of his sisters, he decided not to call her (apparently for reasons of economy). He informs her that he is leaving for a week-long field exercise and enjoins her to write to him (which, he says, based on the tone of his sister's wire, "you should be able to do"). It turned out that she was not. A week later, his mother was dead.

Apparently, neither his mother nor any other member of his family visited Johnson during his four years in Germany. Even when he was a very senior officer, and therefore relatively well-off by the standards of the day, he adhered to the practice of giving a Christmas gift to only one sibling, taking the lead in making arrangements whereby that person gave a gift to only one other, and so on, so that each had to give (and would receive) only a single gift.[3] (But in another case, in a perhaps uncharacteristic act of generosity, he helped a struggling nephew whose parents were divorced get through college, even writing to the college president in his behalf and assisting with his expenses.)

All this rather distant behavior is in marked contrast to Johnson's warmth with his own family, his wife and children. This surprising and not very attractive aspect of his makeup is reminiscent of his mother's insensitive failure to tell Dorothy that she had had word of Johnson's release from captivity after World War II.

DURING THIS TIME, along with Johnson's professional development, his spiritual development continued as well. "Those of us who have seen the grim picture of the battlefield," he said while speaking at a lay service, "have an unusual opportunity to see God in action. Many forget what they have seen when they leave the battlefield, but others are stimulated to further study by their experiences."

He saw himself in the latter category, describing how "in 1956, in Europe, [he] began to read in earnest and to do some serious thinking." He was also the most senior man in the division serving as a Sunday school teacher, leading an adult class. "I find as much uncertainty and confusion in the minds of the class as I have myself," he wrote to his mother. "It is intensely interesting though."

Over time, Johnson visited every regiment in the division to talk to the young officers and their wives. His theme was morality. A status of forces agreement had recently been executed, so U.S. troops no longer constituted an army of occupation. Now they were allies joining in the common defense. "One of our greatest responsibilities," Johnson stressed, "is the example we set for our host nation—our behavior, our morality, how we deal with our children. All this is so important."

Colonel Williamson sat in on some of those sessions and retained a vivid impression of them many years later, saying, "I will always remember a remark he made: 'A man who will cheat on his wife will cheat on anyone. We don't want any cheaters in this division.'"

Johnson himself set a fine example, as described by Sergeant Frank X. Kaiser, who was assigned as his driver. One day, Johnson received as a gift from the local German brewery a case of specially brewed beer. Sending for Kaiser, Johnson instructed him to take it back to the brewery, express his great appreciation for the thoughtfulness, and explain as diplomatically as possible that in his position he was not able to accept such gifts. Kaiser was a beer drinker in those days, and this seemed like a real tragedy to him. "Return the whole case, sir?" he asked mournfully.

"Yes, Sergeant Kaiser, the whole case," Johnson confirmed.

"So," said Kaiser, "with tears in my eyes I returned it."

Johnson and Kaiser became close during this assignment, and Kaiser remained Johnson's driver for the rest of his service. One incident may have cemented the relationship: They were celebrating German-American Friendship Week in Goeppingen, where the division was headquartered. Kaiser and his wife had become friendly with Markus Geiger, the local chief of police, and his wife, who invited the Kaisers to join them across the street from the military housing area, where a carnival and beer tent had been set up. It was after ten o'clock when Kaiser dropped off the general, changed into civilian clothes, and met his wife and the Geigers at the beer tent. There was time for only one stein, because Kaiser had to get back to his quarters by the midnight curfew. He invited the Geigers to come to the house, and the two couples walked across the street together.

Just then a jeep with two military policeman came along. "You cannot come in here," one MP said, indicating the American housing area. Kaiser identified himself and gave his quarters number. The MP asked if the others were krauts.

"No," said Kaiser, "they are German nationals, our guests."

"Well, they can't come in here," the MP insisted.

Kaiser jumped in the back of the jeep and demanded to be taken to see the desk sergeant at the MP station. "By then I was a little hot under the collar," he admitted.

At the MP station, he accosted the desk sergeant. "How about clueing these two monkeys in?" he asked.

"Lock that SOB up," the desk sergeant ordered.

Kaiser jumped over the top of the railing and grabbed the sergeant by the throat. The two MPs promptly began beating on Kaiser with their nightsticks while trying to pull him off the sergeant. The more they pulled, the tighter Kaiser squeezed, and the desk sergeant was definitely running low on air. Finally Kaiser offered a deal: "They let go of me, I let go of you." The desk sergeant nodded his head vigorously. "I did get cell number 1," said Kaiser.

He was just settling in when the desk sergeant, flanked by the same two

MPs, paid him a visit. "We are going to give you a break," he said. "We are going to let you go."

"Like hell you will," said Kaiser. "Close the gate gently. I am trying to sleep."

The next morning, Kaiser's 1st Sergeant came to sign him out, and Kaiser, still dressed in his rumpled civilian clothes and driving his personal automobile, picked up General Johnson and took him to work. "No questions asked by the general," Kaiser noted.

Of course, there was an investigation, the outcome of which was gratifying. General Watlington, the division commander, wrote a personal letter of apology to Herr Geiger. The two MPs were each reduced one grade, and the desk sergeant was transferred. Kaiser received an unofficial reprimand from Johnson, followed two weeks later by promotion to staff sergeant. To celebrate his promotion, the motor officer, Kaiser's nominal boss, gave a party in his honor. Life went on.

JOHNSON UNDERSTOOD the role of an *assistant* division commander very well, and he was a loyal and supportive assistant to General Watlington. His assessment was that the division commander was "very strict, he established very high standards, he expected conformance, he was impatient, he was top within the unit." That did not mean, however, that serving with him was easy.

General Watlington was reassigned shortly before Johnson left the division, so—only days before their own departure—the Johnsons welcomed Major General and Mrs. Philip F. Lindeman to the unit. "They are perfectly delightful people who will be a welcome change from the Watlingtons," Johnson confided to his mother.

Later, an officer he knew well asked Johnson whether he thought that a brigadier general without troop experience should be eligible for promotion to major general. "I wouldn't have said this before I left the Pentagon," Johnson said, "but I now think a man should go out and prove he can get along with a son of a bitch like Watlington for a year." That was unusual language for Johnson, probably reflecting how much diplomacy and self-restraint the assignment had required of him.

In a somewhat parallel inquiry, someone once asked General Clyde D. Eddleman, for whom Johnson would later work, whether he thought that Johnson should be promoted to three-star rank without having had command of a division. "What do you mean?" Eddleman retorted. "Hell, he *had* a division!"

IN SEPTEMBER 1957, after twenty months with the 8th Division, Johnson took up new duties as chief of staff of Seventh Army, the tactical headquarters responsible for controlling combat elements of U.S. Army forces in Germany and their support. This was the first of three senior staff assignments he would fill in Germany over the next three years. Taken together, they would complete his apprenticeship for senior leadership assignments and put him on the path to the culminating assignments of his career.

Commanding Seventh Army at that time was Lieutenant General Bruce C. Clarke, to be followed while Johnson was in the job by Lieutenant General Eddleman. Both men were hard-driving types who subsequently attained four-star rank.

As chief of staff, Johnson was involved in everything the headquarters dealt with. The role of tactical nuclear weapons was high on the agenda. The procedures for release of such weapons, and exercises for testing those procedures, got a lot of his attention. But most of all, Johnson was concerned that the Seventh Army was unduly "kaserne-oriented" instead of concentrating on the terrain and the threat. He was particularly displeased with the performance of Army headquarters itself in getting out into the field when periodic alerts were called. As he saw it, there was "almost complete chaos for a matter of an hour to an hour and a half after an alert was called." He made them do it over and over, until they finally realized that "the standards that we prescribed for the subordinates were the same standards we had to meet ourselves." After that, it went the way he thought it should.

In that matter, he had just kept pounding and pounding and pounding until he got what he wanted, but Johnson could be diplomatic as well. He asked the G-3 people to work up a certain plan, and the staff officers did so, but they could not get the colonel who was G-3 to approve it so that it could be forwarded to Johnson. One day, Johnson buttonholed Donald Bennett, an officer in G-3 who had worked on the plan, and told him to be in his office in ten minutes to brief him on it. Bennett showed up as ordered, and he had Colonel Houston, the G-3, with him. During Bennett's presentation, Houston raised a number of objections. Finally, Houston had to visit the latrine. While he was out of the room, Johnson said to Bennett, "Give me something I can complain about in the plan." Bennett suggested some provision that they didn't much care about one way or the other. When Houston returned, Johnson singled out that aspect for criticism. "It disturbs me very much," he stated forcefully, and Houston quickly agreed. "If you take that out," Johnson immediately added, "then I approve the plan." Bennett was gratified by the outcome. "Colonel Houston's face had been saved, General Johnson had moved the plan forward, and all was well."

While he was in Europe, Johnson became deeply involved in a new movement known as the Protestant Men of the Chapel. Johnson was soon elected president. He perceived that they had been looking for a figurehead, which was not his style. "In all humbleness," Johnson reflected, "I think that I fooled the people who chose me, because I felt an obligation to work, rather than to simply hold the title." Work he did, traveling to many of the chapels in Germany and France, and later Italy as well when they extended the program there. By the time his year in the job was up, he had spoken at forty-five different meetings, influenced the expansion of the movement into the Air Force and Navy, and further extended it to the principal U.S. bases in Turkey and North Africa.

An important relationship for Johnson was with the second Seventh Army commander he served, Clyde Eddleman. "Eddleman played a key part in Johnson's subsequent life," recalled Sitterson, and Johnson's daughter Ellen Kay viewed General Eddleman as her father's mentor. The two men had known each other in the Pentagon during overlapping assignments to G-3 on the Army Staff. General Eddleman "saw and admired the spiritual strength in him," said Charles Brown, who served with them both when he was Seventh Army Chaplain. "And that was meaningful to General Eddleman, who was a preacher's son." Eddleman described Johnson as "the most able chief of staff of my experience."

As in earlier assignments, Johnson was admired and respected by his subordinates as well. He continued to support Boy Scouting, and DeWitt Smith was present when Johnson went down to the train station in Heidelberg one morning to give a departure talk to a group of American Boy Scouts and their British counterparts, off to spend a week together in England. "As I listened to him speak," said Smith, "he seemed so articulate, and so sincere, that I said to myself, 'This is the kind of man who ought to be leading our Army.'" Sitterson made an equally telling observation, saying that Johnson "was one of those people who looked just as good from backstage as he did from out front." In Sitterson's experience, that was not the case with a lot of general officers.

IN APRIL 1959, General Eddleman received his fourth star and was reassigned to be Commander-in-Chief, U.S. Army, Europe (USAREUR). He took Johnson with him to be G-3, the plans and operations officer, of his new command. That job called for him to be simultaneously the G-3 of

Central Army Group, or CENTAG, a NATO headquarters with multinational staffing. It also called for a two-star general, and Johnson was only a brigadier. This caused a furor, recalled Johnson's classmate Steve Fuqua, but General Eddleman said, "I want Johnson for my G-3, and he's going to be it," and that was that. In the autumn, the whole thing was regularized when Johnson was promoted to major general.

When, at the end of the year, CENTAG became a separate, stand-alone headquarters, Johnson was designated its chief of staff. He continued working for General Eddleman in his new capacity, for Eddleman commanded both USAREUR and CENTAG, and Johnson now supervised a staff populated by French, German, and American officers. The USAREUR chief of staff valued the contribution Johnson made to the work of the headquarters, evaluating him as a man who "leads rather than drives."

Staff Sergeant Kaiser accompanied Johnson through this sequence of assignments. In the late spring of 1960, Johnson called him in to ask a question. "Would you like to accompany me to Tacoma, Washington?" he asked.

"Yes, sir," replied Kaiser, "but you are not going to Washington. You are going to Fort Leavenworth."

Johnson didn't think so. "No, I am sure that I am slated for a division," he insisted.

Kaiser was adamant: "No, sir, you are going to Leavenworth."

What Johnson did not know was that General Eddleman's driver had repeated to Kaiser a conversation about Johnson's next assignment between General Eddleman and the Adjutant General, who had told Eddleman, "We've got him slated for the 28th Division in Tacoma."

Eddleman had responded, "We *know* Johnny can command a division, because he ran the 8th Division. Let's shoot for Fort Leavenworth." For some time, Eddleman had been writing in Johnson's efficiency reports things like "especially recommended for Commandant of the Command & General Staff College."

Three weeks later, General Johnson again brought Kaiser in for a little talk. "It seems your G-2 is better than mine," he admitted. "Would you like to accompany me to Fort Leavenworth?"

"Yes, sir," replied Kaiser without hesitation, having had ample time to think it over.

CHAPTER TWELVE

FORT LEAVENWORTH

As Commandant of the U.S. Army Command & General Staff College, Johnson was back where he had begun rebuilding his career after repatriation at the end of World War II. Now he was in charge, and it was the ideal assignment. By this time, he was known throughout the Army as a man of iron will, deep religious faith, unlimited appetite for work, and exemplary character. For the first time, he was in a position where his influence would be felt throughout the establishment. Had he not been a soldier, Johnson once said, he would have chosen to be a teacher.[1] Now he was both, and Fort Leavenworth under his tutelage was going to come to life.

Johnson took up his new duties in August 1960, just in time to welcome two new classes to the College. He had written ahead from Europe, asking for some staff support in preparing his remarks for that occasion, but what he got in return was so parochial and pedestrian that he junked it and started over on his own. He knew exactly what he meant to say. "I wanted to instill pride in the Army and in the Army uniform," he wrote to General Eddleman. "Second, I wanted to establish a tone of general conduct and deportment, including the intellectual and moral attributes of an officer."[2]

Johnson made an immediate and forceful impression on the student body, mostly young majors who were the Army's coming generation of leadership. He let his strong religious convictions show, and he set high standards of personal integrity. "A man who will cheat on his wife will cheat on me," he routinely observed in his welcoming remarks. One allied student who ignored Johnson's warning waltzed across the platform at graduation, only later to discover that he had been handed a blank piece of paper instead of a diploma.

Johnson also observed that excessive use of alcohol was a potential pitfall. "Alcohol is a preservative," he noted, "and this College and the military services have no requirement for the product of a pickled brain."

Maybe as a result of having to deal with problems like these, Johnson developed a jaundiced view of off-duty life. "I always felt," he confessed, "that if the Army day ended with the work day it would be really a great

Army, because an awful lot of trouble tends to grow out of the social side of the Army."

Johnson closed his welcoming presentation with a prayer, just as he had opened his first staff meeting with one. "I'm very sensitive to people who push their religious beliefs in their jobs," said Arthur Brown, a student at Leavenworth during Johnson's tenure as Commandant and later a senior officer. "I don't like that. With General Johnson, that was not a problem. He was very open and forthright about his convictions, but he didn't try to push them on anyone else, except insofar as he demanded honest and faithful service from everyone, regardless of their religion."

Early in this assignment, Johnson decided that the College needed a sports program so people could get to know one another, and at his direction, a softball league was formed. Each student was assigned to one of the teams. In the very first inning of the very first game, with General Johnson in attendance, Bill Livsey, a tightly wound young Infantry officer who would one day become a four-star general, rounded third base and headed for home. There the catcher, another Infantry officer, tagged him with the ball to the mouth. A fistfight ensued, with both benches emptying, moving one gladiator to tell Johnson excitedly, "It's working, General. We're really getting to know these guys!"

Johnson displayed a refreshing irreverence that made him popular with the students. Characterizing the College's guest speaker program as in reality a "guest reader program," Johnson observed that quite often "you got principal officials reading manuscripts that they didn't appear to have any great familiarity with prior to the time that they got up on the platform." The most enjoyable feature of these sessions became Johnson's after-lecture remarks, often introduced by a comment such as, "About half of what General So-and-So told you is open to question." Johnson would then take the lead in a discussion of points that he thought needed to be revisited.

Johnson coined an expression to convey his idea of how students should approach the course of instruction. "Challenge the assertion," he insisted, in a formulation that became known all over the Army. Johnson had been led to this way of thinking by his own mistrust of the Strategic Air Command's claim that it had deterred war. After all, Johnson recalled, some 33,000 soldiers had been killed in action during the Korean War, and "it was hard to see why so many Army people had died if SAC in fact had deterred war." He said, "I just don't believe that threats work all that well," and it was also his view that "bombs don't accomplish very much in the end."

JOHNSON'S PREDECESSOR as Commandant had been Major General Lionel C. McGarr, also known—although probably not to his face—as "Split-head," a reference to the fact that he parted his hair down the middle. "He was a great regimental commander," remarked an officer who had known him in that role, "but not exactly what you'd expect to see as Commandant." He was, observed an officer who served on his faculty, "a concrete general."

McGarr stories were popular cocktail party conversation. On one occasion, when he was out walking in the snow with his two daughters, a passing car splashed them. McGarr, incensed, flagged down the driver. "Do you know who I am?" he demanded. The driver did not. "Well, I'm General McGarr, and I'm the commanding general of this post."

The driver was not impressed. "Well, great, General," he replied. "I'm so-and-so, and I'm the butcher in Leavenworth, Kansas. Just stay out of the road when I'm driving if you don't want to get splashed."

The daughters were so embarrassed by this incident that they slunk away.

The idiosyncrasies of his predecessor were probably not important, but there is no doubt that when Johnson showed up, focused on values and issues and efficient management of the post, he found that approach warmly received, at least in part because of the contrast.[3]

By now, Johnson admitted, he was up to twenty cups of coffee a day, fueling his passion for work. "Work is his only hobby," a friend said of Johnson, and even Johnson agreed with that judgment. Things were busy by nature at Fort Leavenworth, with some 3,500 students a year graduating from the resident courses and about 26,000 enrolled in nonresident extension courses. The staff and faculty included well over 300 officers, and during 1962 alone, the Johnsons entertained 3,300 visitors in their quarters.[4]

Invited by a friend to come to Colorado for a vacation, Johnson declined, explaining that "I feel that I lose touch very quickly every time I go away for even a brief period. I think that I'll do like a good horse does and rest in place." Turning down another friend's invitation to hunt pheasant, Johnson told him that he did not enjoy "killing living things" and was "not a hunter in any sense of the word." Said his daughter Ellen, "Father never seemed to have time to take leave." She thought that if her father had been a ditch digger he would have worked just as hard at that. "It was his way."

Asked what else he did besides work, Johnson would mention church and Scouting, and that about completed the list. He worked with the Kaw Council of the Boy Scouts and received its Silver Beaver Award. While gratefully acknowledging the award, he felt that he had drawn far more from Scouting than he had given to it. "It is a staunch and finite anchor in a world beset by turbulence and unrest," he wrote to a fellow Scouter.

IN THE AUTUMN, Johnson was invited to speak at a banquet in his hometown of Grafton honoring his teacher Cora Lykken, who was finally retiring after fifty-two years in the North Dakota school system. Although billed as the featured speaker, Johnson was listed far down on the program, following an invocation, two welcomes, three sets of remarks, four sets of comments, and two separate interludes of musical selections. When it was finally his turn, Johnson said, "I think I lucked into a career more challenging, more demanding, and more rewarding than any other career that you could name." Later Miss Lykken wrote to thank him for being part of the celebration in her honor, saying, "it touched my heart that you ended with the last stanza from 'Thanatopsis,' " a poem Johnson had been required to memorize in her class thirty-five years before.

LEAVENWORTH PROVIDED THE OPPORTUNITY for Johnson to further explore and expound upon his theories on the role of ground forces, the appropriate balance between firepower and maneuver, and the most effective structure for the infantry division. Clearly these were matters he had long considered, for he spoke of them at the first welcoming address he gave only days after his own arrival. "The Army is unique," he told the newly arrived student officers. "Only the Army [of all the services] has the inherent and organic capability to apply the complete spectrum of force." That was a reference to the limitations of massive retaliation, the strategic concept that dominated the Eisenhower years, and to the Air Force and Navy as custodians— and potential deliverers—of the nuclear arsenal. Johnson's own strategic outlook centered on land power as the source of control—control imposed with the minimum amount of firepower and destruction necessary.

"I was troubled," Johnson explained, "and for a number of years had been troubled, by what I thought was the enormous emphasis on firepower. And what does firepower do? Firepower *destroys*. What else does it do? Nothing, that I can see, really, except *destroy*. Well, the human race doesn't exist to destroy. The human race exists to be *constructive,* and to build." Here, Johnson's strategic and religious views seemed to be cross-reinforcing.

At one point, Johnson selected three officers from his faculty and asked them to study the sources of conflict and what constituted victory, two highly abstruse and illusive questions. Countering the prevailing overemphasis—as he viewed it—on firepower may have motivated his commissioning of this work. The three researchers labored for a year without producing a written report, but Johnson found the exercise useful nevertheless. He conferred with the study team frequently and collected various fragments they came up with for his consideration. But probably the most important outcome was the conclusion he reached about the purpose of armed forces. "Armed forces exist to maintain," he decided, "to restore, or to create an environment of order or a climate of stability within which government under law can function effectively." That was his definitive statement on the matter, and from it much else flowed.

"How do you create order?" Johnson asked. "You create order by establishing control. How do you establish control? By closing with and defeating the enemy." Here he acknowledged having adopted in modified form the classic mission of the infantry: "to close with and destroy the enemy." The change—substituting "defeat" for "destroy"—was significant, and it spoke volumes about both Johnson's strategic outlook and his operative human values.

Next came consideration of how to defeat, rather than destroy, an enemy. "You do that through a process of fire and maneuver," Johnson maintained, and the point was to establish control. Thus, in his view, firepower was not an end in itself but a means of facilitating maneuver, maneuver designed to get a controlling force on the objective. It was an argument for the primacy of maneuver over firepower. It was also a brief for the continuing relevance of the Army to the nation's defense, something that had been called into question, implicitly if not explicitly, during the Eisenhower years. "In the final analysis," Johnson concluded, "armies have the ultimate role in waging war, because only armies can perform the function of closing and of imposing control."[5]

"How do you establish control?" Johnson asked again. "You don't do it by destroying." In a formulation whose exact phrasing, it would later become apparent, was extremely significant, Johnson stated this conviction: "I maintain that control is the object beyond the battle and the object beyond the war."

IN 1961, JOHNSON PRESENTED for consideration by the Army Chief of Staff the Reorganization Objectives Army Division (ROAD for short), an initiative to replace the failed Pentomic division structure with something more workable. The Pentomic structure, brought into being by General Maxwell Taylor during his tenure as Army Chief of Staff, had been designed for wide dispersion, intended to achieve survivability on a nuclear battlefield. Built around five "battle groups" commanded by colonels, it eliminated the usual battalion echelon and went directly to companies commanded by captains. In practice, the Pentomic division was never accepted by the Army's rank and file, indeed was never adequately rationalized to them. When the structure proved both fragile and unwieldy, it was clear that something better was urgently needed.

ROAD built the division around three brigades instead of the five battle groups of the Pentomic approach, also reintroducing the battalion level of command between brigades and companies. Flexible division composition was also stressed, with various types of battalions assigned as needed for the contemplated mission and environment of each division. ROAD was approved and in due course replaced the Pentomic structure throughout the force.

Concurrent with this change, pointed out a subsequent analysis, "Army leaders moved from a doctrine calling for the automatic use of tactical nuclear weapons not only because it had limited the nature of the Army's response and had been accepted reluctantly in the first place, but also because they no longer believed nuclear weapons were the only way to stop a Soviet invasion of Western Europe."[6]

ON THE FACULTY AT LEAVENWORTH, serving as the British Liaison Officer, was Colonel Richard L. Clutterbuck. He was an interesting and perceptive man, a veteran of the campaign to deal with the insurgency in Malaya, and he and Johnson became close friends. Clutterbuck lectured on the Malayan affair and wrote extensively on it for American military publications. Johnson listened to and read what Clutterbuck had to say, and over a period of years they engaged in an extended dialogue on the topic of counterinsurgency.

"We found our ideas to be very much in common," said Clutterbuck, modestly adding that "of course it was I who learned from him rather than he from me. No mistake about that!" Among the points that Clutterbuck and Johnson agreed on regarding Vietnam were the essentiality of rooting out the communist infrastructure in the villages and that, "if the re-establishment of control by force is to have any meaning, it must re-establish government down to village level, protected by viable village police posts and a good police intelligence system."

These ideas would resurface downstream when Johnson moved to a key Pentagon billet, where he would continue to correspond with Clutterbuck on counterinsurgency. Meanwhile, Clutterbuck returned to duty with the British Army, writing to Johnson on his departure that "it was an unforgettable experience to serve under you, and one which will influence me all my life, not only as a soldier but as a man."

ANOTHER KEY PERSONALITY at the College was a colonel named Jasper Wilson, widely known as "Jap." Wilson was an opinionated officer and a thorny personality, but he was smart, and Johnson could depend on him to say what he thought. "Jasper Wilson is my hair shirt," Johnson once told a colleague. "I need him."

As happened from time to time, Johnson found himself having to sort out an incident in order to retain a subordinate's useful services. The matter involved Wilson and his dogs. There were, Johnson once pointed out to the post Women's Club, 608 registered dogs, along with assorted cats, rabbits, and squirrels, living at Fort Leavenworth, mixed in with 3,123 children. Under those circumstances, dog control was a necessity.

Jasper Wilson had a couple of young hunting dogs he was trying to teach to jump into the back of his station wagon when he wanted to go after some birds. One day, Wilson's dogs, all wet and grungy from swimming in the nearby river, happened along just as Jo Birrer, a neighbor, returned from a trip to the commissary. When she opened the back of her station wagon to unload the groceries, they obligingly hopped in, just as they had been taught. By the time Mrs. Birrer ran them out of there, they had done considerable tromping on her purchases, and the lady was not happy.

This led to a complaint against Wilson, who was told that the dogs would have to go. Instead, he requested permission to move off post. He cited the reasonable grounds that where the dogs went, his wife went, and he wanted to continue to enjoy her company. But Wilson was told that, since he fell in the category of key personnel, it was necessary that he continue to live on post—permission denied.

Meanwhile, a sign of uncertain origin had appeared on the Wilsons' lawn. "The dog's a bitch, too!" it proclaimed.[7] Eventually, General Johnson had to get involved. Gaining assurances from Wilson that in the future he would keep his animals tied up, Johnson revoked the banishment decree and allowed both Wilson and the dogs to continue to live on post, where by that time the whole matter had become a community entertainment.

WHILE HE WAS COMMANDANT, Johnson made a new friend in an unusual way. Besides housing the Command & General Staff College, Fort Leavenworth was also the home of the U.S. Disciplinary Barracks, a penitentiary for long-term military prisoners. Those with trusty status did various work around the post, including gardening at General Johnson's quarters. Over time, Johnson noticed that one prisoner assigned to this duty was particularly conscientious and talented. He began talking with the man and found out that Tony Savello had been involved in a family landscaping business in civil life. On several occasions, Johnson invited Savello to have dinner with the family.

Eventually, Johnson asked his driver, Sergeant Frank Kaiser, what Tony was in prison for. Kaiser, who had also come to admire Savello, said that Savello had been on his way home from Korea for discharge from the Army when he was apprehended by authorities and charged with desertion. The duffel bag with his records had been stolen somewhere en route and, unable to establish his status, Savello had somehow wound up in the military prison.

Johnson received this information on a Monday. By the following Saturday, Savello was out of prison, the beneficiary of Johnson's personal interest. Of course, Savello's Army lawyer would have straightened the matter out eventually, but Johnson's involvement streamlined the process remarkably. Thirty-five years later Savello, by then retired from the family business to which he had returned, remembered Johnson with gratitude and admiration: "He was beautiful!"

IN HIS DEALINGS WITH THE STUDENTS, Johnson was professorial in the best sense, instructing and guiding, but also listening and challenging. And he emphasized over and over that the students must question what the faculty presented. "Challenge the assertion," he urged.

Virtually everything Johnson presented to the students had an ethical component, and he had one lecture in particular—it came to be known as the "4 I's" lecture—that was explicit about the professional values he viewed as essential. Intelligence, imagination, initiative, and integrity were the qualities he cited, specifying integrity as the most important. Johnson's impact on the students can be judged from a letter written to him by a Korean student when the course was completed. Thanking Johnson for the inspiration and guidance provided by his 4 I's, the officer said that following these precepts had enabled him to complete the course successfully. "I owe you for it," he said. "I am sure, as long as I believe it, throughout my life I will remember you who gave me so much impression with a few words."

Eventually, even his family could recite the 4 I's. "At some point in high school," recalled his son Bobby, "there was a requirement to give a speech. All of us kids gave the I's. We used his language."

IN AN INITIATIVE that would require much of his time and effort over a period of years, Johnson sought to establish an honors program that would evolve into an accredited master's degree program. Even though the objective had not been fully attained when Johnson left the College, the importance he attached to it is reflected in his comment to a friend that "of all the things that went on at Leavenworth, I am most proud of the progress that we made in that area." He felt that it would have an important impact on the entire officer corps and that it would bring recognition to the "superb Army school system."[8]

JOHNSON ALSO TOOK SERIOUSLY his role as post commander, something that most Commandants left to a deputy. He thought that the students should be educated in installation management techniques, so he decided to conduct his quarterly management reviews on stage in front of the class. This prospect understandably terrified the members of his staff, who envisioned themselves being grilled in front of a huge audience of junior officers. The potential for being embarrassed was substantial.

Nevertheless, Johnson pressed on with the idea. In due course, they were up on the stage as the comptroller, for example, advised Johnson on some matter. Johnson would turn to the class and explain, "Here we have the comptroller telling me I shouldn't do something for fiscal reasons. But it's the right thing to do, and I want to do it. Now here's the background." And he would explain in detail the issues involved and the weight he gave to various factors, illustrating graphically the multiple equities a commander has to take into account and the values that ought to guide him in balancing them.

"Now let's discuss the consequences of doing this," he would say, and they would talk about that. All the while, hundreds of students were listening in, asking questions, and offering opinions, with Johnson functioning as commander, instructor, and master of ceremonies. Finally he would decide the issue, and they'd move on to the next functional area, maybe a presentation by the surgeon or the commander of the Disciplinary Barracks, and deal with his issues. "It took a pretty secure commander to do that, unstructured and unrehearsed, in front of such an audience," observed an officer who had watched the process.

A NUMBER OF ALLIED NATIONS sent students to courses at Fort Leavenworth, and by the time Johnson became Commandant, that included the Japanese. Dorothy said that she would not stand in the receiving line and shake hands with Japanese. "Yes, you will," said her husband, and she did. After the reception was over, Johnson and the Japanese stayed up most of the night, maps spread all across the living room floor, fighting the war all over again. Speaking that same autumn to an audience of military veterans, Johnson said, "I hold no animosity and greatly respect the strength that the present forces of Japan contribute to the Free World."

Another aspect of Johnson's consciously determined attitude toward his World War II experience was demonstrated when one of the organizations of former prisoners of war, styling themselves the "battered bastards of Bataan," held an encampment at Leavenworth. "I am sure they scheduled the meeting there because of General Johnson," said his aide, Bert Turner. "He did not go to one of their meetings. Reason: 'They live in the past, not the present.'"

THE LEAVENWORTH YEARS were good family times. Despite Johnson's commitment to his work and his decided antipathy for social events, parties and receptions and community affairs were part of the job, so he made time for them and enjoyed them. Except for one major temporary duty stint in Washington, he stayed pretty close to home base and—unlike at the Pentagon— was able to come home for meals. He and Dorothy made fudge and peanut brittle, shared popcorn and ice cream. Sometimes they danced a few steps when a song they liked came on the radio. "I remember the good relationship between my parents," said their daughter Ellen, "lots of pats and hugs and touches." Christmas was a special time there, and Dorothy remembered walking through falling snow to the chapel with candles in their hands.[9]

IN THE SUMMER OF 1962, Johnson was tasked to take part in a study commissioned by Secretary of Defense Robert S. McNamara. Soon after taking office, McNamara had issued a list of ninety-nine such projects, to be undertaken in addition to the regular work of the Defense Department, and those tasks came to be referred to informally as his "99 Trombones." Later the list was expanded into the hundreds, on subjects ranging from strategy to procurement.[10] Johnson was pulled in to work on one of the stickiest of these, a study on the use of tactical nuclear weapons.

McNamara was not the only one who had questions about tactical nuclear weapons and their use. Only a few weeks before this study got under way, in fact, General Maxwell Taylor had written to Walt Rostow at the State Department to observe that "some people in government doubt that we have a rational program for the development and employment of tactical nuclear weapons," adding, "indeed, I am one of them." Taylor pointed out, and McNamara acknowledged, the dilemma facing a NATO with inadequate conventional forces to defend against Soviet aggression at a time the United States seemed increasingly unwilling to resort to the use of nuclear weapons.

Johnson, too, was sensitive to the larger issues associated with the use of nuclear weapons. One of the courses periodically conducted at Fort Leavenworth was a Senior Officers' Nuclear Weapons Course, and Johnson customarily opened it with some remarks of his own. One officer who attended later wrote to Johnson, thanking him for what he had had to say. "Your emphasis on the moral and ethical implications of our subject matter struck a responsive chord," he said, "not solely because it was a refreshing change from the more prevalent approaches, but more because I immediately felt this is the kind of lead I want to follow."

While the tac-nuc study was under way, Johnson customarily ate breakfast in the Secretary of the Army's Mess at the Pentagon, often with Secretary Cyrus Vance and Under Secretary Stephen Ailes. Over the bacon and eggs, he got to know both men well. Such meals began what was usually a twelve-hour day, weekends included. Robert Montague worked for Johnson on the study. "We were trying to serve Alain Enthoven and Secretary McNamara," he said, "and they were difficult people to serve. We worked night and day." Montague even went so far as to get a cot and move into the Pentagon for a couple of weeks when things were the most hectic. Johnson later wrote to an associate, "I have never had as grueling and exasperating a job as we had in trying to come up with some sort of definitive answers" in that study.[11]

Montague remembered that their conclusion was that tactical nuclear weapons still had a role, and they recommended wider distribution of weapons that could deliver them. "General Johnson was realistic and practical in his outlook on this, as on all matters," said Montague, who found Johnson friendly and good at listening, a thinker and a doer who thought strategically. "I liked him a lot," he recalled. Colonel Dale Buchanan, another officer who worked with Johnson on the project, came away with a similar impression. "He was my favorite general by far," he said of Johnson. "He was a true officer and gentleman."

Secretary McNamara was also impressed by Johnson's thoughtful and nondoctrinaire approach to the topic, and this certainly played a part in Johnson's selection for much higher office only a short time later. It is somewhat surprising, however, that he would be favorably impressed by Johnson's conclusions, given what we now know about McNamara's own strongly held views on the futility of reliance on tactical nuclear weapons. "Once you use them, you use everything else. You can't keep them limited. You'll destroy Europe, everything," McNamara is reported to have said at a private Pentagon luncheon in June 1961.[12]

Back at Fort Leavenworth, Johnson revised the curriculum to eliminate automatic use of tactical nuclear weapons in favor of a more flexible consideration of their use. He also reduced the 600 hours of classroom time formerly devoted to the nuclear battlefield to less than a tenth of that.[13] These modifications, made possible in part by improvements that McNamara was sponsoring in conventional forces, would also have been viewed favorably by the Secretary in light of his skepticism about the utility of tactical nuclear weapons.

At one point during the study, Johnson accompanied McNamara on a visit to Europe designed to better acquaint the Secretary with some of the nuclear delivery means stationed there. It was a typical McNamara trip, forty-eight hours from start to finish. They started on the West German border and looked back through the whole range of systems the Army and Air Force had deployed there. When they boarded the return flight, Johnson recalled, McNamara leaned back "with a very stout double bourbon on the rocks" and—relaxed and affable, a side of his personality that Johnson had not seen before—engaged him with obvious enjoyment in a spirited academic discussion of the whole issue of tactical nuclear weapons.

The tac-nuc study began on 4 July and kept Johnson in Washington almost full-time until October. Back at Leavenworth, Johnson spoke of the experience. As usual, he was his own severest critic. "I went in with the very best intentions in the world of being objective about the course of the study and the conduct of the study," he told his students. "The deeper we got into this thing, the more I found that it was most difficult to abandon prejudices and to abandon some of the notions that I had acquired over too many years and to be able to look at something really honestly."

JOHNSON LATER CALLED the two tours of duty at Fort Leavenworth "the most satisfying assignments in their totality" of his Army service, writing to friends that "beyond any shadow of a doubt, our happiest years were at Fort Leavenworth." He liked the students, liked their combination of maturity and openness to new ideas, liked the interaction with them, liked challenging them and being challenged by them. He had urged them to "challenge the assertion," and with deep satisfaction saw that become a watchword. In his farewell letter to the last class he served with, Johnson reminded them directly of a core value: "Military service centers around the single characteristic of selflessness."[14] That was exactly what they had seen him teach by example.

Before the academic year was even over, Johnson was pulled out for more Pentagon duty, back in DCSOPS, the Office of the Deputy Chief of Staff for Military Operations on the Army Staff, the staff element where he had done so well as a colonel a decade earlier. This time he was to be the Assistant DCSOPS. General Clyde Eddleman, Johnson's former commander in Europe, was now the Army's Vice Chief of Staff, and his influence was clearly at work here, along with the impression Secretary McNamara had formed of Johnson during the tactical nuclear weapons study, and perhaps all those breakfasts with Secretaries Vance and Ailes.

Johnson managed to get his departure delayed until 22 February 1963. That was his birthday, and also the date on which he had agreed to address the mayor's prayer breakfast in Kansas City, a fitting finale to his years at Fort Leavenworth. "It is important to have some kind of star that can take you through troubled times," he told an audience of 500 business and professional men. For him, he said, that came from prayer. He quoted his favorite passage of scripture, a verse from Matthew: "Let your light so shine before men, that they may see your good works, and glorify your Father which is in heaven."

"What an evangelist he would have made!" marveled one of those present.

But Johnson was a soldier, and he had orders. That valedictory message of faith and conviction delivered, he headed for Washington and the Pentagon, where five turbulent and difficult years would culminate his lifetime of military service.

Descended from pioneer stock, young Keith Johnson was photographed with his father Harold, his mother Edna, his younger sisters Edna Ray and Janet, and other relatives. A brother, Herb, was born later. (Johnson Family Collection)

(*Top*) As a child, Johnson often visited his Grandma Johnson's farm in Lancaster, Minnesota, scene of this wagon ride with dog Queenie. "I've always had a love of animals," he said, attributing it to his early days on farms. (*Right*) From his earliest days, Johnson benefited from a wholesome and supportive community. "I look back on those days as great days," he wrote to an old friend. (Johnson Family Collection)

A rich family life, strong religious influences, and a commitment to Scouting marked Johnson's youth. (Johnson Family Collection)

As a sixth-grade schoolboy in Grafton, North Dakota, Johnson (second seat, near row) grew up where education was taken seriously. He remembered dedicated teachers who brought both "discipline" and "sympathetic understanding" to the classroom. (Courtesy Mrs. H. L. Neagel)

As a senior at Grafton High School, Johnson also worked three jobs, played football and basketball, and was involved in dramatics. "I was pretty busy," he admitted. (Johnson Family Collection)

The first boy from Grafton to attend West Point, Johnson was attracted by the adventure and the educational opportunity. (1933 *Howitzer*)

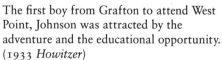

Nicknamed "Olaf" as a cadet, Johnson got an early taste of Army aviation during summer training at Langley Field. (Johnson Family Collection)

As a young officer assigned to the 3d Infantry at Fort Snelling, Johnson was tutored in troop command by 1st Sergeant Frank Cumiskey, remembered by Johnson as "one of my great teachers." (Johnson Family Collection)

At Fort Snelling, Johnson played polo, coached his company basketball team to the post championship, and earned the respect of his soldiers as a young officer with "the qualities to go far in his chosen profession." (Johnson Family Collection)

In 1935, Johnson married Dorothy Rennix, another North Dakotan. At Fort Niagara, while Johnson was with the 28th Infantry, the couple had their first child, named after his father and also called "Johnny." (Johnson Family Collection)

As World War II loomed, Johnson (right) was serving as operations officer of the 57th Infantry (Philippine Scouts). In combat, regimental commander Colonel George S. Clarke (middle) displayed such fear of enemy aircraft that, until he was replaced, Johnson was in effect running the regiment. (Lieutenant Colonel Franklin O. Anders Collection)

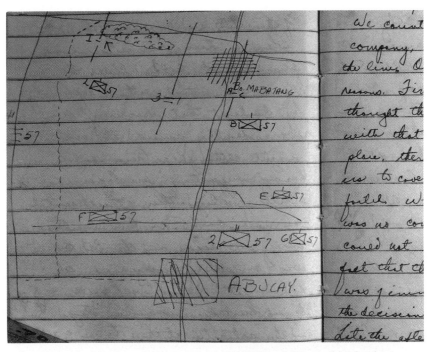

Johnson sketched his battalion's position on the Abucay Line in his clandestine prisoner-of-war diary. (U.S. Army Military History Institute)

After surviving forty-one months as a prisoner of the Japanese, Johnson rebuilt his professional and family life during three good years at Fort Leavenworth, where he and Dorothy celebrated this Christmas with Johnny, Ellen, Bobby, and one of the ever-present dogs. (Johnson Family Collection)

In the Korean War, Johnson commanded a hastily assembled battalion and two successive regiments, then became a corps operations officer, earning a Distinguished Service Cross for valor and a battlefield promotion to colonel. Professionally, he was back in business. (National Archives)

Newly promoted to brigadier general, Johnson as assistant division commander moved the 8th Infantry Division to Germany and oversaw field training that produced record-setting performances on battalion tests. (Johnson Family Collection)

Johnson returned from four years in Germany to become Commandant of the U.S. Army Command & General Staff College, where he urged student officers to "challenge the assertion" and warned them of his belief that "a man who will cheat on his wife will cheat on me." (Johnson Family Collection)

(*Above*) Preparing to become the Army's Deputy Chief of Staff for Operations (DCSOPS), Johnson receives from aide Captain Bert Turner a useful artifact, a wooden turtle that exposes more stars the further its neck sticks out. (Johnson Family Collection)

(*Below*) Johnson's lifelong devotion to Scouting earned him the Silver Beaver and Silver Buffalo awards and involved him in many events like this Eagle Scout recognition dinner. On his desk, Johnson kept two books—the Holy Bible and the Scout Handbook. (Johnson Family Collection)

During a year as DCSOPS, Johnson became deeply involved in all the key Army issues, especially growing involvement in Vietnam and an emerging airmobility capability, and traveled widely, including a visit to the 1st Cavalry Division in Korea. (Johnson Family Collection)

Secretary of the Army Stephen Ailes administered the oath to Johnson, newly appointed Army Chief of Staff. Present were Dorothy Johnson and General Earle G. Wheeler, Chairman of the Joint Chiefs of Staff. Afterward, Johnson quoted the Scout Oath: "On my honor I will do my best to do my duty to God and my country." (Sergeant First Class Frank X. Kaiser Collection)

Johnson with Colonel Jasper J. ("Jap") Wilson on a visit to
Fort Lewis. Wilson, a thorny personality, was also brilliant.
"Jap Wilson's my hair shirt," said Johnson. "I need him."
(Johnson Family Collection)

Johnson, on his first trip to Vietnam as Chief of Staff, with
General Nguyen Khanh, who was then South Vietnam's chief
of state. Jasper Wilson, Khanh's American advisor, had helped
bring him to power. (Johnson Family Collection)

(*Above*) The Joint Chiefs of Staff—Marine General Wallace M. Greene, Jr., Air Force General John P. McConnell, Johnson, and Admiral David L. McDonald —meet with JCS Chairman General Earle G. Wheeler in his office. Johnson described how, "as the adversary relationship [between civilian defense officials and the JCS] hardened, the opposing factions within the JCS "tended to close ranks, and differences that ought to be exposed and analyzed didn't appear." (Johnson Family Collection)

(*Below*) Johnson with General William C. Westmoreland, commander of U.S. forces in Vietnam while Johnson was Chief of Staff. Johnson strongly opposed his conduct of the war, afterward saying, "I don't happen to be a fan of General Westmoreland. I don't think I ever was, and I certainly didn't become one as a result of the Vietnam War." (Johnson Family Collection)

Johnson saluting with new Secretary of the Army Stanley Resor in July 1965. Johnson respected Resor personally, but felt that Secretary of Defense McNamara had unwisely changed the role of the service Secretaries from being primarily spokesmen and advocates for their respective services to being de facto Assistant Secretaries of Defense. (Johnson Family Collection)

Cadets Mark Walsh and Carl Arvin present a copy of the West Point yearbook, *The Howitzer,* to Johnson and Vice Chief of Staff General Creighton Abrams. Before long, Arvin, the cadet First Captain of his class, would be killed in action in Vietnam. Johnson signed a letter of condolence to the family of every soldier lost or missing, sometimes hundreds a week. (Johnson Family Collection)

Addressing a Presidential Prayer Breakfast, Johnson deeply moved his listeners with an account of his prisoner-of-war experiences and closed with his favorite passage of scripture: "Let your light so shine before men that they may see your good works and glorify your Father which is in heaven." (Johnson Family Collection)

Dorothy Johnson was wonderfully supportive of her husband, enduring hard years while he was a prisoner and again as the Vietnam War consumed him as Chief of Staff. Her husband said gratefully that she "makes the friends for the family and restores good relationships with the people that I tend to alienate through an unreasonable brusqueness and bluntness." (U.S. Army Military History Institute)

Johnson traveled extensively, seeking support for the war and encouraging the troops. When an instructor told him that the men in basic training were doing a lot of griping, Johnson replied, "Well, sergeant major, they're infantry privates, and that's one of the few privileges they have." (Johnson Family Collection)

Johnson with General of the Army Omar Bradley, whose advice he sought on resignation. Bradley discouraged that course of action, telling Johnson that he'd just be regarded as a disgruntled general and would be forgotten the next day. (Johnson Family Collection)

On one of the occasions when the Joint Chiefs of Staff were transported to the LBJ ranch in Texas to meet with the President, Johnson took a moment to commune with a resident beagle. (Johnson Family Collection)

At the White House, Johnson confers with Secretary of the Army Resor and Secretary of Defense McNamara during the July 1967 urban riots in Detroit. Johnson found such violent disorders tragic, calling them "a national shame." (LBJ Library)

(*Above*) Shortly after this August 1967 White House discussion with the President, Johnson and other members of the Joint Chiefs of Staff briefly considered resignation en masse to protest LBJ's war policies. (LBJ Library)

(*Below*) Frustrated and unhappy with the way the Vietnam War was being conducted, Johnson's demeanor is grim at a February 1968 White House meeting. (LBJ Library)

Described by Secretary of Defense McNamara as a man with "an iron will, extraordinary toughness of mind and spirit, and a fierce integrity," upon retirement Johnson was awarded the Distinguished Service Medal by the President. (Frontier Army Museum)

His official portrait as Army Chief of Staff portrays Johnson much as he was described at his retirement by LBJ: "gentle, faithful, loyal, wise, and—as the thousands of men who have served under him will all testify —beloved." (Johnson Family Collection)

CHAPTER THIRTEEN

DCSOPS

DCSOPS was the same demanding and fast-paced environment it had been when Johnson was there as a colonel, only now there was a war over the horizon in Vietnam; the cold war was intensified, with the Soviet Union closer to strategic parity; and the Kennedy administration was hard at work rebuilding conventional forces, revamping Pentagon management practices, and reworking the global calculus. If anything, the days were even longer, the issues more numerous and complex, and the tasks more demanding than on the earlier tour. Certainly the civilian leadership was more assertive, more self-assured, and more difficult to deal with, a circumstance that permeated all else that transpired.[1]

Secretary Robert S. McNamara was at the heart of all this, seconded by his assistant secretary for systems analysis, Alain Enthoven, and a stable of other aggressive civilians. Most of them were young, lacking in military experience, and convinced that neither of those two factors made any difference.

A year earlier, General Clyde D. Eddleman, then the Army Vice Chief of Staff, had written to Harold K. Johnson about prospects for "those of you who are going to inherit the top responsibilities of the Army," saying, "I am quite confident that you will be on duty here, possibly sooner than you think."

Now that prediction—helped along, no doubt, by Eddleman's own influence before his retirement—had been fulfilled. Johnson began as Assistant DCSOPS, less than three months into the assignment became Acting DCSOPS, and on 1 July 1963 became DCSOPS in his own right and was promoted to lieutenant general. It had been planned all along that that was the way it would go. "I approach this assignment with many more misgivings than I have ever had on a prior assignment," Johnson wrote to a peer. To another he lamented, "I seem destined to spend the major part of my life away from troops," and that was true—the culminating years of his service were devoted to staff work and schools.

*   *   *

JOHNSON'S FIRST DAY as acting DCSOPS proved to be a memorable one. It was about two o'clock in the afternoon on a Sunday in May—Mother's Day, in fact—when Johnson got a call from his executive officer saying that General Johnson might be interested in knowing that the Secretary of the Army and the Chief of Staff were in the Army War Room. "Yes," said Johnson, he was interested in that, and he hustled over to find out what was going on. When he reached the War Room, Johnson found one of his bosses on the phone talking to the President and the other on the phone with the Attorney General. The topic had to do with deploying Army units, and there seemed to be some controversy over what information had been provided.

What was taking place was a civil rights crisis in Birmingham, Alabama, one of a series of such confrontations during this period, and Army forces— active and reserve—were backing up the federal marshals on the scene. For a time, things were so chaotic that the first flights of troop-carrying aircraft had to fly in circles pending a decision as to their destination.[2]

By eleven o'clock Sunday night, the Army had multiple serials of troops moving toward the scene. That was not necessarily a good thing, as Johnson soon learned in a call from General Paul D. Adams at Strike Command. "Somebody better step in here and stop fragmenting the force," he thundered, "because we've got elements of five divisions moving on Birmingham and Montgomery." At about 1:30 in the morning, with all this in motion, Johnson was pondering the events of the day "and wondering how we were going to do things better." Although the crisis of the moment had been effectively contained, it was clear to Johnson that they needed a better way to manage the deployment of forces and to collate current information about the status of those forces, ensuring that the Army spoke with one voice on such matters and that that voice was an authoritative one.

At that moment the telephone rang. "This is the President. Give me a rundown of the situation," Johnson heard. "From that moment," he said, "we went to work on an improved Army Operations Center."[3]

Later that day, Johnson addressed the people in DCSOPS as their new boss. He spoke of his perception of the working environment, of the values he cherished, of his expectations, and of his profound need for their help in meeting his new responsibilities. "We've had a radical adjustment to make in establishing communication, if you will, with the DOD [Department of Defense] and with our own civilian secretariat level," he said candidly. "We've had to learn . . . a new language."

He stressed, predictably, the need for absolute integrity in carrying out their duties. "The thing that has given me the greatest single pride in the Army over the years (especially the last ten, which have not been particularly happy ones for the Army overall), has been the fundamental honesty of the Army. We've played it straight. We've played it on the basis of what's good for the country. . . . This we must continue to do. We must be honest."

Then he warned them against a common problem in the Pentagon of the day. "There may be occasions when you will be given a directed solution to a given problem." Don't fall for that, he told them. "In each case, I want the starting action officer . . . to present both sides of a problem, to weigh the pro's and con's and let the solution fall out of the analysis. If this isn't what's wanted, there are people who have the necessary authority to change the direction of the paper. But at least they'll know what the consequences are, and they'll know what the fundamentally honest position is."

He wanted the same candor from his people in their dealings with him. "I want you to talk back. Yes-men are no good. If I needed yes-men around, I wouldn't need you at all. When the going begins to get tough, you talk up. There will be times when I'll chop it off, but at least initially I want you to talk up. I can promise you this, I'll hold no resentment."

"I'm going to need an awful lot of your help if I'm going to ride this job rather than have the job ride me," Johnson concluded. "I'd like to meet each of you on your way out." Then he stood at the door and shook the hand of each man as he left the auditorium.

THE JOHNSON FAMILY was assigned quarters at Fort Myer, Virginia, adjacent to Arlington Cemetery and not far from the Pentagon. In his new billet, Johnson was not authorized a driver, so there was the question of what to do with Sergeant Kaiser. Kaiser said he would like to be assigned to the 3d Infantry—the Army's ceremonial regiment, also known as the Old Guard—which was headquartered at Fort Myer, and Johnson arranged for that assignment. He was, in effect, putting Kaiser into storage pending further need of his services. Meanwhile, he told a friend, "my transportation here is a bus."

DURING JOHNSON'S FIRST MONTH on duty with DCSOPS, a drastic change in its organization was implemented. This entailed splitting the existing organization into two parts—one continuing as DCSOPS, and the other becoming a separate staff element known by the acronym ACSFOR, meaning Assistant Chief of Staff for Force Development.[4] Johnson favored the split, or at least accommodated the change. "It will get one agency out of the business of promoting operational readiness while, at the same time, attempting to justify, rationalize, or even hide the errors in reaching a suitable level of readiness," he wrote at the time. It was clear that, as a veteran of DCSOPS, he knew its institutional foibles.

The heart of DCSOPS was the action officer, the man who had primary responsibility for a given matter. He was obliged to become the resident expert on the topic at hand and to carry action on it through to completion. "I intend to assure that our action officers adopt the attitude that the man in the field knows more about his problems than we do in the Pentagon," Johnson declared early in his DCSOPS tenure.

General Johnson, it was universally agreed, invariably treated action officers with respect. He talked directly to them, and they appreciated that. On one occasion, Johnson went to a meeting of the operations deputies after having been advised by the action officer at the prebrief to take a certain stand. As it turned out, the Army lost on that particular issue. At the next meeting, Johnson turned to the action officer and told him, in front of everyone, "It's not your fault. I didn't listen to what you said. I thought I knew the answer." Then they went on with the agenda.

Given the many Joint Chiefs of Staff meetings and the long hours they entailed, it was sometimes quite late in the day by the time an action officer got to give his pitch. William DeGraf cooled his heels until about seven o'clock one evening to prebrief Johnson on some minor matter, and when he finally got in, he didn't hide his annoyance. While DeGraf made his presentation, Johnson rummaged around in his huge desk. Finally he came up with a three- by five-inch card, got up, walked over, and deposited it in the young officer's lap. It was a quotation from a Reverend Lord that read: "Be thankful for the difficulties of your job. If it were not for those, we could hire someone else for much less." DeGraf left with a smile on his face.

When he thought the occasion demanded it, though, Johnson could be quite severe in critiquing his people. "I can find no fact in this study," he wrote concerning one paper he found deficient. "There appears to be a complete absence of understanding of the missions of Seventh Army and United States Army, Europe"—bad luck for the drafter, in that Johnson had held key roles in both headquarters. "The action officer is completely wrong on two specific points that actually govern the findings of the study." Other than that, apparently, a fine piece of work. Johnson remanded it for further consideration.

Johnson was promoted when he became the DCSOPS, but even with his new three-star rank, he was not authorized an assigned driver. He was, however, allowed to have a military gardener. Johnson got hold of Sergeant Kaiser and offered to put him on his staff as the gardener. He left it up to Kaiser whether to stay with the Old Guard or take on these new duties. "I preferred working for him," said Kaiser, "so I bought myself a garden encyclopedia and commenced playing the Jolly Green Giant."

During this period, another soldier who would become an important member of Johnson's military family entered the scene, Sergeant Major George Loikow. He was an administrative wizard, a distinguished-looking and gentlemanly soldier, and also expert at taking dictation. Since Johnson was perennially pressed for time, dictating to Loikow allowed him to at least make a dent in his voluminous correspondence. There were, however, occasional problems when Johnson lacked the time to read over his correspondence, as when he wrote to a friend stationed at Redstone Arsenal, "I understand that northern Alabama is a variable garden spot." For all that, Loikow proved to be invaluable, and would stay with Johnson for the rest of his service.

In late summer, the Johnson's older son, Johnny, was married in Kansas City to Patricia Mesce, known as Trish. Earlier, Johnson had rather ungraciously observed in a "Dear Family" letter that the prospective bride—he never mentioned her first name—was "an only child, and while we are quite fond of her, I must say that she had been somewhat indulged by her parents." Now he gained a new appreciation. He served as his son's best man, Ellen Kay was the maid of honor, and Bobby was one of the groomsmen, so it was an intensely family affair. "Trish is extremely capable and has planned their activities down to the last comma," Johnson observed in his next family epistle.

GENERAL EARLE G. WHEELER was by now the Army Chief of Staff, having succeeded General George Decker in the summer of 1962. Wheeler was the quintessential staff officer, with only modest experience as a commander, and none in the two previous wars. Douglas Kinnard described Wheeler as "gentlemanly, urbane, and highly articulate," saying, "he understood the Washington bureaucracy better perhaps than any active duty officer at that time."[5] As Wheeler's operations deputy, Johnson accompanied him to meetings of the Joint Chiefs of Staff (JCS) and played a key role in the staff work that prepared him for those sessions. Johnson appreciated that JCS meetings were essentially negotiations and that successful negotiating involved some give-and-take.

That was not always easy, he observed, because in the Army Staff, "you've really got some hardnoses there who see everything in terms of black and white and can't give an inch." Johnson took a different approach. "I was not one who pressed General Wheeler to adhere to a position clear down to an outright split among the Chiefs," he said. "And I think that . . . he appreciated that. I wasn't always whispering in his ear, 'You can't give, you can't give, you can't give.' "

Johnson threw himself into the new job with characteristic single-mindedness and energy. "He was there early, he was there late," said Edward C. Meyer, then an action officer. "We worked all day Saturday, and half a day on Sunday." Even in DCSOPS, where such industry was part of the culture, Johnson took it one step further. When he finally did go home at night, he would be lugging two big briefcases stuffed with papers. He customarily got home so late that he did not want any regular dinner, so Dorothy brought him soup and crackers out on the sunporch (which usually had not seen any sun for quite a few hours). Not much disposed to social activity anyway, Johnson now had almost no time for anything unrelated to the job. Even churchgoing suffered, with Johnson telling various chaplains that he had become a "backslider," using Sunday mornings to catch up on his sleep.

It was very much like his earlier Pentagon tour, only more so. "One is hardly conscious of any status change in the Pentagon," Johnson observed, "because the more responsible the position, the more conditions of peonage are found." There were some compensations, however. "This time I have a window, and do not have to wait until evening to get overtime help to do the typing," he admitted.

His West Point class held semiannual dinner dances—"at least a formal dinner dance is usually what it starts out to be," explained a classmate—but Johnson seldom found time to attend. In the spring, he told a friend that he had not yet committed his reserves—he still had Sundays as nonworking days. That was followed shortly by a series of Sunday sessions in the Pentagon. When Johnson went back to Fort Leavenworth to give a talk, a friend who saw him there wrote to say, "I thought how *used* you looked." He urged Johnson to rely on his staff and not try to do it all himself.

All this activity was driven by a relentless calendar of three scheduled JCS meetings a week, each preceded and followed by prebriefs and debriefs for the Chief of Staff. Johnson attended JCS meetings, arranged and attended all the collateral sessions, and went to additional meetings of the operations deputies (called ops deps) from all the services at which they tried to resolve and clear from the JCS agenda as many items as possible.

"A JCS day," Johnson wrote to a friend soon after arriving in DCSOPS, "requires almost a straight twelve hours to prebrief, attend the meeting, and debrief."[6] To Colonel Edmund Lilly, one of his most durable sounding boards, he explained that "there are six separate meetings a week that involve fifteen preliminary or follow-up meetings." And that was solely to deal with JCS matters. Army work "is usually accomplished after 7:00 o'clock at night and on Saturdays." As for the result, Johnson told him, "chaos and all its synonyms would be the shortest version."

Despite the marathon days, the pace was such that "there just isn't enough thinking time in this job," complained Johnson. Given the minimal influence that the Joint Chiefs of Staff were having on defense policy and strategy, especially relating to Vietnam, all this frantic activity has in retrospect an element of sadness to it, no matter how necessary it may have been to fielding and sustaining the forces of the day.[7]

Some insight into the self-discipline that Johnson brought to the job can be derived from a letter he wrote in late May, before he was even well into it, to old friends Colonel and Mrs. George Chapman. "I burrow down to the bottom of my box each Saturday," he told them, "and try to pick up two or three items of business that appear to be most unfinished. Your 4 March letter reached that category today."

He gave them a little flavor of the issues of the day—special forces and psychological operations and the administration's highly personalized way of doing business. The results were not encouraging. "Things have gotten worse here, if that is possible. There is little latitude any more for the Services, with a tremendous centralization in Defense. One wonders sometimes whether he should remain with the resistance group or hang up his spurs and observe from the sidelines. At this point, I still hold the view that someone has to look out for the defense of the country regardless of the views of the economists and management specialists, and so I guess I'll hang on."

Johnson was a beneficiary, if that is the right word, of the current administration's emphasis on youth. In fact, "the accent is on youthful youth, not just youth," he told a friend. "As a consequence, anyone who appears to be dry behind the ears is somewhat suspect." But as usual, Johnson found a compensating advantage. "It is less shocking and less repelling to the younger fellow to be subject to some of the indignities that our people in uniform are subjected to on occasion."

IN LATE AUTUMN 1963, an interesting war game was conducted. Designated SIGMA I, it had to do with Vietnam and included among its participants Maxwell Taylor, George Ball, William Sullivan, and Alexis Johnson, all members of the newly installed Lyndon Johnson administration. The results were not encouraging. According to this five-day game, equating to ten years in actual time, bombing of North Vietnam was essentially unavailing. The enemy was still able to increase infiltration into South Vietnam and, despite deployment of some 600,000 U.S. troops, increase the territory under Viet Cong control. These results predictably outraged General Curtis LeMay, then Air Force Chief of Staff.[8] Perhaps more importantly, they were in stark contrast to the predictions of Secretary McNamara and General Taylor, who had just "reported their judgment that the major part of the U.S. military task [in Vietnam] can be completed by the end of 1965."[9]

THE ATMOSPHERE of Harold K. Johnson's last years of military service was set that autumn. It would be dominated by the personalities and outlooks of three men—Lyndon Johnson, McNamara, and General Earle G. Wheeler—and by one all-pervasive issue, the evolving war in Vietnam.

Even before returning to Washington, Johnson had been concerned about some of the prevailing Pentagon atmospherics. Of course, he had been there on a long stint of temporary duty the previous autumn which had included a lot of firsthand exposure to McNamara. An issue that troubled Johnson greatly was, as he phrased it, civilian "command" of military forces. This was a dubious proposition, in his view, contrasted with the legitimate and indeed essential principle of civilian "control." Over the years, Johnson kept up a correspondence with Colonel Edmund Lilly, his regimental commander in the Philippine Scouts, to whom he explained that "we now not only have civilian control but we have civilian command, and there is a very real difference. It is too early to assess just what the impact of this change will produce in terms of battlefield effectiveness. My own concern is that we may never know until we reach the battlefield, and if the concept has faults, it will be too late."

While still at Fort Leavenworth, Johnson had sent a friend in the Pentagon a pertinent excerpt from Sun Tzu's *Art of War:* "In the Chinese armies one arrangement in command was faulty. Mandarins who had achieved distinction as civil functionaries studied military tactics late in life and directed operations in time of war, while officers of experience could not expect to reach the highest grades. As might be expected, this system frequently brought disaster to Chinese arms."

Uncertainty about the magnitude and duration of the war had always been a difficult aspect of planning for Vietnam, and General Johnson frequently found himself in contention with McNamara's systems analysis staff, headed by Alain Enthoven, on such crucial matters as the Army's force structure and its supporting establishment. In September, commenting on a draft Systems Analysis paper entitled "Determination of Ground Force Requirements," Johnson highlighted some questionable practices. He suggested that, in order to cut costs, the threat was being arbitrarily reduced. In addition, it was wrongly being maintained that there was no limit to the ability of a qualitative superiority to withstand quantitative superiority.

Aspects of the methodology were also suspect, said Johnson. "The procedure of lifting judgments and conclusions from a wide range of studies without reference to the specific assumptions and the cautions that are inherent parts of the studies," he observed, "results in a presentation that could be somewhat misleading. I can speak with firsthand knowledge with respect to the extracts from Project 23," his tactical nuclear weapons study. Further, "the tendency to discount agreed intelligence and substitute what is admittedly speculation will be a major weakness when the study is presented."[10]

A few weeks later, Johnson wrote to a friend to express a more general concern related to the criticisms he had leveled at Systems Analysis. "It seems to me," he observed, "that we are in a precarious position throughout the entire Army, all stemming from trying to do too much with too little." Coming as it did before deployment of major ground forces to Vietnam, that was an ominous judgment. It was also an agonizing question for Johnson personally. "Should argue people as well as forces (structure) and modernization," he wrote in his notes of a 29 October JCS meeting. "Moral question as OPS as to whether I shouldn't be pushing for adequate flesh for the bones."[11]

JUST TWO DAYS after being sworn into office, Lyndon Johnson set the tone for his outlook on Vietnam—and blighted his presidency forever—at a Sunday White House meeting with McNamara, Secretary of State Dean Rusk, Ambassador Henry Cabot Lodge, CIA Director John McCone, and McGeorge Bundy. It is noteworthy that no uniformed military officers, not even the Chairman of the Joint Chiefs of Staff, were present at this fateful meeting.

Agreeing to provide an additional "hundred million or so" dollars to support the South Vietnamese, LBJ added that they could get more if they needed it. But, he emphasized, he expected something for his money. "I want 'em to get off their butts and get out in those jungles and whip hell out of some Communists." Then came the infinitely revealing addendum: "And I want 'em to leave me alone, because I've got some bigger things to do right here at home."[12]

As would eventually become apparent, that was no way to fight a war. Worse yet, inherent in that outlook was the essence of what came to be known as "search and destroy," concentration on combat in the deep jungles while ignoring the hamlets and villages, and preoccupation with "body count." From the outset of his presidency, LBJ demonstrated a lack of understanding of the war, even a lack of interest in it. At least, that was the outlook he communicated to a circle of his closest advisors.

(Later, of course, when things were not going well, LBJ would swing hard over to the opposite pole—up in the middle of the night monitoring reports from Vietnam, personally picking bombing targets, and basically shutting out the uniformed military leadership on the key decisions of the war. That, to his everlasting sorrow, didn't work either.)

Robert McNamara recalled that fateful first meeting in his memoirs. "President Johnson made clear to Lodge on November 24 that he wanted to win the war," he wrote, "and that, at least in the short run, he wanted priority given [in Vietnam] to military operations over 'so-called' social reforms." Thus "two days later National Security Memorandum 273 incorporated the president's directives into policy."[13] But then, only six pages later, McNamara tried to claim just the opposite. "The Joint Chiefs came forward with a proposal for more forceful moves in a memorandum to me on January 22, 1964," he acknowledged. "They asserted that the President in NSAM 273 had resolved 'to ensure victory . . . in South Vietnam.' In fact he had done no such thing, certainly not regardless of the cost in human lives."[14]

Meanwhile, the military leadership was trying, however ineffectually, to influence the action on Vietnam. In January 1964, when American involvement there was still in the advisory stage, the Joint Chiefs of Staff sought relief from what they viewed as crippling policy restrictions. "Currently we and the South Vietnamese are fighting the war on the enemy's terms," they told Secretary McNamara. "He has determined the locale, the timing, and the tactics of the battle while our actions are essentially reactive. One reason for this is the fact that we have obliged ourselves to labor under self-imposed restrictions with respect to impeding external aid to the Viet Cong. These restrictions include keeping the war within the borders of South Vietnam, avoiding the direct use of US combat forces, and limiting US direction of the campaign to rendering advice to the Government of Vietnam."

That wasn't working, the JCS maintained, and they proposed some dramatic changes: induce the South Vietnamese to turn over "the actual tactical direction of the war" to the U.S. military commander and "commit additional US forces, as necessary, in support of the combat action within South Vietnam." The JCS argued that the United States must prepare to conduct "increasingly bolder actions" in Southeast Asia and announced their intention of recommending such actions as in their judgment came to be "militarily required," but stopped short of making such recommendations at that juncture.[15]

Lyndon Johnson, it developed, was supremely ambivalent about what he wanted to do in Vietnam, or at least about what he was willing to commit to the effort. In early April 1964, recalled aide Richard Goodwin, the president complained, "they're trying to get me in a war over there. It will destroy me. I turned them down three times last week."[16] Presumably, LBJ was referring to his statutory military advisors, the Joint Chiefs of Staff.

But the signals on what was wanted, or intended, were incredibly mixed. Only a month earlier, General Johnson had come back from a JCS meeting with this entry in his notes: "Was intent of White House that RVN [Republic of Vietnam] should be used as a laboratory, not only for this war but for any insurgency." Two weeks later, discussing a package of twelve recommendations put together by McNamara following a trip to Vietnam, the JCS were unanimous—with the possible exception of Chairman Taylor—in the opinion that the package amounted to no more than palliatives. Johnson's notes included a strong statement by General Wheeler: "Will not be party to proposals that this action can be done with mirrors."

By late March 1964, General Wallace M. Greene, Jr., Commandant of the Marine Corps, was concerned enough about the absence of JCS input into critical decisions about the war that he went to see Major General Chester V. Clifton, an Army officer assigned as a military aide to the president. Greene protested what he saw as "the insulation, or walling away, of President Johnson from the Joint Chiefs."[17]

Clifton must have been getting similar input from other quarters, for that same day he drafted a "talking paper" on the situation. "I sense a potentially difficult—and even dangerous—situation in the Joint Chiefs of Staff," he wrote. "The major and current problem is the course of action in regard to South Viet Nam. Fundamentally the Chiefs are badly split on this and they do not all agree with what is being done." Where they were in accord, Clifton indicated, was their agreement "that we should not get out and that it would be a disaster to lose South Viet Nam." Generals LeMay and Greene wanted to extend the war to North Vietnam.

Regarding what he called "the present McNamara-Taylor policy which we are pursuing," Clifton said that the Joint Chiefs of Staff "call this the Asian 'Bay of Pigs' around their conference table, and this time they are sure that the Joint Chiefs of Staff cannot be blamed, because each of the members is keeping a careful record of what he has advocated to General Taylor and the Secretary of Defense, and they feel that the things they are advocating have not been presented strongly to the President."

Clifton concluded the paper with some recommendations of his own, obviously intended to assuage these concerns. One was that the present National Security Council document, presumably the twelve recommendations derived from the recent McNamara-Taylor visit to Vietnam, be sent directly to each of the Chiefs for comments to be submitted directly to the President, and that the President then meet with the Chiefs. And, he concluded, "Give some consideration to the replacement of General Harkins by a tougher, more experienced old war horse than General Westmoreland."[18]

Meanwhile, Harold K. Johnson found the situation in Cambodia even more troubling than that in Vietnam. In November 1963, Cambodia had severed economic and military relations with the United States and charged it with attempting to undermine the regime. "This action on the part of Cambodia probably jarred me more than any other single action that occurred in my time in the Pentagon . . . in this whole five-year interval," Johnson said, "for the reason that I viewed this action as a declaration by Prince Sihanouk that he had come to the conclusion that the United States was going to lose in Southeast Asia. He was lining himself up with the force that he thought was going to win, and he was disassociating himself from a loser."

THROUGHOUT THESE YEARS, Johnson maintained an active correspondence with younger officers of his acquaintance who were serving in Vietnam, encouraging them to express their views on all aspects of the conflict. "I would very much appreciate an informal comment from time to time," he told Colonel John Austin. "I correspond now with several of the advisors and it gives me a little more intimate feel of just what transpires. I hold the letters in confidence and do not use them to start a series of crash actions nor undercut the commander on the ground. Somehow, a little different flavor seems to seep through this way."

One of those most willing to speak plainly was Colonel Jasper Wilson, Johnson's associate from Fort Leavenworth, now assigned in Vietnam as advisor to Major General Nguyen Khanh. There he took an active part in planning the coup that would soon overthrow Major General Duong Van Minh and bring Khanh to power as the next in a succession of leaders.[19] "I hope that you will see fit to drop me some of your pungent observations from time to time on a personal basis," Johnson had written to Wilson,[20] who responded with a will.

As 1964 began, Wilson was not pleased with the state of affairs. "I become more convinced daily," he told Johnson, "that in I and II Corps the remaining VC [Viet Cong] are not going to be eliminated with bullets. It is going to take political, economic, and psycho-social action, improvement, and consolidation to cut off the VC source of groceries and intelligence."[21]

IN FEBRUARY 1964, the Johnsons' daughter Ellen Kay was married to Lieutenant James C. Kern, a young officer she had met at St. Lawrence University. Johnson was somewhat bemused by the logistics of the thing, writing of the event in revealing terms to Jasper Wilson. "When one considers the number of people who have been involved over the years in the great institution of Holy Matrimony," Johnson observed, "I can hardly believe the worries that are associated with preparations for a wedding." The good thing was that "the event is over quickly and our recuperative powers are still reasonably good."

The wedding reception was held at home in Quarters 2 at Fort Myer, and the guests included many old Army friends from way back. When Johnson's cadet roommate, Neil Wallace, came through the receiving line, Ellen Kay knew him at once, at least by reputation. "Oh, you're Droopy Drawers!" she exclaimed. A festive spirit prevailed, with Johnson reporting to a friend that they went through eight cases of champagne. Then, all too soon, it was back to the war.

CHAPTER FOURTEEN

VIETNAM TRIP

In late March 1964, Johnson made a trip to Vietnam, the first of ten he would undertake during the next four years.[1] During the visit, he met General Khanh, beneficiary of the recent coup deposing Minh, who had deposed Diem. And of course, he saw his old friend Jasper Wilson, now Khanh's advisor.

"I was most encouraged by the trends which were apparent in Vietnam," he said afterward. "The evident capability and confidence of General Khanh and the strong sense of central direction and purpose that have been instilled by him is the most significant factor." Johnson wrote to Wilson of his favorable impression of Khanh, urging Wilson to "keep up the good work and keep the little man in power." In Washington, he declared himself "tremendously impressed with General Khanh and . . . passed that observation to the Chiefs and the Secretary of Defense."

Those impressions were quickly overtaken by events when Khanh, after hanging by a thread for months, was himself deposed, with a strong American push helping to propel him from the scene. This development could not have enhanced Johnson's credibility.[2]

In tactical matters, Johnson was on firmer ground, coming away from this first visit to Vietnam convinced that "the application of military force alone will not solve all the problems of a country facing subversive insurgency." He did not discount the importance of properly applied military force, however, even while stressing the necessity of dealing with political, economic, and social aspects as well. "The role of military force in internal defense is large," he acknowledged, "and under proper conditions may be decisive."

After the visit, Johnson wrote to General Paul D. Harkins, then commanding U.S. forces in Vietnam (but soon to be replaced by his newly assigned deputy, Lieutenant General William C. Westmoreland). "Unfortunately," Johnson told him, "I do not believe that I was entirely successful in communicating the complexity and variety of problems to the Chiefs and the Secretary of Defense when I reported on my trip. I summed up by giving a picture of modest encouragement without being either optimistic or pessimistic. The Secretary's reaction, in my opinion, continues to be one of attempting to paint your picture in terms of pure black or pure white. I found little of either color, but rather many, many shades of gray."

General Harkins's situation in Saigon had by this time become untenable. For some time he had been under frontal assault by young American journalists covering the war, who charged him with being unrealistically optimistic about progress being made. Sources in the field, including younger American officers serving as advisors, were telling a much different story, one of impending crisis due to the inadequacies of South Vietnamese armed forces, especially when it came to leadership.

Harkins, who before the Saigon assignment had enjoyed a fine reputation going back to his World War II service as a key staff officer for General George Patton, was caught in a bind. He was a protégé of Maxwell Taylor's, and was in fact getting instructions from Taylor through back channels on how he was to report in front channels. "Harkins told me that what he was reporting from Vietnam was what Taylor was telling him to report," confirmed General Donn Starry. "He said to me at one time, 'I couldn't ignore General Taylor's advice.' "[3]

Taylor sought to protect Harkins as long as he could, and that was apparently what motivated the famous cancellation of a JCS briefing by young firebrand John Paul Vann. General Barksdale Hamlett, then Army Vice Chief of Staff, had listened to Vann's briefing and asked that it be presented to the JCS "with tempering of remarks" about General Harkins, reported General William Rosson. But Taylor refused to give Vann a hearing. "The result of Taylor's cancellation of the Vann briefing," wrote Mark Perry, "was an open war in the JCS. The chiefs concluded that Taylor was protecting his good friend Paul Harkins . . . whose reputation for competence was widely and openly questioned by Taylor's Army colleagues, one of whom told the JCS chairman that Harkins was 'just plain stupid.' "[4]

McNamara, it has been argued, concluded that it was something much worse than stupidity. According to Samuel Zaffiri, McNamara told LBJ that "he was convinced [Harkins] had been systematically sending him false information and misleading accounts, all meant to make it appear that the ARVN [Army of the Republic of Vietnam] was winning battles and making progress, when in fact the opposite was the case."[5] It is not clear, however, that McNamara was not a party to the deceptive reporting, at least initially.

David Halberstam, one of the premier field reporters on the Vietnam War, linked Harkins's dishonest reporting not only to Taylor but also to McNamara, further complicating the issue of responsibility. "We always thought the problem was Harkins in Saigon misleading his superiors in

0   100
miles

CHINA

Red River

BURMA

HANOI

NORTH
VIETNAM

Gulf
of
Tonkin

HAINAN

LAOS

VIENTIANE

DMZ

Mekong River

THAILAND

BANGKOK

CAMBODIA

SOUTH
VIETNAM

Gulf
of
Siam

SIHANOUKVILLE   SAIGON

South
China
Sea

© Durfée 1997

Washington," Halberstam later wrote. But when Taylor prevented Vann from briefing the JCS, "we realized how controlled the entire system was, that Harkins was giving Washington what it not only wanted, but what it demanded." Halberstam concluded, in looking back, that "McNamara and Taylor (with Harkins as their proxy) loaded the debate, pressured the field people to report dishonestly, and made sure in the process there was only one source of pessimistic reporting, the American journalists."[6] Of course, those journalists were getting their insights from more junior people in the field, especially advisors working with the South Vietnamese forces.

Harkins, it appears, knew what was really going on in Vietnam. "He lived a spartan military life in Saigon," wrote John Mecklin, who had been

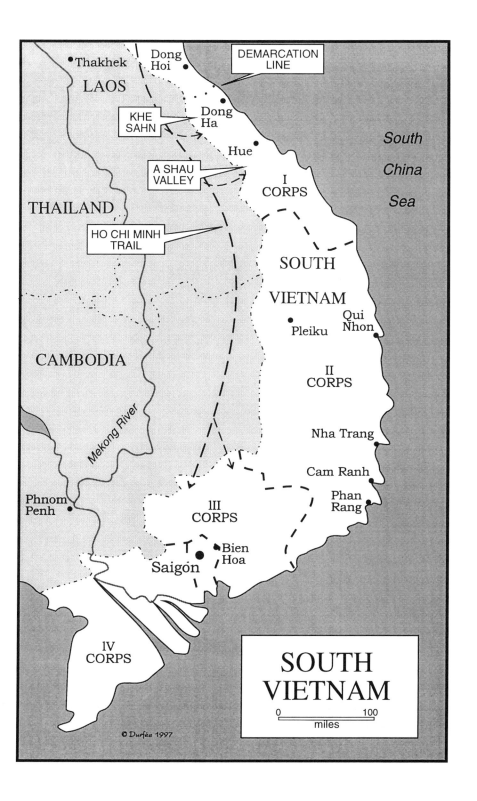

Thakhek

Dong
Hoi

LAOS

DEMARCATION
LINE

KHE
SAHN

Dong
Ha

Hue

A SHAU
VALLEY

I
CORPS

THAILAND

South

China

Sea

HO CHI MINH
TRAIL

SOUTH

VIETNAM

Qui
Nhon

Pleiku

CAMBODIA

II
CORPS

Mekong River

Nha Trang

Cam Ranh

Phnom
Penh

III
CORPS

Phan
Rang

Bien
Hoa

Saigon

IV
CORPS

SOUTH
VIETNAM

0   100
miles

© Durfée 1997

public affairs officer of the U.S. Mission, "traveling almost daily around the country in small planes to keep in touch with the war."[7] Mike Greene served with Harkins as his executive assistant and traveled with him all over Vietnam. "I would sit with the senior advisor," said Greene. "On the plane going back, he'd [Harkins] ask me, 'What's really going on?' " When Greene saw what was happening to Harkins, that he was being subjected to increasing criticism, he kept urging him to do something about it. Invariably, Harkins would thank him kindly, but never act on the advice. Even after Harkins retired, Greene kept urging him to tell his side of the story. "I don't think I want to do that, Mike," was all Harkins would say.

Historian Arthur Schlesinger, Jr., once noted that President John Kennedy "wanted to play down American involvement [in Vietnam], and the military collaborated enthusiastically in the production of cover stories, false claims of battlefield success and other forms of press control." If that is true, it soon got out of hand. According to Schlesinger, "what started as deception of the press the military soon extended to deception of its civilian masters—the Secretary of Defense and the President."[8]

If LBJ and McNamara did *not* know of these arrangements, they were unwittingly sending out as American ambassador to Saigon the very man who had corrupted the reporting process on which decisions about the war were based—Maxwell Taylor.

On an April 1962 visit to Vietnam, General William Rosson tried to warn Harkins discreetly about "unwarranted optimism." Rosson included this in his trip report, fully expecting that it would ignite some fireworks back in Washington. When it sank without a ripple, Rosson began taking a sharper look at the Washington environment of the day. "By the close of 1962," he later wrote, "it was my judgment that optimism had . . . become the recognized position of the Administration." The bureaucratic effect was that contrary views, including some intelligence estimates, were dominated by a syndrome of optimism. "Under McNamara's influence," concluded Rosson, "goals became the product largely of what he perceived to be desirable or necessary, as opposed to being the product of realistic possibilities based on the nature, history and current status of the conflict."[9]

Harkins was subjected to extremely harsh criticism from other sources as well. By the time he was relieved of his post, he was so little regarded that he was not even told directly. He found out about it obliquely when Ambassador Lodge summoned Westmoreland and informed him that he was going to take over the top job. Harkins was brought home, his reputation in tatters, given a consolatory Distinguished Service Medal at a White House ceremony, and retired. He had paid dearly for his loyalty to Taylor, no matter his other inadequacies.

There is evidence that, when Maxwell Taylor left his post as JCS Chairman and went to Saigon as the U.S. ambassador, he continued a pattern of suppressing bad news. General Bruce Palmer, Jr., determined, in the course of an extensive historical study of CIA reporting from Vietnam, that Taylor had approved a coordinated U.S. mission intelligence assessment prepared by the Saigon Station in February 1965 "only after deleting conclusions that forecast discouraging trends." When another special assessment was prepared in April 1965, "Ambassador Taylor deleted the worst news from the outgoing cable."[10]

Secretary McNamara once told a researcher that Harkins "wasn't worth a damn so he was removed."[11] He was replaced with another Taylor protégé. Lyndon Johnson revealed that there had been four candidates to take over as COMUSMACV—Commander, U.S. Military Assistance Command, Vietnam: Harold K. Johnson, who instead became Army Chief of Staff; Creighton Abrams, who became Vice Chief of Staff; Bruce Palmer, Jr., who succeeded Johnson as DCSOPS; and William C. Westmoreland, who got the job. The deciding influence in that fateful selection was Taylor's.[12] Harold K. Johnson stressed that he had no part in the choice of Westmoreland. "I didn't really have any voice in his going or in his ascendancy into the position of the top commander there," he emphasized.

There was much that concerned Harold K. Johnson on his first visit to Vietnam. He was, he revealed, "rather appalled" by U.S. Special Forces activities, particularly the fortified hamlets established in Montagnard territory. "The notion that you could live forever in a barricaded environment," he thought, "had a natural abhorrence." Besides, Johnson concluded, the two Special Forces camps he visited did not seem to be affecting much of anything. "In both cases," he said, "I detected a heavy atmosphere of 'taking in their own laundry.' "

These observations are significant because, in later years, Johnson would be criticized by many in the Special Forces establishment for what they deemed anti–Special Forces bias. It is clear, however, that what put Johnson off was what he saw Special Forces doing. Right or wrong, it was his judgment of their performance that shaped his overall outlook, not any built-in preconceptions.

Those findings in the field had, however, reinforced other concerns about Special Forces, including that their rapid expansion had been at the expense of the rest of the Army structure. Elite units of any kind, Johnson felt, stripped talent from the regular units that could be better used there. Shelby Stanton, who has written sympathetically about Special Forces, recognized this disadvantage. "The retention of thousands of excellent sergeants in such an elite organization," he observed, "especially after the Army's expansion (which had created a grave shortage of noncommissioned officers), deprived the Army's regular units of valuable combat leadership at the most critical time. The hardship was so acute that the lack of available line sergeants, with their potential discipline and experience, ended up being a major factor in the Army's decline."[13]

Johnson also believed that some people were attracted to Special Forces for the wrong reasons. "These were people that somehow or other tended to be nonconformist, couldn't quite get along in a straight military system, and found a haven where their actions were not scrutinized too carefully and where they came under only sporadic or intermittent observation from the regular chain of command," he concluded.

Even so, on balance, Johnson ultimately concluded that Special Forces' accomplishments played a key role, especially under the command of Colonel Jonathan F. Ladd. Shortly before retiring, Johnson wrote to Ladd that "the Special Forces effort is paramount to achieving our aim in Vietnam and, from what I was able to observe, the effectiveness of that effort is apparent in all areas."[14]

Johnson's initial conclusions on the tactics of the war were also significant, and consistent with the position he would maintain over a number of years. In a JCS meeting with the Secretary of Defense, McNamara "raised [the] question as to whether [a] large number of small unit actions was productive or just wheel spinning." Johnson "tried to point out that large-scale patrolling should keep VC on the move and should result in lessened activity on their part as they should be preoccupied with protecting themselves." But, he reported, "Sec Def was not impressed."

After returning to Washington, Johnson submitted a report in which, he subsequently told Major General Richard G. Stilwell at MACV, "we tried very hard to stay away from criticism either direct or implied of the current effort in Vietnam." But Johnson provided Stilwell with a number of critical observations that had been screened out of the report. He cited "the incongruity of CIDG [Civilian Irregular Defense Group] bastions in the face of the MACV effort to free military and paramilitary forces from fixed posts." He questioned "whether or not we have any reliable evidence of the actual present-for-duty strength of ARVN units." He noted "the ostentation of the U.S. effort," saying that the United States had "moved in in the 'grand' style." And he closed with an infantryman's perspective, observing that "it is difficult to rationalize that we will solve the problem of territorial control if we continue to overfly the resistance on the ground."[15] It was a telling and perceptive critique.

Nevertheless, Johnson knew that he did not have all the answers to the complex challenge of Vietnam. "I only regret that I do not have the wisdom to see a solution," Johnson wrote after the visit. "Believe me, we are desperately searching for one." To another friend then serving as an advisor to the Vietnamese, Johnson observed after the visit that "since Vietnam is the first priority interest in government at the Washington level these days, I see no way to reduce the attempts to run the war from here, and it simply won't work that way."

There was one more item of residual business. General Wheeler asked Johnson for his assessment of the morale of American troops in Vietnam. Johnson began with a comment on the nature of the Vietnam War. It was not, he observed, "conducive to the type of morale normally associated with military units in a war environment. There are no spectacular victories; there are no scoreboards; there is no time schedule for conclusion of the war and thus there is not a finite objective to look forward to, as is normally the case." Those accurate observations could have been applied with equal force to an assessment of morale on the home front.

During the visit to Vietnam, Johnson had been assigned a bright young major, Walter Ulmer, as his escort officer. "General Johnson wanted details on everything," recalled Ulmer. "He was easy to talk with. I had no idea he was going to be Chief of Staff so soon, although I suspect he knew." Ulmer accompanied Johnson on a visit to a Montagnard village, advising him to take a gift of a five-pound sack of salt. Ulmer was impressed by this first exposure to Johnson. "He did everything with class," said Ulmer, who remembered that when Johnson got back to Washington, he wrote a note to Ulmer's father reporting on how well his son was performing in Vietnam.

Not everyone was as favorably impressed with Johnson. In the car after seeing him off at the airport, "Kitsy" Westmoreland remarked, "Johnny hasn't changed a bit. After fifteen minutes he thinks he knows more than anyone else." The aide who overheard her recalled that in his experience, Kitsy was never catty, at least in front of the aides—she loved everybody, or said she did—and he was surprised that she would openly make such a remark.[16] Johnson must have ruffled some Westmoreland feathers, distaff or otherwise, during the visit, which preceded by only a few weeks Westmoreland's succession to command of U.S. forces in Vietnam.

EVEN WHEN AMERICAN INVOLVEMENT in the war was still largely advisory, Vietnam had already begun to make an impact on the Army. Even before the buildup of ground forces for Vietnam got into gear, the Army's junior leadership—young officers and sergeants—had been heavily drained by the necessity of sending large numbers of advisors to South Vietnam. They were not replaced with men of comparable rank and experience, and their units had to make do with younger, less experienced, and less mature men acting in the higher grades. Thus began the progressive erosion of leadership, experience, and maturity that was further exacerbated by huge increases in the Army force structure, denial of access to the reserve forces, and repetitive tours in Vietnam over the course of a protracted war.

ON 17 MARCH 1964, National Security Action Memorandum 288 was issued. Based entirely on the results of a recent McNamara-Taylor visit to Vietnam, it prescribed a number of "highly programmatic" steps for conduct of the war. "It is clear with the advantage of hindsight," wrote the *Pentagon Papers* authors, "that these steps were grossly inadequate to the magnitude of the tasks at hand—particularly if the broad U.S. objectives stated in the NSAM were to be realized."[17] Of even greater significance than the puny measures prescribed by the NSAM was the underlying outlook it reflected. "In certain circles in Washington at least," continued the *Pentagon Papers,* "there was what appears now to have been an amazing level of confidence that we could induce the North Vietnamese to abandon their support of the SVN [South Vietnamese] insurgency if only we could convince them that we meant business, and that we would indeed bomb them if they did not stop their infiltration of men and supplies to the South."[18] As was subsequently demonstrated, the North Vietnamese did not care.

MEASURING PROGRESS in the war in Vietnam was one of the most difficult, complex, and frustrating aspects of that long conflict. Given the lack of clear-cut front lines, not to mention the amalgam of conventional and insurgent warfare that made up the conflict, no satisfying advances of blue lines and consequent regression of red lines on battle maps could be displayed as solid evidence of progress. Surrogate measures would have to be found. That search was the subject of endless controversy and debate.

DCSOPS was the early focus of Army work on the problem. "We are still searching for yardsticks," Johnson wrote to Jasper Wilson. "The Secretary [McNamara] will not be satisfied until he has some kind of clear indication as to progress being made, obstacles to progress and the effort required to eliminate or at least reduce the size of the obstacles. Neither of us will rest easy until some sort of program along that line is developed."

In the spring, John Cushman, an articulate and insightful Army colonel, was in Washington on temporary duty from Vietnam. With him he carried a big roll of briefing charts portraying the situation as he had come to understand it while on advisory duty in the Mekong Delta. Cushman went to see Johnson at his office, where Johnson explained that DCSOPS was setting up a facility to track what was going on in the war zone. "I'm going to have the location of every platoon over there in Vietnam in my operations center," he said.

"Sir," Cushman protested, "we didn't have that at *division* level" in Vietnam.

That made no difference. "They're insisting on it," Johnson told him. "McNamara's insisting on it."

"It was kind of pathetic," observed Cushman, "that Harold K. Johnson was being jacked around by McNamara, a man who couldn't hold a candle to him in insight and understanding. I viewed General Johnson as a tragic figure."

Cushman did get a chance to display the contents of his briefing charts and to describe what he believed to be "the essential recipe for pacification." That had to be, first of all, a Vietnamese effort, he concluded, and it would have to be a deliberate and thorough operation. There were no quick fixes. The United States should provide all possible assistance, including well-indoctrinated advisors, "but the Vietnamese should execute it."

That approach was of course not adopted, at least not then. Instead, as Cushman later noted, "the United States introduced its ground forces into the countryside, began a half-hearted air campaign aimed at leading Ho Chi Minh to end his external support, and adopted a self-defeating strategy of attrition."[19]

Meanwhile, Johnson pressed on with the task of satisfying McNamara's appetite for detail about the war and all its works. "I want to have a concentrated effort on the development of devices by which progress in the war in Vietnam can be followed," he instructed his Director of Operations, asking him to "list by province, district and, where available, village the location of Viet Cong individuals and units. This would include both the political structure and the military structure." And he was serious about it.

At the same time, Johnson was canvassing his network of personal contacts in Vietnam for ideas on the subject. "I would welcome any suggestion you might have that . . . would give us a clue as to how progress might be measured," he wrote to Colonel Fred Pierce. "It is difficult for the civilian echelon here to understand how an area can presumably, and theoretically, be cleared of Viet Cong one day and then have attacks by the Viet Cong occur in the same area days or weeks later. I doubt that we can ever satisfactorily explain this one."

IN EARLY MAY 1964, Johnson was designated that year's Kermit Roosevelt lecturer. This would take him to England to deliver a series of talks in a program memorializing the late son of President Theodore Roosevelt, while a British officer lectured at military schools in the United States. This gave Johnson a chance to speak publicly on a number of topics that concerned him before professionally interested audiences at the Imperial Defence College, the Staff College at Camberley, and the Royal Military College of Science.

Johnson began his presentations by stating his determination, as DCSOPS, that he was "not going to become enmeshed in a parochial web." The work so far, he said, had reinforced his conviction that basic Army philosophy was sound, especially in arguing that we must never tie our military policy to a single weapons system or a single concept of war. Then he affirmed his belief "in the pre-eminence of land power as the decisive and ultimate instrument of national power."

Next he expressed, in a deeply felt and almost poetical manner not matched anywhere else in his published works, what constituted an eloquent tribute to the soldier, and especially the classic foot soldier. "Army convictions," he began, "are sober and realistic. They brook no glamour. Their grandeur is only for those who can see grandeur through the grime and wavering gait of a bone-weary infantry battalion moving into regimental reserve—bearing its weapons and wounded with it." These were echoes of that harsh Korean winter of long ago, and of the terrible burden of command he had then come to know. "They have nobility only for those who can see nobility in the rifleman, long worn in combat, gathering his will and drawing on some extra reservoir of strength to go forward once more to the attack. As with all deep convictions, these cannot be put easily into words by the men who hold them." On that day in England, Johnson came pretty close.

Other topics focused on the issues of the day. Johnson had been obliged to have his lectures cleared beforehand by OSD, the Office of the Secretary of Defense, and the changes resulting from that review were interesting. Johnson had written that "some of the arguments which raise my hackles fastest focus on the single-minded and completely unilateral claims on pieces of the environment. In their drive for preeminence, certain individuals forget that national defense is a 'team' affair." That was deleted by OSD. Johnson had argued that infantrymen and helicopters operating in an infantry battalion area were in aerospace, but did not "infringe on the so-called vested interests proclaimed as 'roles and missions.' " That too was deleted by OSD, citing Air Force objection. Johnson had suggested that the Air Force's "first job is to keep enemy air off the back of the Army." OSD changed that to "one of its jobs is to keep enemy air off the back of the Army." And so on.

At the end of these talks, Johnson described what he termed the final "essential ingredient" of effective land combat forces: "the amalgam which cannot be measured by computer techniques—leadership, spirit, conviction, resolve, and fierce pride."

Dorothy had gone along on the trip to England, and they sailed home on the *United States*. It was a five-day voyage and probably the last chance Johnson had to catch his breath before the brutally demanding final four years of his military service.

CHAPTER FIFTEEN

AVIATION

As Johnson's remarks in England had made clear, contention with the Air Force over airpower matters was at fever pitch. Johnson's role in that debate would become more central when he moved up to become Chief of Staff, but even as the DCSOPS he was deeply involved. His outlook is especially important in that, later, some of the most avid exponents of Army aviation would be harshly critical of Johnson, contending that he was lukewarm on Army initiatives to expand its aviation capabilities, too willing to compromise Army interests in the face of Air Force demands, or even antiaviation. The record—and it is robust in this area—demonstrates quite the contrary.

In England, Johnson had stated his position unequivocally. "I view the current U.S. Army position on use of aerial vehicles as logical," he said. "Without question land forces must have the capability for operating comparatively unsophisticated aircraft near the earth's nap and in conjunction with land force operations."

The Air Force was busily arguing the contrary, going on the offensive to claim that anything that flew was an Air Force responsibility. That position would, if accepted, eliminate the already substantial Army investment in aviation—an inventory that had grown to some 6,000 aircraft, mostly helicopters.

Air Force Chief of Staff General Curtis E. LeMay had precipitated this round of the battle in late May 1963. Johnson's notes of a JCS meeting say it succinctly: "AF go back on the offensive—'Everything that flies back in the AF.' "

Reacting to this Air Force initiative, the JCS directed the Joint Staff to take a comprehensive look at the use of "aerial vehicles," as the Air Force was calling them, by both the Army and the Air Force. Meanwhile, the Army formed a special working group, chaired by Lieutenant General Dwight Beach, and in DCSOPS Johnson directed preparation of a paper setting forth the Army's view. "The product," he instructed, "should be a dispassionate statement of what the Army wants and what the Army expects in the way of support from the Air Force."

Johnson provided some of his personal views to General Beach in late

June 1963. "The fundamental concept of using air vehicles to improve the Army's fighting posture is sound," he said. "There have been tendencies to go overboard on capabilities, and tendencies to hide or ignore limitations." He added, "I do not believe that we should be discouraged by outside efforts," meaning those by the Air Force, "to impede Army progress in obtaining a mobility capability that is compatible with the improved lethality of firepower and the increased speed of communications, broadly speaking. Our concepts have not always been practical, but I believe that this is a condition that must be accepted in the evolution of any significantly new concept." In short, he said, "continue to march (fly). The Army has made substantial progress."

By late summer, the Air Force had come up with its own position paper on Army and Air Force responsibilities with respect to aerial vehicles. The matter dragged on into the autumn, with Johnson's notes reflecting as the central issue whether the Army would have some organic aviation. The Air Force's "basic position is that Army will have no aerial vehicles," he recorded at an early October JCS meeting. General LeMay, in making that argument to the Joint Chiefs of Staff, proclaimed, "I have a record of making the most compromises in this body." The Air Force would, he promised, "lay out a paper that will phase out all Army [aviation] and take it over by the AF." (Meanwhile, Johnson said in a note to General Wheeler, the Army had loaned four light liaison aircraft to the Air Force so that it could conduct pilot retraining. Within three weeks, two of the four had "been damaged to the extent that replacements are required.")

LeMay's proposal was about as stark as the issue could get. "Were the roles and missions battle lost," Johnson wrote to General Wheeler, "it can be anticipated that after fifteen years of bitter 'cooperative' experience the Army will lose control and responsiveness of the aerial tactical mobility means which are necessary for the conduct of the land battle." In other words, no less than future tactical viability was at stake.

"The CSAF [Chief of Staff, Air Force] position," said an Army talking paper, "is based on the view that everything that flies should be Air Force because it is the arm for the air dimension." To that, "the Army's counter is that it uses the lower portion of the airspace . . . to execute its traditional ground combat missions." The Air Force tactic was described as one of "embroiling the Army in a fight to *retain* aviation we already possess."

The Army paper suggested that, if the Air Force persisted in questioning whether the Army should have organic aviation, the Army should insist that the same question be raised with respect to the other services. "This should bring about rapid Navy and Marine support for the Army," it was suggested.[1] In retrospect, one wonders why the parallel argument was not raised: that if the Air Force wanted to arrogate to itself everything that flew, the Army should be given similar exclusive jurisdiction over everything on land. That would have given the Air Force something to think about with respect to where its landing fields were going to be put, to say nothing of its officers' clubs.

Johnson came up with another useful parallel, however. "The Air Force," he said, "has for a number of years felt that any flying that is to be done should be done by them. Of course the counterargument by us would be, well, any walking that's to be done should be done by us."

THE ARMY WAS IN THOSE DAYS STRUGGLING, and that is the right word, with the proper role of Army aviation and the closely related issue of developing an air assault capability. Thus intertwined with the Army–Air Force battle over aviation assets was an internal Army debate over the proper amount, type, and allocation of Army aviation assets. One school favored concentration of aviation assets in special-purpose units configured for air assault, while the opposing view was that aviation assets should be more evenly distributed throughout the force, giving all maneuver elements some share in their capabilities.

In DCSOPS, Johnson was "at the center of air assault from the operational point of view."[2] He thus played a lead role in a matter that was critical to the Army's battlefield capability in a time of rapidly changing missions and tactical environments. It would remain for the rest of his service one of the most difficult, and exciting, issues he would deal with.

As early as 1960, the Army had taken a comprehensive look at aviation and its uses, convening in that year an Army Aircraft Requirements Board. It was also known as the Rogers Board for its chairman, Lieutenant General Gordon B. Rogers, an experienced Cavalryman with a distinguished combat record. The board included among its members Hamilton H. Howze, who would soon chair another important board, and its secretary was Robert R. Williams, another officer who would play a large part in the aviation story.[3]

The Rogers Board was tasked primarily to address development of equipment, whereas the later Howze Board concentrated on how the equipment should be used and how much of it was needed. General John Tolson noted that at this point, well before any helicopter companies had been introduced into Vietnam, the Army was already well along in developing its airmobility capability, but these developments "were not necessarily geared to the prospect of an increased involvement in Vietnam, but rather to a new Army structure, worldwide."[4]

Formation of the Howze Board was precipitated by a memorandum from Secretary McNamara in which, said General Tolson, he directed re-examination of tactical mobility requirements "divorced from traditional viewpoints and past policies, and free from veto or dilution by conservative staff review."[5] It amounted to a directed verdict.

McNamara's memorandum had been stimulated by a small group of ac-tivists—Army officers and OSD civilians convinced that airmobility was the wave of the future and that the time had come to exploit it. One of them, then-Colonel Robert R. Williams, had drafted McNamara's memo, a docu-ment described by Delk Oden, another key figure in the aviation panoply, as being "really an insult to the Army." Oden saw Williams as "the damned-est Pentagon politician that ever went around,"[6] and George Seneff agreed. "Bob Williams was a very clever staff manipulator," said Seneff.[7] Williams was clever enough, in fact, to have McNamara specify in his memoran-dum not only that the Army would set up a board but also who would serve on it.

Those suggested were, of course, a who's who of current advocates of airmobility in its widest and most rapid application.[8] Although such tactics forced the Army to move the airmobility question, they also produced the usual negative side effects accompanying such bureaucratic maneuvers.

The Howze Board, formally designated the U.S. Army Tactical Mobility Requirements Board, was convened in the late spring of 1962 under the chairmanship of Lieutenant General Hamilton H. Howze, then command-ing the Army's XVIII Airborne Corps. Among its members were William B. Rosson, Delk Oden, Edward L. Rowny, Clifton von Kann, and Robert Williams, all of whom were or subsequently became general officers. Johnson admired Howze, considering him "a unique person" and "a superb choice" to head such a study, a man of "impeccable integrity" with excep-tional ability to innovate and think creatively.

The Howze Board submitted its final report, a 3,500-page document produced in ninety days, in late August 1962. Its most important tactical innovation was the concept of an air assault division, an element whose 459 organic aircraft would, it was held, give it mobility and self-sufficiency far beyond that of the conventional infantry division. Supporting firepower would include 105mm howitzers, Little John rockets, and aerially delivered fire from armed Mohawks and Huey helicopters mounting 2.75-inch rock-ets. That capability would not come cheap, however; cost of the airmobile division was estimated to be about one and a half times that of a standard division.

The Howze Board concentrated on a European tactical environment, supplemented by some reference to employment of the contemplated forces in counterinsurgency operations. The timing of this study was such, however, that its findings could scarcely avoid being considered with Vietnam in mind, even though, as Oden confirmed, "the Howze Board was oriented towards Europe."[9]

The Board presented Secretary McNamara with five alternative programs, but recommended alternative three, which called for creation of five air assault divisions, three air cavalry combat brigades, and five air transport brigades to go with eleven Army divisions of other types. That recommendation, if approved, would have meant the conversion of five existing divisions of other types to the air assault configuration. That turned out to be a key point.

These results and recommendations were subjected to extensive field testing based on an organization designated the 11th Air Assault Division. General Howze, for one, felt that such testing was not needed, calling it "an unnecessary expense and an unnecessary effort." In his view, "the Board should have been believed more than it was."

Howze described his extensive talks with Secretary of the Army Vance and General Wheeler, then Army Chief of Staff, and noted the politics involved. "They felt," he recalled, "that the overall accomplishment of modernizing the Army, by making it more airmobile, should not be jeopardized in any way by suggesting to Mr. McNamara that he was wrong in requiring the creation of this special division."[10]

General Johnson came in somewhat in the middle of this controversy when he became DCSOPS, but the issues were ones he had been considering for a number of years. "I think that the future battlefield is going to be almost entirely a war of continual movement in the forward area," he had written soon after arriving at Fort Leavenworth. "Any time this battle group sits down it will be gobbled, particularly if we are unable to improve our mobility and gain some mobility advantage over the enemy." Later in the school year, he had told a military audience of his conviction that "there is a requirement that maneuver elements be able to shift more quickly than a speed of Mach .002, which is the speed of the foot soldier."

When Johnson became DCSOPS, the airmobility tests were under way. They were exciting, but they were also putting the Army in a manpower bind. Secretary McNamara had authorized 15,000 additional spaces to support the tests, whereas General Wheeler had determined that the actual requirements were more in the 23,000–24,000 range. The shortfall had to be taken out of their hide. There was also the need for experienced people at every grade, and these could not be provided by new acquisitions. They had to be pulled out of existing units, the same kind of stripping that was being done to provide advisors for South Vietnam.

Besides this, pressure from OSD, along with the inexorable demands of the budget cycle, was forcing the Army to make what it viewed as premature determinations on airmobility issues. "The Army staff," Johnson advised General Wheeler in mid-November 1963, "is in the awkward position of recommending action on the Air Assault Division prior to completion of tests and the development of a fully staffed analysis." Johnson was sensitive to the budgetary implications, stating his "personal conviction that the Army cannot afford three special purpose divisions within a sixteen-division force structure," referring to an airmobile division and the existing two airborne divisions.

Days later, Johnson sent a memorandum to the directors within DCSOPS stating that "there is no reason for any confusion to exist nor should there be any contribution to the confusion that exists outside DCSOPS." He rehearsed for them the current Army position on the air assault division as submitted to the Joint Staff, which was that "the concept has much promise," but "requires a complete and comprehensive test." Then "decisions will be derived from test results."

In December 1963, a report entitled "Army Air Mobility Concept" was published. It began by observing that "increases in firepower since World War II have outstripped improvements in other land combat functions necessary to successful fulfillment of the Army's mission. Therefore, the primary thrust of the Army's efforts in recent years has been to restore balance among these functions and particularly to improve battlefield maneuver. By utilizing aerial vehicles, the Army can make these needed gains in mobility, intelligence and control."[11] That is exactly what Johnson had concluded while he was at Fort Leavenworth.

Soon after this report was published, Johnson gave two important talks in which he addressed the airmobility issue forthrightly. At the Canadian National Defence College in January 1964, he spoke of what the future held for the Army. "A major possibility," he suggested, "is the helicopter, whose capabilities still have not been exploited fully. The helicopter hopefully will get the infantry out of the mud. Hopefully, it will provide an accompanying weapons platform. It is a good airborne relay for communications. It is the answer to a major problem in surveillance, always with the proviso it can survive in this role."

On that last point, he observed that U.S. experience in Vietnam to date indicated that the helicopter "is a much tougher and far less fragile bird than its appearance would indicate." Johnson added that in his professional lifetime he had experienced the evolution of battlefield transport from the mule through several generations of wheeled transport and now into a second or third generation of rotary wing aircraft, so he was not exactly averse to change.

The following month, Johnson told a domestic audience that "in the conduct of operations we are trying to escape the limitations that terrain imposes, and here I think our helicopter is probably one of the things that is coming along best at this particular point in time to give us an opportunity to try . . . to trade off some of the heavy firepower . . . for the ability to move quickly—suddenly—and to have much less exposure time to enemy fires. This hopefully will get engagements over much more quickly and will save lives." Johnson's optimism about the potential of airmobility seemed to be progressing apace with the ongoing tests.

Apparently he was also taking some flak from other quarters for such a nonparochial stance, for he wrote to the Commanding General of the Infantry School, "I carry enough tar marks now for views expressed concerning Army aviation and tanks to be a somewhat suspect doughboy partisan."

In February 1964, Johnson went to Fort Benning to look at a test unit, and he was impressed. "It is quite a picture," he said in a "Dear Family" letter, "to see forty or so helicopters moving around in formation and could very well be a forerunner of the future for the Army." General Edward Rowny maintained retrospectively that General Johnson "as DCSOPS was cool to airmobility, but as Army Chief of Staff changed his mind."[12] Although the evidence shows that, long before then, Johnson was deeply concerned with the need for achieving a mobility differential, clearly what he observed in the tests helped convince him that issues of affordability, survivability, and allocation of assets could be handled.

Not all demonstrations went as well. "Once a week," recalled Rowny, "we would put on a show to which we invited officers and civilians from the Pentagon." Sometimes McNamara and some of his young staffers would attend, as they did on one occasion when a newly developed forward refueling technique was being demonstrated. A Caribou two-engine fixed-wing aircraft had been fitted with a bladder full of helicopter fuel. It was supposed to come in at treetop level, thereby avoiding detection by radar, and land in a cow pasture. Instantly crewmen would leap out, dragging fuel hoses behind them, and spread out to the points of a star. Helicopters could then come in five at a time, set down next to the nozzles, and rapidly refuel. All this had been rehearsed a number of times.

On the day that McNamara attended the weekly show, the Caribou came in too low over the trees, caught its gear, tumbled, and crashed directly in front of the audience. Rowny, standing next to McNamara, had the unenviable task of describing how the refueling would have been accomplished had the crash not occurred. Perennial optimist that he was, Rowny was able to find a bright spot: "The helicopters were able to show their versatility and take the wounded pilot and other crew members to the hospital."[13]

News of that fiasco could not have lessened the concerns of Johnson or others about the hazards of overreliance on the helicopter for tactical mobility. Jasper Wilson, for example, had written to Johnson from Vietnam to say that "Army aviation is doing a wonderful job in Vietnam using essentially the concepts of employment recommended by the Howze Board. I become more convinced every day, however, that we couldn't get by with it against anything other than an ill-equipped guerrilla. It would not be a question of acceptable losses—I believe they would suffer total loss in any opposed landing against a first-class enemy." A few days later, Johnson wrote to another officer to say, "my concern is a basic fear that a total reliance on movement by air will limit rather than improve our ability to move," citing maintenance and weather as limiting factors.

WHEN THE JOHNSONS moved to Washington, their younger son Bobby had been left behind at Fort Leavenworth, living with friends so that he could finish his junior year of high school there. Despite considerable misgivings, it seemed to have worked out satisfactorily. Now his senior year was nearing an end, and Bobby would soon be entering West Point. "I didn't bring any pressure to bear on him," said his father. In fact, his reaction had been negative when, earlier in the year, Bobby had approached him for help in getting what he called a "hip pocket" appointment—one that he could fall back on if his applications to other colleges were not accepted. "I told him that West Point was not a 'hip pocket' choice," said Johnson. Bobby later affirmed West Point as his first choice, whereupon his father helped him get an appointment from a North Dakota senator.

ONE DAY IN MID-JUNE 1964, Secretary of the Army Ailes and General Wheeler sent for General Johnson. Johnson was asked by Ailes, "Johnny, how do you like your job?"

"I like it very much, Mr. Secretary," Johnson replied. "I hope you consider my performance satisfactory."

"You're doing a fine job," Ailes assured him, "but *now* you are going to be the Chief of Staff."

Johnson was stunned by the news. When, moments later, he and Wheeler passed through the connecting door from the Secretary's office into Wheeler's suite, Johnson looked so pale that Sergeant Major Loikow thought he was ill.

It was by then late afternoon, still pretty early in the workday by Johnson's standards. Amazingly, he didn't call Dorothy. As he explained later, "telephones are really broadcasting systems around here," and no public announcement had yet been made. When he got home, late in the evening as usual, he went out to the sunporch. There Dorothy brought him his dinner, a bowl of tomato soup and some crackers. While he was eating, she sat with her sewing in a nearby rocking chair. It was their usual routine. After a few minutes, Johnson said, "A strange thing happened this afternoon. I got a call from 'Bus' [General Wheeler], who asked me to come over to his office. I did, and Bus said that Steve Ailes wanted to see us. We walked over, and I was told that I am going to be the next Chief of Staff." Then he finished his soup. Dorothy was astonished at the news, but not surprised by the manner of its revelation. "That's the way he is," she said.

Johnson had reached the pinnacle of his profession, reclaimed from professional obscurity by character, ability, and incredible industry. "Nobody else has done that—fought his way back from being a prisoner to become Chief of Staff," Dorothy said later with quiet pride. Yet it was anything but a joyous occasion. The responsibilities were too sobering for that, the problems too daunting, the surprise too overwhelming.

The next day, 24 June 1964, there was a White House ceremony for presentation of the Distinguished Service Medal to retiring General Paul Harkins, back from Vietnam. Still nothing was said about Johnson's appointment. Then the Joint Chiefs of Staff met, and around the table there was some idle speculation as to who would be appointed. Johnson kept his mouth shut, and so did Wheeler. Finally, at 4:30 in the afternoon, the appointment was announced. That night at home, the phone rang continually. Finally, at midnight, Johnson pleaded with the operator to hold further calls. They were really going to need their sleep now.

ON 1 JULY 1964, Bobby entered West Point as a plebe with the Class of 1968. Johnson was sympathetic to the difficulties that his newfound prominence was going to cause his young son. "The lot of a Plebe is never an easy one," he wrote to an officer in the Tactical Department at West Point, "and his problem has been compounded a hundredfold by virtue of my appointment just at the time that he was entering." To another correspondent he wrote, "I must say the perspective of a visitor and the perspective of a Plebe are appreciably different. Bobby is in the process of finding out how much, to his shock."

ON HIS LAST DAY AS DCSOPS, Johnson assembled the members of his staff to tell them good-bye. "Obviously," he said candidly, "my selection for the position of Chief of Staff came as a complete shock. One is always hopeful, and in all honesty you have got to say that, but . . . at this stage of my career and with my age I didn't feel that I had any hope at this time."

He spoke of only one action from the past year: the analysis of the Army's forces and the justification for them stimulated by the Enthoven paper, which he had criticized as having fundamental flaws. "The thing that gave me the most pride in that major staff action," Johnson said, "was the fact that we didn't have a 'deal' in the whole thing. What we had in that paper was what we believed was required for the country's defense, and this is important—very important."

Then he thanked them for their help. "When I move out, it isn't me that's making the move. It is you that have moved me, and I can't begin to express my gratitude."

Finally, as he had done after his first talk to them as DCSOPS fourteen months earlier, Johnson asked them all to come by on their way out so that he could shake each person's hand.

CHAPTER SIXTEEN

CHIEF OF STAFF

In the summer of 1964, much turbulence in senior Army ranks followed in the wake of General Maxwell Taylor's appointment as Ambassador to South Vietnam. Army Chief of Staff General Earle G. Wheeler moved up to take Taylor's place as Chairman of the Joint Chiefs of Staff. The Army Vice Chief of Staff, General Barksdale Hamlett, was a superb officer who would have been a strong contender for the top Army job, but he had recently suffered a heart attack and elected to retire.

In the spirit of the "youth movement" being pushed by Secretary of Defense Robert McNamara, he reached far down into the ranks of the Army's senior officers to appoint Harold K. Johnson, then the thirty-second ranking lieutenant general, as Chief of Staff. McNamara considered Johnson a man with "an iron will, extraordinary toughness of mind and spirit, and a fierce integrity," calling him "the best."[1]

Now he moved Johnson into the top job, a decision strongly supported by General Wheeler. Many were surprised by the choice, especially given Johnson's relative youth. Some noted that he had not commanded troops above the regimental level, unless one counted his stint as an assistant division commander.[2] And an officer serving in Vietnam wrote to Johnson expressing surprise on yet other grounds: "I have always believed that you were too intellectually honest and not enough of a politician to become Chief of Staff," he told the new incumbent.

Johnson apparently had no inkling that he was in line for the post. Less than a month before his appointment was announced, he had written in a "Dear Family" letter that, "having survived the first year in this [the DCSOPS] assignment, I would guess that the next two should not be any worse or any more difficult to cope with." Little did he know, apparently, that a new post was about to shoot hell out of those expectations.

There were other more likely candidates, more senior men with good reputations. One was General Hamilton Howze. "There was a sense of some disappointment," he admitted, but the selection was not made from so far down the list as to "shock people and annoy them and make them cry unfair. . . . And everybody recognized Johnson as an extremely capable person."[3] "The action officers were delighted," said Edward C. Meyer. "It meant bringing in a superb staff officer and a superb combat leader."

General Creighton W. Abrams was named Vice Chief of Staff. Abrams was a celebrated battlefield hero who had led a tank battalion across Europe during World War II, often as the lead element of General Patton's Third Army. Although different in personality, he shared with Johnson an admirable set of professional values rooted in integrity and concern for the soldier. "The Army has long needed such a happy combination," wrote noted military affairs commentator S. L. A. Marshall of the Johnson–Abrams team.[4] Johnson was openly delighted to have Abrams at his side. "I must say without any bravado whatsoever," he wrote to his close friend Harry Lemley, "that Abe and I ought to be able to cut it if any combination can! At least, this is the way I feel."

Johnson and Abrams were in personality about as different as two men could be—Johnson spare, quiet, serious, even-tempered, circumspect in speech; Abrams beefier, volatile, colorful, a man who, observed a journalist, "let the goddamns fall where they may." Nevertheless, the two established an unusually close personal and professional relationship, one founded on shared values and outlooks, on integrity, modesty, selflessness, religious faith, physical and moral courage, compassion, love for the soldier, and extraordinary competence. "We had about as close a relationship," said Johnson, "as any two men can have." Of Abrams he said, "the more you know about him, the more you'll know about what it takes to be a top, top flight commander. He was a man of great integrity, a unique man."

Meanwhile, another top-performing officer, Lieutenant General Bruce Palmer, Jr., succeeded Johnson as Deputy Chief of Staff for Military Operations. "I picked General Palmer because of his brightness, because he knew his way around the joint arena, and he was not a 'yes-man.' He spoke up," said Johnson.

ON THE MORNING OF 2 JULY 1964, Johnson appeared for his confirmation hearing before the Senate Armed Services Committee, Senator Richard B. Russell in the chair. Responding to the Chairman's question, Johnson said, "I hold the view that my first obligation is to the defense of my country, that when I appear before this committee or any committee of the Congress, it is incumbent upon me to be completely honest with the Congress and to respond to any questions that I am competent to answer." And, Johnson said, he had discussed this very matter with Secretary of Defense McNamara and had his assurances that he had complete freedom to do so.[5]

McNamara had called Johnson out of a meeting of the operations deputies to congratulate him on his selection and had asked whether he had any
questions. "I have a part question, and perhaps it's a part statement,"
Johnson responded. "I presume in my relationships with the Congress that
I can be totally candid with them."

"Oh, of course you can," McNamara assured him.

Later, reflecting on that, Johnson said, "Well, I don't think he *really*
meant it, but *I* took it as a license."

Some measure of how Johnson was regarded by the Congress can be
discerned in the fact that his confirmation hearing was scheduled for the
morning of the day before he was to be sworn in to office. Total elapsed time
for the hearing was eighteen minutes, and confirmation by the full Senate
was conferred later the same day.

Harold K. Johnson was promoted to full general and sworn in as Army
Chief of Staff on 3 July 1964, youngest man—with the sole exception of
Douglas MacArthur—yet to hold the position. Afterward, he quoted to assembled family, friends, and associates the opening words of the Scout Oath:
"On my honor I will do my best to do my duty to God and my country."
He added a prayer for the strength, courage, and wisdom he would need to
do the job. He described his concept of the role: "I intend to be the Army's
staunchest defender and its severest critic. I intend to be both nourisher and
pruner somewhere along the line." Then he thanked his friends and closed
with another prayer.[6] He was ready to get on with the work at hand.

EXPRESSIONS OF ENCOURAGEMENT AND SUPPORT poured in from all the far-
flung Army outposts, and not only soldiers voiced their backing for the new
Chief of Staff. One of the most gratifying messages was from Forrest Pogue,
the biographer of General George Catlett Marshall, who said to Johnson,
"your experience and background put you definitely in the Marshall tradition." Senior officers, some of whom Johnson had leapfrogged to take his
new post, weighed in with assurances of their support. Whether these were
pro forma or not, Johnson accepted them at face value and, in so doing, laid
the groundwork for harmonious working relationships with these key players. To General Paul Freeman, commanding the U.S. Army, Europe, Johnson
cabled: "Grateful for your message. Deeply conscious of fact that distinguished officers with experience and wisdom far beyond mine have been
jumped by virtue of my nomination, including you. Thus I am deeply appreciative of your pledge of support." The press reported that at least two senior officers were sufficiently miffed about being jumped by Johnson that they

were considering retirement, but none did. His sensitive handling of the situation apparently defused their resentment.

One less than enthusiastic view came from Colonel George McIntyre, en route to an assignment in DCSOPS, who wrote to lament "having my boss promoted out from over me." To an officer who wrote from Thailand, Johnson responded that he was "pleased that the tempo of activity . . . is such that you did not have time to sign the letter." And a politician from Kansas added his input to the flood of incoming congratulations, leading Johnson to succinctly instruct the drafter of his reply: "Pro forma. A name dropper and upstart."

The thread running through all these endorsements was a common view of the kind of man Johnson was. "He had a moral center to him," said Edward C. Meyer. "His moral compass was headed north, it wasn't headed northeast or north-northwest. He had a hard core ethical approach to problems." And, said John McPherson, "he wore his rank so lightly."

THE RANGE OF JOHNSON'S INTERESTS was apparently limitless. On his second day in the job—incidentally, the Fourth of July, which did not discourage him from working until late afternoon—Johnson got off a letter to the Commanding General of the Military District of Washington (MDW). That officer's duties included responsibility for the housekeeping of Forts Myer and McNair. Johnson had a few problems in that realm. "The grasscutters going over the grass leave large tufts at odd places and do nothing about some of the tougher types of growth that seem to withstand the blade," he noted. Also, the trees needed pruning, and no new tree plantings had been done in the past year. And, he said, some of the cars coming out of the Pentagon motor pool, also an MDW responsibility, had dirty seat covers.

The "mayor" was not intimidated. In a "Dear Johnny" reply, he observed that tree pruning was done on a three-year contract, and that no new plantings had been done because they were trying to maintain the cleared area to give a vista of Washington City, as requested by Mrs. Eisenhower during her residence at Fort Myer. In any event, "most of the existing large trees are estimated to have over a half-century of life remaining. Planting of replacement trees at this time would be futile as the existing trees would tend to stunt and starve the new ones." In addition, he had inspected the motor pool and found only one minor deficiency. "It has been good to learn of your wishes regarding Myer, McNair and the Motor Pool," he concluded.

Johnson, although impressively zinged, couldn't quite give it up. Perhaps too embarrassed to have it typed up, he lamely replied by handwritten note:

"I would question the estimates of life remaining in some of the old trees on Washington Avenue. The tops are going too quickly to support the estimate." Then, presumably, it was on to other things.

JOHNSON KNEW what he was getting into as Chief of Staff, that the challenges involved would be personal as well as organizational. "I felt that I walked in here as an honest man," he told a friend soon after taking on the new assignment. "I am going to endeavor to go out the same way." After only a few days in office, he wrote to another friend that the earlier assignment at Fort Leavenworth had been the most enjoyable tour of duty he had ever had, adding, "I expect this one will have too much heartache associated with it to fall into the same category." As he had already demonstrated, Johnson knew where to turn for sustenance in difficult times. In his office he kept a Bible and a copy of the Scout Handbook. "Sometimes when it was getting late at night," remembered General John A. Wickham, who as a colonel had been Johnson's executive officer, "we'd look through the small peephole in the door to his office and he'd be in there reading the Bible."

"After Bataan," said his classmate General "Jimmy" Polk in describing Johnson, "he got very serious, and his hobby was work." Johnson now set about pursuing his hobby with single-minded intensity. The issues were not new to him, having spent the previous year as DCSOPS, so he was able to take informed positions on the Army's behalf right from the start.

WHEN JOHNSON TOOK OVER, the Army outwardly appeared to be in excellent shape. There were underlying problems, however, that were quite severe. During the Eisenhower administration, with its emphasis on massive retaliation and strategic forces, the Army's share of defense resources had been meager. Conventional force capability had been allowed to atrophy, along with essential elements of airlift, sealift, tactical air support, and other capabilities for which the Army depended on the other services.

This was the state of affairs that had led General Maxwell D. Taylor to direct that the Army reorganize into Pentomic divisions. Soon after Taylor retired to publish *The Uncertain Trumpet,* a book criticizing prevailing defense policy, the Army scrapped the Pentomic division. That brought on yet another reorganization so that, with one thing and another, there had been quite a lot of backing and forthing over recent years. Meanwhile, a very significant number of experienced junior and midlevel leaders, both officer and enlisted, had been stripped out of units to meet requirements for advisors in Vietnam.

The effects of these organizational changes were compounded by other changes in the Army's support echelons, especially doing away with the technical services and reorganizing along functional lines. In 1961, in another McNamara-mandated study—this one designated Project 80 and having to do with the organization of the Army management structure—the Army had been extremely self-critical. Wrote Leonard Hoescher, Deputy Comptroller of the Army, who headed up the study, "The pattern of organization that was satisfactory in the early days of the Army's existence no longer gave the Army sufficient flexibility for future growth. The Army needed better long-term guidance, greater unity of purpose and effort, more closely related programs and resources, decentralized operations, more flexible personnel actions, an improved development process, a better organized development-procurement-production area, a single supply system and improved supply service, better coordinated individual and unit training, better guidance to Reserve units, a readjustment of the ROTC program, and better relations with higher authority, industry, and the scientific world."[7]

These findings were briefed to General Taylor, by then serving in the White House as Military Representative of the President for John F. Kennedy and out of the job of Army Chief of Staff for only a couple of years. Taylor remarked wryly that he had not known that "the Army was so bad off."[8]

There was much evidence, though, that the problems were real. When the Brown Board looked into the Army logistics system, the results were sobering. It essentially concluded, Johnson later noted, that "we didn't have a system. That's kind of a horrifying thing to find out . . . when you are . . . about six or seven months into a war. No system!" There were, instead, about six or seven different systems, and they weren't all talking to one another. "You wonder how the Army has run, really," said Johnson.

In early 1962, a reorganization of the Army, based on results of the Hoescher study, was ordered. One of its most significant features was abolition of the venerable technical services, so that the Chief Signal Officer, the Adjutant General, the Quartermaster General, the Chief of Finance, the Chief of Ordnance, the Chief Chemical Officer, and the Chief of Transportation suddenly found themselves out of jobs.[9] Of course, the activities they had overseen did not go away, so other organizational arrangements for their direction had to be devised. As a result, it was for a time literally not clear where to find the institutional memory on certain critical functions.

Adding to these internal difficulties were the demands of a management style brought to the Pentagon by Secretary McNamara and his civilian associates. They required large amounts of data that the Army was not equipped to provide in the detail and with the timeliness desired by OSD. Then there was the need to adapt to the new system of programming and budgeting also introduced by the McNamara team. These realities necessitated further internal reorganization.

Meanwhile, the administration's initiatives aimed at rebuilding conventional force capabilities, although welcomed by the Army, absorbed more adaptive capacity. This was especially true when it came to Special Forces and counterinsurgency capabilities—not necessarily where the Army would have chosen to apply the added resources. Thus, during a period of transition extending from 1961 to 1964, the Army expanded from eleven to sixteen divisions, converted to a new divisional structure, experimented with yet another concept for an airmobile division, created two new major functional commands, expanded its special warfare capabilities, and supported Vietnam requirements.[10] The cumulative effect of these factors was that, managerially, the Army was in some disarray.

"DOROTHY IS HAPPY here in Washington. I wish I could say the same," Johnson had observed only a couple of weeks before he was appointed Chief of Staff. In correspondence, he sometimes referred to Dorothy as "Mama," and often as "my tomato." He wrote to a friend soon after becoming Chief of Staff, "You can just bet that 'tomatoes' play a very significant role in the ability of an officer to meet the range of responsibilities that are thrust upon him these days." In a much more personalized tribute, he said of Dorothy, "I have a strong feeling that she makes the friends for the family and restores good relationships with the people that I tend to alienate through an unreasonable brusqueness and bluntness."

Now Johnson was responsible for dealing with all this unfinished business, and he perceived the state of affairs clearly. "I had a feeling . . . that the Army was uncertain as to where it was going," he said later. "The Army was uncertain about its role. The Army was uncertain as to just what its function was within the Department of Defense." That would have been challenge enough for a new chief of staff, but it was soon to be compounded by massive Army involvement in the war in Vietnam. And unfortunately, Johnson had inherited an Army whose "most important problem," said Secretary of the Army Stephen Ailes only days before Johnson took office, was the "readiness of the Army."[11]

EARLY IN HIS NEW ASSIGNMENT, Johnson had occasion to demonstrate his ethical stance in a case involving a major general who had, according to the findings of an investigation, acted improperly in seeking modifications to his headquarters building. When the matter was investigated, the officer tried to evade responsibility and obfuscate the facts. "The weight of the evidence in the report of the Inspector General," Johnson wrote to this officer, "suggests strongly that your statements border upon falsification and certainly are misleading." "You have forfeited my personal confidence in your ability as a commander," he added. Accordingly, he reprimanded this officer—who was one of his West Point classmates—and relieved him from command.

When another senior officer, a major general, became involved with the wife of one of his subordinates, Johnson took the opportunity to send another message on standards. Calling the offending man in, Johnson arranged for his prompt retirement, an action that the officer understood completely. "I really don't see how, in light of his beliefs, he could have done less," he said.

JOHNSON HAD AN ARTIFACT that he kept in his office, a wooden turtle. If you pulled the turtle's head out a little, exposing a portion of the neck, one star showed. The further you pulled, the more stars appeared, so that when the neck was sticking out all the way, four stars were visible. Showing the turtle to a friend one day, Johnson told him that that was about the way he had found it to be. Early in his tenure Johnson decided that he would stick his neck out all the way, risking those four stars on the issue of military pay.

Secretary McNamara maintained that comparability between military and civilian pay had previously been achieved, so all that was necessary in the coming year was a keep-even pay boost. Johnson didn't see it that way, even though he was under strong pressure to support the OSD view.[12] That pressure included being closeted in Secretary Ailes's office from 10:45 in the morning until 3:20 in the afternoon for "pay testimony review" on the day before Johnson was scheduled to testify, followed by another hour in Secretary McNamara's office late that afternoon.

That night Johnson called in his military stenographer. It was already about 11:00 P.M. "The heck with it. I am the spokesman for a million and a half men and I can't let them down now," his driver heard Johnson say. Then he began dictating a revised statement that would present his own evaluation of the issue. Pacing up and down, he laid out the case as he saw it, point by point. By the time he finished, it was 2:00 A.M. They were due on the Hill at 10:00. Obviously, nobody in OSD was going to clear this material before it was presented.

"I didn't dispute figures or the conclusions that were reached," said Johnson. "I just said that I came to different conclusions with the same data." One of his objections was that OSD calculated the individual soldier's pay by averaging the pay of all soldiers, even though some received special incentive pays that were not available to others. "I couldn't send my daughter to college with General Westmoreland's jump pay," he complained, "but I was being charged with the share of his jump pay."

Johnson made that point in testimony before the House Armed Services Committee, providing a detailed analysis to back up his argument. In so doing, he was the only member of the Joint Chiefs of Staff to take an independent position. When Johnson finished, Committee Chairman Mendel Rivers came over to the witness table and put an arm around his shoulder. "General," he said, "that is the truest from-the-heart statement in defense of the American soldier I've ever heard." Soon thereafter, Congress enacted a substantial military pay raise that approached genuine comparability.

Soldiers appreciated that kind of support. "To us out in the pasture," wrote one retired officer, "the knowledge that our No. 1 soldier laid his job on the line by speaking his convictions is unbelievably heartening." Johnson knew that he was risking his job, because he had gone to General Omar Bradley seeking counsel. "I felt that if I could not support the policies of the administration I really had no part—I had no *place*—being in that administration," Johnson recalled. So he went down and talked to General Bradley when he "decided that in the interests of the people in the Army . . . I had to speak up on the pay issue. And I said to him, 'General Bradley, should I request relief and resign or retire?' "

"No," the old soldier counseled. "If you resign you're going to be a disgruntled general, you'll be a headline for one day, and then you'll be forgotten. What you do is you stay and you fight your battle and you continue to fight it to the best of your ability inside." Johnson followed that advice.

Not everyone was happy that he did. "Johnny was a hell of a fine guy," said Secretary of the Army Ailes, "and a real soldier. But I had a problem with him: he would be unhappy about a decision, and he would feel loyalty to the system required him to say so—on the Hill, for example. I told him, 'You don't have to *volunteer* every little pet peeve you have.' "

As CHIEF OF STAFF, Johnson continued working closely with General Earle G. Wheeler, now Chairman of the Joint Chiefs of Staff. Johnson felt a certain inhibition in following his boss into his former job and still having him as his boss, each of them one step further up the ladder. "I was always conscious of quite a number of forces at work," Johnson said. "Force number one was that my predecessor as Chief of Staff of the Army was the Chairman of the Joint Chiefs of Staff, and he had certain views with respect to joint positions, so I would consult with him." Of course, Johnson as DCSOPS had helped Wheeler formulate most of those positions, whether he agreed with them or not, so it was going to be hard to establish himself as an independent persona on policy matters.

Profiling Wheeler at the time he assumed his new duties, *Time* magazine observed that in thirty-two years of service he had only five months of combat duty, and that was as a division chief of staff, so he had never commanded in combat at any level.[13] He was called variously a "military politician" and "a consummate professional." John McPherson, who worked closely with them both, contrasted Johnson and Wheeler. "Johnson was such a conscientious guy," he said, "and bright, and he had the courage of his convictions. Wheeler was a different type. There were no expressions of enthusiasm from him. He'd never say 'Charge!' "[14]

Given how disastrously things went while Wheeler was Chairman, it would be easy to write him off as not up to the job. Some of his contemporaries had a different view, however. Marine Commandant General Wallace Greene, for example, said that in the twelve years he had been associated with the JCS in one capacity or another, General Wheeler was "the best Chairman I knew. He was very fair, understanding, hard-working, and bore up under his physical disability," a heart condition.

Wheeler had other physical problems, including the aftermath of cataract surgery, which left him with no depth perception. And, recalled Phil McAuliffe, who worked closely with Wheeler, "light bothered him very much. He would have a partially darkened office because of his sensitivity to light." McPherson sympathized with Wheeler on two counts: "He was annoyed" more or less constantly during those years, "and he was sick a good part of the time."

Stephen Ailes knew Wheeler well and contrasted his work habits with his own and Johnson's. " 'Bus' would leave there about six with an absolutely clear desk," he recalled. "He'd go home, have a drink, look at a movie. Yet he was clearly on top of his job. Meanwhile, I was there until nine. Johnny would go out of there every night with two briefcases bulging."

A fascinating source of commentary on General Wheeler is a Soviet sketch done for intelligence purposes (and probably propaganda as well) during the Vietnam War. Noting that Wheeler was a native of the District of Columbia and thus supposedly lacked the patronage enjoyed by others who had senators and congressmen to push their fortunes, this study concluded that "the fact that Wheeler was able to advance so far without all these career-promoting circumstances is indicative of his unusual aggressive character." And: "A pushful staff worker, Wheeler knew very well how to read between the lines."[15]

"Bus" Wheeler, said General Ralph Haines, who served as Vice Chief during Johnson's last year as Chief of Staff, "was a man of conviction, but I do think McNamara felt he was a man who—." Haines let his thought trail off, unsaid, but seemed to imply "could be finessed," or maybe "co-opted." Lyndon Johnson provided what might be viewed as substantiating evidence: "This business of the military keeping things from me and trying to influence me—Buzz Wheeler never tried to influence or force a decision on me from the day I took the Presidency until I left. . . . If there was ever a judicious, fair man, he was that man. Now, he'd say, 'Here are the arguments for it, here are the arguments against it. Here's why I believe you ought to do this.' And that was it. And then Mr. McNamara might tear him to pieces."[16]

Perhaps the most insightful comment of all on Wheeler was an observation by John McPherson: "There was no color. No color there."

DEALING WITH ACTION OFFICERS, Johnson as Chief of Staff continued to be accessible and receptive. "I've seen great numbers of Indians in his JCS briefings back him off of a position," said General Lemley. "It's not at all unusual, and he expects you to speak up."

General Haines observed how Johnson "was deeply involved in the joint arena. He really enjoyed the pre-brief and the de-brief. There's where, out of character, he'd pull out a big black cigar, clip off the end, and light that up as the first order of business. He found the jousting very interesting. He liked interacting with the young lieutenant colonels." Haines learned that, contrary to his surface impression, Johnson was not humorless, that he had a keen and wry sense of humor that he often let show in these sessions. And, he saw, Johnson often knew more about the action officers' papers than they did. "He inspired real confidence on the part of the young officers that he would carry the ball when their papers merited it."

WHEN HE WENT FOR HIS ANNUAL PHYSICAL at the Fort Myer clinic, Johnson was examined by an old and valued friend, Dr. Walter A. Kostecki. He had been Johnson's literal savior when, as an emaciated prisoner near death, Johnson had dragged himself off a ship in Japan. Kostecki was now a colonel and in command of the clinic. And Kostecki once again came to Johnson's rescue, recalled General Oren Hurlbut, carrying out some simple instructions from the Chief of Staff: "Keep the general officers, and their families, off my back." Kostecki's fine care ensured that there would be no complaints to Johnson about the quality of the medical treatment they received.

WITHIN WEEKS of becoming Chief of Staff, Johnson was formulating some innovative proposals concerning Vietnam. He viewed the first task as getting South Vietnamese units up to strength. Next was to get some U.S. forces in on the ground, preferably in the highlands region. And then, "if you wanted to reverse the trend and stop the infiltration," an operation should be run straight across Vietnam all the way to the Mekong River, using four divisions to "just stop the Ho Chi Minh trail."

In late July 1964, recorded Marine Major General H. W. Buse, Jr., at a special JCS meeting, "the President requested the Joint Chiefs of Staff to recommend actions which would obtain maximum military results with minimum U.S. participation and minimum risk of escalation."[17] Harold K. Johnson proposed the interdiction operation to the Joint Chiefs of Staff in August 1964. Reflecting on it later, he said, "I regret very much that I didn't push that a lot harder than I did . . . at the time. Of course," he added, "politically it was something not possible. It was only two years after the Laos Accords of 1962, and they had been come by pretty hard. And it denied completely the Air Force theory that we could stop movement of men and supplies by bombing alone, so that you have that argument, too." But Johnson was convinced that the four-division operation could close the area off to any significant enemy infiltration.

In August 1964, an article written by Johnson, probably before he was nominated to be Chief of Staff, was published in an Army journal. Entitled "Land Power!" it was a strong articulation of Johnson's views on the essentiality of ground forces for the resolution of armed conflict. In it, he emphasized another essential aspect of successful war fighting, saying that the soldier in combat "prays for the full support implicit in an aroused national determination to sustain him over the distance between his foxhole and his objectives."[18] When Lyndon Johnson sent U.S. ground forces into Vietnam the following year, he not only failed to rally the people to such support but also specifically decided as a matter of policy not to do so.

General Johnson made another key point in this essay that demonstrated how divorced in outlook he was from the reigning civilian defense hierarchy, highlighting what he called "the catalyst that has defied quantification— leadership, spirit, conviction, resolve, fierce pride. These are," he stressed, "essential ingredients of the driving force organic to the human element of land combat."[19]

IN SEPTEMBER 1964, another Vietnam-oriented political-military game was conducted, this one designated SIGMA II-64. It seems likely that a game that used Americans to play the Red Team, representing the North Vietnamese and the Viet Cong, would be inherently flawed, given the failure of Americans to understand the outlook, motivations, psychology, and actions of their opponents. But in the case of SIGMA II-64, it worked better than might have been expected—in fact, rather well. The Red Team was, for the most part, unperturbed by the Blue Team's actions—even when they dispatched a number of U.S. combat divisions to the theater of war—and by the fact that the game postulated declaration of a national emergency and at least partial mobilization by the United States.[20] In fact, the Red Team acted pretty much like the actual enemy did throughout most of the war. Red Team members went on with what they were doing, stoically accepting whatever costs that entailed, confident that in the end they would prevail. It turned out to be a valid indication of what lay ahead, although of course not all players—especially on the Blue Team—perceived it as such.

The U.S. approach in this game was the same "graduated response" that, only a few months later, would guide its actual deployment of forces. The application of airpower against North Vietnam was a facet of particular interest. "Several Blues felt further annoyance during the game that the air attacks against the DRV [Democratic Republic of Vietnam, or North Vietnam] had not yielded more positive results and voiced resentment against the scenario and Control," said a summary of the game's results. "Since this was the 'name of the game' (SIGMA II was a look at the situation *if* such measures fail to work)," it was observed, "Control accepted the comments philosophically."[21]

Many elements of reality were injected into this game. "A question was raised," for example, "regarding how long the American public, with the current flavor of press coverage, would support the commitment of ground forces in such strength"—a postulated six plus division forces.[22]

Harold K. Johnson was on the Red Team. It is interesting to speculate how much the experience may have influenced his thinking on the course of the war. Only a few months later, he launched the PROVN Study, about which more later, the results of which were so condemnatory of the way the war was then being fought.

As the autumn wore on, Johnson reported to various friends on his younger son's progress. "Bobby is adjusting slowly to West Point," he said at an early point. "As is usual," he wrote a bit later, "he spends a great deal of time griping and not enough time organizing his activities so that he stays out of the hands of the sheriff. As a consequence, he gets what I consider to be more than his share of demerits, all of his own creation." That put Bobby solidly in the mainstream of plebes.

Johnson enjoyed telling a story about his son the plebe: On weekends, many people were away for various reasons, so some tables in the Cadet Mess would be closed, and the cadets normally seated there would "float" until they found a vacant seat at another table. One Sunday morning, Bobby wound up at a table with people he didn't know and a friendly second classman as the table commandant. This man went around the table quizzing each plebe, finally getting to Bobby.

"Where are you from, Mister?"

Bobby, bracing at the foot of the table, responded, "Arlington, Virginia, sir."

"Are you a member of a military family?"

"Yes, sir."

"What was your dad, a colonel?"

"No, sir."

"A brigadier general?"

"No, sir."

"A major general?"

"No, sir."

"A lieutenant general?"

"No, sir."

"Oh, you're *that* one!" A pause, then: "Mister, do you know me?"

"No, sir."

"Well, let's keep it that way."

Johnson got a lot of mileage out of that story, even telling it to cadets at The Citadel when he went to lecture there.

"The Army means people," Johnson often said, and now that he was Chief of Staff he set about doing everything he could for those people. Early in his tenure, he included in the Chief of Staff's *Weekly Summary*, a publication that went to all Army general officers, a message about "putting the personal into personnel." Johnson believed that anyone having anything to do with the Army personnel system should treat people not as "personnel" but as individuals who were entitled to personal attention to their well-being. He kept pounding on that theme in every forum available to him. Evidence that the message was being received came from a commander in the field who wrote that "these three words [personal into personnel] which everyone now associates with you, and which I am certain will go down in history with you, have become almost a creed or motto here at the Infantry School."

Johnson adopted as his own a program of self-help that became known as Army Community Service, a way of providing support to soldiers' families who were experiencing problems that they couldn't handle alone. Staffed primarily by volunteers, ACS centers at Army posts all over the world provided counseling on budgeting and family finance, child care, relocation, consumer affairs, and other social services, growing so fast that in a single year, 160,000 cases were handled.[23]

Only a couple of months into the new job Johnson lost someone close to him when 1st Lieutenant Richard T. Lynch, a young West Pointer who had been his aide-de-camp at Fort Leavenworth, was killed in action in Vietnam. Stimulated by the father of another soldier killed in Vietnam who had complained that the notification he received was impersonal and did not address him properly, Johnson tore into his Adjutant General. "It is imperative that actions involving family feelings of any sort be handled with the utmost discrimination and taste," he emphasized. "I expect people to be handled like people and not like a group of numbers or a herd of cattle."

Johnson followed that up with a handwritten note. "I want to keep uppermost in people's minds that they are dealing with human tragedy," he said, "that there are individuals and families at the end of the line to whom one problem is the major fact in their lives, overwhelming all others. They should be able to detect that we know it, too. That's all I ask. Our only job here is to solve problems—most of the time for other people."

Also, Johnson said, "effective immediately, I would like to sign a letter of condolence to the next of kin of individuals killed or missing in action." And he did, for the rest of his tenure, sometimes hundreds of them a week. He would wait until late in the day, when he was virtually alone, and often added a personal handwritten note below his signature. Sometimes his executive officer would go into Johnson's office and find him standing at the window, looking out at the great vista of the city of Washington and all its monuments. He had been signing all those letters, and when he turned from the window, his eyes were full of tears.

ONE AUTUMN DAY, Johnson had some special guests for lunch in his office: Colonel Frank Anders and his father, retired Major Frank L. Anders, then eighty-nine years of age and a holder of the Medal of Honor. The younger Anders had been with Johnson in the 57th Infantry of the Philippine Scouts. At Johnson's invitation, he had come to lunch at the Pentagon, bringing with him his distinguished old soldier father, a fellow North Dakotan. Later, as the two men emerged from the Pentagon, Major "Pops" Anders said, "Sonny, this was worth the whole trip—one of the finest experiences of my life." Afterward, the younger Anders wrote to Colonel Lilly, their regimental commander in the 57th Infantry, to tell him about Johnson's "heartwarming kindly attentiveness to an old man."

IN THE SPRING OF 1964, the Joint Chiefs of Staff began work on a paper that considered the options available to the United States with respect to Vietnam. At one extreme was the option of cutting losses and getting out; on the other was "bombing North Vietnam back into the Stone Age." General Curtis LeMay, then Air Force Chief of Staff, advocated the latter—and "he used this term quite frequently in the Chiefs," said Johnson.[24] An invasion of North Vietnam was also one of the options. Recalled Johnson, "the option that was *chosen* of a graduated response, and a wait until the enemy reacted before you added your next element of force, was described in this paper . . . *precisely* as it happened, that is that the American public would become disenchanted, there would be a loss of support for the effort and . . . a question as to whether there could be a favorable outcome." Even so, Johnson acknowledged, "after the commitment was made, I don't recall any military challenges being made to the policy, and this, of course, could *well* be the fatal error."

The senior military leadership had, Johnson pointed out, all been schooled in the professional ethic "that you argue your case up to the point of decision. Having been given a decision, you carry it out with all the force that you can, put all your effort behind carrying it out." That was essentially what the Joint Chiefs of Staff sought to do—make the most of the policies established by their civilian leaders. It was what they were *supposed* to do, it was what they had been *trained* to do, and it was a sure route to disaster.

"So what I say now," Johnson observed a number of years after the war, "is that there was no way that we could be successful in Vietnam in light of the policies that we had."

Be that as it may, in early November 1964 the Joint Chiefs of Staff met with Secretary McNamara and were told: "I want the Chiefs to reexamine the forces which would be required to support a major effort in South Vietnam and the logistics to back up those forces." The troop deployments of the following spring and summer had their antecedents at least this far back.

IN DECEMBER 1964, Johnson made a second trip to Vietnam and other points in the Far East, his first as Chief of Staff. "This is a combination 'showing the flag' and defensive maneuver," he wrote to General Hamlett, "because I feel that I must be able to say to the Congressional committees that I have just visited the Far East and have firsthand information of developments there." Dorothy accompanied her husband on the trip.

At this time, the CIA Station in Saigon cabled a year-end assessment that was unrelievedly bleak. "Enemy activity was intensifying while ARVN combat effectiveness was deteriorating, and government control of the countryside was steadily eroding while the military regime in Saigon showed continued disunity and instability. The assessment concluded that unless the South Vietnamese were soon bolstered by external military forces, an ARVN defeat in the near future was likely to take place."[25]

EN ROUTE TO VIETNAM, Johnson explained to soldiers at Fort Wainwright, Alaska, why they were experiencing some shortages: "Everybody in the Army is helping fight that war, even if they're not in Viet Nam." In Okinawa, he told a group of young officers that they might have to begin thinking about a second unaccompanied tour in Vietnam, because he foresaw "a bitterly long struggle." In Korea, he had an equally sobering observation about Vietnam, saying that "there probably will be people going out there [on assignments] ten years from now."

The headline-grabbing stop on the way out, though, was in Hawaii, where Johnson observed some training of the Army forces stationed on Oahu. In a skit depicting how to deal with interrogation if captured, the sergeant in charge used language that Johnson considered so inappropriate that he stepped in to correct the man. When he got back from the trip, Johnson put out a message about this type of conduct and his strongly negative views on it, followed up by a letter distributed Army-wide entitled "The Image of the Army."

That occasioned a great deal of comment, much of it public. In fact, the *Washington Star* was moved to ridicule Johnson on its editorial page in a piece entitled "Is nothing sacred? Not even the profane?"[26] Johnson got a lot of mail, too, including letters from young enlisted men supporting his position. "One reason I am not going to reenlist," one man told him, "is that I don't like the moral tone of the leadership."

Johnson himself commented further on the matter when he spoke at service schools in succeeding months. "There's been a good bit of misinterpretation of an instruction I put out . . . concerning profanity," he said at the Infantry School. "I'm a fairly practical fellow, and I don't believe that I have the power to stop people from swearing. However, I can stop planned, deliberate use of off-color stories and profanity in instruction and in training."

On a return visit to Fort Leavenworth, Johnson reinforced the message he had meant to send: "It is what you do in your duties, mundane as they might be, day after day that creates the picture that people have of us. This is what you must look at."

The reaction to Johnson's more overt manifestations of his moral outlook was mixed, as shown by the views of able and experienced senior officers who were widely respected for their own principled leadership but reached quite different conclusions. "General Johnson had that evangelical religious outlook," said Lieutenant General DeWitt C. Smith, Jr. "People were put off by it, even if they shared his values." In contrast, "It was a source of strength," said General Donald V. Bennett. "People appreciated that we had a Chief of Staff who believed that, his religious convictions and his ethical commitment." Another senior officer, though perhaps revealing more about himself than Johnson, observed succinctly and dismissively, "He was a Christer."

Yet another perspective, perhaps the most representative, was provided by Colonel Lloyd J. Matthews, who, as a lieutenant, had served in the 8th Infantry Division when Johnson was assistant division commander. "With many, if not most, people," he wrote, "overt religiosity carried over into their professional lives can be a big turn-off in this secular age. But I never heard HKJ criticized for it. People understood the ordeal that lay behind it. They accepted it. And it is possible that they respected him more *because* of it rather than *in spite* of it." Maxine Clark, Johnson's civilian secretary during his final years of service, reflected that view. "He was a dedicated Christian," she said, "which was the foundation for his greatness. It set him apart morally, spiritually, and professionally."

SHORTLY BEFORE DEPARTING for Southeast Asia, Johnson had written to Colonel Lilly about the situation there, saying, "it will be a long, slow, painful haul and require an infinite patience on the part of the American public." Once in Vietnam, he crisscrossed the country from top to bottom, visiting multiple installations in all four of the corps areas.

Returning to Saigon after his forays into the countryside, Johnson learned that General William C. Westmoreland, now the Commander, U.S. Military Assistance Command, Vietnam (COMUSMACV), had issued an order mandating "the maintenance of an optimistic outlook on the part of all advisors." Also, perhaps unaware of the recent CIA assessment of the military and political situation, Westmoreland had just sent a message to his senior advisors stating that "an opportunity for birth of new era in counterinsurgency war is at hand." Johnson brought back a copy for the JCS.

Back in Washington, Johnson drafted—but never sent—a report to Secretary McNamara. In it, he pointed out as problems the insensitive conduct of some South Vietnamese forces toward their own civilian populace and the inhibiting effects of certain operational constraints. On balance, though, he observed that "though I see no quick or simple solution, I am quietly optimistic about the military progress being made. Given political stability and widening popular support, this military progress offers real hope for drying up the sea in which the VC must live."

Johnson did forward a trip report to the JCS, however, stating that "on balance I believe the conflict in Vietnam can be brought to a successful conclusion in a military sense, provided some semblance of a national governmental structure can be maintained." That was an important qualification, however, for Johnson also noted that "General Khanh appeared to have a somewhat dog in the manger attitude by voicing his intent to take recourse in resignation or retirement from the scene in the event his subordinates do not follow his orders."

Of more lasting significance, perhaps, Johnson strongly stated his belief "that it is the duty of the Joint Chiefs of Staff individually to seek opportunities to make public explanations of the military situation in Vietnam and to express publicly their belief that the military aspects of this conflict can be won, provided the American people demonstrate patience and express their determination to assist in the defense of the right of men to be free." That was a mission he would undertake personally with almost evangelical zeal in the coming months and years. So frequently did he make this case, Dorothy remembered, that she could have given the speech from memory.

A WEEK AFTER HE GOT BACK from the Far East, Johnson joined other members of the Joint Chiefs of Staff for a ceremonial visit to the LBJ ranch in Texas, where theoretically deliberations on the defense budget were to take place. Given that the Chiefs flew out of Washington close to eight o'clock in the morning, and Johnson was back in his office at the Pentagon a little past five-thirty, it is clear that there was not much time for substantive discussion. Photographs of the occasion show the Joint Chiefs in full uniform, seated uncomfortably on folding beach chairs around an outdoor picnic table, LBJ and McNamara presiding in shirtsleeves. The President, said news accounts, sided with McNamara's recommendation that eight billion dollars be cut from the defense budget. Lady Bird gave them lunch, then the Chiefs headed for home.

Lyndon Johnson followed up by cabling Ambassador Taylor to complain that "every time I get a military recommendation it seems to me that it calls for large-scale bombing: I have never felt that this war will be won from the air, and it seems to me that what is much more needed and would be more effective is a larger and stronger use of . . . appropriate military strength on the ground and on the scene. I am ready to look with great favor on that kind of increased American effort." LBJ invited recommendations for such an endeavor, "even though I know that it may involve the acceptance of larger American sacrifices. We have been building our strength to fight this kind of war ever since 1961, and I myself am ready to substantially increase the number of Americans in Vietnam if it is necessary to provide this kind of fighting force against the Viet Cong."[27] With the election behind him, Lyndon Johnson had obviously changed his conception of himself as a man fighting doggedly against a military establishment eager to drag him into a war.

But, as a MACV analysis forwarded by Ambassador Taylor to the President made clear, the current outlook in Saigon was decidedly not supportive of major involvement by American ground forces. The advisory effort had concentrated on giving the South Vietnamese both the skills and the motivation they needed to succeed, read the analysis. "If that effort has not succeeded there is less reason to think that U.S. combat forces would have the desired effect. In fact, there is good reason to believe that they would have the opposite effect by causing some Vietnamese to let the U.S. carry the burden while others, probably the majority, would actively turn against us."[28]

Thus diametrically opposed positions on the major American decision of the war were clearly staked out. Bombing policy, potential troop deployments, and escalation were all in the air as 1964 came to a close. From that point on, at least for Harold K. Johnson, Vietnam would dominate virtually every aspect of life.

CHAPTER SEVENTEEN

MARCH 1965

In March 1965, President Lyndon Johnson sent General Johnson to Vietnam to make a personal assessment of the situation. Johnson was accompanied by a number of others, including representatives of each of the services and John McNaughton from McNamara's office, but it was his personal and individual responsibility to report his findings to the President.

On the day before he was to depart—which was also the day he learned he would be going—Johnson joined LBJ and others for breakfast at the White House. LBJ made it clear that he wanted to stabilize the situation in Vietnam, and that he was not going to lose there. Afterward, going down in the elevator, the President bored his finger into Johnson's chest and told him, "Get things bubbling, General!"

While Johnson was en route, McNamara cabled Ambassador Taylor to say on behalf of the President that, "in developing list [of additional actions needed], you may, of course, assume no limitations on funds, equipment or personnel. We will be prepared to act immediately and favorably on any recommendations you and General Johnson may make."[1]

As Johnson was arriving in Saigon, McGeorge Bundy sent the President a memorandum marked "Personal and Sensitive" in which he reported on a lengthy meeting the previous evening with McNamara and Dean Rusk. "Last night," Bundy said, "Bob McNamara said for the first time what many others have thought for a long time—that the Pentagon and the military have been going at this thing the wrong way round from the very beginning: they have been concentrating on military results against guerrillas in the field, when they should have been concentrating on intense police control from the individual villager on up."[2]

During the visit to Vietnam, Johnson stayed at Westmoreland's villa in Saigon. The day after his arrival, two battalion landing teams of U.S. Marines came ashore in the I Corps area of South Vietnam. Before long, Johnson had firsthand confirmation of the validity of McNamara's observation. "We've listened to briefings for two and a half days" at MACV, he observed to other members of his trip section, "and security at hamlet level hasn't been mentioned." He described how he had awakened at three o'clock in the morning and decided to have a tree chart made, with the base at hamlet level. "We have this top-heavy structure which all people here are trying to keep track of at the top," he explained, "but they can't give attention to the root of the tree."[3]

Ambassador Maxwell Taylor had a better grasp of the situation. "Taylor," recalled the *Pentagon Papers,* "saw the basic unresolved problem as the provision of adequate security for the population. Without it, other programs were either impossible or of marginal effectiveness at best." Taylor went on to explain how "occasional military successes achieved in clearing operations too frequently went unexploited. Areas were cleared but not held. Other areas were cleared and held—but were not developed; the VC infra-structure remained in place, ready to emerge when the troops moved on."[4] That was it exactly, and search and destroy wasn't going to touch it.

Delk Oden recalled one MACV briefing for General Johnson and his party that was distinctly out of the ordinary. "We gave him a regular briefing for about two hours," he said, "and then he asked everyone to leave the room but the generals. Then he said, 'Gentlemen, as you know, I don't come as the Army Chief of Staff. I am here as a representative of the President of the United States. Mr. Johnson asked me to come, and to tell you that I come with a blank check. What do you need to win the war?' " And, added Oden, "that's when the buildup started, for better or worse."[5]

This was Johnson's third visit to Vietnam and, as on the previous occasions, he traveled widely to units and installations, both U.S. and Vietnamese. He began with visits to two of the top leaders at that time, Major General Nguyen Van Thieu, then Minister of Defense, and Air Vice Marshal Nguyen Cao Ky.[6] (Nguyen Khanh, the chief of state who had favorably impressed him on an earlier visit, had by now been swept from the scene, forced into exile.)

In Pleiku, Johnson talked with the local commander, General Co, who later became South Vietnam's Minister of Defense. Co, Johnson said, "impressed me above all others with the depth and extent of his concern." Co pointed out that his troops were equipped, for the most part, with the M-1 rifle and a sprinkling of M-2 carbines, leftover weapons of World War II vintage, and were coming up against enemy forces wielding the new and far superior AK-47 assault rifle. Being so decisively outgunned, his men were breaking and running in every engagement, unable to withstand the shock of initial contact with their pathetically inferior firepower. Johnson found Co seized with "what almost might be termed despair," but Co was not alone in his concern. "Everybody says they need more firepower, that they're outgunned by the enemy," read a handwritten note in Johnson's trip file.

ON HIS RETURN FROM VIETNAM, Johnson stopped in Hawaii long enough to outline his preliminary findings at CINCPAC (Commander-in-Chief, Pacific) Headquarters. "I think really that our policy there is pretty clear," he said. "We are going to keep Vietnam free regardless of what it costs. We are going to try to do that without broadening the war or widening the war." He continued, "The first job is security. I must never get away from that."

He was asked about the possibility of there being a blank check for the war in Vietnam. "I will tell you the confidence I have in a blank check," he responded. "I haven't spent a nickel. Now Mr. McNamara has said all along, 'Money is no object.' Every time you get down to paying them you have to dig into your other pocket. This has happened every time."

UPON HIS RETURN, Johnson submitted a report containing twenty-one recommendations in a category of actions designed to "arrest the deterioration," including an intensified air war against North Vietnam. In a separate category, he proposed deployment of much larger ground forces to Vietnam. "The report in its entirety is representative of my viewpoint alone," Johnson stated.[7] That was correct, but only up to a point, because the twenty-one recommendations came from a list of twenty-eight provided by OSD's John McNaughton before they even left Washington.[8]

At least that helped explain why many of these particular recommendations appeared feeble, futile, or appropriate to some lower staff level. They included, for example, streamlining construction procedures and doing some harbor dredging. Later Johnson candidly admitted that many of them were "bandaids of a sort," although scattered among them were several recommendations of greater substance and significance. These included increasing the scope and tempo of air strikes against North Vietnam and removing self-imposed restrictions on the conduct of such strikes.

Also significant were the recommendations on McNaughton's list that Johnson did *not* endorse. One was a proposal to "send assassination squads after VC leaders," while another proposed rewards to South Vietnamese leaders "to induce them to accept U.S. instructions." On behalf of the Department of State, William Bundy indicated "no policy problem" with respect to these initiatives—it was all right with him to assassinate enemies and bribe allies.[9] Johnson didn't think so and scrubbed these proposals from the McNaughton list.

The recommendations that really counted, Johnson stressed, were those aimed at getting South Vietnamese units up to strength, putting some U.S.

forces in on the ground, and mounting an operation to cut the Ho Chi Minh Trail. Johnson had been in Vietnam only three months earlier, but, he now reported, "it is clearly evident that the situation in Vietnam has deteriorated rapidly and extensively in the past several months." This he attributed to an inability to provide adequate security for the population, the instability of the government, and apathy and low morale among a population "which will not commit itself until the government can demonstrate a capability to protect the people and provide for their basic needs."[10]

In later testimony before a congressional committee, Johnson referred to "the low point, which I establish as March of 1965," adding "you can take the 1st of July 1965 if you wish."[11] He told a military audience much the same thing, saying, "in March of 1965 I saw a pretty desperate nation, and a pretty disconsolate group of leaders. As a matter of fact I think the word would be 'despairing' rather than 'disconsolate.' And they were on the verge of collapsing. Vietnam was on the verge of collapsing at that time."

Of particular concern were local defense forces, which had been provided scant training, equipped with only light weapons, and given little status or incentive in comparison with regular forces, even though "these are the forces which are bearing the brunt of Viet Cong attacks in the countryside today," said Johnson.[12] He praised the work of U.S. advisors, calling them "the glue which is holding the military effort together."[13]

In addition to the steps included on the McNaughton list, Johnson saw the need to deploy a tailored division force of U.S. troops, which he suggested should take over security of the Bien Hoa-Tan Son Nhut complex near Saigon, plus Nha Trang and Qui Nhon up the coast and Pleiku in the highlands. He conceded that this would not be adequate to reverse the deteriorating trend, but the proposal was "not made because it is militarily sufficient but because it may be the maximum action which is politically feasible within the U.S. at this time."

An alternative, which Johnson preferred, was to give the U.S. division responsibility for the security of Kontum, Pleiku, and Darlac Provinces, all in the highlands.[14] Whichever version was accepted, deployment of U.S. ground forces to Vietnam in division strength represented a major crossroads, and it was Johnson's recommendation that precipitated, if not originated, that fateful decision.[15]

Johnson in effect brought back a new intelligence estimate of enemy capabilities, along with a recommended set of reactions to the new appraisal, and put those directly and immediately before the decision makers in Washington. "It was in this institutionally unstructured context and by such ad hoc processes," held a later study, "that one of the basic issues of the war arose, was dealt with, and a decision reached."[16]

It was also essential, Johnson concluded, to cut enemy land infiltration from the north by establishing a force stretching from the sea across Quang Tri Province, just south of the 17th Parallel, and from there entirely across the Laos panhandle to the Mekong River. That would take an international force or, if only U.S. troops were employed, an estimated four-division force.[17]

This was a key point, and it restated a recommendation that Johnson had first made in August of the preceding year. After the war, many retrospective analyses would conclude that choking off the infiltration of men and materiel from North Vietnam was a sine qua non for successful prosecution of the war, but this was never achieved. It was, in fact, never even attempted on the ground, while intensive efforts to do so by air interdiction were never more than partially successful, driving up the cost to the enemy, perhaps sometimes slowing his operational tempo, but no more, certainly nothing decisive. Johnson understood how critical this was. "Isolate the battlefield, isolate the battlefield," he kept saying,[18] but it was never done.

In the wake of this trip, Johnson saw the situation in Vietnam in regional, or perhaps global, terms. He told an audience shortly after his return that the war in Vietnam was "a test of the greatest issue of our times: whether any non-communist government of an emerging nation can be overthrown by externally supported, covert armed aggression even when that emerging nation is backed by U.S. economic and military assistance."

MEETING WITH LBJ and his principal advisors at the White House, General Johnson also predicted that it could take 500,000 U.S. troops and five years to win the war. "His estimate shocked not just the president and me but the other chiefs as well," recalled Robert McNamara. "None of us had been thinking in anything approaching such terms."[19]

Most of General Johnson's proposals from the McNaughton list were approved, although not necessarily implemented as he had envisioned. "It wasn't a blueprint of what happened later," said Johnson, "but all that was proposed in there ultimately was adopted, but certainly not within the time frame that I assessed. I would guess . . . that I was guilty of an unstated assumption in that, when you commit forces, you commit them at the most rapid rate possible and not apply them at the rate of application of an eyedropper."[20] In other words, Johnson felt, he had failed to specify the obvious, and soon gradualism held sway.

In closing his report, Johnson raised the question of how much more the United States would have to contribute in support of South Vietnam. In the margin, McNamara wrote a prophetic blank check: "Policy is: anything that will strengthen the position of the GVN will be sent."[21] If a watershed had not yet been reached, one certainly impended.

"I felt that if something weren't done," said Johnson later, "Vietnam would fall within a matter of about six months, that it would require the commitment of ground forces in order to arrest the deterioration, and that something on the order . . . [of] about three divisions were going to be required in order to just establish a balance, and that it was going to take something above seven divisions to turn it around."

AN ANNUAL WASHINGTON EVENT is the Presidential Prayer Breakfast. It draws a large audience, mostly people in government, and features a prominent speaker. In February 1965, shortly before his directed trip to Vietnam, Harold K. Johnson had been that speaker, the first layman to be so honored, and of course the first soldier.

Johnson had been scouted for the occasion by Dr. Abraham Vereide, leader of the sponsoring International Christian Leadership. Vereide came to Johnson's Pentagon office and began the conversation by asking a direct question: "What kind of a man are you?"

Johnson was a little taken aback by the query. "Well, I guess I'm human," he began, then recited the whole history of his religious outlook from boyhood on. "The important thing to me," he concluded, "is to believe in the God Almighty." That was clearly a good enough answer.

Johnson moved his audience deeply with an account of his experiences as a prisoner of war, concluding with his favorite passage of scripture, a quotation from Matthew: "Let your light so shine before men that they may see your good works and glorify your Father which is in heaven."

The reaction to Johnson's presentation was overwhelming, and led to his deep involvement in the prayer breakfast movement in succeeding years, even when the press of business squeezed out most other outside activities. "Your message at the Presidential Prayer Breakfast was as 'apples of gold in pitchers of silver,' " wrote one approving correspondent. "We thank God that the head of America's army is yoked to the God of victorious battles."

There were invitations to address other religious audiences as well, giving Johnson an opportunity to tell a "Religion in American Life" conference in New York City about his nondenominational approach to religion. "I've spent a lot of time with a great many Chaplains and a lot of civilian pastors searching for a denomination," he said, "but which one of the 361 should I join? I don't know. The important thing to me," he said, reiterating what he had told Vereide, "is to believe in the God Almighty."

Dating at least from his days as Commandant at Fort Leavenworth, where in each succeeding year he was more overt in profession of religious convictions, Johnson brought the tenets of his faith into his dealings with soldiers. At the Army Infantry School at Fort Benning, for example, he told student officers how faith and service fit together. "I don't seek a zealot who is out recruiting for the Lord," he emphasized. "I don't seek someone who is criticizing his fellow man. I seek one thing among our people, and that is to conduct themselves so that they can face themselves in the mirror every morning and be proud of what they see. Religion is living and doing and giving."

A MONTH AFTER Johnson's return from Vietnam, LBJ brought the Joint Chiefs of Staff, along with McNamara, to the White House for an Oval Office meeting. "You're all graduates of the Military Academy and you should be able to give me an answer," the President said. "I want you to come back here next Tuesday and tell me how we are going to kill more Viet Cong." There it was again—body count; attrition; the whole sorry, unworkable, head-down, brute-force approach to prosecution of the war—and the troops were only just being launched. "I find myself, as I dictate this memorandum," Marine Commandant General Wallace M. Greene, Jr., wrote sadly of this event, "considerably alarmed over the current situation in Vietnam—the failure to understand it on the part of members of Congress and the American public—the lack of backing for the President in many quarters—the clear worry which he shows . . . and the fact that he does not seem to grasp the military details of what can and cannot be done in Vietnam."[22]

SOON HAROLD K. JOHNSON was back at Fort Leavenworth, speaking to the current class of student officers about what lay ahead. "Our basic purpose in the Army is not destruction," he counseled. "Our basic purpose is control" so as to establish a climate of order and stability in which government under law can function effectively. "We destroy only to the extent required to create this condition of order."

He knew, perhaps at this point better than anyone else, the sacrifices that lay ahead for these young officers. "We don't have a job," he told them. "We don't have a profession. We have within the Army a way of life that is an integral part of our country."

JOHNSON WAS NOW ACCEPTING a large number of speaking engagements, acting on his earlier prescription that the Joint Chiefs of Staff had an obligation to get out and inform the people about what was happening in Vietnam and to seek their support for it. One swing took him to the West Coast, where he was a dinner speaker at the Presidio of San Francisco, a historic old Army post. In the audience was a special soldier, and Johnson introduced him and spoke of their earlier service together. As a second lieutenant, he began, "I was granted the privilege of commanding a company in the 3d Infantry at Fort Snelling." He recalled how he had had a splendid first sergeant, a man named Frank Cumiskey, who had sat him down every afternoon and coached him on how things ought to be done in a well-run company.

That man was the finest teacher I ever had, Johnson said, and he is here tonight. Then he asked Colonel Frank Cumiskey, who had been commissioned during World War II, to stand and be recognized. It would be difficult to say which man was more proud of the other, but afterward, Cumiskey wrote to Johnson that "it was the most touching experience of my life. I don't know how many there saw my eyes when I arose and took a bow; but, I am sure, they fully revealed my feelings."

DURING LATE MARCH AND APRIL, Johnson sought the President's agreement to a full-scale mobilization. An assistant, Colonel Edward C. Meyer, was tasked to draw up a proposal. "The basis of it was that the war could not be won without calling up the reserves," Meyer later told Mark Perry. "It would show the American people we were serious." In May, the Joint Chiefs of Staff endorsed Johnson's initiative and asked for a private meeting with the President. LBJ received them, listened to the argument, then leaned across the table and said to Johnson, "General, you leave the American people to me. I know more about the American people than anyone in this room."[23]

DURING THAT BUSY SPRING OF 1965, Johnson also made a trip to Fort Bragg, North Carolina, to visit the Army's Special Warfare Center and School, then commanded by Major General William P. Yarborough. Johnson was given one of the demonstrations that had been raised to an art form by the Green Berets. As they were walking away, he turned to Yarborough and said, "I'm relieving you."

"But why?" Yarborough asked in disbelief.

"I thought he was end-running me and he wasn't being loyal to me," Johnson said later. He believed that Yarborough had a personal pipeline to the White House, and that's what he told him straight out.

Johnson had a point, but Yarborough was in a difficult situation. His classmate "Ted" Clifton was an aide to the President, and he was calling Yarborough on almost a daily basis with some input or another and, as Yarborough noted, "the interest of the President in Special Forces didn't really leave me much of an option." Yarborough realized that this was a problem for the Chief of Staff. "Johnny felt this very deeply, but it was in reality less me than it was the whole situation with a lot of political overtones."

Yarborough perceived that Johnson had probably come down intending to "tear a strip off me," as he put it, but when Johnson witnessed such a fine display, and found the men impressive in their appearance and attitude, his demeanor toward Yarborough had softened. "Just remember, I'm in command and you're not," Johnson reminded him.

Nevertheless, Johnson reassigned Yarborough to Korea to be chief of the United Nations Military Armistice Commission—"to his horror," said Johnson. After a few months, he brought Yarborough back into the Pentagon as an Assistant DCSOPS, and then made him one of his staff principals as the Army's Assistant Chief of Staff for Intelligence. From there, Yarborough went on to command of I Corps Group in Korea, with promotion to lieutenant general before concluding a distinguished career. Johnson hadn't held a grudge, but instead had given this talented officer an opportunity to work his way back into good standing.

Meanwhile, back at Fort Bragg, Johnson was told, things were looking up under a new commander, Brigadier General Joseph W. Stilwell, Jr. "He has taken action, with my support," reported XVIII Airborne Corps commander Lieutenant General John W. Bowen, "to disembarrass himself of certain individuals of limited ability and questionable loyalty. This metamorphosis has indeed been interesting to observe as an exhibition in revitalization after a prolonged period of inbreeding and organizational incest."

At one point, air assault field tests were conducted in a maneuver area based on Fort Jackson, South Carolina. "General Johnson came down from Washington and conducted a large-scale critique of the test activities," recalled Lieutenant General Robert E. Coffin, who was serving as chief of staff of the test and evaluation group of the 11th Air Assault Division. Unit commanders down to company level attended the session, and then, after dinner, Johnson gathered all the general officers involved in the living room of a little cottage where he was staying.

Johnson revealed that the President had asked for a recommendation about whether to send combat divisions to Vietnam, and he wanted to discuss whether an air assault division would be the best division to send. Johnson went around the room, asking each officer for his views, starting with the most junior. General Robert Williams remembered the occasion vividly, because what they had conducted was "a test of the air assault division in a mid-intensity conflict, and . . . we really hadn't given too much thought to how we would fight as an airmobile division in a counterinsurgency, or say a Vietnam-type of operation." When General Johnson posed the question, said Williams, "actually we had to stop and think and debate a little while. We hadn't even really thought about the airmobile division like the 11th Air Assault Division fighting in Vietnam."

General Johnson "listened intently to each of us," said Coffin. Some argued that the air assault concept had been fully developed and was ready to be implemented, but others thought that more time was needed. Each man had his say, with no discussion by the others. Finally General Charles Rich, who headed up the tests, summed up what the final written report was going to say.

The session lasted until one o'clock in the morning. "General Johnson courteously thanked us all," said Coffin, "said good night at the door, calling each of us by name, and said we had given him a great deal to think about in arriving at a decision."

When the tests were complete, it was time to decide whether to operationalize what had been achieved. All during the tests, said General Jack Wright, "we believed that we were going to Vietnam." While the written report was being prepared, Rich kept getting calls from Johnson asking about different aspects of the tests. It soon became apparent that he was wrestling with whether to recommend deployment of the division to Vietnam. Eventually he decided that it should be the first division sent. "General Johnson," said Coffin, "felt that an air assault force in Vietnam could change the whole nature of the war over there."

By early April 1965, the proposed deployments to Southeast Asia had, as the result of a CINCPAC planning conference in Honolulu, grown to a force of thirty-four maneuver battalions and supporting air and logistical forces, with the United States to provide twenty-four battalions, the Republic of Korea nine, and Australia and New Zealand a combined one. This amounted essentially to a three-division force. Later that month, McNamara went to Honolulu, where he met with Taylor and Westmoreland, out from Saigon, and other officials. From that conference came agreement to provide roughly half the forces being requested, although as it turned out, the rest would eventually be authorized. "The experience," observed an insightful study, "would prove to be a precedent for what became thereafter a characteristic pattern of the buildup—formal military requirements severely cut back, rejected, or ignored when tendered, then eventually fulfilled de facto in piecemeal increments."[24] By early July 1965, the proposed force had grown to forty-four maneuver battalions, thirty-four U.S. and the remaining ten primarily Korean forces, about a five-division force.[25]

At this point, the Joint Chiefs of Staff were tasked by McNamara to come up with a comprehensive strategic review of the Vietnam situation to determine what assurance the United States could have of winning the war "if we do everything we can." Lieutenant General Andrew J. Goodpaster was put in charge of an ad hoc staff group to conduct the study. The resulting "concept and appraisal," completed in less than two weeks, indicated that victory was possible given the establishment of a military force capable of seizing and retaining the initiative.[26] This result, noted the *Pentagon Papers,* was a *conditional* affirmative. " '*Within the bounds of reasonable assumptions . . . there appears to be no reason we cannot win if such is our will—and if that will is manifested in strategy and tactical operations.*' "[27]

The day after the ad hoc report was submitted, the JCS were authorized to alert the airmobile division and procure transportation in anticipation of moving it to Vietnam.[28]

AT THE END OF APRIL, another crisis, this one much closer to home, erupted in the Dominican Republic. President Johnson ordered U.S. forces, including the entire 82d Airborne Division, into the midst of a volatile situation. Lieutenant General Bruce Palmer, Jr., left his post as Army DCSOPS to take command of XVIII Airborne Corps and direct the operation, depriving General Johnson of his key deputy just as crucial decisions on Vietnam were pending.

So rapidly did Palmer move out that he missed a dinner in his honor that the Johnsons were hosting at Quarters One. In the Dominican Republic, Colonel Frank Linnell told Johnson, General Palmer was "the rock around which the shallow civilian waters babble and trickle."

There wasn't much discussion in advance of that deployment, Johnson recalled. LBJ "was convinced that this was another Castro-type operation, and he wasn't going to be tarred with losing the Dominican Republic to the communists, so he took the actions necessary to see that that didn't happen. And that was it." Those actions included establishing a reasonably neat and clean chain of command, sending an overload of troops, and gaining rapid control of the situation. A major advantage was the skilled State Department representative on the ground, Ambassador Ellsworth Bunker. Nevertheless, it was not until early December 1965 that the bulk of the 82d Airborne got back to Fort Bragg, and one of its brigades stayed in the Dominican Republic until late September 1966.[29]

"The Dominican Republic," said General Edward C. Meyer, "shows that General Johnson knew how to do it right, and how frustrated he must have been by not being allowed to do it right in Vietnam."

ONE EVENING IN LATE MAY, during a White House military reception on the South Lawn, the President told those present that he had recently been given a quotation from a Roman consul, and he read from it. Should any wish to advise me, the consul said, "Let him come with me into Macedonia and he shall be furnished with a ship, and a horse, and a tent, and even his traveling charges shall be defrayed. But if he thinks this is too much trouble and prefers the repose of city life to the toils of war, let him not on land assume the office of pilot."

"I know," LBJ told his military listeners, "that all of you in the services have made and are willing to make sacrifices wherever and whenever you are asked to make them. So I would like to present this quotation, as an expression of appreciation to every man in the service of his country, civilian and military, to a man who exemplifies the best in all of you, a man who is courageous but compassionate, a man who respects our civil institutions and yet always honors to the fullest his military duty, a man that I welcome to the role of assuming the office of pilot—General Johnson."[30] What occasioned that particular tribute is a mystery, but the amicable relationship it seemed to imply—if it ever had existed—was not going to last much longer under the strain of war.

IN MID-JUNE, McNamara announced additional Vietnam deployments to a level of 75,000 men. That proved to be merely preliminary to the fateful decisions of July. McNamara traveled to Saigon, where he conferred with Ambassador Taylor, General Westmoreland, and other senior U.S. and South Vietnamese officials. Upon his return, he put on the table a recommendation for additional troop deployments, a call-up of reserve forces, and extension of tours of duty.[31] The point of irrevocable commitment was at hand.

CHAPTER EIGHTEEN

JULY 1965

On 28 July 1965, Lyndon Johnson told the nation that he was sending 50,000 more troops to Vietnam and that draft calls would be increased. "Additional forces will be needed later," he added, "and they will be sent as requested."

The events leading up to this announcement are both profoundly troubling and fascinating, constituting a stew of expectations raised and shattered, decisions reached but concealed, and fateful choices made whose consequences were only dimly perceived. The antecedents went back as far as the previous autumn, but more immediately, the events stemmed from a 1 July memorandum from McNamara to the President in which he stated that "the situation in South Vietnam is worse than a year ago (when it was worse than a year before that)."[1]

McNamara consequently recommended that the President authorize building up to a forty-four-battalion force of U.S. and allied maneuver elements in Vietnam over the next several months, mining North Vietnam's harbors, and calling up about 100,000 men from the reserves. It was going to be a long-term commitment, he said, and "the test of endurance may be as much in the United States as in Vietnam."[2]

On Tuesday, 13 July, the day before McNamara departed on a hurried trip to Vietnam, his assistant John McNaughton sent to McGeorge Bundy at the White House a draft of the trip report McNamara intended to submit upon his return from Saigon. This somewhat unusual procedure was later explained by Adam Yarmolinsky, who helped draft the pre-trip version of the report, on the basis that McNamara "regarded his trips as theater, and, in fact, the report was usually drafted before he left and then revised in the light of what assessments they made of what people told them." In this case, the draft report included a recommendation that reserve forces be called.[3]

As McNamara left for Vietnam, an ad hoc study group headed by Lieutenant General Andrew J. Goodpaster, Special Assistant to General Wheeler, submitted a report that McNamara had requested twelve days earlier. The task had been to estimate the United States' chances of success in Vietnam "if we do everything we can." The study found that victory was possible, but convincing the enemy that they could not win would "require the de-struction as effective fighting forces of a large percentage of the main force battalions."[4] The report added that bogging down "in inconclusive jungle combat" would "represent failing rather than winning." And, in a wonder-fully prophetic insight, the study's authors observed that "if the war drags on and the VC are not effectively rooted out, popular sympathy could turn against the United States and a desire to end the war on any terms would grow."[5]

McNamara was in Saigon 16–20 July. There, he and General Wheeler met with Ambassador Taylor and General Westmoreland and were briefed on a forty-four-battalion plan (requiring thirty-four U.S. battalions, with the rest to be provided by allies) that, it was argued, would suffice to prevent defeat. An additional twenty-four maneuver battalions would be needed to seize the initiative in 1966, Westmoreland said. "Those meetings," McNamara later wrote, "reinforced many of my worst fears and doubts."[6]

The decisions being made at this juncture were fateful indeed for Harold K. Johnson and the Army he led, particularly when it came to mobilization of reserve forces. The Army, of all the services, was most dependent on its reserves, and was so structured that all contingency plans for commitments of any size were premised on full or partial reserve mobilization. Thus it is instructive to review the events of the next ten days as they pertain to the reserve forces.

During the deliberations in Saigon, McNamara received a cable from Deputy Secretary of Defense Cyrus Vance informing him that President Johnson had decided to go ahead with the first part of Westmoreland's troop request, and that he was "favorably disposed to the call-up of reserves and extension of tours of active duty personnel."[7] The President recognized that there would be resistance to such a call-up in Congress, but said that they would just have to "bull it through." Also, said Vance, "yesterday I met three times with highest authority [the President]. . . . I asked highest authority whether request for legislation authorizing call-up of Reserves and extension of tours of duty would be acceptable in light of his comments concerning domestic program, and he stated that it would."[8]

This cable is extremely significant in considering President Johnson's fail-ure to call up the reserves. Later accounts routinely attribute it to his reluc-tance to get into a fight with Congress and his fear that calling the reserves would jeopardize his much-prized domestic programs, explanations that have come to be the received wisdom on the matter. But only days before he turned down reserve mobilization, the President considered these factors and decided to go ahead and call the reserves anyway. This is a clear indication that, when he subsequently reversed himself and declined to call the reserves, there was a more proximate cause.

On Saturday, 17 July, having been informed by Vance that the President was going to approve Westmoreland's request, Assistant Secretary of State William Bundy prepared a checklist of actions that would need to be taken. Included on the list was preparation of legislation for calling up reserve forces and extending tours of duty of those already in active service.[9]

Late Monday evening, 19 July, McGeorge Bundy sent the President a memorandum in which he reported that Vance had gone ahead with "planning for the Reserve call-up, the extension of tours [of duty], and the increased draft calls which are foreshadowed in the military planning." In another memorandum sent to LBJ only minutes earlier, Bundy had referred to "those things which we have to do (like calling reserves)."[10]

On Tuesday, 20 July, McNamara issued a memorandum stating that, as noted by Marine Commandant Greene, the anticipated call-up of reserves "would be for a two year period; but his intention would be to release them after one year, by which time they could be relieved by regular forces if conditions permitted."[11]

On Wednesday, 21 July, the President met with McNamara, just back from Vietnam, Wheeler, and many others at the White House. McNamara summarized Westmoreland's requirements, noting that satisfying them would seriously reduce the Strategic Reserve and that, as William Gibbons phrased it, "action should be taken in 1966 to reconstitute the Strategic Reserves by calling up 235,000" from various reserve forces. "The President replied that when the time came to call up the Reserves 'he wanted a full statement of the situation in Vietnam which required additional troops.' "[12]

McNamara told President Johnson that in his judgment, "if the military and political moves are properly integrated and executed with continuing vigor and visible determination," the course of action recommended in his written report "stands a good chance of achieving an acceptable outcome within a reasonable time."[13]

On Thursday, 22 July, the President held a conference at the White House that included McNamara, the service Secretaries, and the JCS. Marine Commandant Greene told the gathering that in his opinion it would take five years and at least half a million U.S. troops to achieve victory in Vietnam,[14] the same prediction Harold K. Johnson had made in March. Responding to the President, General Johnson said that the least desirable alternative was getting out of Vietnam, and second best was doing what they were doing. "Best is to get in and get the job done."[15] Then LBJ asked, "What is your reaction to Ho's statement he is ready to fight for 20 years?"

General Johnson was unequivocal: "I believe it."[16]

Although there is much to criticize President Johnson for in his conduct of the war, one cannot help having some sympathy for him, in light of the often wildly conflicting advice he was getting from his senior aides and advisors, including those in uniform. General Wheeler, his senior military advisor, was often just flat wrong in what he told the President, and the meeting of 22 July provided a stunning example.

Major ground force deployments to Vietnam were the central issue on the table, and the President worried that North Vietnam would respond by pouring in more men of its own. "If we put in 100,000 won't they put in an equal number?" The President need not be concerned, soothed General Wheeler, because the "weight of judgment" was that the enemy "can't match us on a buildup."[17] That turned out to be one of the classic misjudgments of the war, comparable in wrongheadedness—and in grievous consequences—to General MacArthur's assurances to President Truman that Chinese forces would not intervene in the Korean War.

On Friday, 23 July, the U.S. Intelligence Board issued Special National Intelligence Estimate 10-9-65, which concluded that "if the U.S. sent large-scale troop deployments to South Vietnam . . . the Communists would respond by augmenting their own forces, including sending more North Vietnamese troops to the South, and by avoiding direct confrontation with U.S. forces. In response to heavier bombing of the North, the North Vietnamese would ask the Russians for greater air defense assistance, but even with heavier bombing of military and industrial targets their will to persist would not be significantly affected."[18]

Also on 23 July, McGeorge Bundy sent the President a revised version of the 19 July memorandum in which he had included calling reserves as an example of those things that had to be done. In this later version, calling reserves was no longer mentioned.[19] Something had apparently happened in the intervening four days.

And on 23 July, the President held a long meeting at the White House with McNamara, Wheeler, and a number of others. This session was devoted to consideration of three alternative plans presented by Wheeler, two of which included call-up of reserve forces. McNamara expressed a preference for one of those involving reserve forces. "The President, however," states Gibbons, "had decided that he should not call up the Reserves."[20]

Finally, late that same afternoon, General Greene was called to the office of Secretary of the Navy Paul Nitze, where he was told that Nitze had "new instructions which he had just received from the SecDef." The objective of the new instructions, Greene noted, was to meet Westmoreland's requirements for additional troops "and to hold down the political noise level (CHICOM [Chinese Communist] and Soviet reaction). The Reserves would not be mobilized."[21]

On Saturday, 24 July, General Johnson and Secretary of the Army Resor, along with their counterparts from the other services, met with McNamara in his office and were briefed on the announcement the President would make on 28 July. Johnson, knowing that such a session was imminent, had earlier that morning convened an emergency meeting of Army Staff principals to go over the kinds of problems they might have to deal with if Army forces were committed to Vietnam.[22]

McNamara covered the units that were going to be sent and their deployment schedule. Then he added, "And you'll do this without calling up the reserves." That was a bombshell. It "came as a *total* and *complete* surprise," said Johnson, "and I might say a *shock. Every single contingency plan* that the Army had that called for any kind of an expansion of force had the assumption in it that the reserves would be called." Moreover, OSD had approved all those plans, so the availability of reserves was not even thought to be in question.

Johnson immediately raised a caution flag. "Mr. McNamara," he began, "I haven't any basis for justifying what I'm going to say, but I can assure you of one thing, and that is that without a call-up of the reserves that the quality of the Army is going to erode and we're going to suffer very badly. I don't know at what point this will occur, but it will be relatively soon. I don't know how widespread it will be, but it will be relatively widespread." That was, as it turned out, an absolutely accurate prediction. McNamara just looked at Johnson, without any reaction or response, then moved on.

Admiral David L. McDonald, the Chief of Naval Operations, also challenged the decision not to call up the reserves. "The Secretary of Defense," noted General Greene, "exhibiting his usual suave side, smilingly replied that mobilization of the Reserves would indeed cause considerable debate, that a lot of minority votes would result, that there was certain to be a strong vote against a call-up, and that the Communists might get the wrong impression regarding division among our ranks."[23]

Following that session, Johnson discussed with Assistant Secretary of Defense Ignatius another serious problem: his concern about the inadequate amount of logistical support in the package LBJ was approving. The two men discussed the issue for hours. Finally, said Johnson, "I told him that if I were asked whether the money was adequate, that my response . . . [would be] that it was not adequate in my professional judgment."

Johnson returned to his office, only to be summoned by McNamara to explain his problem. "He told me that it was my job to tell him what I needed, when I needed it, and that it was his job to provide the material," said Johnson. "He asked if that were satisfactory to me." Johnson said that it was, whereupon McNamara "called in a secretary and dictated a brief two-sentence note."[24]

The President spent Sunday, 25 July, at Camp David, at one point meeting in Aspen Lodge with McNamara, Clark Clifford, and Arthur Goldberg, an Associate Justice of the Supreme Court who had just agreed to leave the Court and become U.S. Ambassador to the United Nations.[25] "Goldberg," wrote George Kahin, "joined Clifford in opposing McNamara's recommendation that the president call up the reserves. He recalls feeling so strongly on this point that," he said, " 'I advised the President that if he accepted this recommendation that I would withdraw my resignation from the Supreme Court.' "[26]

It is not known whether LBJ had prior knowledge of Goldberg's opposition to calling up reserve forces. If he did, however, and it preceded the decision not to call reserves announced by Johnson on 23 July, the question arises as to how much Johnson's desire to preserve the Supreme Court vacancy for his old friend Abe Fortas entered into the decision. It is apparent that some factor that came into play late in the game reversed Johnson's intention to call up reserves. All the general factors usually cited, such as desire to protect his Great Society programs and unwillingness to signal to the nation that we were going to war, pertained throughout this extended decision-making process and are thus unsatisfying explanations for the last-minute change of heart.

On Monday, 26 July, a politico-military game designated SIGMA II-65 began. It was the fifth in an ongoing series of games conducted over the past three years that had all concluded that "the bombing of North Vietnam and the use of large-scale U.S. ground forces in the South would not defeat the Communists, who would respond with greater force in an effort to inflict increasing casualties and to compel the U.S. to withdraw."[27] (When this game concluded on 5 August, General Wheeler directed a closing comment to McGeorge Bundy, Averell Harriman, Walt Rostow, Harold K. Johnson, other JCS members, and the rest of the senior-level discussion group: "As usual, we are frustrated. We haven't solved anybody's problems. We have just kicked them around again.")[28]

On Tuesday, 27 July, the National Security Council met in the late afternoon. "If Russia, England, etc. wouldn't get all excited about calling up reserves," said the President, "I would do it right now."[29] Afterward LBJ spent two hours with a group of congressional leaders. At that session the

President said that there were "good reasons for not calling Reserves. If you call 'em now you won't be really ready. You'll have it worked out better in January."[30]

Senator Everett Dirksen expressed concern that "we are stripping Europe components." McNamara responded heatedly: "Baloney on stripping. We are *not* stripping. It is not necessary."[31] That was a disingenuous assertion, as General Johnson could have confirmed. Just a month before, on a visit to Army forces in Europe, he had been briefed on problems in logistics, personnel, and facilities. The shortage of captains, in particular, was having a "severe impact," and platoon leaders were in such short supply that 23 percent of platoons were commanded by sergeants. And this was *before* the major deployments of troop units to Vietnam began.

At noon on Wednesday, 28 July, President Johnson told the American people that he was sending 50,000 more troops to Vietnam, for a total of 125,000, and that more would be needed and sent as requested. This would be done, he added, without calling up reserve forces. He did not mention that he had already approved the deployment of an additional 50,000, and that 100,000 more than that were already scheduled to deploy during 1966.[32]

LBJ had let his Defense Secretary think that he was going to call the reserves, had let him recommend that he do so, and had then at the last minute pulled the rug out from under him. And of course there would be no call-up of reserve forces in January, either, or in response to repeated recommendations from the Joint Chiefs of Staff in the coming months. This was clearly the President's doing, not that of McNamara, who later told Larry Berman that "because of what I considered to have been the essential role of the Reserves in resolving the 1961 Berlin crisis, I strongly favored calling them up in 1965."[33]

Nevertheless, when McNamara came to write his memoirs of the Vietnam era, he ignored the matter of mobilizing reserve forces. "It was not a key issue," he said. "I'm not even discussing it in my book."[34]

Others, particularly those who lived through the decision's impact on the Army, have a different outlook. "It's clearly a watershed in American military history," said Brigadier General Harold Nelson, a former Army Chief of Military History.[35] Harold K. Johnson agreed, saying of the failure to call reserve forces: "That was, I think, the greatest single mistake that was made." For his part, Westmoreland, the field commander, was totally uncomprehending. "It was General Johnson's decision to meet my relatively modest requirements by cadreing the Army rather than by insisting on a reserve callup," he maintained two decades later.[36]

There was one more thing. At his 28 July news conference the President also announced that he was appointing Abe Fortas to the Supreme Court seat being vacated by Arthur Goldberg.[37]

THE SUPERSTRUCTURE was growing apace, but no foundation had ever been established. Instead, as a later study noted, "the original introduction of ground combat units, the subsequent increases in numbers of troops in-country, and the projected deployment programs to commit yet more forces all, so far, lacked policy context or strategic perspective."[38]

In separate attempts, Johnson, Marine Commandant Greene, and Air Force Chief of Staff McConnell tried to remedy that crippling oversight, and in late August the JCS forwarded to McNamara a "Concept for Vietnam." The opening statement was: "In the light of the introduction of major U.S. combat units into Southeast Asia, the Joint Chiefs of Staff consider it essential that we further formalize our concept for the future conduct of the war."[39] In their paper the JCS stated the U.S. objective as that set forth in NSAM 288, "a stable and independent non-communist government" in South Vietnam, and postulated the steps they considered necessary to achieve that end.

The paper was never acted on by civilian authorities. John McNaughton shot it down, recommending that McNamara take no action on the grounds that the paper contained elements that were "clearly controversial and raise far-reaching policy issues."[40] William Gibbons called this JCS paper "the most definitive statement of its kind during the entire course of the U.S. involvement in the war."[41] Yet, found a definitive later study, it had had "no discernible impact."[42]

There was one significant result, however—a negative one—later pointed out by General Bruce Palmer. The failure of the civilian leadership to make any decisions on the basic strategic issues of the war, he said, "left Westmoreland in Vietnam to invent his own strategic concept, which he did."[43]

THE PRESIDENT'S REFUSAL to call reserve forces struck Army planners like a bombshell. As General Johnson had stressed, all contingency plans for an operation of this magnitude had been based on recourse to reserve forces. All the preliminary preparations had been made for a call-up. The Joint Chiefs of Staff had recommended a call-up, as had the Secretary of Defense. It was understood that the President was in agreement; indeed, he had told

Vance that he was. Then, at the last minute, LBJ went ahead with the buildup and deployment without reserve forces.

The President "met again at the White House with his key military and civil advisers," according to one account. "He announced he now favored a graduated military escalation that fell short of a decisive mobilization and proclamation of an emergency. McNamara made it clear he backed the President. General Harold K. Johnson and his JCS colleagues sat through this meeting in shocked silence. Their civilian superior, Robert McNamara, had abandoned them."[44]

Rapid and massive buildup of the Army without access to reserve forces quickly depleted the leadership pool and diluted maturity and experience levels. "While we tended to meet statistically the objectives of the expansion in terms of numbers," observed Johnson, "the individuals with whom we filled these slots, a lot of times, simply didn't have the requisite qualifications. They were promoted before they were ready." General Creighton Abrams succinctly characterized the increases as consisting entirely of privates and second lieutenants. It showed.

Johnson viewed this issue as evidence of cynicism and duplicity on the part of McNamara and his associates: "By assuming the call-up of reserve forces in an emergency," which had been the policy and the expectation, "OSD analysts could avoid creating support forces in the regular establishment, at a substantial annual reduction in the cost of the total active force."

When the Vietnam buildup was ordered without the use of reserves, "the creation of an active support force from a zero base proved to be costly to the Army in the sense of creation of new skills at the expense of the people involved. Unfortunately, computers and the people who manage them have little sensitivity to the personal problems of people." Here Johnson was undoubtedly referring to Enthoven's people in OSD Systems Analysis, and for him, it was more than an academic issue. "Since the attitude of people is the main determinant of willingness to fight, the cost of this attitude is enormous, and perhaps determines the fate of the nation."

MARK PERRY CONCISELY DEFINED General Johnson's approach to the war as "the Johnson plan—declare a national emergency, mobilize the reserves, get in, win, and get out."[45] Instead, Lyndon Johnson and Robert McNamara were going to try to do it incrementally, tangentially, almost surreptitiously. It would not work.

General Johnson, and probably the rest of his colleagues on the Joint Chiefs of Staff as well, knew that it would not work. Denial of access to reserve forces hurt the Army most of all among the services, for it had become the most dependent on reserve forces, especially for combat service support, in the event of war. Thus General Johnson persistently sought the call-up of reserve forces, and President Johnson stubbornly kept turning him down.

Besides denying access to reserve forces, LBJ also declined to extend the tours of duty of those currently serving. This was a body blow for units about to deploy, since it meant that they could not take with them their "short-timers" whose obligated service was nearing an end.

This news reached the 1st Cavalry Division, newly reorganized as an airmobile unit, virtually on the eve of its departure. Harold K. Johnson had visited the division earlier and, in a private meeting with the division commander, had advised Major General Harry W. O. Kinnard that the division would be going to Vietnam. The President was going to announce on television that the airmobile concept had been proven a success, that an airmobile unit designated the 1st Cavalry Division was being formed, and that it would be sent to Vietnam at once. And, Johnson said, "most important of all from the point of view of the Army and the country, was that [the President] was planning to announce that a state of emergency was in effect as of the time he made the statement."[46]

When LBJ came on television to address the American people, Kinnard and the handful of others at Fort Benning who had advance notice of what he was going to say were watching intently. They heard him say that the airmobile concept was a success, and that an airmobile division was being sent to Vietnam. And, said Kinnard, "we very expectantly leaned forward for the announcement about a state of emergency, and it never came."

The result was cataclysmic, with the division stripped of many of its trained personnel, replaced by fillers who lacked specialized training in airmobile tactics and operations and who had not been part of the extensive training and maneuvers that had developed essential teamwork and cohesion within the division's units. This came at "exactly the worst time," said Kinnard, "namely just as we were preparing to go to war." Aviation units had to give up more than 500 highly skilled pilots, crew chiefs, and mechanics.

The effect was devastating, recalled Lieutenant General "Hal" Moore, who was then a lieutenant colonel commanding a battalion in the division: "We were sick at heart. We were being shipped off to war sadly understrength, and crippled by the loss of almost a hundred troopers in my battalion alone. The very men who would be the most useful in combat—those who had trained longest in the new techniques of helicopter warfare—were by this order taken away from us."[47]

Under this policy, the situation was like trying to stop a hemorrhage with a perforated compress. During Fiscal Year 1966, for example, the Army had to induct and train more than 488,000 men in order to meet its strength objectives, because during the same period some 250,000 were released to return to civil life.[48]

The problems confronting Johnson and his staff were huge, even this early in the buildup, and they would soon become much worse. The shortage of qualified noncommissioned officers was a particular problem, said Johnson, that "continued to haunt the Army." There were just not enough NCOs to fill newly activated units and at the same time provide an adequate rotation base. As the war dragged on, "the difficulty was exacerbated by the growing disillusionment of the noncommissioned officers and their families, who could foresee repetitive tours to Vietnam with no relief in sight. The predictable outcome was a massive exodus from the Army."

FOR HIS RAPIDLY GROWING TROOP CONTINGENT, General Westmoreland settled on a strategy of attrition and tactics of search and destroy. The measure of merit under this approach became the body count, and the defining objective the so-called crossover point, that point at which enemy soldiers were being killed at a greater rate than they could be replaced by infiltration from the north or in-country recruitment in South Vietnam. To that end, Westmoreland mounted numerous multibattalion operations aimed at bringing enemy main force units to battle.

The 173d Airborne Brigade was the first major U.S. Army ground combat element sent to Vietnam, arriving in early May 1965. Thus, it was one of the first units to try out this approach. "After our thrashing around in the jungle on our first large-scale operation," said Brigadier General Ellis W. Williamson, the brigade's commanding general, "I was convinced that large operations of that type were not the way to go except when we knew in advance what the objective was. Having thousands of men fight in the high grass, brier bushes, large overlapping layers of vegetation, etc. is not productive in proportion to the effort expended."[49]

By August, Williamson was even more strongly convinced that this was not the way to fight the war. "I hope," he openly observed in a Commander's Combat Note, "that we have conducted our last 'search and destroy' operation. I am thoroughly convinced that running into the jungle with a lot of people without a fixed target is a lot of effort, a lot of physical energy expended. A major portion of our effort evaporates into the air."[50]

The 1st Cavalry Division (Airmobile) was the Army's first division force sent to Vietnam. Johnson had chosen the name, an adaptation of one of the Army's oldest designations, and it was a good one. General Paul D. Adams, commanding Strike Command, called the unit "a good cavalry division using helicopters for horses." Deployed in the immediate aftermath of LBJ's 28 July announcement, it closed in Vietnam by mid-September 1965. Only ninety-five days after being created from the reorganized 11th Air Assault Division, elements of the 1st Cavalry were engaged in combat.[51]

Things got off to a rocky start on the first day when General Kinnard, the division commander, reported in to Westmoreland, who greeted him by saying that he had "the perfect solution" for employment of the division—break it down into three brigades and scatter them around the country. Kinnard was horrified. "The fact is," he said, "Westy really did not understand the airmobile division. . . . He had been out of the country while we were doing this testing, and frankly did not understand it."

Several months before the 1st Cavalry deployed, General Johnson had visited the division. While he was there, he met privately with the division commander. "The one specific thing that I remember vividly," said Kinnard, "was again a mission-type order in which he said: 'Harry, your job with your division is to prevent the enemy from cutting Vietnam in two through the Vietnamese Highlands,' period."

Now Westmoreland wanted to fragment the division. Kinnard quickly made two points. "One was that H. K. Johnson, the Chief of Staff, U.S. Army, had made it very clear to me that my principal role was to keep the North Vietnamese from cutting the country in two, roughly from Pleiku right on down to Qui Nhon. Secondly, I said that the way this thing is tailored—like, for example, two lift battalions—the whole name of the game is to be able to concentrate your lift assets to give great mobility to all these people at once. Now, if you penny packet them all over the country, you have lost it. Fortunately," said Kinnard, "I was able to convince him of that."

IN THE AUTUMN, General Amano, the Japanese Chief of Staff, paid an official visit to the United States. In Washington, he was rendered honors in a ceremony at Fort Myer, then called on Johnson in his office at the Pentagon. That night the Johnsons gave him a black-tie dinner, and the next night they attended a dinner for Amano hosted by Ambassador and Mrs. Takeuchi at the Japanese Embassy. There Johnson made some remarks.

"He got up and without any rancor at all made a really very fine address," recalled Lieutenant General William Yarborough. "I thought that showed that he was a great Christian, and listening to him we all had lumps in our throats." How Johnson was able to do such things, given his long ordeal in World War II, was baffling to many people, but Johnson's daughter Ellen understood it. "He had a tough inner core," she knew. "He just went on with his life. He willed himself not to be bitter."

ONCE THE INITIAL ground force deployments had been approved, the command in Vietnam quickly submitted requests for even more forces, and the buildup of U.S. troops moved into high gear. As early as mid-October 1965, recalled Robert McNamara, "Westy's troop requests troubled us all. We worried that this was the beginning of an open-ended commitment. . . . I sensed things were slipping out of our control."[52] During the month leading up to the President's 28 July announcement, recalled McNamara, he had "spent countless hours with the Joint Chiefs in 'The Tank' debating Westy's shifting plans and requirements."[53] As soon became clear, that was only the beginning.

At this time, the *Washington Post* noted in an editorial that "General Harold K. Johnson, Army chief of staff, has introduced into the contemplation of events in South Vietnam an appropriate and timely note of realism to balance some of the enthusiastic and premature exultation over recent 'victories.' " It was important, stressed the *Post,* to demonstrate that the United States was "prepared for a prolonged commitment in South Vietnam if that is necessary to achieve our purposes. General Johnson's sober estimate of future requirements ought to help make that clear."[54]

It was also at this time, we learned much later, that Robert McNamara gave up on the war. McNamara's grudging testimony in the Westmoreland versus CBS libel trial included the admission that he had reached the conclusion "no later than mid-'66," and possibly "as early as the latter part of '65," that the war could not be won militarily.[55]

In his mid-October request, Westmoreland asked for 325,000 troops by July 1966, up from the 275,000 he had previously estimated that he would need. On 23 November 1965, he cabled that he would need 200,000 more troops in 1966, twice the number he had estimated as recently as July, for a total of 410,000 instead of 275,000. "The message came as a shattering blow," said McNamara, reflecting Westmoreland's outlook that the commitment was virtually open-ended, and bringing with it the probability of much higher U.S. casualties.[56]

In a special Joint Chiefs of Staff meeting the day after Westmoreland's message came in, Johnson commented on the impact of providing more replacements on short notice, including delays in activating new units being formed. "This looks like a shell game to me," he said. "He [McNamara] deals with the Joint Chiefs in one vein and then deals with the Service Secretaries in another way."[57]

In February 1966, only months after the first major increases, Westmoreland's requirements would raise the troop ceiling to 429,000. In 1967, he would be back with further requests for major augmentation beyond the 470,000 that by that point had been authorized. At that time, he presented two alternatives: one was described as a "minimum essential" add-on of 80,500 troops; the other was an "optimum" of some 200,000 additional troops, which would have brought the total to 670,000. In Washington, neither of these packages was approved; only a scaled-down addition to a new total of 525,000 was authorized.[58] Tolerance for additional commitments was running out.

DANIEL ELLSBERG, later infamous as the leaker of the *Pentagon Papers,* entered government service in August 1964. "I found myself with some surprise surrounded by a mood almost of conspiracy," he reported, "a situation where the people on the inside felt a great tension and discrepancy between what they thought was necessary for the nation and perhaps for their Administration, and what the public would allow them to do."[59] Certainly the uniformed military leadership confronted a similar situation in their dealings with the President and his defense secretary. Bill Moyers, a quintessential White House insider, told historian Henry Graff that President Johnson "relies less on military advice than any President since Wilson."[60] And LBJ, widely perceived as having nothing but disdain for military advisors, was quoted as saying dismissively: "The generals know only two words—spend and bomb."[61]

Besides hostility, the civilian hierarchy confronted their military counterparts with an admixture of arrogance and ignorance. "Military judgment was a term you just never even mentioned," said General James Woolnough, "because military judgment didn't mean anything to any of those people. They were new, and they just discovered the wheel." General Johnson cautioned Woolnough on this point when he first took over as the Army's personnel chief: "Your military judgment doesn't count for a thing. You have got to prove it statistically if you are going to sell it to these directors of today."[62]

Lieutenant General Harry Lemley, who succeeded Johnson as Commandant at Fort Leavenworth and later was brought in by him to be DCSOPS, laid it on the line about the Pentagon atmosphere. During the McNamara and Clifford regimes, he said, "there was an atmosphere of total dishonesty in the civilian hierarchy of the Pentagon." That didn't make prosecuting the war any easier. "Being in the Pentagon at that time was a pretty unpleasant sort of business," especially given the character of McNamara, whom Lemley came to regard as both "arbitrary and ruthless."[63]

Besides the lack of integrity permeating the civilian hierarchy, said Lemley, there was a strong antiwar element within the Pentagon itself. "I mean," he said, referring to the civilian staffers, "some of these people didn't really want us to win that war. I could see it from an official capacity."[64]

IN LATE AUGUST 1965 the Joint Chiefs had given McNamara a package of recommendations on basic U.S. strategy for Vietnam, including stronger air and naval pressures aimed at military targets, the supply base, and lines of communication. They asked that their views be laid before the President "without delay." McNamara refused to approve this package, very possibly setting up a dramatic—and humiliating—encounter between the Joint Chiefs of Staff and Lyndon Johnson only a few weeks later.

At some point the Joint Chiefs of Staff exercised their right to go to the President directly with their concerns about how the war was being fought. Lieutenant General Charles Cooper, who has detailed this traumatic event, dates it in early November 1965.[65] Cooper, then a major serving as the Marine aide-de-camp to Admiral David L. McDonald, Chief of Naval Operations, went along to handle the map when the Joint Chiefs of Staff met with LBJ, McNamara in attendance, at the White House. "This was," said Cooper, "to be the meeting to determine whether the U.S. military would continue its seemingly directionless Vietnam buildup to fight a protracted ground war or take bold measures designed to bring the war to an early, favorable conclusion."[66]

The primary objective of the Joint Chiefs of Staff was an increase in the scope and intensity of actions against North Vietnam, including mining and blockading the principal ports and more intensive bombing. "It was," thought Cooper, "make or break time for the Chiefs."[67]

The President did not offer his guests a seat. Instead, they stood around the map, with Major Cooper serving as a human easel. General Wheeler spoke first, then Admiral McDonald, with General McConnell adding a brief comment. All this took only a few minutes. LBJ asked Generals

Johnson and Greene if they agreed with what their colleagues had suggested. They did. Then, said Cooper, he witnessed one of the most disturbing and distasteful displays imaginable. LBJ turned away for a moment, then whirled on the assembled senior military leadership and attacked them in the most vile and despicable terms, cursing them personally, ridiculing their advice, using the crudest and filthiest language. They were, said Cooper, subjected to the worst side of a "venal and vindictive man." Dean Acheson had spoken of Lyndon Johnson's "swinish bullying boorishness which made his last three years unbearable,"[68] and the nation's senior military leadership was getting an undiluted demonstration of these appalling qualities.

Still screaming and cursing, LBJ told the Joint Chiefs of Staff that "he was not going to let some military idiots talk him into World War III" and ordered them to "get the hell out of my office!"

Those officers—Wheeler, Johnson, McConnell, McDonald, and Greene—continued to serve after this humiliation, Wheeler for almost five more years. It is difficult to imagine, though, that they retained any influence, any effectiveness, or any self-respect in future dealings with their Commander-in-Chief, or with the Secretary of Defense who had witnessed their degradation. "They were cowed, I'm totally convinced," said Cooper. "That was," said the Marine Corps' General Greene, "just the beginning of the President's treatment of the Joint Chiefs."

IN DECEMBER 1965, *Time* made General Johnson the subject of a cover story, featuring a portrait painted by Boris Chaliapin. John Mulliken, who had won a Silver Star while serving in the 7th Armored Division during World War II, reported the story. He quoted Johnson's view that "you can do whatever you will yourself to do," and he quoted Abrams on Johnson, "the toughest man I have ever known." Stripped across the cover was Johnson's observation that "the battlefield is a lonely place." And an editorial sidebar sympathized with Chaliapin, who had to accommodate Johnson's insistence that sittings for the cover portrait be scheduled at 7:30 A.M.[69]

DECEMBER 1965 ALSO FEATURED the annual pilgrimage of the Joint Chiefs of Staff and other officials to the LBJ ranch for a symbolic day of budget deliberations. This iteration was particularly painful. "I can recall vividly, vividly," said Harold K. Johnson, "when we were formulating the Fiscal Year 1967 budget . . . knowing [that] the money we were asking for was inadequate to the tasks that we saw ahead." For one thing, the strength increases announced by the President were, General Johnson knew, already overtaken by yet additional increases that had not yet been publicly revealed. "Now, then," said Johnson, "I have to ask myself, 'What should my role have been?' I'm a dumb soldier under civilian control who supports or doesn't support the budget that's advanced. I could resign, but what am I? I'm a disgruntled general for forty-eight hours, and then I'm out of sight. Right? Or, I can stay and try to fight and get the best posture that we can during this time." It was the same dilemma that confronted Johnson and the other members of the Joint Chiefs of Staff over and over on one issue after another. Johnson decided to stick it out—again.

WHEN HE WENT to Vietnam to spend Christmas 1965 with the troops, Johnson was very candid in discussions with senior officers. One of them later reported Johnson's views in a letter home. "He said that Mr. McNamara is beginning to show the strain," wrote Colonel Sidney B. Berry, then advisor to the 7th ARVN Division in My Tho, to his wife. "Growing more rigid and combative. Showing less and less give." Congress was gearing up to put McNamara through the wringer. "General Johnson says that he dreads this coming Congressional session more than any yet," Berry added.[70]

WITH THE BUILDUP of U.S. ground forces in Vietnam proceeding at a rapid clip, the next pressing questions—one could have argued that they were prior questions—were what those forces were there to do and what strategic concept their actions were meant to further.

The dismaying reality seems to have been that the senior civilian leadership did not think that a real war would be necessary. "There was an unstated assumption," suggested Harold K. Johnson, "that was held by many people, particularly among the civilians, that a demonstration of force on the part of the United States, a demonstration of determination, a willingness to react and respond, would so impress the other fellow that he would stop his subversive efforts. And of course this was a lousy assumption." What it led to was a perfunctory effort at going to war, doing it almost on the sly with no declaration of national emergency, no mobilization of reserve forces, only a piecemeal commitment of forces, indemnification of the enemy from any real threat to his own interests, and no enlistment of the national will to get the job done in a reasonable span of time.

As early as November 1964, Major General William R. Peers, then assigned in Army DCSOPS, had published an essay in *Army* magazine arguing that internal security in an insurgency environment could be attained only if the people wanted it. Thus the key task was to mobilize those human resources, not long-term deployment of large numbers of U.S. forces.[71] Harold K. Johnson understood this. Creighton Abrams understood it as well, as did Bruce Palmer, Jr. They were the three candidates to lead U.S. forces in Vietnam who had been passed over by Lyndon Johnson. William C. Westmoreland, LBJ's choice, did not understand this fundamental imperative, but was allowed by the Commander-in-Chief, the Secretary of Defense, and the Joint Chiefs of Staff to proceed as he did, disastrously.

It may be argued that it was not the prerogative of the Joint Chiefs of Staff to dictate tactical concepts to the field commander, and there was a high degree of self-inhibition on the part of individual members of the JCS in this regard. "The Joint Chiefs did not prescribe for General Westmoreland, generally speaking, the disposition of his forces and the manner in which his forces could be employed," said Johnson. "I don't think that the Joint Chiefs of Staff can run a war," he indicated, "nor do I think that a war can be run from Washington. . . . The trouble is that communications make it very tempting to run a war from Washington. Your information is sketchy, the pressures on you don't reflect the conditions on the battlefield. There are different kinds of pressures, and for the most part I don't think that they're consistent with what is going on on the battlefield."

The fact is that the Joint Chiefs of Staff were in a decidedly anomalous situation. They were not in the chain of command, but functioned as a sort of message center in passing directives from the Secretary of Defense to the unified and specified commands. As individual service chiefs, they had responsibility for raising, training, and equipping the forces deployed to those commands. They had some input, often largely cosmetic, when it came to budget formulation, and they were constantly being called on to testify before congressional committees, often on matters over which they had little or no influence.

Their statutory duties as a corporate body were confined primarily to the provision of military advice to the President and the Secretary of Defense, who were at liberty to ignore any or all of that advice, a privilege they exercised regularly. It could be, and often was, an immensely frustrating circumstance to be in. For "a group who by law are supposed to be [the President's] military advisors," said Johnson, "we saw him with a dreadful infrequency, particularly when you figure that there was a war going on for three of the years that I served."

Johnson maintained his own tabulation of the times he had met with the

President. Excluding ceremonial occasions, it amounted to thirty encounters during his four years as Chief of Staff. If sessions such as "luncheon honoring Westmoreland" and the National Security Council meetings that were largely stage-managed affairs are eliminated, there were at most thirteen occasions when General Johnson had an opportunity to talk about the war with his Commander-in-Chief: once in 1964, five times in 1965, once in 1966, four times in 1967, and twice in 1968.

Confirmatory testimony came from another member of the Joint Chiefs of Staff, Marine Commandant General Wallace M. Greene, Jr. Appearing before a House subcommittee in August 1967, Greene was asked to recall the last time the Joint Chiefs of Staff had met with the President to discuss the situation in Vietnam. "I told them in June 1966," fourteen months ago, said Greene.[72]

Military affairs commentator Hanson Baldwin later pointed out how dramatically different this situation was from the close contact between Presidents Roosevelt, Truman, and Eisenhower and the senior military leadership. "The Chairman of the Joint Chiefs of Staff," he wrote, "was the only member of the Joint Chiefs who saw the President with any regularity in the crucial years 1965–1968." As for the individual service chiefs, they "seldom saw the President privately. In the crucial twelve months from June 1965 to June 1966, when large numbers of US ground troops were committed to Vietnam . . . the Chief of Staff of the Army saw the President privately twice."[73]

"I don't think anybody understands the role of the Joint Chiefs of Staff," General Johnson once said, "including most of the Joint Chiefs of Staff. And I'm not sure I understand all that I ought to about them, although I think I understand it as well as almost anybody that's worked in that position." Certainly he devoted himself as assiduously to the role as any man ever has.

But just as surely the JCS had a mandate to advise the President on military matters, and if they perceived that the commander had embarked on a losing course of action, their responsibility as advisors could scarcely allow them to remain silent. At least one, Harold K. Johnson, now set out to do something about this situation.

CHAPTER NINETEEN

PROVN

The Westmoreland approach to fighting the war in Vietnam, as later events demonstrated conclusively, was not going to achieve allied objectives. Harold K. Johnson was strongly convinced of that fact, and early on. General William E. DePuy, who played a key role in development of that approach as MACV J-3, acknowledged that Johnson "was a counterinsurgency man 100 percent. He thought, and there were a lot of people in Washington that agreed with him, that Westmoreland and DePuy and his other henchmen out there didn't understand the war, that the war was a counterinsurgency and that . . . we were trying to get prepared for a big bashing of the North Vietnamese Army."[1]

That was right on target. Johnson was convinced that Westmoreland's approach was not working—indeed, could not work—and he had a sound basis for his views in a study he commissioned soon after returning from Vietnam in the spring of 1965. Entitled "A Program for the Pacification and Long-Term Development of Vietnam," and known as PROVN for short, that study was complete by March of the following year. Its conclusions would prove to be stark and disturbing and would have an enormous, although much delayed, impact on the American involvement in Vietnam.

Although the directive to undertake the study went out soon after Johnson's return from his March 1965 trip to Vietnam, the initiative had its origins much further back, reaching at least to Johnson's intellectual inquiries while he was Commandant at Fort Leavenworth.

Two men who were with Johnson at Leavenworth were particularly important in terms of the PROVN Study, Colonel Richard Clutterbuck of the British Army and Colonel Jasper J. Wilson. Clutterbuck had served in Malaya during the insurgency there and while assigned as British Liaison Officer at Leavenworth was doing some insightful thinking, writing, and lecturing on counterinsurgency. He and Johnson became good friends and kept up a dialogue on this topic. Much of what they discussed is reflected in a book Clutterbuck wrote, *The Long, Long War: Counterinsurgency in Malaya and Vietnam.* Not surprisingly, he asked Johnson to contribute the foreword. Clutterbuck's central point, one as applicable in Vietnam as in

Malaya, was simple and straightforward: "The first reaction to guerrilla warfare must be to protect and control the population."[2] But, he observed wryly, "the predilection of some army officers for major operations seems incurable."[3] That would not do the job and, in fact, got in the way of doing it. In Vietnam, observed Clutterbuck, "massive airmobile operations against big Viet Cong units have left few men available for harassment patrols," the real key to success.[4]

While he was Commandant, Johnson had assigned three officers the year-long task of researching the concepts of conflict and victory, and from that he drew some strongly felt conclusions. "I maintain that control is the object beyond the battle and the object beyond the war," he wrote in late 1964. "Destruction is applied only to the extent necessary to achieve control and, thus, by its nature, must be discriminating." That outlook, as soon became apparent, would inform every aspect of the PROVN Study.

Jasper Wilson went from Leavenworth to Vietnam, where he wound up as advisor to General Nguyen Khanh, helping plan the coup that brought Khanh—briefly—to the head of the South Vietnamese government. During this assignment, Wilson kept up an active correspondence with Johnson, who solicited his ideas on every aspect of the war. Johnson conferred with Wilson during a December 1964 trip to Vietnam, writing some further impressions while he was still on the road. "As usual," he told Wilson, "you gave me a good clue as to one of the studies we should undertake with regard to a long range outlook. I intend to do just that when I return, but it will require a good deal of thought and some breakaway from rather stereotyped thinking. I suppose that will be the single most important thought that I picked up on the entire trip." Interestingly, there is nothing about this in Johnson's trip reports. He had apparently decided that it was time to strike out on his own in seeking a solution to the problem of Vietnam.

Johnson's own observations during the four trips he had by now taken to Vietnam were also important in shaping his outlook, and even before this most recent foray he was expressing the view that "unfortunately, the heavy armament of the aircraft is largely wasted against the type of target found out there, unless our basic purpose is to flatten the countryside. At this point, that isn't our purpose." From what he had seen, though, that wasn't understood in the field. "General Johnson once observed dryly," said Sergeant Major Wooldridge, "that the attrition war worked against his soldiers more than the enemy. I believe this 'flawed' policy, as he referred to it, was what led to the decision to launch a full study of the war and attempt to turn around a policy that simply was not working."

When Wilson came back from Vietnam, he found himself assigned to the Office of the Chief of Staff as Special Assistant to Harold K. Johnson. "General Johnson gave him an office, a desk, a pad and a pencil. 'Write on Vietnam,' he told him. That was the beginning of PROVN," recalled Tom Hanifen.

Another precipitating factor of the PROVN Study took place in late April, when Johnson scheduled a discussion with Bernard Fall, a journalist known for his expertise on Southeast Asia. The staff sent in a talking paper for Johnson's use during the conversation, but every time Johnson mentioned something the staff had told him, Fall pointed out how it was erroneous. Afterward, Johnson described the experience for Wilson: "As a result of my discussions with Dr. Fall, I conclude that I am the victim of appreciable misinformation concerning cliques, claques and the variety of outlooks and objectives of the diverse elements that comprise the population of Vietnam."

Johnson asked Wilson to talk with Fall and then—drawing on the work he had already done—prepare an expanded outline of a study that the staff could undertake. "I do not want this to take a dialectical form," Johnson specified. "I want it to address specific problems and specific actions that are designed to alleviate specific problems. If a problem is complex, I want it broken down to proportions which are manageable. I would like a practical time schedule, even if it takes fifty years."

The resultant PROVN Study was conducted by ten carefully chosen and talented officers of diverse backgrounds and experience, two of whom eventually became four-star generals. The specified mix was a historian, a political scientist, an economist, a cultural anthropologist, and specialists in intelligence, military operations, psychological operations, and economic assistance, and the group that was assembled matched up pretty well.

Of the nine working members, three were West Pointers, one of them a Rhodes Scholar, while others were graduates of Washington, St. Lawrence, Wichita, Notre Dame, Michigan, and Harvard. All but one had master's degrees, earned at Tulane, Vanderbilt, Alabama, Pittsburgh, Georgetown, Harvard, and Oxford in such fields as international relations, psychology, and political science, and one held a doctorate in anthropology from Harvard.

All but one had graduated from the Army Command & General Staff College. Three were also graduates of the Armed Forces Staff College, one was a graduate of the Air War College, and another was an Army War College graduate.

One woman and eight men made up the team, and they ranged from thirty-two to forty-five years of age. Their branches included Infantry, Armor, Signal Corps, Women's Army Corps, Military Police, Engineers, and Army Intelligence & Security. Most had already served in Vietnam, their assignments there ranging from sector advisor to MACV staff officer. One had served there with the Agency for International Development, and the deputy director had spent two years with a military assistance group in Thailand. Six were qualified parachutists; two others were Ranger qualified, one of them also a senior parachutist.

The nominal chairman was the Director of Strategic Plans and Policy in the Office of the DCSOPS, but the de facto chair was Colonel Thomas J. Hanifen, an Armor officer also working in DCSOPS.

Hanifen had been handed one very hot potato. As the pressure of time and the import of how the study's findings were shaping up weighed on Hanifen, he became increasingly distraught, on at least one occasion weeping in frustration at the team's inability to reach agreement on some point. "We pulled Tom back and forth across the sharp edge of our discussions—without mercy," recalled one team member. Sometimes, unable to sleep, Hanifen would get up in the middle of the night and go back to the Pentagon, where other members of the team would see that his safe had been signed open at 2:30 in the morning or some such. Sometimes he slept on his desk. Hanifen "felt terrible pressures," said Art Brown, the historian of the group. "He had trouble riding herd on this very diverse and opinionated group."

The anthropologist was Don Marshall, a Harvard-trained Ph.D. and a reserve officer on extended active duty. "Don Marshall was in a class by himself," exulted Hanifen. "Goddamn, he was a worker!" Marshall also proved to be the connecting link between the PROVN Study and PROVN implementation when General Creighton Abrams had him head up long-range planning later in the war. Hanifen encountered Marshall then and found that he hadn't slowed a step. "He was sleeping on a cot in the J-5 office when I went to MACV," he said.

Dan Schungel, who would later kill a Russian-made tank with an LAW light antitank weapon at Lang Vei Special Forces Camp, was recognized by everyone as the warrior in the group. Art Brown had been brought from the Combat Developments Command. Ames Albro was en route to England, with his household goods already shipped, when he was pulled in to be the economist. Anne Doering, born in Hanoi when her father was there with Standard Oil, was the WAC member. Volney Warner had just returned from a tour as a province senior advisor in the Delta. Chuck Emmons was the intelligence man, John Granger a Military Police member, and Harry Jackson another Infantryman.[5]

The study directive was published in late June 1965. A month later the team was assembled and at work. "The time has long since passed when a broader look at this situation [in South Vietnam] should have been taken," Johnson told them, for the directive reproduced exactly his language in the memorandum to Jasper Wilson. "I would like you to stand away from the problem and examine it from the broadest possible perspective."[6]

While the study was under way, Johnson sometimes dropped in on the team in what Don Marshall called their "airy dungeon under the Mall parking lot"—really a sort of shelf or balcony located in a big computer room in a subbasement of the Pentagon. There was constant background noise from the whirring of all the machines, and it was hot in summer and cold in winter, reminiscent of being in the bowels of a big ship. Hanifen set the official duty day as seven in the morning to seven at night, six days a week, but even so, a lot of overtime got logged.

Some members of the study team met with Henry Kissinger once or twice; a couple of them had a session with Bernard Fall—meeting with him secretly for some unknown reason. They also had people talk with General Edward Lansdale at Airlie House. Some members of the team made an extended research trip to Vietnam, and others analyzed completed questionnaires from several hundred officers who had served in Vietnam, many as advisors to the South Vietnamese. "Almost none of the respondents," said the final report, "recommended the use of 'large sweeps' against the VC."[7]

There was a lot of cross-fertilization taking place, because in speeches Johnson used things that later showed up in PROVN, and PROVN incorporated things he had espoused before the study began. Harry Jackson put together some maps that proved to be of interest, with one set of overlays showing where the resources—rice, fish, and so on—were located, and another set showing what areas were controlled by the Viet Cong. "Naturally," said Art Brown, "they were the same areas. The VC were in there with the rice and the fish. What we had was the places where nothing was." During work on the study, said Hanifen, "I dropped off pieces to General Johnson that he could use." Pieces like those maps really drove home the futility of beating around out in the boondocks.

As the study was nearing completion, Johnson went to Vietnam to spend Christmas 1965 with the troops. While there, he assembled a group of colonels and sought their views on how the war was progressing. "We just didn't think we could do the job the way we were doing it," recalled General Edward C. Meyer, one of those who met with Johnson and himself a future Chief of Staff. Many others told Johnson that it wasn't working, a view reinforced by another commander who said that he had pleaded with Westmoreland to "end the big unit war" and told Johnson, "we're just not going to win it doing this."[8]

"It was clear that General Johnson was not happy about how the war was being fought. He looked at that huge base camp at An Khe. He said that was not what he had envisioned—a third to a half of the division tied up on base camp security. He had wanted the forces to be dispersed throughout the area of operations. That troubled him," said Meyer. Thus the visit strongly reinforced Johnson's misgivings about how things were going in the combat zone.

EVEN THOUGH eight months had been allowed for the study, its scope was so comprehensive that intensive effort was required to get the work done on time. Near the end, a major crisis threatened to destroy the timetable. Ben Heck was a junior enlisted man assigned to the team as a graphic artist. Before getting drafted, he had been with *U.S. News & World Report,* and he was a terrific artist, if not a very enthusiastic soldier.

At some point, Heck got tired of parking in the far reaches of the Pentagon lot, so he took to parking wherever he felt like it, much closer in. This netted him a steady stream of parking tickets, all of which he tore up and threw away. Then Heck noticed that a privileged few were able to park right at the entrance to the Pentagon, and that they had special little colored windshield stickers authorizing them to do so. Heck was an artist. Pretty soon he had a decal of his own, and every day he parked in close-in splendor.

Unfortunately for Heck, he did not know that periodically the decals were changed to a new color, and that all authorized parkers were issued new decals in advance of the changeover date. When that day came, he stood out conspicuously as the sole parker with the old color, and they nailed him. That brought the pile of outstanding parking tickets to light, and Heck was fined $100—a lot of money in those days, especially for a junior enlisted man. Heck couldn't pay, and it looked like he was headed for jail.

The plain fact was that the PROVN team needed Heck, and they needed him right away. A conference was held, and a solution arrived at. Each officer put ten dollars into the kitty, Heck was bailed out, and the study was back in business.[9]

WHEN THE PROVN STUDY was finished and briefed to General Johnson, he made only one change, directing that a chronological tabulation of statements by various U.S. presidents, a listing that demonstrated considerable inconsistency over the years, be dropped. "I will not put into print something that would embarrass the President," he told the study team.

THE PROVN STUDY'S RESULTS were published on 1 March 1966. Their tone was revealed by the following quotation, prominently displayed at the top of the title page:

> Modern wars are not internecine wars in which the killing of the enemy is the object. The destruction of the enemy in modern war, and, indeed modern war itself, are means to obtain that object of the belligerent which lies beyond the war.
>
> War Department
> General Order No. 100
> 24 April 1863

That was familiar language, and Johnson had been using it since his Leavenworth days in speeches on the war. The previous year, for example, he had told the National Guard Association that "military force ... should be committed with the object beyond war in mind." And, he said, "broadly speaking, the object beyond war should be the restoration of stability with the minimum of destruction, so that society and lawful government may proceed in an atmosphere of justice and order."

That opening also made it clear that body count, the centerpiece of Westmoreland's approach to waging war, was not going to be high on the study's list of priority objectives in Vietnam. What was at the top of the list—indeed, the heart of the entire study—was security for the people living in the hamlets and villages of South Vietnam. "PROVN contends," read the foreword, "that people—Vietnamese and American, individually and collectively—constitute both the strategic determinants of today's conflict and 'the object ... which lies beyond' this war." Thus the imperative was clear: "The United States ... must redirect the Republic of Vietnam–Free World military effort to achieve greater security."

"The critical actions are those that occur at the village, the district and provincial levels," read the study's summary statement. "This is where the war must be fought; this is where the war and the object which lies beyond it must be won." And, recalled Secretary of the Army Ailes, "the guy who said 'the object beyond the war' was Johnny." PROVN was very clear on what that object was: "a free and independent non-communist nation."[10]

As early as 1964, Johnson had expressed at a military symposium his view that "the time appears to be at hand to extend our thinking to embrace counterinsurgency operations ... [as] a normal third principal mission of the Army, going hand in hand with [missions for] nuclear warfare and conventional warfare"—comments that the PROVN Study quoted approvingly.

By contrast, as Johnson subsequently observed, search and destroy operations in remote jungle regions produced no lasting effects and were irrelevant to security in the villages. He called the large unit action "something like the elephant tromping down, and a lot of stuff sprayed away." He was totally in accord with the PROVN Study, which held that the battle for the villages was the central battle, that "all other military aspects of the war are secondary." "At no time," said PROVN, "should US-FW [Free World] combat operations shift the American focus of support from the true point of decision in Vietnam—the villages."[11]

It seemed clear to Johnson that the effort expended in the large search and destroy operations would have been more effective if it had been spread out over a larger area and maintained for a longer period. What being more effective meant to Johnson was "being effective in digging out the infrastructure of the Viet Cong, and being more effective in that with the infrastructure gone the legitimate government could govern effectively in those areas."

Early on Johnson had been appalled by the enormous amount of unobserved firepower being splashed around in Vietnam, and things didn't seem to be getting better. On a visit in August 1967, Johnson asked how much of the artillery fire was observed, and he was told 6 percent. This, too, was reflected in the PROVN Study, which noted that "aerial attacks and artillery fire, applied indiscriminately, also have exacted a toll on village allegiance." In other words, the very operations that were supposed to be protecting the villagers were harming and alienating them. This was clearly no way to "win the hearts and minds" of the people. "Discontinue unobserved artillery fire in populated areas," PROVN flatly recommended.

Operationalizing the strategic, tactical, and political insights of PROVN were a total of 140 near-term recommendations, along with others that applied to midterm and longer-range objectives.

THE STUDY WAS PREPARED under the nominal supervision of the DCSOPS, and when it was finished, the team took it to Lieutenant General Vernon P. Mock for approval. Mock was well-known for his caution and self-protective skills as a bureaucratic politician—"he spent his time on the puce-colored tabs," said Hanifen, rather than the substance of a paper—and he apparently lacked a sense of how this study was going to be received. He also seemed unaware of the ongoing interaction between Johnson and members of the team and of how much Johnson's own views and values permeated the final product.

In any event, Mock refused to sign off. "If you want it signed," he told the young officers who had just devoted eight months of their lives to the project, "you can get one of the char force to do it." Eventually someone signed off on the thing, maybe one of Mock's assistants, and the study went to meet its fate.

Lieutenant General Charles Bonesteel, a cerebral and immensely respected officer then serving as Director of Special Studies for General Johnson, provided some thoughts on how PROVN should be presented. "First," he began, "I want to say that I think the study is a highly professional, profound and useful analysis which really has dug into the real-life problems." As for uses to be made of it, said Bonesteel, "I would personally recommend that it receive selective distribution outside the DA. . . . It could be distributed on the basis of being a thinkpiece rather than any 'Army position.' " Bonesteel added that "timing is vitally important today and I feel that if we try to reconcile all the many divergencies which will arise within the Army family if we try to come up with a fully staffed and approved 'position,' we will find that we have missed the boat and failed to influence the Presidential level decisions which are already being made and which will have to be expanded in the near future. Time and tide wait for no man—not even the Army!"[12]

In classic Pentagon fashion, PROVN was briefed at one layer of command after another. The Joint Chiefs of Staff were an early audience, with Don Marshall making the presentation. He began by referring to "the current lack of understanding of what the war in Vietnam actually is all about," probably not what the JCS wanted to hear or how they perceived their own grasp of the situation.[13] "The thing that caused the most interest by far," remembered Marshall, "especially in General Wheeler—they were just fascinated by it—was a display where I had put all the province maps together on a single overall map. My interpretation was that they had had no idea of the smallness of the blue and the largeness of the red and the orange."[14] But fundamentally the Joint Chiefs of Staff were more concerned with limitations on the larger war—bombing restrictions, prohibition of attacks on enemy sanctuaries and mining of enemy harbors, restrictive rules of engagement—than they were with the war inside South Vietnam.

General Wheeler was clearly more interested in those matters than he was in pacification, as he had indicated when he took over as Chairman. "It is fashionable in some quarters to say that the problems in Southeast Asia are primarily political and economic rather than military," he said. "I do not agree. The essence of the problem in Vietnam is military."[15]

An officer who was close to him suggested that Wheeler also was reluctant to push PROVN's findings actively to the Secretary of Defense or within the JCS because of how critical PROVN was of the way the war was being conducted. Those findings would open up another avenue of attack for the OSD civilians to use against the military services.

Beyond that, the JCS were loath to interfere with the field commander's conduct of the war, an outlook with deep roots in military custom and tradition. All this meant that with respect to PROVN, the JCS, whose endorsement of the study might have made a difference, laid low. "In any event," said Marshall, "the PROVN Study was not forwarded to the White House by the JCS. Instead, it made its way there by other means. We used to say that, instead of going over the river to the White House, PROVN went under the river."

Things did not go well when the study was briefed to McNamara, either, or so the study team concluded at the time. "It was a miserable briefing," said Volney Warner. "McNamara didn't like what he heard, and didn't want to hear it." Plus the power failed for the overhead projector, and they wound up passing the visual aids hand to hand. Nevertheless, as would soon become apparent, the outcome was not as unpromising as it first appeared.

PROVN briefers also went to the Far East for presentations in Honolulu and Saigon. The briefing at CINCPAC Headquarters in Hawaii was particularly rough, because PROVN pointed out the need to simplify the chain of command for Vietnam and recommended that CINCPAC be taken out of that chain. "We wanted a unified command that would control all air, ground and naval operations in the theater," said Art Brown, "and that guaranteed opposition from CINCPAC [at the time Admiral U.S. Grant Sharp] when the study went forward."

Westmoreland heard PROVN briefed in Honolulu, where he was on leave when it was presented to CINCPAC.[16] "Westmoreland knew all about PROVN," confirmed Volney Warner. "He'd read PROVN." The briefers went on to Saigon, where they made a presentation at MACV Headquarters, and in due course MACV was called on to provide comment on the finished report. "I wrote Westmoreland's response to PROVN," recalled Colonel Herbert Schandler. "We all thought it was great stuff, but we couldn't say that. We had to write things like 'there are some good ideas here for consideration' and so on." Schandler also included comments such as "we are implementing many of these programs already" because, he said, "General

Westmoreland wanted to show he was ahead of the game." It was painful
to have to draft such a response, said Schandler, because at the working level
of the MACV Staff the reaction to PROVN was enthusiastic. "We thought
it was great!"

The PROVN team saw MACV as a second enemy. "I think General
Johnson was not able to communicate with Westmoreland," said General
Donald V. Bennett, who as a brigadier in DCSOPS had helped oversee the
PROVN Study. "Even later Westmoreland didn't understand what he was
talking about."

In any event, Westmoreland's headquarters was obliged to reject out of
hand the PROVN findings, because they repudiated everything Westmoreland was doing. "The COMUSMACV recommended the study be presented
to the National Security Council for use in developing concepts, policies,
and actions to improve effectiveness of the American effort in Vietnam,"
Johnson said in the *Weekly Summary*. Meanwhile, said Thomas Scoville,
Ambassador Lodge heard about PROVN "and demanded of MACV that if
they didn't give him a copy, he would go to much higher sources and make
them give him one."[17]

Lieutenant General Phillip Davidson, who had served as Westmoreland's
J-2, wrote that "the study deserved more mature consideration. Its execu-
tioner was General Westmoreland, and while he does not even mention
PROVN in his memoirs or in his *Official Report on the War,* his reasons for
throttling it are obvious. PROVN forthrightly attacked his search and destroy concept. . . . He could not embrace the study's concept . . . without ad-
mitting that he and his strategy were wrong." But later, said Davidson—
who had an excellent vantage point, as he stayed on for a year as J-2 for
General Creighton Abrams—the study "would rise again as 'Son of
PROVN' in 1969, and then, under different circumstances and a different
commander, would gain support and credence."[18]

By July 1966, Johnson told his general officers via the *Weekly Summary*
that the study had been briefed to the Joint Chiefs of Staff; the Commander-
in-Chief, Pacific; the Commander, U.S. Military Assistance Command; the
Commander-in-Chief, U.S. Army, Pacific; the Commander-in-Chief, U.S. Air
Force, Pacific; the Secretary of the Army; and the Secretary of Defense.
Johnson provided a summary of the study's key findings in this publication,
which was distributed to every Army general officer worldwide. So even at
this early date, PROVN's essence was widely known.[19] Subsequently, the JCS
authorized distribution of PROVN within the Department of Defense, and
in September 1966 Secretary McNamara authorized distribution to government agencies outside Defense.

Once the study had been published, Johnson made its conclusions a staple of his public remarks. At Fort Benning the month after the final report was released, he observed that "the Viet Cong political cadre structure throughout the countryside has by no means been put out of action. It is very much intact, and will continue to be a threat to stability in South Vietnam until it is rooted out by the Vietnamese themselves."

Besides the emphasis on neutralizing the enemy infrastructure, Johnson stressed the importance of local security as opposed to operations of the regular forces. "In the last analysis," he explained, "it is this fellow that's guarding the peasant night after night and keeping his throat from being slit that is going to be the important security factor out there." Jasper Wilson kept hammering on the basic theme as well, stressing to Johnson a year after PROVN that "the basic objective . . . remains the *people and their security. We must offensively take this objective.*"

IN THE SUMMER OF 1966, not long after PROVN was published, Secretary McNamara made another of his periodic trips to Vietnam. Afterward, recalled General Donn Starry, who was then a colonel assigned to the MACV Staff, "Westmoreland had us do an analysis of the prospects for conclusion of the war," responding to a question McNamara had posed during his visit. "We said that it would take one million Vietnamese, half a million US, and ten years." That wasn't a very palatable forecast, and "Westmoreland wouldn't send our analysis. He said it was politically unacceptable." Meanwhile, McNamara's staffers kept demanding that MACV respond to the Secretary's question. "So finally," said Starry, "Westmoreland sent it, but with a disclaimer. He said the war was going to be over in the summer of 1967."

DURING 1966, Secretary McNamara's Systems Analysis office, under Alain Enthoven, analyzed combat operations in Vietnam and determined that the strategy of attrition was not working and could not work, not least because of the enemy's ability to control his losses and to make up losses far greater than those the allies were able to inflict. Those findings were conveyed to McNamara.

Systems Analysis also completed work that was severely critical of the effect of huge amounts of unobserved fire delivered by U.S. forces on the Vietnam battlefield, an aspect of the war that had greatly troubled Harold K. Johnson since his earliest visits to Vietnam. These findings were also brought to McNamara's attention by Enthoven.

Yet other work in Systems Analysis documented the far greater effectiveness of small long-range patrols as compared with the multibattalion sweeps favored by Westmoreland. McNamara was made aware of this work, too. In Vietnam, meanwhile, American forces continued the operations that Systems Analysis found so flawed.[20]

IN MID-NOVEMBER 1966 the real impact of PROVN, at least within the inner councils of government, became apparent in the pages of a Draft Presidential Memorandum prepared by McNamara. "We now face a choice of two approaches to the threat of the regular VC/NVA forces," he began. One approach would involve further increases in deployed U.S. forces, using them "primarily in large-scale 'seek out and destroy' operations to destroy the main force VC/NVA units." That was what MACV was busy trying to do. McNamara laid out the "distinct disadvantages" to that approach, including "very strongly diminishing marginal returns" as more and more U.S. troops were put in the field.[21]

A second approach would involve building U.S. forces only to that level necessary "to neutralize the large enemy units and prevent them from interfering with the pacification program." A portion of the U.S. force, in a departure from the current practice, would "give priority to improving the pacification effort. The enemy regular units would cease to perform what I believe to be their primary function of diverting our effort to give security to the population." And, added McNamara, "I believe it is time to adopt the second approach."[22]

In this key document, perhaps for the first time on the record, McNamara expressed dissatisfaction with the effectiveness with which Westmoreland was using the troops he already had. "It may be possible," McNamara wrote, "to reduce enemy strength substantially through improved tactics or other means . . . , but further large increases in U.S. forces do not appear to be the answer."[23]

Then, in words that could have been drawn directly from PROVN, McNamara critiqued the current tactical approach. "The large unit war," he argued, "at which we are succeeding fairly well, is largely irrelevant to pacification as long as we keep the regular VC/NVA units from interfering and do not lose the major battles." Furthermore, search and destroy missions, by definition, enter an area and then move on, failing to provide any lasting security for the people. Thus, said McNamara, "the most enduring problems are reflected in the belief of the rural Vietnamese that the GVN [government of South Vietnam] will not stay long when it comes into an area but the VC will; the VC will punish cooperation with the GVN; the GVN is indifferent to the people's welfare; the low-level GVN officials are tools of the local rich; and the GVN is excessively corrupt from top to bottom."[24]

Search and destroy didn't help solve these problems. "Success in changing these beliefs," McNamara stressed, "and in pacification, depends on the interrelated functions of providing physical security, destroying the VC organization and presence, motivating the villager to cooperate, and establishing responsive local government." A new approach was urgently required. "Physical security must come first and is the essential prerequisite to a successful revolutionary development effort. The security must be permanent or it is meaningless to the villager, and it must be a well organized 'clear and hold' operation continued long enough to really clear the area and conducted by competent military forces who have been trained to show respect for the villager and his problems."[25]

The key task was to provide "permanently secure areas" in which to "root out the VC infrastructure and establish the GVN presence," McNamara concluded. "This has been our task all along. It is still our task. The war cannot come to a successful end until we have found a way to succeed in this task."[26] That was exactly what PROVN had been advocating. Before long, with McNamara's backing, Robert Komer would be deployed to Vietnam as a deputy to the COMUSMACV for pacification support, and the formerly disparate elements of American support for pacification would be pulled together under the COMUSMACV, just as recommended by PROVN. McNamara had been listening after all.

THERE WERE OTHERS who became PROVN supporters. One was Marine Lieutenant General Victor Krulak. "Brute" Krulak had a personal relationship with Secretary McNamara that he sometimes used to advance a policy viewpoint. In January 1966, just two months before the final PROVN report was issued, Krulak wrote to McNamara to urge that a pacification-oriented approach replace Westmoreland's search and destroy operations. Attrition, said Krulak, was "the route to defeat." In Vietnam, "the Vietnamese people are the prize." Thus "our self-declared victories in the search-and-destroy operations are not relevant to the total outcome of the war."[27]

Krulak, who commanded Fleet Marine Forces, Pacific, had also contacted senior Marine commanders in Vietnam—in a cable marked "Marine Corps Eyes Only"—to say that "I am sure that he [Westmoreland] has not altered his view that 'find, fix and destroy the big main force units' is really the answer, and that patrols, ambushes and civic action are all second class endeavors more suitable for the ARVN and the paramilitary." "I disagree with this," stressed Krulak, "and know that you do too."[28]

This outlook was entirely compatible with PROVN's findings, and when Krulak was given a copy of the PROVN briefing in Honolulu, he reportedly sat up all night reading it, then cabled Marine Commandant General Wallace Greene the next morning to say that it was the best thing he had seen on how the war should be fought.

Another PROVN enthusiast was Robert Komer, who since May 1966 had been working the pacification account in the White House and a year later would be sent out as a deputy to Westmoreland for pacification support. When Komer came on the job, he was already familiar with PROVN, published two months earlier, and General Johnson made sure he had a copy.[29] Early in the new assignment, Komer charged out to Vietnam for his first look around, then came back to tell LBJ that "chasing the large units around the boondocks still leaves intact the VC infrastructure, with its local guerrilla capability plus the weapons of terror and intimidation."[30]

One study team member wound up working in Komer's office, and General Johnson seeded others in key places around the Pentagon where they could be advocates for PROVN's recommended approach. Lieutenant Colonel Dave Hughes, a recent graduate from the Army War College and on orders to Vietnam, wrote to Hanifen: "I'm soon off to the jungles. Have been running a mile a morning, practiced on my .45, have black insignia on my fatigues, have memorized PROVN, and am rarin' to go."

"Komer took PROVN and rode it like a horse," said Hanifen, and in July 1967 former PROVN team member Volney Warner wrote to Hanifen from the White House, where he was assigned to Komer's old office, that "PROVN concepts are very much alive and our organizational proposals are now very much in being." But it was not until General Creighton Abrams took command of MACV in the spring of 1968 that PROVN became the touchstone for operations there—operations reconfigured for the conduct of "one war" with population security as its goal.

CHAPTER TWENTY

TROUBLES

As 1966 began, *Time* magazine named General Westmoreland "Man of the Year."[1] The PROVN Study was nearing completion, and Johnson believed that what Westmoreland was doing in Vietnam would not be successful, no matter how lionized he might be at the moment. Far from agreeing that security for the people in South Vietnam's hamlets and villages was the key objective, Westmoreland was actively resisting efforts to get him involved in that. There were, he later said in an oral history interview, people in Washington who were pushing for emphasis on pacification. "I mean they had a one-sided view of the war—unrealistic, in my opinion, and as it obviously turned out unrealistic. And very unrealistic for me at the time, and I was fighting them off constantly, just fighting them off. I took steps to demonstrate that I was not against pacification, but I certainly was not going to become so obsessed with pacification that we would give the North Vietnamese Army and the main forces of the Viet Cong a free rein and allow them to attack when and where they chose."[2]

Furthermore, Westmoreland argued, "pacification was oversold in the United States and oversold to the Johnson administration, where it was the 'end all.' It was never the end all with me, and I got pressure after pressure after pressure to put emphasis on pacification at the expense of allowing the main forces to have a free rein."[3]

Lieutenant General Phillip Davidson, Westmoreland's J-2, noted how successful his boss was in evading such pressure. "Westmoreland," he wrote, "wanted to fight the 'big unit' war now emerging on the battlefield. To him, pacification was a bore and a distraction."[4]

The results of that outlook showed as 1966 wore on, with McNamara's Systems Analysis shop observing that "physical security was the essential prerequisite to a successful pacification effort" and that such security had to be permanent to be meaningful. "It had to be established by a well-organized 'clear and hold' operation, and conducted by competent military forces trained to show respect for the villager and his problems." That was exactly what PROVN had argued. "This prerequisite had not been shown by late 1966," said Alain Enthoven, "so we did not trust the pacification statistics that glowingly reported progress."[5] That conclusion went to problems on two fronts: neglect of the essential aspect of the war and accurate reporting.

Johnson's concerns after his December 1965 visit to Vietnam included "a steady but discernible erosion of the support provided to the ARVN as this support is absorbed by US Army units entering the theater." Most noticeable, Johnson judged, was the reduction in helicopter lift provided to the South Vietnamese. U.S. forces were taking over the war and, instead of improving the capabilities of South Vietnam's armed forces, were both shouldering them out of the way and hogging the combat assets.

This came at a terrible time for the South Vietnamese, because the enemy was equipped with a splendid new range of weaponry, judged by the JCS historian as "among the world's best," including the AK-47 assault rifle. By 1966, "an enemy unit armed with the new family of 7.62mm weapons and the K-50 submachine gun far surpassed in firepower an opposing friendly unit equipped with such semi-automatic weapons as the US M-1 rifle or the M-14," he said.[6]

These problems would only be exacerbated by Westmoreland's requests for the deployment of more U.S. troops early in 1966 and in succeeding months. Meanwhile, Ambassador Henry Cabot Lodge argued for more attention to pacification at the Honolulu Conference of February 1966. "We can beat up North Vietnamese regiments in the high plateau for the next twenty years," he said, "and it will not end the war—unless we and the Vietnamese are able to build simple but solid political institutions under which a proper police can function and a climate created in which economic and social revolution, in freedom, are possible."[7] Lodge's views were reflected in the conference's outcome, for, observed the *Pentagon Papers,* "from Honolulu on it was open and unmistakable U.S. policy to support pacification and the 'other war,' and those who saw these activities as unimportant or secondary had to submerge their sentiments under a cloud of rhetoric."[8]

JOHNSON HAD HIS OWN PROBLEMS, occasioned by his Auntie Ray's dissatisfaction with how the Army Corps of Engineers was dealing with floods ravaging her hometown of Bowesmont, North Dakota. Naturally she brought this matter to her nephew's attention, confident that he could arrange immediate resolution. "The Army Engineer did write me," she began, "and informed me that it would cost more than one million dollars to protect Bowesmont and considering the fact that we would have an expected flood recurrence frequency of once in about 100 years. (So what am I worrying about? We have had our quota for 400 years.)" Enclosed was a clipping showing that year's flooding of the Red River.

The Engineers told Johnson that, according to their calculations, the annual benefits if a levee were constructed would be only half the annual costs of providing the protection. They didn't want to go for it. Johnson didn't think that he could take that rationale back to his aunt. "It is my view," he told the Engineers, "that you do not really have any very good answers to the questions that were raised. I suggest that you think this problem through again and give me something more persuasive in my response to my Aunt." The record is incomplete as to how Johnson managed to get off the hook with Auntie Ray.

THROUGHOUT THESE YEARS Johnson continued a backbreaking schedule of public speeches, now invariably and exclusively having to do with the war in Vietnam. By mid-December 1966, he told a correspondent, "I have personally made 58 formal speeches with a Vietnam motif." In fact, he told another officer, "I now have a travelling map (that rolls up) to show Southeast Asia as a backdrop for talks on the subject." Invited to be the featured speaker at the centennial celebration of Pembina County, North Dakota, Johnson talked about Vietnam—sadly, and of course—delivering a *long* speech, more than eight single-spaced pages, manifestly inappropriate to the occasion. Clearly he had become a driven man on the subject.

Speaking to the American Ordnance Association in Chicago, Johnson began by saying, "Tonight I want to talk about Vietnam. I wish I could talk about something else." Then he gave a typical performance, going on and on and *on* about the war, twenty pages of densely argued text. Later Johnson got a moving letter from someone who had been more struck by who he was than what he had to say. Alluding to Johnson's ordeal at Bataan, this correspondent said that "no one in that room, I felt, had more right to be there than you. To be the guest speaker. To be honored. To partake of prime ribs."

Johnson's correspondence continued to be as robust as his speaking schedule, including this postcard from New Jersey: "Dear Sir, I've traded your autograph, so would be so kind as to send me another. Thank you." Johnson did.

"A DOUGHBOY ALL THE WAY" was how his classmates had described Johnson, and Johnson's affection for the foot soldier was an enduring part of his outlook. Asked to write a foreword for *The U.S. Infantry: Queen of Battle,* Johnson paid a tribute to such soldiers: "The men in these pages," he wrote, "personify the Army's most precious intangible asset—our integrity. It is this integrity in its individual and collective aspects which gives the Army its moral and spiritual greatness and which guarantees that no matter how long the march nor how tough the fight, our will to win and our drive to prevail shall never falter."[9]

Johnson wanted to play fair with the soldier, as he demonstrated when a group of officers came by to show him some new recruiting posters that depicted all the benefits of joining the Army. "They are all mighty nice," said the Chief of Staff, "but not one of them says that you might get killed fighting for your country." Asked by a Washington reporter whether he favored having women in the combat arms, Johnson answered graphically: "When the American public is ready to have their girlfriends, wives and mothers come home in body bags, then I will say yes."

THERE CAME, in the late spring of 1966, a personal blow so harsh, so cruel, and so unexpected that it would have driven a lesser man under. Johnson's younger son Bobby, nearing the end of his second year at West Point, was found guilty of violating the Cadet Honor Code and was forced to leave the Military Academy.

West Point's Honor Code is powerful in its simplicity: "A cadet will not lie, cheat or steal, nor tolerate those who do." It is the last part, known as the nontoleration clause, that Bobby had violated. Learning that a classmate had cheated, he failed to report it. When that became known, he was found guilty of an honor violation and forced to resign. It was devastating for him, for his father and mother, and for the senior Army leadership close to Johnson. "I can remember being just absolutely crushed by that news," said former Secretary of the Army Stephen Ailes.

General Johnson had made clear his own stand on such matters when he was Commandant at Fort Leavenworth. In a lecture on leadership he mentioned a case of suspected plagiarism that had been investigated the previous year. One officer's excuse was, "But other people are doing this." Challenged to identify them, he declined. "Well," said Johnson, "when I read that, that guy was cooked, for the simple reason that he wasn't measuring up to his responsibility." Johnson cited the biblical story of Cain and Abel, asking, "Am I my brother's keeper?" His answer was very simple: "Yes."

If members of the officer corps would not accept responsibility for enforcing standards of professional conduct, they were not worthy of belonging to that brotherhood. "Of all the things that we have in the Army," Johnson emphasized, "our most treasured possession is the integrity of the Army as a whole, and each one of these instances that we let somebody skip by is an erosion of this integrity. When you don't have integrity in the Army, you don't have an Army."[10]

Bobby's truncated cadet career had been a somewhat troubled one. "The only reason he went to West Point was because his father wanted him to go so badly," said a tactical officer who knew him. "He didn't say it, but it was so obvious." In recent months Johnson had written to others that his son was evidencing "rebellious attitudes" and that he was "just skimming by" and "hanging on at West Point." Now all that had come to an end.

Those who had to tell General Johnson what had happened were heartsick. Lieutenant General James Woolnough, then the Army's Deputy Chief of Staff for Personnel, knew that it was his duty to inform Johnson, but he dreaded doing so. "I waited until after six o'clock one evening," he said, "then went in to see him. He wouldn't believe me—couldn't believe it—and became angry with me. Then, when it began to sink in, he said, 'Of course, I'll have to resign.' I spent two hours trying to talk him out of it, but I really think what settled him down was Dorothy. She was a sound lady. Two days later he apologized for having been angry with me. He said it was a cadet determination, and he'd have to accept it." Added Woolnough, "I view his having thought he should resign over this as an example of why he was the most honest man I ever knew."[11]

"I told the father the truth," said Arch Hamblen, then a regimental tactical officer at West Point and a friend of the Johnson family. "He cried. He accepted it, and believed it. He felt the value of one on one to people, treating each one individually, and he hadn't done that with Bobby. He felt he had let his son down. 'I've done that to him,' he said. 'I should never have let him go.'" It was, Hamblen knew, devastating for General Johnson. "Duty-Honor-Country was everything to him, and he *lived* that way."[12]

The Superintendent of the Military Academy at the time was General Donald Bennett, and he too called General Johnson to discuss what had taken place. "Thank you very much," Johnson told him.[13] Tom Irwin, Johnson's aide-de-camp, was listening on an extension. "It pointed up to me the general's integrity," he remembered. "He said to General Bennett, 'He's like anybody else. You handle him like anybody else. Your word is your bond.'"[14]

It was General Johnson who had chosen Bennett to be Superintendent, and Bennett had been coming to Washington about once a month to have lunch and bring him up to date on happenings at West Point. "That continued after Bobby was found," said Bennett. "He never raised the subject with me, except once to say that 'this was awfully hard on Mrs. Johnson.' "[15]

Bobby's own account of what happened is heartbreaking. "It was outside his realm of understanding—deplorable, despicable," he said of his father. "I called him on the phone and told him I was leaving. He asked me if I had done anything. I said I had not. I told him I'd be home in a couple of months. I didn't know what I was going to do—maybe enlist in the Army."[16]

His father wouldn't hear of that. "The first thing you've got to do is come home," he told his son. "You *must* come home." Bobby agreed to do so, and his father pointed his face toward the future. "I know a crackerjack school," he said, and "you need to get back into school right away." The school was Dickinson College, and in the autumn Bobby began his junior year there. Then he joined ROTC. "I wanted to graduate at the same time as my former classmates at West Point," Bobby said, "and to get the same date of rank when I was commissioned as a lieutenant. I had every intention of staying in the service."[17]

IN JULY 1966, Johnson created a new position, Sergeant Major of the Army, as a means of bringing to the top echelon a better appreciation for what concerned the soldier. According to Johnson, "The position was established on the premise that, if we were going to talk about the noncommissioned officers being the backbone of the Army, there ought to be established a position that recognized that this was in fact the case." The job of the Sergeant Major of the Army, he added, would be "basically dealing with people." We created in him "what might . . . be called an ombudsman." Sergeant Major Loikow, Johnson's invaluable administrative assistant, had urged that he establish such a position, noting that the Marine Corps already had a similar post.

Major Army commands around the world were invited to make nominations, and from those Johnson made the choice. The man selected was Sergeant Major William O. Wooldridge, then serving as sergeant major of the 1st Infantry Division in Vietnam, who was General Westmoreland's nominee. Wooldridge had been a private in the 1st Division during World War II, with the legendary Ted Dobol as his squad leader in Company K, 26th Infantry, where he worked his way up to first sergeant.

Johnson knew that Wooldridge had been involved in some scrapes when he was a young soldier, including robbing a pay telephone in England during pre-Normandy invasion training. But, he said, "I still hold quite strongly to the view that once a man has paid the price you don't forever hold him to account for that, particularly where subsequent service has been exceptional in nature and so recognized."

"Johnny was charitable," said Major General Charlie Brown, the Army's Chief of Chaplains. "He would look at the best that was in people. I think he remembered Wooldridge as a fighter, and a good fighter. And in the 1st Infantry Division they had made Wooldridge the command sergeant major, and recommended him to Johnny. He trusted the officers who made that recommendation." Besides his excellent record, Wooldridge was well-spoken and likable, and Johnson thought that he would represent the Army well. He got the job.

"I'm kept informed on matters of all kinds by my staff," Johnson told his new sergeant major. "They don't always tell me what I want to know. They don't always know what's going on at the end of the line." Wooldridge's job was to help with that problem. Johnson provided some fairly condensed instructions that he had written on a three- by five-inch card, a card that Wooldridge carried in his wallet for years to come.

Johnson set Wooldridge up in an office on the E Ring of the Pentagon, right across the corridor from his own office, and told him that he needed no one's approval to see him at any time; he was just to use the private entrance and come right in. When a photograph and accompanying article describing these arrangements appeared in the *Washington Post*, Wooldridge was later told by Herb Sweet, the top Marine noncommissioned officer, the effect was dramatic: "That morning I was working for a colonel in the basement. The next morning I had an office up next to General Greene's." Greene was then Commandant of the Marine Corps.

Johnson put Wooldridge, literally just back from Vietnam, on leave for a few days to see his family in Junction City, Kansas. Wooldridge hadn't been home more than a day or two, however, when he got an urgent call from Major Tom Irwin, Johnson's aide. "Come back to Washington at once," Irwin said, "the President wants to see you."

Wooldridge caught the next flight and reported to the White House, where Bill Moyers greeted him and took him in to meet LBJ. There was a photo session, then the President took Wooldridge in to see the assembled cabinet. Afterward LBJ said, "I'm going to Fort Campbell tomorrow. I'd like you to go with me."

"I'll have to ask my boss," Wooldridge blurted out.

"Who's your boss?" the President demanded.

"General Johnson, the Chief of Staff of the Army," said Wooldridge.

"That's all right," said LBJ, "he's going, too."

When Wooldridge got back to the Pentagon, he was met by General Johnson, who came out of his office, took him by the hand, and said, "You have done the Army a service this morning, Sergeant Major." Apparently, Moyers or someone had telephoned to relate how Wooldridge had told the President that he would have to ask his boss about going to Fort Campbell, and there were delighted grins all around at the Pentagon.

When a command sergeants major program was put in place throughout the Army, Johnson authorized a worldwide conference, chaired by Wooldridge. That produced twenty-one recommendations, sixteen of which Johnson approved at once. One of those established a Sergeants Major Academy at which selectees for the top enlisted grade would get capstone training similar to that provided officers at the War College level. Regarding those recommendations that General Johnson did not sign off on, said Wooldridge, "he went over with me personally each disapproval, explaining the reasons."

When they traveled to Vietnam together, Wooldridge recalled, General Johnson would be dealing in the highest councils of war in the morning. Then in the afternoon, by his own request, "he was standing in a paddy somewhere in the coastal plain discussing rice farming with three elderly Vietnamese. He asked them whether the sea came in and soured their land. They agreed that was a problem, and everyone stood around talking about whether there was some way of blocking that."

WHEN COLONEL JASPER J. WILSON came back from Vietnam, General Johnson assigned him to his own office as a special projects officer. "He is my hair shirt, and I need him," Johnson said. Some such explanation was necessary, because in certain other respects, Wilson did not seem like Johnson's kind of fellow. Dorothy Johnson and Wilson became good friends, and she had some insight into his strengths and weaknesses. He had a brilliant mind, she said, but conspicuous faults as well: "He was profane, and he just couldn't keep his mouth shut."

It is not an overstatement to say that Wilson was the intellectual father of PROVN, first in his correspondence with General Johnson from Vietnam, reinforcing Johnson's own theoretical conclusions and his observations, then in the conceptualization of such a study prepared at Johnson's request. That was not the limit of his contribution. "I've said frequently that you need one person close to you who is pretty thoroughly abrasive," said Johnson, "and the one that I selected for that role was one that I had come to know and respect at Fort Leavenworth when I was Commandant there. That was Colonel Jasper ('Jap') Wilson, and Jap in some cases had an affinity for annoying people, but I knew that in his relationship with me he would tell it like it was, and in his relationship with others he would sort of keep things stirred up so that problems wouldn't be concealed. He was of very special value to me."

In July 1966, Jasper Wilson became involved in a special project indeed. It began with a letter from former South Vietnamese Lieutenant General Nguyen Khanh, then living in exile in France. Khanh said that he would be arriving in New York aboard an Air France flight early on the afternoon of 12 July, bringing his daughter to the United States for medical treatment. "I hope that I will have the opportunity to see you," he told Wilson, "because I have some *very important thing* to discuss with the olds friends over there."[18]

Wilson immediately informed Johnson, who discussed the matter with Secretary Cyrus Vance. It was decided that Wilson should meet Khanh when he arrived in New York, which he did. Khanh and Wilson had dinner together that evening. The next morning, they took a long walk together, then talked at Khanh's hotel. Khanh revealed, in bits and pieces over two days, that two months earlier he had been contacted by a Vietnamese he had once known as a Viet Minh, and that since then they had met several more times. Wilson learned that this man, designated by him "Mr. Out," was one of three who controlled the National Liberation Front in Vietnam. A second was the overt leader, Nguyen Huu Tho. And, Wilson learned, there was a third—"Mr. In," he called him—who was described to him as "a bourgeois intellectual following a profession (not medicine) in Saigon. Mr. Out cannot enter Viet Nam & Mr. In cannot leave," Wilson noted, "both are covert." Khanh now knew both by name.[19]

Mr. In, a communist, was not aware of Khanh's contact with Jasper Wilson, but Tho knew about it, said Khanh. Both Tho and Mr. Out recognized that the Viet Cong (as opposed to North Vietnamese forces) could not win the war, and they were very much concerned that the North Vietnamese and the Chinese were going to take over and subjugate the Viet Cong—many of whom, including Mr. Out, were not communists.

These concerns led Mr. Out to seek out Khanh as a possible intermediary to arrange negotiations between the Viet Cong and the United States, with a view to U.S. withdrawal from Vietnam. Khanh refused, arguing that he had fought the communists for twenty years and intended to continue to do so. And, Khanh suggested, continued U.S. presence would be necessary to defend even the Viet Cong from the North Vietnamese and Chinese following any negotiated settlement. Finally, after Khanh and Mr. Out had discussed the matter repeatedly, a mutually agreed position was worked out.

Wilson understood the offer from Mr. Out to be as follows: "The noncommunist elements of the VC under Tho & Mr. Out want to defect to the GVN & U.S." Just how large this element was, General Khanh did not know. Under their proposal, U.S. forces could remain in South Vietnam, and noncommunist Viet Cong would be permitted to participate in upcoming elections.

Mr. Out sought to discuss this possibility with the right American representative. Khanh was willing to make the connection, but wanted no further role. In his opinion, though, the right American should be someone who could deal directly with President Johnson and who would be authorized to make decisions within guidance. Khanh suggested one of the following: William Colby, General Harold K. Johnson, Ambassador Alexis Johnson, or Secretary Robert McNamara. Khanh stressed, said Wilson, that "it was essential that GVN know nothing of this because of extremely poor security which resulted in compromise & failure of previous defection possibilities."

All this Wilson reported to General Johnson, who undoubtedly informed his superiors. But, said General Khanh, no meeting ever took place between Mr. Out, subsequently identified as Le Van, and any American negotiator. "I don't think Washington was ready then to explore negotiations," said Khanh.[20] So ended Jasper Wilson's special project.

Ironically, within weeks of the Khanh initiative, Secretary McNamara, just back from a trip to Vietnam, forwarded an October 1966 memorandum to the President in which he recommended the following course of action: "Try to split the VC off from Hanoi."[21] And in May 1967, McNamara's assistant John McNaughton drafted a memorandum that recommended certain actions to be followed in September 1967, including this: "Move the newly elected Saigon government well beyond its National Reconciliation program to seek a political settlement with the non-Communist members of the NLF—to explore a ceasefire and to reach an accommodation with the non-Communist South Vietnamese who are under the VC banner; to accept them as members of an opposition political party, and, if necessary, to accept their individual participation in the national government—in sum, to transform the members of the VC from military opponents to political opponents."[22] But Khanh's initiative had met with no such responsiveness when he made it.

General Khanh returned to France, then later came to live in the United States, where for a time he and Jasper Wilson were in business together as co-owners of the Panda Steak House, a Tucson watering hole. That venture was short-lived, however. "They were not businessmen," said Wilson's daughter sympathetically.

Mr. In remains unidentified, although it is possible that he was Huynh Tan Phat, a Saigon architect. Truong Nhu Tang identified Phat in his memoirs as one of the small group of original organizers of the Viet Cong, also stating that he was chosen first vice president when a presidium was formed. And his vocation would accord with Khanh's description of someone "following a profession (not medicine)."[23]

IN MID-1966, HALFWAY through Johnson's four years as Chief of Staff and for no apparent reason, Secretary of the Army Resor decorated him with the Distinguished Service Medal for his accomplishments from July 1964 to July 1966. "As Chief of Staff, United States Army, during this period," read the citation, "General Johnson played a key role in the rapid expansion of the Army to meet the Communist threat in Vietnam while ensuring the Army's ability to fulfill its many other commitments throughout the world."[24] Of course, that was absolute hogwash. Neither Johnson nor anyone else could have achieved such an outcome under the constraints imposed on the buildup. In fact, meeting the ever-increasing requirements in Vietnam had ripped hell out of the Army's readiness, cohesion, and morale in every other part of the world.

WHILE JOHNSON WAS STATIONED in Washington, living in the big Chief of Staff's quarters, his brother Herb brought his family on a vacation visit to the capital. But Herb did not even call his brother, either at Fort Myer or in the Pentagon. "We had little kids, and we figured those were no places for diapers," he said by way of explanation. Neither did Johnson's sister Janet and her family visit Quarters 1 while Johnson was Chief of Staff. Only sister Edna Ray, who lived nearby, seems to have been a part of Johnson's life during these difficult years. Even when his career culminated with a White House retirement ceremony, she was the only sibling present. Thus continued the pattern of distance between Johnson and his siblings.

IN LATE JULY 1966, Johnson made his sixth trip to Vietnam. His itinerary for the ten days in-country gives some idea of the pace he maintained. He met with the Secretary General of the National Leadership Council, Lieutenant General Chieu, at Gia Long Palace; with Ambassador Lodge at the Embassy; with the Army Concept Team in Vietnam; with Minister of Revolutionary Development Major General Thang; and with General Westmoreland. He went to Sunday services at the Rex Chapel, then to Cho Ray Hospital and the post exchange in Cholon, then to see Lieutenant General Engler, the 18th Engineer Brigade, the 1st Aviation Brigade, the 97th Artillery Group, the Minister of National Defense at the Joint General Staff (JGS) compound, and then the Chief of the JGS there. Next came the 525th Military Intelligence Group, the 1st Signal Brigade, Lieutenant General Momyer of Seventh Air Force, the commercial port and customs warehouses, 1st Logistical Command, the Back Beach and Australian area in Vung Tau, Vung Tau Support Command, the Republic of Korea's MASH, the R&R center in Vung Tau, the 21st ARVN Division in Bac Lieu, the 13th Aviation Battalion and the Chieu Hoi Center in Soc Trang, Can Tho, the Commanding General and Headquarters of IV Corps, the Special Forces "B" Detachment at Chau Doc, the commanding general of III Corps, a prisoner of war camp, the commanding general of the 5th ARVN Division in Phu Loi, Major General DePuy and the 1st Infantry Division, Tay Ninh and the Special Forces "C" Detachment there, Major General Weyand and the 25th Infantry Division at Cu Chi, commanding general of the 25th ARVN Division at Duc Hoa, Commanding General of the 10th ARVN Division at Xuan Loc, the 1st Australian Task Force and New Zealand Forces, the Chieu Hoi Center at Ba Ria, Major General Larsen and I Field Force Vietnam Headquarters, Colonel Kelly and the 5th Special Forces Group Headquarters, Brigadier General Pearson and the 1st Brigade of the 101st Airborne Division, Brigadier General Walker and the 3d Brigade of the 25th Infantry Division, the Duc Co CIDG Camp, Major General Vinh Loc and II Corps Headquarters, 7:30 A.M. church services with Major General Norton and the 1st Cavalry Division, Binh Dinh Sector Headquarters, a hamlet being reconstructed in Tuy Phuoc, Major General Lam and I Corps Headquarters, Lieutenant General Walt and III Marine Amphibious Force Headquarters, a Marine regimental command post on Hill 55, the An Hoa industrial complex, the 2d ARVN Division, and a few other stops. This was a fairly typical agenda.

When he was in Washington rather than on the road, Johnson said, he spent an hour and a half to two hours a day, including Sunday, reading the cable traffic, most of it dealing with Vietnam. "I felt that it was important to do that so that my knowledge of what transpired in Vietnam would be just as complete as I could make it." This paid off, especially on his trips to Vietnam, where Johnson sometimes found that he "knew more about the content of the cable than most of the staff out there did."

Johnson later said that during this period he felt like an "observer" and that, "despite a sense of responsibility for what was happening, had little feeling of control over the war itself."[25] Immersing himself in the cables, making frequent trips to the war zone, and attending as many JCS meetings as possible were apparent attempts to overcome that problem.

EVEN-TEMPERED AND GENTLEMANLY, Johnson was for the most part an easy man to work for. "He always had a little smile on his face, a chuckle," said Sergeant Major Loikow, "a nice man to be around."[26] Johnson did have some peculiarities, though. One had to do with the photographs he was always being asked to sign or inscribe to one person or another. Glossy prints, he found, were hard to write on. "I despise glossy prints," he told a friend.

He had a more extensive dislike for certain words or phrases. Johnson was, said an associate, "a first-class wordsmith who actually read all of the papers—enclosures, footnotes, and all." And he read with a critical eye, pouncing on offending usages. For example, he disapproved of phrases such as "get in *contact* with," insisting that to get in contact with someone you had to touch him, and he questioned the use of "we" in such formulations as "we agree." "Who is 'we'?" he would demand. "Etc." was also proscribed, and pretty soon there was an actual list passed around for the benefit of those who drafted material for Johnson's use. Inevitably, there was a counterattack in the form of a fake letter. "Dear General Johnson," it began, then incorporated every term he detested, several to a sentence. "*You will recall* the officers of War Plans Division who presented *the Army position adequately,*" it stated. "They *desire* that your *departure* be *enhanced* by *ideal* weather." Johnson was probably amused, but his vocabular preferences remained intact.

SERGEANT MAJOR WOOLDRIDGE came to revere Johnson, calling him "the finest soldier and officer that I was privileged to serve with in the Army." Johnson, in turn, developed a great deal of trust in Wooldridge, so much so that late in 1966 he confided to him his uneasiness about the integrity of the reporting coming out of Vietnam. Wooldridge had himself gotten several letters from noncommissioned officers in Vietnam asking him to "look into false reporting of enemy strength and casualties that, according to these men, had gotten completely out of line and had become standard operating procedure from battalion to MACV level."[27]

Wooldridge spent several months probing the matter, becoming "convinced that there were false reports on enemy strengths and casualties being filed." None of the unit sergeants major would talk to him about it, perhaps being too close to the unit commanders, but the battalion and brigade operations sergeants and the intelligence sergeants were willing to do so. Wooldridge briefed Johnson on his findings, "and he was obviously upset. He told me," said Wooldridge, "that things like this happen when you are following a policy that is not working and such actions are the result of trying to justify that false policy."[28]

JOHNSON WAS BACK in Vietnam at Christmas 1966, his third trip to the war zone that year, visiting units all over the country. His son-in-law, Captain Jim Kern, was serving in Vietnam as an advisor with the Vietnamese Airborne Division, and Johnson asked that the young officer be assigned to travel the country with him. "I was a cocky captain talking to a four-star general who was his father-in-law," said Kern. As a result, he wound up having Christmas dinner at Westmoreland's quarters with the likes of Johnson, Westmoreland, Cardinal Spellman, and Billy Graham.

Kern remembered a particularly dramatic moment during a visit to the 1st Infantry Division. There Johnson was briefed on an action involving enemy infiltration of a listening post. "We only lost two," said the briefer.

Johnson responded, "For those two kids, that was the biggest battle of the world, wasn't it?"

"The briefer just crumpled," said Kern.

Johnson was proud of his son-in-law, writing in a "Dear Family" letter that Kern had been in a tough fight and had been awarded a decoration for gallantry by the Vietnamese government. As they traveled the country together, they also talked about the war. Kern did not think that it was going well, and in fact eventually left the Army because of his disillusionment with the way the war had been conducted. Later, when he learned of Johnson's own misgivings, he concluded that Johnson had hidden most of them in their talks so as not to undermine the morale of a young officer who was stuck in the midst of the thing.

During this trip, a drama that had been building played out to a conclusion of sorts. After serving as MACV J-3 for General Westmoreland, Major

General William E. DePuy had been given command of the 1st Infantry Division. He promptly set about making a name for himself by summarily relieving subordinate commanders in impressive numbers. Reading about DePuy's command techniques in press accounts, General Paul Freeman, Commanding General of the Continental Army Command, wrote to Johnson. "With the entire officer and noncommissioned officer corps of the Army outside Vietnam reduced to approximately cadre strength that we might provide our Army in Vietnam with the best talent we can produce under present difficult circumstances," he observed, "it seems to me that flagrant relief as an instrument of command is a wasteful abuse of our most precious and limited asset."

Johnson forwarded Freeman's letter to Westmoreland in Vietnam, adding his own comment that when he had visited the 1st Division the previous April he "got a strong sense of change for the sake of change" and that he had talked to General DePuy about the need to develop the available leadership. "I wound up pointing out that in my view a good leader is an individual who can bring out talents in people that they themselves frequently do not know that they have and that any commander would do a good job when he is provided with all of the top talent. The real commander is the one who performs well by developing people who under some circumstances might be disposed of."

After the April visit, Johnson also wrote to DePuy to comment on a cable and news release indicating that DePuy and one of his assistant division commanders, Brigadier General James Hollingsworth, had been out chasing Viet Cong in their helicopters. "If I had wanted a lead scout in command of the 1st Division," Johnson said, "you would not have gotten the job. Your value and Holly's is proportional to the responsibility that you have for something over 15,000 men. Your job is not to shoot VC. Your job is to see that other people shoot VC. At least, that is the way that I look at it."

During the Christmas 1966 visit to Vietnam, Johnson had another encounter with DePuy. One afternoon in Lai Khe, recalled Colonel Eugene R. Cocke, "I came out of the 1st Division TOC, the Tactical Operations Center, which was right next door to the general officers' mess, where I could hear a heated argument going on. It involved General DePuy and General Harold K. Johnson, the visiting Army Chief of Staff, and also General Hollingsworth, one of our assistant division commanders." Cocke, then a young major, was fascinated and astounded by the acrimony of the dialogue. He stood outside and listened to an exchange concerning DePuy's having relieved a large number of officers, especially battalion commanders, from their posts. "I'm not here to run a training ground," General DePuy shouted. "They get people killed!"

"I can't have you be the filter for all the best officers we have in the Army to see if they meet your approval," General Johnson retorted. They went back and forth like that for what seemed to be a long time, maybe half an hour.[29]

Shortly after General Johnson's departure from the division area, recalled Lieutenant General Sidney B. Berry, then a colonel commanding the 1st Division's 1st Brigade, "DePuy landed by helicopter at a defensive position I was visiting. DePuy looked dejected. 'The Chief of Staff just left, and I'm probably going to be relieved,' he told me. 'Nonsense!' I said. Then DePuy told me that HKJ had said, 'I can't afford another Big Red One [the 1st Division's nickname]. You get the Army's best officers assigned, and then you relieve them. I need division commanders who make the best of the human material they are assigned.' "[30]

To another division commander, Johnson wrote that "to the extent possible I intend to have division commanders who look upon their jobs as one of teaching, training, guiding and advising, particularly in the officer and senior noncommissioned officer field, rather than driving, whipping and demanding. It is my own conviction that our troops function better when led, rather than driven."

When, early the next year, DePuy came home from Vietnam, he wanted to be assigned as Commanding General of the Infantry School. "I told him that I couldn't afford him at Fort Benning," said Johnson, "because I didn't have enough people to replace those that were down there that I knew he was going to fire." DePuy was not welcome on the Army Staff under Johnson, either, and wound up in a Joint Staff billet.

WHEN JOHNSON RETURNED from a trip to Vietnam, he invariably sent out a raft of letters, most of them to the wives and parents of soldiers he had met, saying how well they looked and what a grand job they were doing. On this occasion, however, he was the recipient of an interesting letter. "I have long wanted to get to know you better," wrote Billy Graham. "Your Christian witness is spoken of throughout the Christian world, and thousands of Christians here in America would join me in saying 'Thank you' for the faith in Christ that you so openly express."

Johnson made a lasting impression on young Jim Kern as well. Even later, when his marriage to Ellen had ended in divorce, Kern retained his admiration for his former father-in-law. "I met three presidents, and Billy Graham, and a number of other prominent people," he recalled. "Johnny was the most inspirational man I ever knew."

AT THE HONOLULU CONFERENCE early in the year, General Westmoreland had been given a set of quantitative goals for accomplishment during the rest of the year. One was to "attrit, by year's end, VC/NVA forces at a rate as high as their capability to put men into the field." In other words, Westmoreland was tasked to reach what was referred to as the "crossover point," that point at which enemy losses exceeded the ability to replace them, resulting in a net decline in enemy strength. That goal proved well out of reach, for during 1966—despite heavy losses inflicted—enemy strength actually rose substantially.[31] Said General Westmoreland in a year-end television interview, "Well, I do indeed see the light at the end of this long tunnel."[32]

CHAPTER TWENTY-ONE

SLOGGING

Even before the deployment of ground forces began, Vietnam was having a heavy impact on the Army. "We have about 4.8 divisions worth of majors and captains, 3.5 divisions of lieutenants, and 3 divisions worth of master sergeants in Vietnam today," General Johnson told an audience in January 1965.[1] And, he said, over the past three years the Army had taken on around 40,000 man-years' worth of additional work without getting any additional people.

That drain was creating a significant strain in the sixteen-division deterrent force, and in the training establishment, he explained, for "in the Army today it appears that we have a small conceptual gap . . . between the missions for which our Army is now generally organized and the disruptive realities, such as in Vietnam, which have required an increasing share of critical Army resources."[2] Because of the need to pull people out of units to meet Vietnam requirements, he said, "we've got substitutes backing up substitutes backing up substitutes in a lot of places."

By the time the buildup was all over, the Army had increased in size by about 50 percent, later characterized as "one of the largest and most controversial military buildups in U.S. history."[3] Beginning at some 960,000, it reached 1.5 million at the high-water mark. "I come somewhat out of breath," Johnson told a military audience in the midst of all this, "because for the last year and a half or so I have found myself in the position of trying to keep a bathtub filled with the plug out." Every month, he explained, the Army was losing about 30,000 trained people.

"This weighed on Johnny more than anything I ever saw weigh on him," said Lieutenant General Charlie Corcoran, "trying to expand the Army under the restrictions laid on by LBJ and McNamara. His feeling was that the way the Army had been forced to expand was a disaster."

Although the Army's buildup for the war in Vietnam was substantial, it was modest in comparison to the buildup for World War II. What made the Vietnam buildup so difficult was President Johnson's refusal to call up reserve forces, or to put the nation on a war footing, meaning that all the growth had to come from inexperienced new acquisitions and that trained people could not be retained for the duration of the conflict. This meant that training had to be repeated as each cohort finished its two years of mandatory service and left the Army, only to be replaced with a whole new complement of new and untrained inductees. These disadvantages, Johnson once told a colleague, made the task like going from Washington to Baltimore along old U.S. Route 1 rather than being allowed to use the new Baltimore-Washington Parkway—it would be slower, but you would get there eventually.

Much of Johnson's concern stemmed from his compassion for the men who had to do the actual fighting. "The Army is like a funnel," he used to say. "At the top you pour in doctrine, resources, concepts, equipment, and facilities. And out at the bottom comes one lone soldier walking point." Johnson cared passionately about what happened to that solitary soldier. "The single most precious element of combat power is the life and the energy of the individual soldier," he maintained. "We all exist, every one of us, to keep some rifle squad doing what it has to do."

During 1965, over 500 new Army units were activated, and in the first months of the following year, more than 600. For example, when it was determined on 1 July 1965 that thirty combat engineer battalions had to be deployed to Vietnam by 1 July 1966, the Army had only ten such outfits worldwide. This meant that within twelve months it had to activate, man, and equip thirty new battalions while maintaining the existing ten. Before long, some engineers were facing back-to-back tours in Vietnam, and equipment was being stripped from nondeploying units, both active and reserve.

The strategic reserve—known as the STRAF, for Strategic Army Force—suffered grievously during this process, declining in strength from about 227,000 in May 1965 to only about 96,000 in trained strength by January 1966.[4] During approximately the same period, the Army increased its strength in Vietnam by nearly 70,000.[5] By June 1966, the majority of major combat units outside Vietnam were rated C-3, meaning marginally combat ready, or C-4, not ready.[6] "The Chief of Staff fully appreciates the fact that providing cadres for new units, expanding the training base, and providing replacements for overseas commands will have a drastic impact on the units of the STRAF," Johnson told his general officers, in the process also putting them on notice that there was no use griping about it.[7] When a new readiness reporting system was introduced, said Secretary of the Army Ailes, "we could see graphically what the Vietnam deployments were doing to our forces. We had 93–94 percent readiness, and then 30 percent—shocking!"

Meanwhile, the Army's Vice Chief of Staff, General Abrams, was giving the same message to young leaders, many of them bound for Vietnam. "In the Army," he told a Leavenworth graduating class in December 1965, "the war in Vietnam is being fought with what we have." The necessity of taking much of what was needed for Vietnam out of their hide greatly concerned the Joint Chiefs of Staff and was one of the primary reasons for their repeated efforts to get the President to call reserve forces.

At Fort Benning, where many soldiers went through Officer Candidate School, they were constructing new facilities as fast as they could throw them up. "It was not unusual," said General Ellis Williamson, "to finish a building on Friday, furnish it with beds, kitchen equipment, etc. on Saturday and Sunday, and fill it with 240 students on Monday. I saw it happen time and time again."

Even more of a problem than building facilities was finding qualified people to conduct the instruction. Things got to the point where there were instructors whose total service consisted of sixteen weeks of basic and advanced training as enlisted men, two weeks of leave, and three months in OCS. With that background, they turned right around and became instructors in the very courses they had just completed. "There we were," said Williamson, "turning out officers with instructors who had less than a year's total service."

Two years into the buildup, General Johnson described some of the effects to a conference of Army lawyers. As a result of not having mobilized reserve forces, the Army had brought in well over a million men to cover expansion and the replacement of those who had completed their terms of service. "Now," he said, "you wonder why you have problems. Basically, [it is] because something over 70 percent of the Army today has less than two years' service. You can complain about this all you want to, but there is one hard fact—this is what we have."[8]

Very early in the process, the readiness of Army elements outside Vietnam began to be degraded because of Vietnam requirements. At one point, the Department of Defense ordered that units stationed in Europe be filled to only 90 percent, and those in Korea to 80 percent. Units were also removed from Europe and sent to Vietnam—first logistical outfits, and later combat formations. Said Lieutenant General Frank Sackton, "It was not unusual for scores and scores of trucks and tanks to be put on blocks in order to provide the manpower."

General Johnson and General Abrams resisted these encroachments on European readiness as long as they could, but with no access to the reserves, no extension of the terms of service of those already in the active force, and a turnover rate in Vietnam that reached 120 percent a year, the forces in the continental United States were simply unable to sustain the Vietnam deployments.

This brought Johnson into conflict with the civilian hierarchy. Sackton remembered "extremely difficult and turbulent periods of discussion with the Army Secretary, who was supporting the Secretary of Defense. The [Under Secretary] was supporting the Secretary of Defense and, of course, the Secretary of Defense and his organizations naturally [were] supporting themselves. So we were in a kind of a losing fight here, but it was a traumatic period. The discussions were harsh, they were very bitter. It was during this period . . . where it got so bitter with the Under Secretary of the Army . . . where there was an actual explicit threat on the part of the Chief of Staff to resign his office under these circumstances. It got that bitter."

"Now finally," said Sackton, "the Army leadership did what historically it has done, and that is to acquiesce to the requirements of civilian authority and provide the forces, even though it made known to the civilian authorities that it would require a substantial drawdown of Europe. Here again there was a risk. It was an extremely serious military risk, but in the wisdom of our civilian masters they considered it not to be a political risk."

Johnson had a horror of sending men into combat before they were ready, and this was the source of some of the most heated controversies with civilian leadership. When the 9th Infantry Division was being readied for shipment to Vietnam in early 1966, Johnson was in his office late one night and buzzed General Charlie Corcoran on the intercom. "Anybody there?" he asked. General "Hook" Almquist answered. "You two come in here," Johnson instructed.

When they entered Johnson's office, they found Under Secretary of the Army David McGiffert with him. They had obviously been in some kind of a heated discussion, and returned to it at once. "I still don't understand," said McGiffert, "why you don't deploy the 9th Division that's been requested out there." Johnson explained again that it was simply not ready. McGiffert wanted to know when it would be ready. "May," answered Almquist.

"You gave us 'cadre' to train," added Johnson. "You gave us 1,600 people, most E3 and below—all in lieu of sergeants. And the officers were mostly second lieutenants. We had to train the trainers. We've been at it six months so far, and it usually takes a year. This division is not ready to go."

By this time it was 10:30 or 11:00 at night, but McGiffert continued to work on Johnson about deploying the division. "Finally," said Almquist, "Johnny slammed the one open space on his desk. 'I'll be goddamned if I'll do that!' McGiffert's response was, 'If you feel this strongly about it, I think you ought to take it up with the Secretary of Defense.' 'Mr. Secretary,' Johnson said, 'I don't deal directly with the Secretary of Defense. I deal with him through the Secretary of the Army.' " End of conversation. (The 9th Infantry Division began deploying to Vietnam in December 1966 and had all elements in place by the end of January 1967.)

Later Johnson revealed to a friend another issue that he considered non-negotiable: the well-being and development of junior officers. There was great pressure to defer schooling in order to recycle career officers through Vietnam more rapidly, and in fact this was done with aviators at one point. "My depth of feeling on that subject," said Johnson some years later, "is such that I had promised myself that if the career courses at branch school level, Leavenworth, and the Army War College were closed or curtailed significantly that I would depart in protest."

On his birthday Johnson wrote to a friend: "My one wish is to have the strength—physical-mental-moral—to do the things required by the Army this next year." When nearly another year had passed, he wrote to Major General Arthur S. Collins, Jr., then taking command of the 4th Infantry Division, to tell him, "You will have problems in the months ahead simply because I have permitted the resources of the Army to be spread desperately thin."

Secretary of the Army Resor acknowledged the bind. "We were always behind in meeting General Westmoreland's requirements as agreed to by Secretary McNamara," he said. As a result, the Army was basically in the business of "allocating shortages." It needed a larger training base to generate more output against future requirements, but was hard-pressed to provide the assets needed to expand that base while trying to organize and deploy units to meet the current requirements. And, thanks to terms of service not being extended for those on active duty, it was also necessary to replace the entire force, less the careerists, every two years.

Secretary Resor and General Johnson, recalled General Ferdinand Chesarek, "had a falling out on calling the reserves and (more nasty, bitingly) the readiness of the force issues." Reports were prepared every month, said Chesarek, and the issue turned on how ready the forces in the United States were, and how ready the reserve forces were. "Resor said he would not call the reserves, but he wanted on paper to show them as ready." General Johnson "was too ethical to agree, and would not sign off." Chesarek blamed Under Secretary of the Army McGiffert for pushing this, noting that at one point attitudes became so bitter that he had to function as a go-between for Johnson and Resor.[9]

In an effort to keep up, by April 1966 Johnson had increased the number of companies providing basic training to sixty and expanded OCS to turn out 3,500 new second lieutenants a month.[10] Inevitably, there was some degradation of standards, reflected in a bitter joke of the time: "OCS has not lowered its standards, they just no longer require the candidates to meet them."

Inevitably the massive deployments to Vietnam brought pleas from people who wanted to be exempted. One came in the form of a letter from a soldier who said that he had been on the Bataan Death March and suffered a long period of captivity at the hands of the Japanese. Instead of going to Vietnam, he would like to be sent to a noncombat area. Johnson wrote back to say that he had undergone a similar experience, "and in addition I served in Korea during the dark, bitter days of that conflict. I expect," he said, "to go wherever I am called. I expect each soldier in the United States Army to do no less. The Army is not a welfare institution." Request denied.

When a colonel wrote to Johnson to ask his opinion about what assignment would be most beneficial to his career, Johnson's answer was equally straightforward. "My advice," he responded, "is that you play them as they come."

After the war, Westmoreland would refer to his "relatively modest" requirements for men in Vietnam, requirements that eventually reached 549,500, of whom some 543,000 were deployed at the high-water mark. Others viewed his repeated troop requests as anything but modest. Alain Enthoven, McNamara's assistant secretary for systems analysis, spoke of the "huge catalogue of units requested by General Westmoreland,"[11] and Charlie Corcoran remembered how Enthoven's people used to complain that "what Westy wants, Westy gets." Regardless of differing perspectives, the reality is that meeting the ever-increasing levies for deployments to Vietnam ravaged the Army everywhere else in the world, so much so that a decade after the war was over the effects were still being felt.

KEEPING TRACK of all this activity was an enormous task, and it proved to be a task the Army was not quite up to. By the time of the autumn 1966 budget process, said General Chesarek, who was then the Army's Comptroller, "the Army was in real bad shape. We were trying to build our forces up to accommodate Vietnam (without knowing what the requirement was eventually going to amount to), and they were trying to maintain some kind of sobriety with respect to our commitment to Europe."

In OSD, there was dissatisfaction with the speed and accuracy of data being provided by the Army in response to a flood of questions. OSD Systems Analysis, said Chesarek, prepared a series of draft memoranda that "more or less indicated that the Army was incapable of managing its affairs, and that they [Systems Analysis] would take over this responsibility." Chesarek conferred with Generals Johnson and Abrams, and it was decided that some integrating mechanism at the Chief of Staff level had to be created. Although Johnson was concerned that such a "super staff" might downgrade the effectiveness of his deputy chiefs of staff, it was clear that dealings with OSD had to be improved and, said Chesarek, a means found to "bridge, also, the gap between the Chief and the Secretary [of the Army], which had grown during some very, very troublesome months."

Chesarek was given forty-eight hours to draft a charter for what they had decided to call the office of the Assistant Vice Chief of Staff. He was cautioned to do the work alone, since the proposal was obviously going to be controversial. Chesarek came back the next night with a proposal for an OAVCSA that basically would have left Johnson, Abrams, and the deputies with nothing to do. Abrams sent him back to the drawing board. The next night he was back with a charter they could live with.

The following day was a Saturday, and Johnson called a meeting of the Army General Staff principals. Copies of the charter were passed out, and everyone was given time to read it. Johnson asked for comments. All agreed that it was necessary to do something, but nobody wanted to go that far.

Johnson recalled how at one of his first appearances before a congressional committee as Chief of Staff, he had been asked what the Army's major problem was. There was no answer for such a question in his backup book, said Johnson, but he knew—"basically it was trying to know what our resources were." Now, two and a half years later, that was still a problem.

The Chief of Staff emphasized that he had no intention of encroaching on the authority of his deputies, but he also insisted that there must be an integrative mechanism. After a lot of discussion it was clear that only Johnson, Abrams, and Chesarek favored establishing the new office—every single deputy opposed it. Johnson approved it, the Secretary of the Army concurred, and the office of the "A-Vice" was in business.

Chesarek, having invented it, was put in charge. Two existing staff elements were folded in, a Force Planning Analysis Office and a Special Studies Office. To these were added newly created offices for Management Information Systems and for Weapons Systems Analysis. Johnson's late February 1967 announcement in the *Weekly Summary* said that the new office would "provide for the central management and control of the three systems which have a major impact on all functional areas—management information systems, weapons systems analysis, and force planning analysis."[12] One of the things he hoped to do, said Johnson, "was to tie all those things together at a level above the infighting."

When this amalgam was up and running, it provided a valuable means of generating timely, consistent, and integrated data for Army management and for dealing with OSD. Johnson had described expansion of the civilian staffs of the Secretary of Defense and the Secretary of the Army as resulting in an enormous increase in the number of "question askers," but without any additional "question answerers" being provided. Now he had some help in getting answers. "I am persuaded," Johnson later wrote, "that the establishment of the Assistant Vice's office was the coordinating mechanism that every Chief of Staff since WW II has been looking for."[13]

The mechanism that did the most good in taking the load off the Chief and Vice Chief of Staff was also the most controversial. The Assistant Vice Chief of Staff met weekly with the Secretary of the Army to prepare him for his weekly meetings with the Secretary of Defense, and these sessions covered the whole range of managerial issues. Chesarek was a brilliant man, and a disciplined one. His contribution during this period was invaluable. During endless hours of interaction with the civilian secretariats at Army and OSD levels, he also developed some insights into the Pentagon bureaucracy, particularly as concerned the Secretary of Defense. "In forcing his business concepts on the military services," observed Chesarek, "which he deemed essential to obtain political and public support for an unpopular war, Mr. McNamara had neither the time, patience or understanding to consider tradition, morale and the other intangibles that contribute so importantly to the makeup of a fighting force."[14] The A-Vice dealt in numbers and, during much of its short life, did good service for the Army.

But, just as the A-Vice was a powerful position, it was also one with the potential for end-running and usurpation of power. Johnson and Abrams were both conscious of this yet still felt obliged by current exigencies to create such a position. In fact, said Johnson, "it was clear that there was a danger of this office taking over the responsibilities of the staff. I felt so deeply about it that this was the single point upon which I cautioned my successor—be sure that it doesn't get out of hand." Later, with a new Chief of Staff and different personalities in the senior civilian positions, more robust management capabilities in the principal staff sections, and a different operating environment, the calculus changed. "I was delighted when General Abrams wiped out the position," said Johnson.

THE COMPASSION Johnson felt for soldiers was known throughout the Army. Usually it was viewed as a good thing, an excellent thing, but on occasion there was a small problem. One such problem came to light early in 1967 when a soldier who had deserted twice and was missing from his base at Fort Ord got into trouble in Las Vegas. While a guest at the Orbit Inn Motel, he fired a .25-caliber pistol into fifty sticks of dynamite he had stashed in his room, killing himself, his wife, and four other people, and also ripping apart thirty units of the three-story building in the heart of the casino district.

Subsequent investigation revealed that the man had twice been court-martialed, entitling him to spend quite a bit of time incarcerated in the U.S. Disciplinary Barracks at Fort Leavenworth, where he had accumulated twenty-four offenses involving disciplinary action. Sentenced to a bad-conduct discharge, he appealed for another chance to be a soldier, asking for a waiver so he could reenlist. That request made its way to the desk of Harold K. Johnson, who sent it to the Deputy Chief of Staff for Personnel with a handwritten note. "I know our policy," wrote Johnson, "but why not take a chance and keep track of this one?" That turned out to be a pretty easy thing to do—they could read all about him in the *New York Times*. "Afraid I made a mistake on this one," Johnson acknowledged with impressive understatement.[15]

BEGINNING IN EARLY 1967, there were efforts in several quarters to remove General Westmoreland from direct command of ground forces operations in Vietnam. One proposal would have made him the U.S. Ambassador to Vietnam, and President Johnson even asked General Maxwell Taylor, by that time back in private life, to consider how this might be accomplished. (Apparently nothing so straightforward as simply making the appointment had occurred to the President.) Taylor told the President that he favored making Westmoreland the Ambassador but proposed a complicated scheme in which he would still be Commander-in-Chief of U.S. military forces, reporting through the Secretary of State as Ambassador and through CINCPAC and the JCS as Commander-in-Chief.[16] Fortunately, that ponderous arrangement never came to pass.

Harold K. Johnson advanced a different solution, one that would leave Westmoreland as the joint theater commander but divest him of his dual role as Army component commander. "Under this organization," said General Bruce Palmer, "the deputy commander of MACV would remain at three-star level and a separate four-star field army commander would be established." This would have had the effect of removing Westmoreland from direct day-to-day tactical command of Army ground forces, or at least putting one headquarters between him and those forces. Westmoreland opposed this arrangement, however, and his desires prevailed.[17]

WITH RESERVE FORCES OUT OF REACH, agonizing things had to be done to compensate, such as taking active-duty units of types that were not required in Vietnam and retraining them to become units of the kinds that were required. And all the while, perfectly good units of the types needed were languishing in the reserve components. But LBJ was adamant that he would not call them up. "The Chiefs," said John Wickham, "had counted on it. They even talked about resigning."

Certainly Harold K. Johnson contemplated resignation in protest. He even had a staff officer working on a letter that would say not just that he was stepping down but also exactly why. Perhaps that would precipitate a debate on the underlying issue. "I remember Johnny expressing these feelings about possibly resigning on many different occasions and on several issues," said General James K. Woolnough, his Deputy Chief of Staff for Personnel. "I remember his saying, 'Every night I go home, and I wonder if I should resign. They're asking me to do things that frighten me. But if I resign, they'll just put somebody in who will vote the way they want him to.'" Thus, time after time, the possibility was considered, then discarded.

"The Joint Chiefs of Staff," said Johnson, "never did abandon their initial recommendation of moving in more quickly with a greater level of force, but the Chiefs didn't make any public outcry and publicly supported the administration's decisions in that regard, because the reservations that were expressed about hiking tensions, creating a more crisis[-like] atmosphere worldwide, and arousing public outcries outside the United States appeared to be legitimate concerns on the part of the people that were supporting that position. But the Joint Chiefs of Staff never did agree with that kind of philosophy to the extent of agreeing with its validity, but did support the decisions that were based on the philosophy."

When the President elected not to follow the advice of the Joint Chiefs of Staff, they had little choice but to go along or resign. "We had made our recommendations," said Johnson. "Our advice had been rejected and other courses of action were chosen, so we simply were good soldiers and did what we were told to do."

Plenty of people were uninhibited about raising the issue with the senior military leadership, as they did when Johnson lectured at the Army War College. A student asked the Chief of Staff why reserves had not been called for Vietnam. Johnson said that he'd been to the White House five times trying to get that done, but obviously without success. Then they asked him why he hadn't resigned or retired in protest. He said that he had considered doing so, but ultimately decided that it would have been disruptive, deciding instead to serve on and do the best he could under the circumstances. He acknowledged that others might not agree with his decision, but that was what he had decided to do.

That decision, it is clear, was hard to reach and revisited repeatedly. For an extended period, Major General Michael Davison was the acting ACSFOR—Assistant Chief of Staff for Force Development—the staff element where all the newly created units had to be planned and tracked. It was a nightmare of a job, and it brought him into frequent contact with Harold K. Johnson. One evening about eight o'clock, Davison went in to get approval of a recommended deployment and commented in passing on the difficulty of fielding units under the circumstances.

Johnson picked up on it at once. "If the President would only call the reserves," he said, "it would not only solve this problem, but alert the American people to the magnitude of our involvement in Vietnam, and the matter could be debated." After a pause, he continued: "Two or three times I've been up the chain to ask the President to call the Guard and Reserves, and he's refused to do it. I'm so upset about it that I'm considering resigning."

"General Johnson, you can't do that," blurted out Davison. "Your leadership is too important for the Army as it is today."

Johnson quietly thanked the younger man for his views, ending the conversation.

Lieutenant General John McPherson, an Air Force officer, served in the office of the JCS for a number of years. "I sat in the tank with the JCS when, several times, they talked about resigning," he said. "Johnny Johnson felt the strongest about it. But always they concluded, 'What the hell—it wouldn't take them five minutes to get someone to replace us.' Their philosophy was 'we'll do the best we can.' And, they asked, 'How can we quit when we have those kids out there dying?' "

Speaking at the War College several years after his retirement, Johnson was asked the usual question about resignation. This time he spoke of the events of July 1965, and especially the President's refusal to call reserve forces. "I was totally opposed to the commitment without mobilization," he recalled. "I expressed my view to the Chairman. We were scheduled to go to the White House to meet as a group with the President the next day.

I had a very sleepless night. I was very determined that I was going to resign if it came to that. But the more I thought about it, the more I came to believe that I could not walk away from the Army and the soldiers we were sending to Vietnam. I finally concluded that I could do more good by staying in the job."

This rationale was entirely consistent with the advice that Johnson had been given by General Omar Bradley. Johnson also may have been influenced by his outlook on what had befallen General MacArthur during the Korean War. The historical record, Johnson thought, made it clear that President Truman had no choice but to relieve MacArthur. "No military commander can set himself up as higher than his president," Johnson observed. "Each time that this confrontation takes place, the man in uniform had better lose, or we're not going to have the kind of government we now enjoy."

While he was Commandant at Fort Leavenworth Johnson had candidly addressed the issue of obedience to higher authority. "I've gotten further than I ever expected to be," he told students in a lecture on leadership, "and I'm further than I ever deserved to be. Any time they want to fire me they can. Now I'm here to get a job done, and I'm doing the very best I know how to get the job done. And I go lashing back, but lots of times I'm overruled on something. I don't fight it. I see what they want, and this is what I do. Sometimes I wonder whether I'm right or whether I'm wrong."

JOHNSON FOUND HIMSELF CAUGHT in a cruel dilemma. Convinced that Westmoreland's tactics in Vietnam were not working and could not work, he had been unable to get them changed. Meanwhile, he had to publicly support what Westmoreland was doing, even though it was anathema to him. He could scarcely do otherwise and remain in office. Thus, day after day, to one audience after another, Johnson had to praise an effort that he viewed as massively incompetent. It must have been agonizing for him, the most moral of men, to have to do this. Again and again, he contemplated the alternative, resigning in protest, and always he reached the same conclusion—he could do more good by continuing in office.

FINALLY, in the late spring of 1967, General Creighton Abrams was sent to Vietnam as Deputy COMUSMACV. The plan was that after a short stint in the second slot, Abrams would replace Westmoreland as COMUSMACV sometime in the summer of 1967. The evidence for this includes not only the expectations of Abrams and his closest aides who accompanied him, but also the fact that Abrams was allowed to choose Major General Walter T. Kerwin to go along as his prospective chief of staff. Kerwin remembers being called in by Harold K. Johnson and told that he was going to Vietnam in three days. Kerwin was stunned, but Johnson explained the reason. "General Abe was going over to replace Westy," he was told. "It didn't happen that way, but that is what he was supposed to do."

Cyrus Vance, who was then serving as McNamara's deputy, also recalls clearly that the plan was for Abrams to succeed Westmoreland within two or three months. Other confirmation comes from Westmoreland himself, who after the 1968 Tet Offensive told reporter Keyes Beech, "You know, I was supposed to leave before this. Now I'm going to be looked on as the guy who lost the war."

But after Abrams was sent to Vietnam, LBJ changed his mind and left Westmoreland in command, meaning that nothing much changed in the conduct of the war. Meanwhile, Abrams devoted himself to improving South Vietnam's forces, achieving results that would be demonstrated dramatically in the Tet Offensive, when those forces stood their ground and performed far better than anyone had expected. Soon after that, Abrams was in de facto command, and in July 1968, officially so. How matters would have played out had he taken over a year earlier can only be imagined.

The delay in Abrams's ascension to the top command seems entirely attributable to LBJ. In the months before Secretary McNamara's July 1967 trip to Vietnam, he and his senior aides had increasingly focused on the need to make better use of the forces in Vietnam. OSD Systems Analysis, critiquing Westmoreland's March 1967 request for 200,000 more troops, recommended that Westmoreland be directed to submit a plan for more effective use of the forces he already had, including "consideration of changes in tactical employment (e.g., greater use of long-range patrols, fewer battalions in static defense, and more efficient use of available helicopter resources)."[18] And, Enthoven told McNamara, "our analysis has shown that present forces could be employed more effectively (and at less cost) if greater emphasis were given to small unit operations."[19] Thus this recommendation was made: "Tell MACV to start making good analyses of his operations and feeding them back into his planning so that we can get more out of not only the U.S. and allied forces, but the ARVN as well."[20]

In a 19 May 1967 Draft Presidential Memorandum McNamara asked this question: "Can we achieve the same military effect [of adding more forces] by making more efficient use of presently approved US manpower?"[21]

During his July 1967 visit to Vietnam, McNamara again addressed this issue. The press soon got wind of the criticism. Before McNamara even left Saigon, one dispatch stated that he "reportedly said that resources now available in Vietnam are not being well used: despite the presence of 464,000 troops in South Vietnam, only 50,000 troops are available for offensive ground operations."[22]

When McNamara returned to Washington, he raised the issue of more effective use of the available troops again, this time publicly. Westmoreland complained to the President of hurt feelings and being unappreciated. "The President said General Westmoreland was upset last night because of the press reports," read Tom Johnson's notes of a Cabinet Room meeting that included McNamara, Westmoreland (back in the United States for his mother's funeral), and Wheeler. "The press indicated to General Westmoreland that Secretary McNamara had questioned the General's management of the war when the Secretary briefed the press at the White House on July 12."[23] Indeed he had. Now the President summoned Westmoreland to the White House for some consoling. McNamara was also brought over, and LBJ presided over a "consensus" meeting.[24] "The President said he told General Westmoreland Wednesday night [that] we would carefully review everything. Secretary McNamara, General Westmoreland, and the President feel that General Westmoreland's team in Vietnam is the best we have ever seen, and the President said he has never heard anybody who has ever been critical of General Westmoreland in any way."[25]

Some insight into the complexity of Lyndon Johnson is provided by the fact that it was he who had directed McNamara to brief the press, specifying that he should include a statement "that the troops currently [in Vietnam] should be used better."[26] The next day, the President made his own statement to the press: "I think it is fair to say that at no time during my Presidency have I been more pleased with the quality of leadership, namely, the leadership being provided by General Westmoreland and the leadership being provided by Ambassador Bunker, there than I am now."[27]

In addition to this ringing endorsement, after having publicly committed himself to Westmoreland for so long, the President would have found it difficult to relieve the general when he was under siege—not because of any concern for Westmoreland, but because it would call into question LBJ's own judgment.

General Bruce Palmer suggested yet another reason—potentially an important one—for not bringing Westmoreland back to the United States at that time. Late that spring, he said, "it began to dawn on them that Westy was a political threat. It was obvious to me that Westy was bitten by the presidential bug as early as the spring of 1967. They wouldn't want Westy back in the US under those circumstances."

Complementing these factors was widespread speculation in the press that Abrams was about to take over for Westmoreland. One fairly typical press treatment suggested that Abrams would replace Westmoreland by the end of the year, adding that "the unvarnished truth is that an increasing number of senior government officials—including Robert McNamara—have wanted to replace Westmoreland for some time, and that only the political need to present him as a victorious and successful returning hero has prevented the changeover from taking place before."[28]

This speculation would have motivated LBJ to change his mind about replacing Westmoreland, as evidenced by Chester Cooper's portrayal of him. "Nothing pleased him more than to 'surprise'; nothing angered him more than to have a 'surprise' spoiled by premature exposure. It was common knowledge that the President would change his mind on a pending policy decision or personnel appointment if there was advance, accurate speculation in the press," observed Cooper, who further illustrated LBJ's character by quoting a description of Henry II: "It pleased him to vex his stewards with the pandemonium and uncertainty of his plans."[29]

ALTHOUGH VIETNAM drove Johnson every day that he was Chief of Staff and pervaded all aspects of the Army elsewhere, there were issues outside Vietnam that had to be addressed. Mostly these concerns had to be left to others. In June 1967, Johnson made his first trip to Europe in over two years. What he found there could have been neither surprising nor encouraging. In a visit that included all the U.S. divisions, Johnson told a friend, "I cannot recall having seen so many second lieutenants in all of my service."

After the trip Johnson wrote a sympathetic letter to General James H. Polk, commanding general of U.S. Army, Europe. "I come away with mixed emotions," Johnson said, "because the condition in which you find yourself with regard to noncommissioned officers and company grade officers differs so markedly from the Seventh Army that I knew in the late 1950's. In addition, the uncertainty of when modernization might be resumed tends to place a somewhat different complexion on the way in which commanders report their accomplishments and aspirations. It is hard to put your finger on a specific and I am simply recording an impression that I have difficulty in describing."

The reality was clear enough—Vietnam had stripped Seventh Army of talent and experience, its equipment had deteriorated to something pretty close to junk, and the whole thing was just heartbreaking to someone who had served in the great Seventh Army of less than a decade earlier. "Everybody was obviously dedicated and doing his best with what he had," Johnson told Polk compassionately.

BY THE AUTUMN OF 1967, Harold K. Johnson's anguish over the course of events in Vietnam had become extreme. "Are freedom and stable government for a diverse group of warring Asians worth the life of several thousand . . . of a hundred . . . of even one American soldier?" he asked while addressing the Association of the United States Army's annual meeting, the most public forum within the Army family. "This thought tears mercilessly at the heart and soul of every thinking person. I read the casualty lists as they come to me day by day. I write a personal letter to every family that loses a son, or a husband, or a brother. . . . I can assure you from the bottom of my heart that I ask myself this question day and night, and if I did not have an answer I would not be able to take the first step each morning that leads from my quarters to my office."[30]

CHAPTER TWENTY-TWO

AIRPOWER

Perhaps the most dominant issue running through JCS deliberations during the long years of the war was the bombing of North Vietnam. This was a matter in which members of the JCS had unequal equities. The Air Force and Navy chiefs, given their responsibility for carrying out the bombing missions (and their services' interests in demonstrating their capabilities, a concern not lacking in budgetary implications), were the strongest advocates of a robust and rapidly escalated bombing campaign.

Initially Harold K. Johnson did not see this as centrally important to what was going on in South Vietnam, and he said so early on. According to recollections of Secretary McNamara, only two months after becoming Chief of Staff "Johnson argued that the rationale for air strikes was gravely flawed" and that "the war against the insurgency will be won in South Vietnam and along its frontiers."[1] Recalled McNamara, "This question of bombing's effectiveness that General Johnson had raised became a fundamental issue between the president and me, on the one hand, and the chiefs and military commanders in Vietnam on the other, for the next three and a half years."[2]

Perhaps nothing could more vividly underscore the bizarre way in which this war was conducted. John Schlight calculated that "a mere 6.7 percent of the Air Force's effort in the war went north." Three-quarters of the missions were flown in South Vietnam, including close air support, airlift, search and rescue, defoliation, and courier service; the rest involved interdiction and close air support in Laos and Cambodia.[3] Yet, as McNamara acknowledged, that 6.7 percent was what divided him and the President from their principal military advisors—isolated them, really—and absorbed huge amounts of their time and energy in the minute details of target selection, rules of engagement, and other operational details. It was perhaps the most enduring item on the Tuesday Lunch agenda.

The bombing issue also illuminates another factor that has sometimes been hinted at but seldom addressed head-on: that Lyndon Johnson was afraid. Doris Kearns captured some of this in her interviews with LBJ, who told her that he was afraid that there were secret treaties between North

Vietnam and China or the Soviet Union. As a result, she wrote, "Johnson lived in constant fear of triggering some imaginary provision of some imaginary treaty." Johnson recalled how he would lie awake at night agonizing over whether one of the targets he had picked that day would trigger a Chinese or Soviet reaction. "What happens then?" he asked fearfully.[4]

As McNamara later admitted, "there was a constant controversy between me and others about particular targets and—let's put it this way, I was trying to hold the bombing down."[5] Later, asked why he undertook the bombing if he didn't think it would work, McNamara gave as his primary reason "because we had to try to prove it wouldn't work."[6] During the first half of 1966, McNamara doggedly blocked the bombing of North Vietnam's POL (petroleum, oil, and lubricants) supply system, an issue that was debated so publicly that by the time authorization was finally and grudgingly given, the enemy had been able to disperse the system and make it redundant to such an extent that it was much less vulnerable to air attack.

At one point McNamara ordered the production of air munitions cut by 30 percent, an action he rationalized by saying that it was "designed to avoid wasteful accumulation of excessive inventories such as the $12 billion surplus of ammunition and equipment with which we ended the Korean War."[7] These tactics had enormous effects, one of which was to condition the Joint Chiefs of Staff to scale down their proposals before submitting them, in anticipation of their probable reception.[8]

"THE JCS WERE SHARPLY SPLIT on the issue of the utility of strategic bombing," noted George Herring, "but they submitted unified recommendations so as not to give Secretary of Defense McNamara a wedge to drive between them."[9] Harold K. Johnson acknowledged that there was "growing unanimity on the actions that would be taken . . . I think [there] was a very substantial closing of the ranks in the face of a growing criticism of the military action."

When CIA produced its now-famous assessment entitled "The Vietnamese Communists' Will to Persist" in late August 1966, its analysts observed that intensified air attacks against the north would be more effective than the lukewarm campaign then being waged. "Although expanded air attacks would not stop activities essential to support of the war," CIA said, "they could cause a drastic decline in the level and efficiency with which the economic and military sectors function."[10] LBJ suppressed the assessment, even keeping it from the Joint Chiefs of Staff.[11]

It seems clear that as the war went on, Harold K. Johnson changed his outlook on the strategic bombing campaign, becoming much more favorably disposed toward it. Later, discussing LBJ's March 1968 cutback of Rolling Thunder, Johnson said, "I viewed it with a great deal of distress, because I felt at the time that the louder the North Vietnamese were yelling, the more they were hurting, and that the outcries at that particular time were rather significant on their part. And I felt that we were cutting out the bombing at a time when it was probably beginning to have its most devastating impact, and that cutting it back was an acknowledgment really of defeat in many respects."

Johnson was not arguing that bombing North Vietnam would by itself win the war, only that it was an important element in the overall prosecution of the war. This bombing cutback, as he described it, was just one more bad decision in a chain of bad decisions stemming from "failure to take strong action with the forces you had available, in contrast to applying force in a selective and limited way."[12]

In retrospect, Johnson expressed disappointment in what airpower had been able to achieve. "There were always differences among the Chiefs with respect to what was going to get the job done," he said. "The Air Force, supported for the most part by the Navy, were reluctant to see the commitment of ground forces in any numbers to Vietnam. The premise here was that airpower could do the job. I think that if anything came out of Vietnam it was that airpower couldn't do the job." And, added Johnson, "I think that we'd better get off the kick that bombs and destruction are going to achieve the ends that military forces are designed to achieve."

In the end, concluded a Joint Chiefs of Staff history of the war, the bombing campaign known as "Rolling Thunder" had not substantially reduced the capacity of North Vietnam's fixed military establishment. No major military target system, including barracks, airfields, surface-to-air missile sites, naval bases, radar installations, and supply depots, had suffered as much as 25 percent damage, and North Vietnam retained the capacity to support its forces in the field. "Much of this," noted the JCS historians, "was owing to the fact that most of the major military facilities were in 'sanctuary areas.'"[13] An assessment by CIA took similar note of the impact of self-imposed restrictions on the bombing campaign, observing that "no target system can be reduced to its critical point under existing rules."[14]

McNamara and his civilian associates continually sought to limit the scope and intensity of the bombing, eventually claiming that it was ineffective. To the extent that this was true, it was at least in part because of the limitations they had imposed. But the North Vietnamese considered the bombing neither ineffective nor inconsequential, as evidenced by their repeated efforts to get it stopped, frequently as a precondition to negotiations.

That the air war against North Vietnam could have accomplished more in support of the overall war effort seems beyond dispute. Whether that would have made any difference in the long run is impossible to determine.

ONE SUBPLOT in the issue of the use of airpower was the campaign by Air Force Chief of Staff General Curtis E. LeMay to strip the Army of *all* aircraft. Had he had his way, LeMay might have gone even further. After World War II, when LeMay was assigned to the Strategic Air Command, he was invited to lecture at Fort Leavenworth. In the Commandant's office before his talk, LeMay startled those present by blurting out, "I don't know why you invited me down here to talk to you. To start with, I don't believe you need an Army. We have SAC. We'll take care of them [the enemy]."[15]

Meanwhile, the Army was industriously expanding its aviation assets. Army experiments in arming helicopters particularly enraged the Air Force. Johnson had struggled to maintain the Army's options, and when General John P. McConnell replaced LeMay as Air Force Chief of Staff in 1965, some room for negotiation developed. McConnell, one year ahead of Johnson at West Point, had been manager of the football team. As an assistant manager, Johnson had gotten to know him well. Now, a lifetime later, they found themselves chiefs of their respective services.

The two men eventually reached an agreement on fixed-wing and rotary-wing aircraft. In April 1966, they signed the formal agreement. The Army relinquished claims to "the Caribou and to future fixed-wing aircraft designed for tactical airlift," while the Air Force agreed "to relinquish all claims for helicopters and follow-on rotary wing aircraft which are designed and operated for intra-theater movement, fire support, supply, and resupply of Army forces," thus resolving what Lieutenant General John Tolson called "one of the most emotionally packed debates" of the day.[16] One powerful spur to reaching agreement was the fear that OSD was about to impose a solution in terms of roles and missions that neither service would be happy with.

Some in the Army were critical of Johnson for giving up the transport aircraft, but those who were best informed understood that in doing so he had protected the Army's right to unimpeded development of the airmobile concept and of the whole range of rotary-wing aircraft that have been centrally important to the Army ever since.[17]

General Tolson, noting that "the keystone to airmobility was—and is—the helicopter," emphasized that the "helicopter—specifically the tactical transport as represented by the Huey—was the absolute *sine qua non* of the Army's concept of airmobility. General Johnson . . . was keenly aware of this basic fact."[18] Tolson noted that the agreement achieved by General Johnson "was far broader than the Caribou problem alone and essentially established without doubt the Army's claim to the helicopter, and especially to the armed helicopter."[19]

"The Army–Air Force trade-off cost us the Caribou," noted Major General Ellis "Butch" Williamson. "On balance it was good. General Johnson, in my opinion, made the decision he should have. But Army aviation would have gone considerably further if he hadn't had to make that decision." According to Williamson, it was well on the way to becoming a separate service, following much the same route the Air Force had taken late in World War II. "General Johnson got the most he could under the circumstances," said Williamson.[20]

"I really think that Johnson traded the Caribou to the Air Force in the hope, in the honest hope, that they would lay off our armed gunships," said Lieutenant General George Seneff, an important figure in the development of Army aviation. "It didn't turn out that way, but I think he really felt that he had done the right thing by the Army." What Johnson had gotten was Air Force agreement to the Army's *entitlement* to arm helicopters. After that, every time the Air Force sought to revisit the issue, challenging what the Army was doing, the Army could cite this pact and press on. That is exactly what it did.

"Very shortly thereafter," recalled Lieutenant General Robert R. Williams, when the Air Force began a violent attack against the Cheyenne, "General Johnson . . . who had agreed to transfer the Caribou, indicated that he had understood that the trade-off for transferring the Caribou to the Air Force was the withdrawal of their opposition to the Army's having armed helicopters—gunships—and that they really were defaulting on their agreement in continuing to attack."

Williams readily agreed that if he had been asked whether he "would be willing to give up all the Caribous to have a clear path without having to go through so much blood, guts, delay and so forth to get a helicopter gunship, I would have said it's worth every ounce of it." But the Air Force still fought against Army armed helicopters. "I think General Johnson made a perfectly honest, well considered judgment to do it," concluded Williams. "I just think he thought there was more honesty on the other side than [there] turned out to be."[21]

In the same general series of agreements, noted General Seneff, Johnson agreed to stop arming Mohawks, a fixed-wing aircraft being used primarily for surveillance. That turned out to be not much of a loss. "The Mohawk really didn't produce for us," said General Tolson, "and this sort of just died a natural death . . . rather than transferring them to the Air Force or anything of that nature."

Johnson had persisted, and eventually he and McConnell reached an agreement that both sides considered satisfactory. Bob Williams also found it to his liking. "I don't think there is any question about the fact that we are going in exactly the right direction," he said a decade later, "and I think it is most heartwarming, most encouraging, that the Army and the Air Force have been able to get together to the degree they have in cooperation and harmony. It has been the most encouraging thing I have seen."

RESOLUTION OF THESE ISSUES with the Air Force was essential if Army airmobility were to prosper. Advancing in parallel with Johnson's struggles in the JCS was the Army's program of testing the Howze Board's findings and recommendations, begun while he was serving as DCSOPS and continuing during his years as Chief of Staff. The impact of these tests on Johnson's outlook on airmobility and Army aviation in general was dramatic. Earlier, although appreciative of the potential of air assets to provide an increase in maneuver capability, he was also conscious of a range of limitations. While at Fort Leavenworth, addressing a combat developments conference, he had gone through the issues of reliability, maintainability, and vulnerability of helicopters, expressing concern over each aspect. But his conclusion was positive. "We're going to have to give up something to get something," he stated. "This is inevitable. We've got to lean toward the side of advancing the art."

THERE WAS ONE OFFICER, Major General Edward Rowny, who was, as Johnson saw it, a big part of the problem rather than a contributor to a solution. In a directed assignment as a special assistant for mobility, Rowny in effect worked for Deputy Secretary of Defense Cyrus Vance, despite being part of the Army Staff. Johnson perceived Rowny as the master of the "end run"—bypassing Johnson and going directly to his patrons in the civilian secretariat.[22] Johnson didn't have many enemies, but he surely had one in Rowny, who subsequently completed an oral history replete with factual misstatements concerning Johnson. In fact, he blamed Johnson for not giving him an assignment he aspired to at a time when Johnson had already been retired from the Army for over a year.[23]

Rowny had been an advocate of what General Charles Corcoran characterized as the ACSFOR view, "that at least half the Army's divisions should be air assault." A contrary view prevailed in DCSOPS, where "they thought it had to be more flexible, and relate the types of divisions to the missions . . . they would have to perform." Eventually the matter was briefed to Secretary of the Army Stanley Resor and, according to Corcoran, "it was agreed that we would stand back from the ACSFOR view and instead take what was best of the air assault concept and integrate it into the overall force structure. Johnny was very strong on this and instrumental in getting that decision."[24] As a result, although a second airmobile division was later organized, airmobility assets and to some extent airmobile concepts were integrated into many combat elements, proving invaluable when they deployed to Vietnam.

"General Johnson was very definitely anti-aviation at one stage of the game," observed General George Seneff. "He made a resounding turnaround during the 11th Air Assault operation, largely because he saw something that he didn't realize was going to be possible." At one point Johnson observed the 11th Air Assault Division in action and then, only a few days later, a conventional division with Air Force support in a parallel set of maneuvers. As a result, the 11th Air Assault clearly won a convert. "I would make a comparison," said Johnson, "of perhaps a gazelle and an elephant."[25]

Johnson visited the tests on several occasions, once bringing along his DCSOPS, Lieutenant General Bruce Palmer, Jr. During a welcoming briefing, Palmer began to question some of the things that were being said. Johnson interrupted him and said, "Bruce, you are not going to believe what you are going to see tomorrow." Seneff later told that story about General Johnson to illustrate "the extent to which he swung around. He became a leading proponent of aviation before we got into Vietnam."

The pacing element in expansion of Army aviation became, and remained, the availability of aviators, even though the helicopter manufacturers were also hard-pressed to keep up with escalating requirements for aircraft.[26] The fleet to be manned was large and growing rapidly. Whereas in July 1965 the Army had about 600 aircraft in Vietnam, that number was programmed to increase to more than 2,000 by early 1966.[27]

By mid-June 1966, the Army's projections showed a serious pilot shortage. At the end of that fiscal year, there would be about 9,700 in the force, against a requirement for some 14,300. In the next fiscal year, the requirements were going to increase to approximately 21,500, with only 12,800 available. The Army was losing ground in providing enough pilots to man the aviation fleet, even though it was turning them out at an unprecedented rate.[28] But not until late March 1966 had McNamara approved the Army's plan to increase the monthly output of its flight training program from 120 to 410 aviators, and it would still take until April 1967 to reach that rate.[29] At the peak of the Vietnam War, the Army was turning out 7,200 pilots a year and, incredibly, Fort Rucker was graduating a class of enlisted aviation mechanics every day, seven days a week.

At one point Johnson had a study done on the most important issues concerning Army aviators. When the results were briefed to him, his response was: "Well, that's a little thin. What statistics do you have to back that up?"

"Sir," said Delk Oden, "we just couldn't get any statistics, just plain common sense and judgment."

Johnson looked over at his Vice Chief of Staff, General Creighton Abrams, smiled, then turned back to the briefer. "Approved," he said.

Johnson eventually was satisfied that all his earlier concerns about the helicopter in combat had been resolved. "On the battlefield," he said, "the helicopter is being used to give the foot soldier a victory over three of his oldest foes—time, terrain, and fatigue." And, he added, sounding a classic Johnsonian theme, "the real success of anything we do in the Army can best be measured in terms of what it does for the rifle squad."

When Johnson was about to bring General Kinnard back from Vietnam after a highly successful tour as commanding general of the 1st Cavalry Division, he wrote to inform him of an impending assignment on the Army Staff. "It will," he observed, "give you a certain tempering with regard to facts of Washington and Pentagon life, as well as give you a direct exposure to the many individuals who now are helping us with our business."

RUNNING THE ARMY was a full-time job. Functioning as a member of the Joint Chiefs of Staff was a full-time job. Rather than delegating either to his Vice Chief of Staff, Johnson tried his best to do them both. When General Curtis LeMay retired[30] and was succeeded as Air Force Chief by General John P. McConnell, *Time* magazine ran a cover story on the JCS with a banner strip reading "Thinkers and Managers Replace the Heroes."[31] Johnson, holder of the Distinguished Service Cross, might not have appreciated that, but he now felt comfortable in the company of his fellow JCS members.

Johnson took his duties as a JCS member seriously, scrupulously blocking his calendar for the thrice-weekly meetings in the "tank," as the JCS
conference room was known, scheduling talks and other outside activities
so as not to interfere with these sessions, and missing meetings only when
such things as trips to Vietnam made it unavoidable. He even passed up the
funeral of his former aide, who had been killed in action in Vietnam, because it would have required him to travel to West Point on a JCS meeting day. "General Johnson had the reputation of being the best prepared
chief when he went to the tank," said an aide to General Wheeler. Martin
Blumenson called him "a moderating and stabilizing influence in the Joint
Chiefs of Staff . . . because his intellectual and moral leadership consistently
advocated the balanced view."[32]

Explaining his commitment to the enterprise, Johnson cited the need
for "maintaining a very essential continuity in attendance at JCS meetings.
From my own observation, I think that the Army suffers the most from a
lack of continuity in the Joint Chiefs of Staff deliberations. Deviations that
occur during the absence of a Chief sometimes appear to be relatively minor,
but when the cumulative effect takes hold we frequently find ourselves in a
position of a long fight back to a position that we never should have lost in
the first place." The incessant battles with the Air Force over Army aviation
may well have produced this outlook.

THE MOST TRAUMATIC CONFRONTATION between the Joint Chiefs of Staff
and their civilian superiors since that 1965 thrashing in the Oval Office took
place in August 1967, this time in public. The occasion was a series of hearings on the air war convened by Senator John Stennis and his Preparedness
Subcommittee of the Senate Armed Services Committee. McNamara was
called to testify, as were all the members of the Joint Chiefs of Staff, in a
deliberate effort by the committee to demonstrate how dramatically the uniformed and civilian leadership were split on conduct of the war.

The hearings ran intermittently through much of August, with
McNamara scheduled near the end, followed only by General Johnson and
General Greene. Wheeler testified on 16 August in carefully crafted terms.
"With the exception of the three major ports of North Vietnam, targets
in the buffer zone along the Chinese border, and targets located in heavily
populated areas, the majority of known military fixed targets in North Vietnam have been struck," he said. In other words, except for the most lucra-
tive targets, and targets on the move, over half the remaining targets had
been struck. He omitted any discussion of the multiple constraints applied

to even those strikes, including timing, ordnance, and direction and weight of effort.[33]

When McNamara's turn came, he took refuge in a straw man, claiming that critics of the bombing campaign maintained that, if properly conducted, it could either break the will of the North Vietnamese or cut off the movement of war materiel to the south.[34] In fact, nobody was claiming any such thing. Rather, more robust bombing was considered an essential part of the overall campaign, especially in reducing (not cutting off) the influx of supplies and making it more costly for the enemy to support his forces in the field.

Along the way, McNamara took a position on the enemy's logistical needs in South Vietnam that revealed how low his credibility had fallen. Maintaining that the amount of externally supplied material, other than food, required to support Viet Cong and North Vietnamese forces in South Vietnam was only fifteen tons a day, McNamara was immediately challenged by Senator Jackson, who observed that for the enemy strength currently estimated in South Vietnam, that would work out to about two ounces per man per day. "These figures don't quite add up," he told the Pentagon's greatest devotee of figures.[35]

McNamara also reported intelligence estimates that North Vietnam was receiving imported military equipment at the rate of 550 tons a day and total imports of 5,800 tons a day.[36] That made it seem even more unlikely that he was right about only fifteen tons a day being needed in the south.

McNamara then described the large numbers of enemy trucks being destroyed and the equal number being brought in to replace those lost—some 9,200 since February 1965. Senator Miller observed that a truck fleet that large seemed to provide "evidence that there is much more tonnage being furnished the south than 15 tons per day."[37]

James Kendall, the committee's chief counsel, had also been doing some calculations as McNamara spoke. He figured that the fifteen tons a day amounted to just 1.6 ounces per man, then offered a comment that demonstrated McNamara's lack of credibility: "They are firing a tremendous amount of mortars, artillery rounds, and rockets down there."[38]

The assertion that probably did the most to damage McNamara, at least with the Joint Chiefs of Staff, was this: "I think it will be a successful war, if we maintain our pressure and our patience."[39] That statement branded McNamara a liar, because the JCS knew that he had been arguing for perhaps as long as two years that there was no way the war could be won militarily. When McNamara subsequently said, responding to a question from Senator Symington, "I don't believe that there is this gulf between the military leaders and the civilian leaders in the executive branch," his last shred of credibility disappeared.[40] Worse yet, from his standpoint, he lost ground with his most important patron. "The President," said Townsend Hoopes, "was jolted and displeased by McNamara's statement before the Stennis Committee."[41] As George Herring has pointed out, what upset LBJ was not McNamara's statement that there was no gulf between the JCS and the Secretary of Defense, but the revelation from McNamara's statement that there was indeed a sizable gulf.[42]

In its report, the subcommittee stated that McNamara and the Joint Chiefs of Staff held "diametrically opposed" views on conduct of the air war against North Vietnam, although McNamara had maintained that their differences were "very narrow" and did not involve fundamental strategy.[43] McNamara was apparently slow to grasp the significance of the revealed split, perhaps only doing so in light of press coverage following his testimony. After Wheeler's earlier appearance before the committee, McNamara had described himself as gratified. Wheeler "did a helluva good job," he told President Johnson in Wheeler's presence at an 18 August White House meeting.[44]

By the time, a number of years later, of the Westmoreland versus CBS libel trial, however, McNamara saw things differently. The Stennis hearing, he said, personalizing the matter, "was an extraordinarily trying ordeal in which the Chiefs and the Committee were against me."[45] The Joint Chiefs of Staff, he said, "were unanimous in believing that the bombing was effective, and this poor, inexperienced civilian didn't know what the hell was going on and had a different view. That was the conclusion of the hearing."[46] Still later, in his memoirs, McNamara claimed that "President Johnson considered [the hearings] a political disaster. He later told Bus: 'Your generals almost destroyed us with their testimony before the Stennis Committee. We were murdered in the hearings.' "[47] After the hearings, however, LBJ approved many of the things the Joint Chiefs had been pushing for, including some measures that McNamara had specifically recommended against, so there appears to be an element of self-serving in McNamara's recollection of the matter.

A dramatic event followed that was first reported by journalist Mark Perry many years after the war: consideration by the Joint Chiefs of Staff of resignation en masse. On the evening of Friday, 25 August 1967, the day on which McNamara had testified, Wheeler is reported to have called the Joint Chiefs of Staff together, not in the "tank" where they usually met, but in his office, and with no aides present. Asking each man never to mention the meeting, Wheeler told them that McNamara's testimony—characterized by

Perry as his "bad-faith defense of a clearly discredited strategy"—was simply false, and that it was time for resignation in protest.[48] He proposed a press conference the following morning at which they would make the announcement. After discussion that continued late into the night, they all agreed. By the next morning, however, Wheeler had had a change of heart. Reconvening the Chiefs, he talked them out of doing what he had persuaded them to do the night before. All this Perry reported without attribution in *Four Stars*, an insightful 1989 history of the JCS.

There is evidence substantiating his account. Before his death, General Wheeler spoke of the episode to his wife and to his grown son, and also discussed it with General Bruce Palmer. "It was at that point that General Wheeler, who was Chairman at the time, told me that the Joint Chiefs considered resigning," said Palmer. "*En masse.* But Wheeler talked them out of it. Thinking back on it now, I think we should have made the effort. We should have turned in our suits," Palmer added.[49]

Lieutenant General Dennis P. McAuliffe, who worked in Wheeler's office during this period, also had some knowledge of the event. "In talking the JCS out of it," he said, "General Wheeler told them if they resigned 'they'd put some stooges in' who would do whatever they wanted them to do."[50] Air Force Lieutenant General John McPherson, also close to Wheeler, confirmed that "people around Wheeler were aware of the JCS discussion of resignation. Wheeler was the one the next day who called it off."[51]

General Johnson, said Palmer, also "discussed it with me several times." Added Palmer, "after first denying that this ever happened, Admiral Moorer later told me that the Chiefs had in fact come close to resigning en masse." Further, after dinner at his quarters at Fort Myer one evening in 1968, General Wheeler told Palmer "that he planned to write a series of essays about civil-military relations which would indirectly bring out the whole story."[52]

General Wheeler's widow also knew the story. "I think Johnny was the one who first talked about it," she said, referring to Harold K. Johnson. "They changed their minds because of what Bus said: 'Who would they put in that could do better? And it would be mutiny. Do we want them to get cat's-paws?' "[53]

"My recollection is it's true," said Wheeler's son Dr. Gilmore Wheeler. "They discussed resigning and more or less decided to do it. Then they slept on it and began discussing it again. And the issue became 'who will step into this mess behind us?' And someone told my dad that no other military officer had the respect of the President and the Congress to the extent that he did. Later he came to doubt that, but there was absolutely no question that the Joint Chiefs as a group discussed resigning, and came very close to doing so."[54]

One apparent outcome of the hearings was that General Wheeler, who had been largely excluded from LBJ's Tuesday Lunch meetings of the inner circle, was added to the guest list. How much good that did is unclear, since the Tuesday Lunch was an unsatisfactory forum for any kind of coherent planning or decision making. Chester Cooper summed it up when he said that the Tuesday Lunch had "much of the character of a cabal: no agenda, no minutes, no regular subsequent communication or follow-up with staff officers and subordinate officials."[55] William Bundy agreed, calling the Tuesday Lunch "a procedural abomination—rambling, lacking in a formal agenda or clear conclusions, infinitely wearing to the participants, and confusing to those at the second level who then had to take the supporting actions"—all in all, "a nightmare."[56]

CHAPTER TWENTY-THREE

EXPLOSIONS

During 1967, General Westmoreland made a series of trips back to the United States to report optimistically on developments in Vietnam. These appearances, along with those of other members of the administration, came to be known collectively as the "progress offensive." Whatever effect this first round of the progress offensive was having on the press, the public, and the Congress, it was apparently not convincing its principal sponsor, LBJ himself, who in a Memorial Day proclamation called the war a "bloody impasse."[1]

At almost the same time, Ambassador Bunker was submitting a paper entitled "Blueprint for Viet-Nam," which included an assessment that was jarringly contrary to what was being said publicly. "We still have a long way to go," it began. "Much of the country is still in VC hands, the enemy can still shell our bases and commit acts of terrorism in the securest areas, VC units still mount large scale attacks, most of the populace has still not actively committed itself to the Government, and," most tellingly, "a VC infrastructure still exists throughout the country."[2]

This bleak assessment casts considerable doubt on McNamara's claim that "the optimistic briefings I had heard in Saigon" the preceding month "eased my long-standing doubts about the war's progress in the South" and led him to tell the president, " 'There is not a military stalemate,' and . . . if we stuck to our program we would win—contingent, of course, on the performance of the South Vietnamese government."[3]

In November 1967 Westmoreland returned to the United States to continue the progress offensive, telling reporters who greeted him in Washington that he was "very, very encouraged. I have never been more encouraged during my entire almost four years in country." Then, in a speech at the National Press Club, Westmoreland said reassuringly, "I am absolutely certain that whereas in 1965 the enemy was winning, today he is certainly losing. We have reached an important point when the end begins to come into view."

Harold K. Johnson was unimpressed by Westmoreland's actions, cabling General Abrams through back channels to observe, "I only hope that he has not dug a hole for himself with regard to his prognostications. The platform of false prophets is crowded!"[4]

Later, Westmoreland would claim that he had been an unwilling participant in the progress offensive, that he had been ordered to take part by the President. "As I was reluctant to go to Washington for public appearances, so I sought no public exposure for personal aggrandizement," he wrote in his memoirs.[5] The record shows otherwise; it shows, in fact, that the progress offensive was at least partly Westmoreland's idea. In a cable to General Wheeler, Westmoreland argued the need to counter public perceptions of lack of progress in the war and to orchestrate a public-relations campaign to rally public support for the war. "Of course we must make haste carefully in order to avoid charges that the military establishment is conducting an organized propaganda campaign, either overt or covert," Westmoreland cautioned.[6]

General Bruce Palmer also perceived Westmoreland's enthusiasm for the mission. "Since it was obvious that Westmoreland was being used for political purposes," he wrote, "many of us in Vietnam at the time resented having our field commander put on the spot in this manner. Westmoreland enjoyed these occasions, however, and would return to Saigon still 'up on cloud nine.' "[7]

These representations by Westmoreland helped set the stage for the disillusionment of the American people, government, and media in the wake of the enemy's widespread attacks at Tet 1968. There followed a concatenation of events precipitated in large measure by the shock of that offensive. Westmoreland was replaced as MACV commander, U.S. troop withdrawals began, public support for the war progressively dwindled, and eventually the South Vietnamese were abandoned altogether.

These developments left Harold K. Johnson embittered. Earlier, returning from his fifth trip to Vietnam, he had spoken publicly of his views on the possibility of American withdrawal from Southeast Asia. "To do so," he told an audience in New York, "would be to abandon everything we have been fighting and dying for in Vietnam. To do so would be to close for all time the book of our American heritage." Two years later, as his retirement drew near, Johnson could see that very prospect on the horizon. "I don't happen to be a fan of General Westmoreland," he said in an oral history interview. "I don't think I ever was, and I certainly didn't become one as a result of the Vietnam War."[8]

The trauma of dealing with McNamara's OSD had also left its mark. "He really hated arrogance," Johnson's son Bobby said of his father, "and he felt there was a lot of that around."[9] General Andrew Goodpaster provided pertinent insights into civil-military relationships at this juncture in an oral history interview. "You had here, on the civilian side," he noted, "a group of very intelligent people who were completely unaware of the limits of their competence. Those limits in terms of understanding the military art were quite severe—that is, in terms of understanding the extent of unknowns in a situation of this kind, the need for making decisions that provided for flexibility and a certain measure of redundancy in order to meet problems that could not be foreseen in precise terms and in detail—an awareness and a recognition of the nonquantifiable factors that enter into military affairs, such as the value of human life, for example."[10]

Systems Analysis in OSD earned Johnson's particular disdain. "Now I was a believer in asking questions," he said. "Where I became disenchanted with the system was when they began to provide conclusions and then build studies around them to support the conclusions."

In Johnson's view, another key problem was that Secretary McNamara had altered the traditional role of the service secretaries, changing them from primary spokesmen and advocates for their respective services into no more than assistant secretaries of defense, working de facto for one of McNamara's principal associates. This, thought Johnson, put the full burden of explaining and defending the Army's mission, needs, and performance on the uniformed leadership, a role that he thought they were illequipped to perform and that the Secretary should be performing.

Johnson also blamed the adversary relationship between OSD and the services for an adverse impact on effective functioning of the Joint Chiefs of Staff. "The Joint Staff, at least at the time that I left it," said Johnson, "had not matured to the extent that they could produce a paper in which I had a great deal of confidence." This internal problem was greatly exacerbated by the externals. "As criticism rose, the tendency was [for the JCS] to close ranks more tightly, and not to let divisions between them or differences between them come to the surface and be exposed where they might be exploited."

This had extremely serious consequences in terms of a whole range of defense issues, from strategy and tactics through budget and acquisition decisions to the evaluation of everything from the threat to progress in the war. "As the adversary relationship hardened, the opposing factions tended to close ranks, and differences that ought to be exposed and analyzed didn't appear, and there's a deliberate effort to submerge them so that they don't appear. I don't think this is good for the defense effort," Johnson concluded.

As for dealings with McNamara himself, Johnson recalled that the Secretary's meetings with the Joint Chiefs of Staff tended to be cosmetic, con-

ducted primarily to answer criticism that JCS advice was not being sought
or heeded; the meetings were devoid of any serious consideration of substance. "They were sort of like a mating dance of the turkeys," he once
suggested. "You went through certain set procedures, but you solved no
problems."

In short, Johnson's experience with the senior civilian leadership in OSD
left him unadmiring of their professionalism, competence, and ethical
grounding. With authority should go accountability, Johnson believed, but
"this regrettably was not something that the Assistant Secretaries of Defense
during the McNamara and Clifford regimes were prepared to accept, in my
humble opinion. As a matter of fact," said Johnson, "I think in many respects they were intellectual prostitutes whom I cared little for, or respected,
because they simply were not prepared to assume the responsibility for their
actions. . . . I think they were a sorry lot of people."

AT THE END OF JANUARY 1968 the enemy launched what came to be known
as the Tet Offensive, striking installations and cities all over Vietnam. The
shock of these widespread, coordinated attacks was heightened by the effects of the previous year's progress offensive, as Walter Cronkite made clear
in his questioning of the President. "Don't you feel that perhaps we were set
up psychologically for that defeat by the optimistic statements from Vietnam and from Washington?" he asked.

LBJ could not deny it. "I'm certain that that may have contributed to it,"
he admitted.[11]

General Westmoreland sought to reassure the President, the press, the
public, and the Congress, but severely undermined his own efforts by claiming a victory and then saying that he needed 206,000 more troops.[12] This
set off the most intense reexamination of the American commitment to Vietnam since ground forces had first been dispatched nearly three years earlier, and was a true watershed in terms of that commitment.

IN THE SPRING OF 1968 an interesting Army staff action was being worked
in the nuclear division of ACSFOR. Known as "Oregon Trail," it had to do
with battlefield nuclear weapons employment in the European environment.
The primary action officer was Albion Knight, who besides being a colonel
in the Army was a priest of the Episcopal Church.

One day Knight received a note from General Johnson that said something like "I've been looking through my Bible and I can't find justification

for continuing a study based on the tenets of Oregon Trail." Johnson was concerned about the spillover effect of such weapons on the civilian population. This was a serious matter, because in those days, allied forces in Europe, outmanned and on the defensive, counted on being able to use tactical nuclear weapons to deter aggression and to help repel it if deterrence failed.

Knight wrote up a justification for continuing the study, based on *his* reading of the Bible. "In effect I told the Chief of Staff that he was full of beans," he said. Forty-five minutes passed, then Knight got a call telling him to report to General Johnson. When Knight arrived, he found that the Chief of Staff had gathered in anticipation of his arrival the Vice Chief of Staff, the commanding general of the Combat Developments Command, and some other senior officers, "about twenty stars in all."

Johnson had Knight's memorandum on the table in front of him. "So you think I am wrong?" he asked.

"Yes, sir, I do," Knight replied.

Johnson went around the table, asking each man whether he agreed with Colonel Knight's position. The first said that he did. So did the second, and the third, and so on around the table. What Johnson may not have known was that several of those queried were members of the congregation at St. Paul's, Knight's church in suburban Virginia, or had been communicants of a church he served earlier in El Paso. Johnson thought for a few moments, then said quietly, "All right, continue with the study."

IN COUNTERPOINT to the war in Vietnam was a succession of violent demonstrations in U.S. cities, crises that increasingly necessitated intervention by troops when civil authorities were no longer able to maintain control. "Civil disturbances" they were called euphemistically, but the hard truth is that an epidemic of rioting, arson, looting, maiming, and killing ravaged the nation. In city after city it fell to the Army, both active and reserve components, to deal with this. Thus Harold K. Johnson found himself with his own domestic war to contend with, even as the war in Vietnam continued to rage.

On 4 April 1968, Martin Luther King was assassinated, setting off another round of violence. Johnson's last weeks in office were immersed in the grim task of putting down insurrections by the citizenry he had devoted his professional life to defending. He mobilized Army forces that same night, and on Friday night put troops in Washington. Saturday night, troops went into Chicago, and Sunday night into Baltimore. Meanwhile, he had troop commanders reconnoitering Pittsburgh and Kansas City on a precautionary basis. Describing these events contemporaneously, Johnson spoke of "the tragedy of our cities—a national shame—that our country could fall to this state." He was close to tears. "I tell you, it's something one doesn't like to contemplate at all."

WHEN GENERAL JOHNSON RETIRED, Sergeant Major of the Army Wooldridge was reassigned to Vietnam. It subsequently came to light that for years he had apparently been involved in a conspiracy to defraud Army clubs and messes of large amounts of money. Indicted by a federal grand jury, Wooldridge was allowed to retire. Some of those charged as his co-conspirators received dishonorable discharges and heavy fines.[13]

"The Sergeant Major of the Army was a tremendous shock to Harold K. Johnson," remembered General William Knowlton. "He just could not believe that his confidence would have been so violated by a man." Johnson had indeed trusted Wooldridge, and admired the job he had done as the first incumbent Sergeant Major of the Army. "You have shouldered a large burden and I am most appreciative of the way you've done it," Johnson told him in a handwritten note midway through their service together.[14] When Wooldridge left the Pentagon assignment, Johnson presented him with the Distinguished Service Medal. It was, said Sergeant Major Loikow, "the only DSM presented to an enlisted man since they gave one to the fellow who spotted the Japs coming over Kola Kola Pass."

"I feel very badly about the Sergeant Major," Johnson said some years after his retirement, "because I thought he did a very splendid job in an awkward position where he was establishing the ground rules for what would be done in subsequent years. He had the trust and confidence of a substantial body of the enlisted population of the Army."[15]

A second case of misplaced trust was equally devastating to Johnson. It involved Major General Carl C. Turner, who had been his Provost Marshal General and was closely involved with Johnson in Masonic observances and prayer breakfasts. Turner—"a real crook," said Chief of Chaplains Charlie Brown—had gathered confiscated weapons from civilian police agencies, then sold them for private gain. This, too, came to light after Johnson's retirement but had taken place on his watch. Turner was convicted of tax evasion and fraud and sent to prison.

What is more, these two cases were eventually found to be linked in a sinister way, for it was determined that Turner had apparently suppressed the early investigation of the Wooldridge case.[16] When this came to light, the Criminal Investigation Detachment was converted to a major command, the U.S. Army Criminal Investigation Command, to give it more independence and less susceptibility to influence from the Provost Marshal General.

"The one great failing of General Johnson," concluded General Knowlton, "was that he was himself so honest and so honorable that he didn't recognize dishonesty or lack of honor on the part of others. He got taken to the cleaners by General Turner . . . and by Sergeant Major of the Army Wooldridge." Brigadier General James Piner, who had been Johnson's aide, suggested that people in high positions are inherently vulnerable to such exploitation and that Johnson "had fewer of these mistakes than most senior officers."

It would have been no comfort to Johnson, but his able Vice Chief of Staff, General Creighton Abrams, had been similarly misled. "General Abrams used to say," recalled his longtime aide Tom Noel, "that the only two people he ever totally misjudged were Colonel Turner and that Sergeant Major. Abrams was a tremendous judge of character . . . [but] he was wrong on Wooldridge and Turner. He never really got over the fact that he had been wrong."

JOHNSON HAD HIS OWN CRISIS with suspicion and mistrust. One day he had been testifying before some committee on the Hill. When he came out, Sergeant Kaiser had the car waiting for him at the curb. As Johnson prepared to get in, a reporter stepped up to Johnson and asked whether he could ask him something. He was late for another appointment, Johnson said, but he'd answer one question. The reporter wanted to know what Johnson thought about mining Haiphong harbor. "Militarily it should be done," Johnson told him, "but politically it can't be." Then Johnson got in the sedan, and Kaiser drove him away.

The next morning, the headline in the *Washington Post* was "Army Chief of Staff Advocates Mining Haiphong," or words to that effect. Early in the day, Johnson had Sergeant Kaiser drive him to the White House. Johnson went inside, and after a few minutes, Kaiser, too, was summoned to the Oval Office. LBJ shook his hand, then asked, "What did General Johnson say to that reporter yesterday?"

"The truth, Sergeant Kaiser," said General Johnson. Then he turned and looked out the window.

Kaiser told the President exactly what had taken place, that General Johnson had said that militarily Haiphong ought to be mined, but that politically it couldn't be done.

"Thank you, Sergeant Kaiser," said the President. "You just saved your boss's job."

On the way back to the Pentagon, General Johnson said to Kaiser, "I'd appreciate it if you'd keep that conversation under your hat."

"What conversation?" Kaiser responded. "With who? Where?" And, said Kaiser in an interview nearly three decades later, "I've never told anyone about it until now."

ONE CRUCIAL RITE OF PASSAGE for the Army's leadership is selection for brigadier general, a very narrow gate to pass through. Johnson paid particular attention to the instructions that these newly selected members of the top leadership received, especially in his own remarks. "There is just one charge I would like to leave with you," he told them, referring to the Army's most precious possession, its integrity. "That is that your job is to uphold that integrity—just play it straight."

On other occasions, Johnson assembled Army officers who were working on the Joint Staff or in other assignments outside the Army in the Washington area. "I want to make it crystal clear that when you are working outside the Army you haven't an obligation to any so-called Army 'party line.' We do not have a party line. We would prefer that you look at whatever problems confront you from the point of view of what is good for the country." Once you have figured out what that is, he said, "You do what is right for the country, and the Army will live with it." And whoever you work for, Johnson emphasized, "your loyalty has to be to that person."

DURING THESE LAST YEARS of his service, Johnson thought a lot about the meaning of individual responsibility, especially when he saw some young men stepping forward to serve their country when called to do so and others who rioted, burned cities, or ran away to escape such a call. "Those who accept responsibility in our country contribute to America and all that it stands for," he told an audience at John Carroll University. "Those who dodge it or dally with it are people who just happen to live here—who partake of a feast that others have sown, harvested, prepared, cooked and served."[17]

CHAPTER TWENTY-FOUR

COMPLINE

As Chief of Staff, Johnson made nine trips to Vietnam, flew nearly half a million miles, and spent in the aggregate almost an entire year of his four years in the job on the road, visiting troop units and installations, speaking in support of the nation's effort in Vietnam, showing the flag, looking after soldiers.

He never lost his quiet sense of humor, an attribute not well known to people who were not close to him, but greatly enjoyed by those who were. At the end of a visit to one of the Army's basic training centers, he stopped to talk with the senior noncommissioned officer. "Any problems?" Johnson asked.

"None we can't handle," he was told, "but some of these trainees do an awful lot of griping."

"Well, sergeant major," observed Johnson, "they're infantry privates, and that's one of the few privileges they have."

Johnson always insisted on the primacy of the Army's people, on the essentiality of "putting the personal into personnel" and making real the concept that "the Army takes care of its own." His conviction was that the soldier deserved no less. "It is the soldier who fights; it is the soldier who bleeds and dies if he must; it is the soldier who brings the victory home," he emphasized. "Where does he get this devotion? I wish I could say that we issue it to him in the Army, but we can only help him find it. He brings it with him from family, the church, and schools of his hometown, or he doesn't bring it at all."[1]

As the war dragged on, Johnson worked behind the scenes to bring about essential change in the way the war was being fought on the ground in South Vietnam. "I felt in 1962," he said, "and I still felt in 1968—with virtually no way to influence it—that what was required was a lot of scouting and patrolling type of activity by quite small units with the capacity to reinforce quickly. We didn't get into much of that." But in the last months of his tenure, Johnson succeeded in implementing the strategy and tactics that he thought could win the war under a commander who shared those views. It was one of his least known and most important accomplishments.

Historian Martin Blumenson characterized the four years during which Johnson served as Chief of Staff as "one of the most militarily frustrating periods in U.S. history. And yet," he added, "it was a time when the Army scored some of its most impressive achievements."[2] The leadership and example of Harold K. Johnson were at the heart of that performance.

IN THE SUMMER OF 1968, many people thought that Johnson would be appointed Chairman of the Joint Chiefs of Staff. Instead, General Wheeler was reappointed and Johnson was retired. This came as a surprise, even a shock, to people close to both Wheeler and Johnson. As far back as the summer of 1966, said General Bernard Rogers, who had been Wheeler's executive officer, "Wheeler was already exhausted and ill. I was frankly quite surprised when he stayed on."

Wheeler had a heart attack while on a visit to Vietnam in July 1967, but it was not discovered until a physical examination upon his return to the United States. He was hospitalized and then on convalescent leave for several weeks, during which time Johnson was Acting Chairman of the JCS. When Wheeler got out of the hospital he went to see the President. "I suggested to him that I should retire and that he should appoint somebody else as Chairman of the Joint Chiefs of Staff," said Wheeler. But LBJ told him that he didn't want anybody else, and that if the physicians said that Wheeler could do the job he wanted him to stay on.[3] So Wheeler finished out what everyone thought would be the final year of his term as Chairman. When that ended, he was reappointed by LBJ for an additional year, and then for yet another year by President Richard Nixon.

The evidence is mixed as to what Johnson wanted to see happen. As far back as December 1964, he had apparently asked for staff advice on his tenure as Army Chief of Staff. A memorandum from the Army's Deputy Chief of Staff for Personnel indicated that he had not been appointed for a specific term, so, in consonance with the statute, his tenure was at the pleasure of the President, "but not for more than four years" unless reappointed.[4]

Early in his tenure, he had written to General Hugh Harris, who was on the point of retiring, that "it comes home pretty forcibly to me from time to time that I have no next assignment to look forward to either, and a somewhat uncertain tenure in this one!"

Lieutenant General Harry Lemley, who had been close to Johnson since Fort Leavenworth days, was certain that Johnson was retired because he was not compliant enough to suit the civilian leadership. "He was fired," said Lemley, "and it was a terrific blow to him." Lemley, who was DCSOPS at the time, said that the White House also chose "a very dirty way to do it." General Wheeler had been over at the White House, and when he returned he said, "Johnny, I've got to see you right away." They went into Wheeler's office, where Johnson was told that he had a choice of being assigned as U.S. Representative to the NATO Military Committee—a huge comedown from his status as Chief of Staff—or retiring.[5] That is one version.

Sergeant Kaiser, Johnson's driver, provides another. "Towards the end of General Johnson's term as Chief of Staff," he recalled, "we were in the back of the White House when President Johnson came out with him and said, 'Johnny, you know we got you pegged for the next Chairman of the Joint Chiefs.' General Johnson replied, 'I humbly decline, Mr. President, on the grounds I would have that much *more* responsibility and that much *less* say so.' "[6]

Dorothy Johnson confirms her husband's reluctance. "I know people say Johnny wanted to be Chairman of the Joint Chiefs of Staff," she acknowledges, "but he *didn't!* He'd had enough of those whiz boys!"

On 23 March 1968, LBJ announced that General Johnson would retire when his term ended in July, that General Westmoreland would be nominated to succeed him, and that he was asking General Wheeler to stay on for a year as Chairman.[7]

Naturally, Johnson was inundated with correspondence from people who had hoped, and expected, that he would be moving up to be Chairman. His answers were moderate and reasoned. "I have consistently maintained that my tenure as Chief of Staff would complete my service in the Army," he wrote to former aide Tom Irwin. "This is the only logical course."

To General Polk he wrote that "many months ago I decided that when my time came I should step aside and make way for the next generation unless there was some reason that I would have to stay in the national interest. Such a case is hardly conceivable to me." To his former executive officer Johnson disclosed that he had been offered a couple of other assignments that "held virtually no attraction." He admitted, "If the senior commander were in a position to influence the course of events somewhat more than is the case now, I would probably have a different outlook. However, I see little change in the offing and since this is the case I believe that I should be fully honest with myself and my superiors and step aside." To General Mike Davison, Johnson said, "I do not have the qualifications required of a Chairman so I will make my departure with pride in the performance of the Army."

In a tantalizing footnote, Johnson's office calendar shows that on Friday, 5 April, two tailors came for uniform fittings—one green uniform and one white. Since the White House had already announced Johnson's impending retirement, why would he need two new uniforms? Had he ordered these uniforms earlier in anticipation of a different outcome? If so, his hopes, or expectations, had been dashed.

OVER SEVERAL YEARS the Army had been called on to deal with civil disturbances in such places as Detroit, Watts, Baltimore, Chicago, and Washington, including a march on the Pentagon by antiwar protesters. Near the end of Johnson's tenure, a new round of violence was precipitated by Martin Luther King's murder in April 1968, and in late June, the situation became so threatening that a Military Police battalion was ordered to Fort Myer. That was where Johnson lived, and two weeks before he was due to retire, he was practically under siege. In some perverse way, that seemed appropriate, commensurate with the rest of the experience.

NEAR THE END, Johnson wrote to a friend that his plans for retirement were not yet complete. "However, there's one thing I am not going to do; that is, to create any more problems for the President. He has enough already. Consistent with this I may have something to say from time to time."

AT FORT SILL IN MID-JUNE, Johnson spoke to the student officers, then got some gratifying feedback from a father who forwarded his son's account of the event. "General Johnson was down here to talk to us last week," he began. "He arrived twenty minutes late, spoke for an hour and twenty minutes, including some of the lunch period, and you could have heard a pin drop the entire time. He is, without a doubt, one of the most fascinating people we have seen out here, or anywhere else for that matter. He spoke about Nam, the M-16, riots, and our role as professional officers and our responsibilities to the country, to include our legal position in the structure of government, a thing which has never been clearly put to most of us. His presentation is the first one that I have left with a feeling of confidence and a smile on my face. The entire group was smiling, which is extremely unusual. The whole thing was very gratifying and stimulating."

EVENTUALLY, in correspondence with friends and later in oral history interviews, Johnson expressed some summary judgments about the war in Vietnam. "I leave with no regrets," he said, "except that we have failed to reach a solution in Vietnam in my tenure."

He identified "two very significant mistakes," one political and one military. Politically, "we tried to please everybody, and as a consequence we pleased nobody." And militarily, "we simply didn't get there first with the most, a fundamental military axiom. When you violate it, you're in trouble."

Underlying those mistakes, Johnson suggested, was "an underlying assumption in the minds of most of the people involved, and this includes the President and his advisors and the people at the State Department and the people in the military departments, including the Joint Chiefs of Staff, that if the United States demonstrated a fairly hard line of support for South Vietnam that our power and prestige in the world would be so awesome that the other side would have really no alternative but to cave in."

Much later, Johnson wrote that "Vietnam turned out about as badly as it might have except that I have no regrets at all about the action that we took when we went in initially. My principal regret is that I was not much more forceful in attempting to deal with the Secretary of Defense and the President with regard to the objectives that were established in Vietnam and the restrictions with respect to national policy that we imposed upon ourselves, such as no overthrow of the government in North Vietnam, no invasion of North Vietnam, and no violation of the Geneva Accords of 1954 and 1962. In retrospect, it is reasonably clear now that the Joint Chiefs of Staff did not have their wits about them when they failed to oppose the President's determination that the folks in charge in Hanoi would not be thrown out."

A SERIES of dramatic and emotional events crowded the last days of Johnson's active service. In early June he spoke at the ROTC commissioning ceremony at Dickinson College, where his son Bobby was graduating and, as a Distinguished Military Graduate, receiving a Regular Army commission in the Infantry.[8]

Three days later Johnson was at West Point to give the graduation address to the Class of 1968, Bobby's former class, on what must have been a bittersweet occasion. He recalled the graduation address his own Class of 1933 had heard, thirty-five years before. "I shall never forget General Douglas MacArthur as he stood before us and described the perils of the then current wave of pacifism: 'any nation that would keep its self-respect must keep alive its martial ardor and be prepared to defend itself.' "

Now this class, he said, was going out into a "tough, cruel demanding world of reality where advantage, gain and privilege are accompanied by work, sweat, tears and accountability for our actions." He offered them the words of the Apostle Paul: "Whatsoever things are true, whatsoever things are honest, whatsoever things are just, whatsoever things are pure, think on these things."

That afternoon, back in his Pentagon office, Johnson administered the oath of office to Bobby, then helped Dorothy pin on their son's second lieutenant's bars.

In Vietnam, Creighton Abrams penned a handwritten letter. "I would like somehow to convey to you what it has meant to me to serve for you," he began. "I simply feel inadequate to the task. I will say at least that my service as your vice chief of staff was the most rewarding experience I have had. I have never felt more trusted." And, he wrote, "You have made a great and lasting mark on the Army."

At the end, Johnson thanked his personal staff, pinned well-earned decorations on them all, then went to say farewell to the Army Staff. The papers he had worked on the preceding Saturday, he told them, carried numbers in the 8,000s. That meant that for the past four years, about forty papers a day, seven days a week, had crossed his desk.[9]

"Every one of us—*every one of us*—has always got to bear in mind 'to thine own self be true.' You have got to live with yourself," Johnson told them. "One of the things that I am going to take away with me at noon today is that I think that I am still my own man. I have not been captured. I have been manipulated, perhaps, a little bit, but not too much. You must not permit this. Sometimes it is awfully hard—awfully hard. Sometimes you will suffer. But this is just one of the hazards."

He continued, "So I want to leave this injunction with you: draw your truth line up there, and keep your toes on it—always on it—and maintain that integrity." He concluded, "There just aren't words to express my appreciation to you. Finally, just a farewell. I'll see you somewhere, sometime. Good luck to you all."

EPILOGUE

General Harold K. Johnson retired from the United States Army on 2 July 1968. "I don't believe there is any more interesting way to make a living than what we do in the Army," he had once observed. "I don't think there is any more challenging way. And I don't think there is any more satisfying way." Now, after thirty-five years as a soldier, he made a quiet departure, declining a parade or other formal ceremony. On his last full day in office he worked his usual long hours and then, noted an aide, just closed his briefcase and left. The next morning, at a small White House gathering, President Johnson awarded him an Oak Leaf Cluster to the Distinguished Service Medal.

On that occasion LBJ recited some words that he said fit General Johnson well, words like "gentle, faithful, loyal, wise, and—as the thousands of men who have served under him all testify—beloved." Johnny Johnson made a few remarks of his own. He had begun his service as Chief of Staff by reciting some lines from the Scout Oath, and at the end he returned to that touchstone, observing that he had sometimes been described as having approached his duties like a Boy Scout. "I accept the charge and am honored by it," he said, "because I have seen no Boy Scout tear down the flag of our country, nor attack the values and the standards that have made our country great."[1] Then he called it a career.

PUBLIC SERVICE had been Johnson's life, and in retirement he turned again to that course. For three years he headed the Freedoms Foundation at Valley Forge, until the demands of fund-raising became "downright demeaning." Then he embarked on yet another career as a banking executive before retiring for a final time.

He and Dorothy spent much time at a cottage on Lake George, a soul-restoring refuge for them both. From their earliest days together, Dorothy's love and support had been major factors in Johnson's life. His assignment as Chief of Staff had in many ways been an ordeal for them both, perhaps especially for Dorothy. "She led a horrible life those four years," said Tom Irwin sympathetically. Now—for the first time, really, since she sailed home from the Philippines almost a lifetime ago—they could be together without the pressures of rebuilding a shattered career or trying to deal with one un-yielding crisis after another.

Meanwhile, in Vietnam, remarkable things were happening. General Creighton Abrams, finally in command, set about implementing the recommendations of the PROVN Study that he had helped Johnson see through to completion. In what proved to be an absolutely splendid combination of talent and character, Ambassador Ellsworth Bunker, Abrams, and Ambassador William Colby coalesced the multiple aspects of the campaign into "one war." They progressively turned responsibility for it back to the South Vietnamese while helping them improve their ability to handle it, coped with the simultaneous progressive redeployment of their own forces, and in essence saw the internal war against insurgency successfully completed.

When virtually all American ground troops had been withdrawn and Abrams—a renowned tanker—had only air and naval elements to throw into the battle, the South Vietnamese stood up to a ferocious assault by enemy conventional forces amounting to some fourteen divisions in the 1972 Easter Offensive. It took the communists three years to mount another comparable onslaught. By then the United States had withdrawn all its military support, and finally its financial assistance as well, while China and the Soviet Union continued to supply their North Vietnamese surrogate abundantly. With those the prevailing realities, the outcome of the final offensive in 1975 was foreordained, and South Vietnam succumbed.

Johnson lived to see all that, as Abrams mercifully had not. And in his last years, Johnson revisited an issue that had long nagged at him: resignation in protest. It is certain that Johnson's personal example of principled leadership constituted one of his most meaningful contributions to the Army he led in those troubled times. He characteristically held himself to extremely demanding standards, and sometimes concluded that he had not measured up. During the course of his stewardship as Chief of Staff, he had on a number of occasions contemplated resignation in protest, but each time he drew back, concluding that he could do more good by continuing to serve.

In retirement, as a frequent speaker at the Army War College and elsewhere, he was invariably questioned on this matter, and answered as he had rationalized it to himself while in active service. Resignation would be a meaningless act, making at best a brief splash in the newspapers, then would be quickly forgotten, while others more amenable would be brought in to do the administration's bidding. Better to serve on, faithful to the Army and the soldier, and do what one could to make things better.

Late in his life, however, Johnson reached a different conclusion, one he confided to a number of people. The most fully articulated version was elicited by Brigadier General Albion Knight, the unusual officer who was also an Episcopal priest, the man who had matched biblical interpretations with Johnson over the "Oregon Trail" study. He and Johnson had by now known each other well for a number of years, and there came a point at which Knight posed a searching question. "General," he asked, "if you had to live your life over again, what would you do different?"

General Johnson responded by observing that there are sins of omission and sins of commission. He recalled that the Army had reached down quite a few files to make him Chief of Staff, and he believed that the Lord had pulled him up to do a job. He mentioned resignation in protest, asking, "Was that the job He wanted me to do?"

Then, very quietly, Johnson spoke of the conclusion he had reached. "I remember the day I was ready to go over to the Oval Office and give my four stars to the President and tell him, 'You have refused to tell the country they cannot fight a war without mobilization; you have required me to send men into battle with little hope of their ultimate victory; and you have forced us in the military to violate almost every one of the principles of war in Vietnam. Therefore, I resign and will hold a press conference after I walk out of your door.' "

Then, added Johnson with a look of anguish, "I made the typical mistake of believing I could do more for the country and the Army if I stayed in than if I got out. I am now going to my grave with that lapse in moral courage on my back."[2]

Whether anyone else would be so harsh in judging Johnson is questionable, for he was widely admired as an exemplary soldier and a man of inspiring decency and honor. General Bruce Palmer, Jr., reflected the views of many. Johnson, he said, was "one of the noblest men I have ever known. He was my beau ideal."

Harold K. Johnson passed from this life on 24 September 1983 at Walter Reed Army Medical Center in Washington, dead of cancer at the age of seventy-one. His body was cremated and his ashes laid to rest at Arlington National Cemetery, side by side forever with those young soldiers whose early deaths had filled his eyes with tears.

NOTES

The documentary record of Harold K. Johnson's outlook and exploits is very rich. Beginning with his prison camp diaries, it includes some 149 boxes of papers, including extensive correspondence, in the Archives of the U.S. Army Military History Institute. His primary oral history, also at MHI, is the most extensive in its large collection, running to more than 600 pages covering sixteen interview sessions conducted by three different interviewers over thirty-three months. In addition, there are four other specialized oral histories: one conducted for the U.S. Army Center of Military History, one by scholar D. Clayton James while Johnson was heading the Freedoms Foundation at Valley Forge, one in the "Abrams Story" series at MHI, and one by Colonel George H. Gray as part of a student research project.

These materials have been supplemented with some 200 interviews by the author, along with reference to the oral history interviews and in some cases the personal papers of dozens of others who knew and worked with Johnson at various stages of his career, as well as official records and collateral materials in the holdings of a number of depositories.

Given this abundance of material, it would have been possible to footnote virtually every line, but that seemed unnecessarily distracting and pedantic. The author has, however, prepared a fully annotated copy of the manuscript and will gladly respond to inquiries through the publisher as to the source of any quoted material. All materials drawn from the work of other scholars have of course been credited in the notes.

Abbreviations

CARL:	Combined Arms Research Library, USAC&GSC
CMH:	U.S. Army Center of Military History
HAAC:	History of Army Aviation Collection, MHI
HKJ:	Harold K. Johnson
HKJP:	Harold K. Johnson Papers, MHI
MCHC:	Marine Corps Historical Center
MHI:	U.S. Army Military History Institute
NA:	National Archives and Records Center
NPRC:	National Personnel Records Center, St. Louis, Missouri
USAC&GSC:	U.S. Army Command & General Staff College

VF OH: Oral Reminiscences of General Harold K. Johnson, Interview, Valley Forge, Pennsylvania

1. Early Life

1. Johnson's sister Edna Ray Hinman, the family historian, provided much of the detail on the early days. When Johnson was two years old, his family relocated to Edinburg, North Dakota; four years after that they moved to Hampden, North Dakota, where they lived for two years before finally settling in Grafton.

2. Harold K. Johnson, Jr., "Obituary," *Assembly* (June 1984): 136.

3. That cadet was Harry D. McHugh from Devils Lake, North Dakota, USMA Class of 1924. He had the distinction of commanding three different infantry regiment during and after World War II and then retiring as a colonel. Johnson received his appointment from Rep. O. B. Burtness of North Dakota's First District.

2. Cadet Days

1. A and M Companies had the tallest cadets, known as "flankers" because when the Corps lined up on parade they were on the left and right flanks of the formation. F and G Companies were assigned the shortest cadets, the "runts," and were in the middle of the formation. Thus the gradations in height were small from one company to the next, giving the impression that all cadets were the same size. Johnson, in C Company, was of about average height.

2. *Grafton News and Times*, 31 December 1930.

3. The account of this matter is based primarily on materials in the cadet records of Harold K. Johnson, USMA Office of the Registrar, West Point, New York.

4. *New York Times*, 14 June 1933.

3. Depression Army

1. This section is based on Association of the United States Army, *The U.S. Army between World Wars I and II* (Arlington, Va.: AUSA, March 1992), pp. 2–8.

2. Pamphlet, "Historic Fort Snelling," Minnesota Historical Society, n.d.

3. Herbert G. Sparrow, *The Times of Our Lives: Story of a West Point Class* (n.p.: privately printed, 1983), p. 44.

4. Dorothy Helen Rennix was born 28 May 1909 in Hankinson, North Dakota. When she was a high school sophomore, her family moved to Fargo, North Dakota, where she graduated from high school.

5. The marriage was performed by Judge R. M. Carson, variously described as an uncle or great-uncle of Johnson's.

6. Captain Coates also commanded a machine-gun company, and it won all the gunnery prizes. Eventually, people began to wonder if there might be some hanky-panky involved. An investigation was conducted, and what it revealed was Coates's

superb understanding of the soldier. He had rigged a light source, attached it to a machine gun, and set up one of the panoramic targets on the far wall of the company day room. Squeezing the trigger momentarily activated the light, which cast a beam the same size as a bullet. The soldiers got to playing around with this, and pretty soon they began placing bets on the results. Then it became a rage, and there was always a group of men competing on the machine gun, laying bets on the side. Naturally, in the process, they got more practice than any other troop. When it came to real firing on the range, they ate up the competition. Col. Maury S. Cralle served in the regiment and related this story.

7. As quoted in Martin Blumenson, "A Most Remarkable Man," *Army* (August 1968): 21.

8. Per Janet Johnson Levy. Another source identifies the man as Wilbrod Gourde.

9. USMA Class of 1933, *Golden Anniversary Book,* p. 45.

10. Sparrow, *The Times of Our Lives,* p. 46.

4. Philippine Scouts

1. John E. Olson, *Anywhere-Anytime: The History of the Fifty-seventh Infantry (PS)* (n.p.: privately printed, 1985), p. 6.

2. USMA Class of 1933, *Golden Anniversary Book* (n.p.: privately printed, 1983), p. 49.

3. Interview, *U.S. News & World Report,* 18 January 1982, p. 25. At the time of this interview, Johnson had been retired from the Army for fourteen years, but it is obvious that he still felt strongly about the conditions of unreadiness the nation had allowed to develop in the Philippines prior to World War II.

4. Gen. Jonathan M. Wainwright, *General Wainwright's Story,* ed. Robert Consadine (Garden City, N.Y.: Doubleday, 1946), p. 9.

5. Martin Blumenson, "A Most Remarkable Man," *Army* (August 1968): 22.

6. Wainwright, *General Wainwright's Story,* p. 10.

7. D. Clayton James, ed., *South to Bataan, North to Mukden: The Prison Diary of Brigadier General W. E. Brougher* (Athens: University of Georgia Press, 1971), p. 5.

8. Brig. Gen. Wm. E. Brougher, undated one-page essay entitled "57th Infantry Lieutenants," HKJP.

9. Louis Morton, *The Fall of the Philippines* (Washington, D.C.: Office of the Chief of Military History, Department of the Army, 1953), p. 21.

10. Obituary of Miller P. Warren, Jr., *Assembly* (April 1947): 13.

11. Wainwright, *General Wainwright's Story,* p. 8.

12. Ibid., p. 12.

13. Morton, *Fall of the Philippines,* p. 79.

14. Olson, *Anywhere-Anytime,* p. 25.

15. Wainwright, *General Wainwright's Story,* p. 9.

16. Later studies have confirmed these views. For example, historian Richard Meixsel found that when the ill-prepared Philippine Army forces and the able but outnumbered Philippine Scouts were forced back into the Bataan Peninsula, it was "thanks in part to MacArthur's ill-considered abrogation of WPO-3 earlier, [that]

they fell prey to disease, malnutrition, and the Imperial Japanese Army" (Richard B. Meixsel, "Major General George Grunert, WPO-3, and the Philippine Army, 1940–1941," *Journal of Military History* [April 1995]: 304). D. Clayton James noted that "in many of MacArthur's radios to Washington, he frequently spoke of the overwhelming odds that he was facing." But, added James, later scholarship revealed that General Homma actually had about 43,000 troops, as compared with the 80,000–100,000 MacArthur had under his command (see VF OH, comments by James as the interviewer). Stanley Falk observed that "there is little doubt that [MacArthur's] hesitation, vacillation and delay on the war's first day, his faulty tactical scheme and his strange relationship with President Quezon contributed significantly to the disaster that befell him" ("Review," *Army* [December 1995]: 61).

17. When it quickly became apparent that MacArthur had been wrong, that the defending forces could not hold on the beaches, "the awful consequences of the shifts in . . . defense plans became clear," wrote Jennifer L. Bailey in an official history. "The hasty withdrawal forced the retreating units to leave most of their supplies and equipment behind," material that had been moved up from depots throughout Bataan and Corregidor to support the beach-defense strategy. Now they were precipitously lost, and "the resulting lack of food, ammunition, weapons, and medical supplies would prove to be the critical factors in the subsequent operation" (*Philippine Islands: The U.S. Army Campaigns of World War II* [Washington, D.C.: U.S. Government Printing Office, 1992], p. 15).

18. 1st Lt. Mark Herbst, a surgeon with the 3d Battalion, 57th Infantry—the unit Johnson would take over late in the campaign—said that at Fort McKinley he had been issued "a case of medical instruments that had been used by the 31st Infantry in their 1918 Siberian expedition. The instruments were in cosmoline and the medications were in hard-rubber bottles." Herbst tried to use some of the medicines, but they were too old to be effective (quoted in Donald Knox, *Death March: The Survivors of Bataan* [New York: Harcourt Brace Jovanovich, 1981], p. 30).

5. Japanese Invasion

1. John E. Olson, *Anywhere-Anytime: The History of the Fifty-seventh Infantry (PS)* (n.p.: privately printed, 1985), p. 36.

2. Ibid., p. 42.

3. Douglas Brinkley, "Review," *Washington Post Book Review,* 18 December 1994, p. 2.

4. Louis Morton, *The Fall of the Philippines* (Washington, D.C.: Office of the Chief of Military History, Department of the Army, 1953), p. 157.

5. Olson, *Anywhere-Anytime,* p. 45.

6. "I don't view General MacArthur as a great captain as far as the defense of the Philippines was concerned," Johnson later said. "He was a masterful leader, a masterful figurehead, but there was a great deal of ridicule in the subordinate echelons of the differences between the press releases that were issued by his headquarters and the conditions as we knew them on the ground, and the gap between private and general in this particular case was very, very substantial. Disrespectful comments were widespread." John Olson, in *Anywhere-Anytime,* recalled a bitter stanza

that gained currency shortly after the outbreak of hostilities: "We're the battling bastards of Bataan, no mama, no papa, and no Uncle Sam. No uncles, no aunts, no nephews, no nieces; no pills, no planes, no artillery pieces. And nobody gives a damn." It was apt, he observed, for they had indeed been "cast adrift."

7. Association of the United States Army, *The Early Stages of World War II* (Arlington, Va.: AUSA, March 1992), p. 3. See also Ronald H. Spector, *Eagle Against the Sun* (New York: Free Press, 1985), p. 110; Spector dates the order to withdraw at a point early on 24 December.

8. Olson, *Anywhere-Anytime*, p. 31. Actually, the war with Japan lasted just four months short of four years.

9. Ibid., p. 49, as to the toast. The description rendered here is based on General Johnson's oral history; Colonel Olson's account details more intermediate moves by the regiment.

10. Olson puts the reduction in rations at 6 January in *O'Donnell: Andersonville of the Pacific* (n.p.: privately printed, 1985), p. 106.

11. Colonel Olson noted that Clarke was the only man in the regiment with any combat experience, and that "the other officers of the regiment, especially the staff, had great respect for the regimental commander's experience and judgment." But Clarke soon forfeited this advantage through his conduct. He was, said Olson, "unfortunately . . . a very emotional and highly imaginative person who was prone to exaggerate the risks and magnify the dangers in every shadow. He was determined that every measure would be taken to safeguard his command, and himself" (*Anywhere-Anytime*, p. 30).

12. John Whitman reported that when MacArthur visited the 57th Infantry's command post on 10 January, Clarke "was effusive in his conversation with MacArthur, referring to him as 'My General.' He assured MacArthur that the Scouts would defend their positions to the last man." But Clarke "believed airplanes had so changed the nature of warfare that foot soldiers had no hope of survival at all." By the next day, said Whitman, Clarke lay against the wall of the dugout with a blanket over his head. "When some 75mm self-propelled mounts fired from directly behind the dugout, Colonel Clarke collapsed and left Major Johnson to run the battle" (*Bataan: Our Last Ditch* [New York: Hippocrene, 1990], pp. 123, 134, 139–40).

13. This account relies primarily on Morton, *Fall of the Philippines*, pp. 251ff.

14. Olson, *Anywhere-Anytime*, p. 70. In an article published after the war, Johnson wrote that "withholding artillery support was a grave error" ("Defense Along the Abucay Line," *Military Review* [February 1949]: 50).

15. Olson, *Anywhere-Anytime*, p. 75.

16. Ibid.

17. Morton, *Fall of the Philippines*, p. 270.

18. Ibid., p. 295.

19. Olson, *Anywhere-Anytime*, p. 92. Johnson was very candid in describing this incident in his prison camp diary: "I wish that I could record my own feelings and reactions during the period from the 21st to the 27th of January," he wrote. "I was superseded as S-3 by Col. Brokaw when Col. Frye [*sic*] assumed command. At the time I was offered the 3d Bn. but declined. I was about all in mentally and physically after our first prolonged period under fire. Why we weren't chewed up during our Abucay withdrawal I'll never know. I think my own despair was as deep as it was at

the end. When we started around to the west side life looked a whole lot brighter. I was terribly sick for a couple of days. Spent most of the time on my cot except when I had to be up and around. The night of the 30th a new saga in my own life started" (Diary, 15 December 1942).

20. Johnson, "Defense," pp. 5–6. See also Olson, *Anywhere-Anytime,* p. 139.

21. Johnson, "Defense," p. 3.

22. Ibid., pp. 7–8.

23. Johnson's short-term replacement in that job, Lt. Col. Frank E. Brokaw (described by Olson as an "epicurean" rather than a fighter), was made regimental executive officer, the position Lilly had filled before being given command of the regiment. Brokaw was soon hospitalized with dysentery, however, and did not return to duty until the Battle of the Points was over (Olson, *Anywhere-Anytime,* p. 139).

24. Ibid. The assigned forces also included the 17th Pursuit Squadron and a Philippine Air Corps detachment.

25. Johnson, "Defense," p. 12.

26. Ibid., p. 16.

27. Jennifer L. Bailey, *Philippine Islands: The U.S. Army Campaigns of World War II* (Washington, D.C.: U.S. Government Printing Office, 1992), p. 19.

28. Morton, *Fall of the Philippines,* p. 257. See also Olson, *Anywhere-Anytime,* p. 156.

29. Olson, *Anywhere-Anytime,* p. 155.

30. At this juncture, very near the end of the fighting on Bataan, Johnson and others who were holding positions calling for lieutenant colonels were promoted to that rank. Johnson's promotion was dated 7 April 1942, the same day that the tactical situation is described in the official history as "disintegration." These orders were gratifying to the officers affected, for they had long resented the actions of MacArthur's headquarters in imposing "very restrictive promotion policies" on the premise that these officers were too young to be promoted. Johnson cited as victims of this policy battalion commanders such as Ganahl, Babcock, and Trapnell, who were doing the job but were denied the rank to go with it. When they were promoted to lieutenant colonel, Trapnell was thirty-nine years of age, Ganahl was forty-one, and Babcock was forty-five, providing an interesting contrast to MacArthur's World War I promotion to brigadier general, two grades higher, at the age of thirty-eight. Johnson, at thirty, was much younger when he received his promotion (*1995 Register of Graduates and Former Cadets* [West Point, N.Y.: Association of Graduates, 1995], pp. 205, 217, 218; *1990 Register of Graduates and Former Cadets* [West Point, N.Y.: Association of Graduates, 1990], p. 325). These officers were grateful to Wainwright for breaking the logjam. "He was," said Johnson, "viewed by the people who were left behind as a warm and concerned commander," an obvious contrast to the departed MacArthur.

MacArthur departed the Philippines by submarine on 12 March when, according to Wainwright, the tactical situation on Bataan was "simply desperate" (Gen. Jonathan M. Wainwright, *General Wainwright's Story,* ed. Robert Consadine [Garden City, N.Y.: Doubleday, 1946], p. 4). The troops didn't learn about it until two or three days later. After that, said Johnson, "we had an expression, 'Crafty Mac, he'll never be back.' " Even before his departure, MacArthur had been viewed as a distant and uninvolved commander. "He never appeared to have gotten much dust on his boots," was the way Johnson expressed it (VF OH). Resentment increased, observed H. W. Brands, when the troops later learned that MacArthur had been awarded the Medal of Honor for "heroic conduct of defensive and offensive operations on the Bataan Peninsula" (*Bound to Empire: The United States and the Philippines* [New York: Oxford University Press, 1992], p. 196).

Brig. Gen. William E. Brougher, who had commanded the 57th Infantry before being promoted out of the job in September 1941, wrote scathingly, without ever mentioning MacArthur by name, in a prison diary that the American defenders of the Philippines had been devoted to a hopeless task from the beginning. "Who took the responsibility for saying that some other possibility was in prospect?" he asked, with the obvious answer being MacArthur. "A foul trick of deception has been played on a large group of Americans by a Commander in Chief and small staff who are now eating steak and eggs in Australia. God damn them!" (D. Clayton James, ed., *South to Bataan, North to Mukden: The Prison Diary of Brigadier General W. E. Brougher* [Athens: University of Georgia Press, 1971], p. 32).

31. Many years later, Brig. Gen. Clifford Bluemel wrote to Johnson: "I well remember the night Colonel Lilly brought you to me at the formation of the San Vicente Line and I placed you on the flank. I always regretted that the next morning when the line broke that I was unable to get that information and order to you."

32. Morton, *Fall of the Philippines,* pp. 445, 448.

33. Very near the end, on 7 April 1942, Maj. Paul D. Wood was killed in action when the forward command post was struck by artillery. He was the first member of the Class of 1933 lost in combat.

34. As quoted in *Time* magazine cover story, 10 December 1965, p. 32. In his prison diary Johnson stated that he took command of the battalion on 6 April. Three days later, it was all over. Johnson concluded a long retrospective analysis of the campaign, and his part in it, having found some resolution: "I believe that I did the best I could as conditions arose and will have to be content with that" (Diary, 15 December 1942).

35. Maj. Royal Reynolds, Johnson's West Point classmate who succeeded him as operations officer of the 57th Infantry, had a different experience and consequently opted for a different course of action. On the morning of 8 April, while moving cross-country behind Japanese lines, he and his companions came across a clearing containing the bodies of 200 or 300 Philippine Army soldiers who had been shot or bayoneted to death. With that impression of the possible consequences of surrender, Reynolds and the others decided to try to escape. "We headed north," he said, "relying on a compass and following pig trails, and got away safely."

The experiences of others who escaped tended to support the wisdom of the decision made by Johnson and Fendall. Pvt. Walter R. Connell escaped from the Cabanatuan farm detail and made his way to a nearby barrio. There he was turned in by a pro-Japanese Filipino and "beaten to death." Three naval officers who escaped from Cabanatuan "were turned in to the Jap military by bounty hunting Filipinos." According to the historian of an organization known as American Defenders of Bataan and Corregidor, only two men successfully escaped from Cabanatuan and remained at large (*Quan* [July 1966]: 4).

36. Harold K. Johnson, "Col. Johnson Tells about Death March," *Aberdeen American-News,* 9 November 1945.

37. By virtue of their aborted truck ride, Johnson and Fendall and their Air Force passengers began the Death March closer to their eventual destination than others did.

6. Death March

1. Harold K. Johnson, "Col. Johnson Tells about Death March, Atrocities in Jap Prisons," *Aberdeen American-News,* 9 November 1945.

2. Observed Brig. Gen. Kenneth F. Zitzman: "It was infinitely, infinitely more difficult being a Japanese POW than a German one."

3. Johnson, "Col. Johnson Tells about Death March."

4. Ibid.

5. Ibid.

6. Ibid.

7. In his MHI Oral History Interview, Johnson says that he began the death march on 11 April, whereas in a foreword to the published version of General Brougher's prison diary, he says that he began on 12 April. The latter date seems more likely to be correct.

8. John E. Olson, *O'Donnell: Andersonville of the Pacific* (n.p.: privately printed, 1985), pp. 18–21.

9. Ibid., p. 21.

10. Diary of Col. A. S. Quintard, quoted in Olson, *O'Donnell,* pp. 24–25; Olson, p. 29.

11. It was nearly two years before details of the Bataan Death March became known to the American public. There had been rumors, but only when the Army and Navy made a joint announcement on 27 January 1944 was the extent of the tragedy understood. The announcement took the form of a sworn statement based on the testimony of three American officers who had escaped from Japanese prison camps in the Philippines. "Nearly 30,000 Americans were in Japanese prisons at this time," reported the Associated Press. "The United States had been trying desperately, by political pressure, by threat, and by cajolery, to get food and medicine to them, and to force the Japanese to improve their treatment. When all efforts failed, the story was told." Richard F. Newcomb, AP, *Seattle Times,* 26 March 1967. A copy of this article in the Johnson family's possession has been annotated in longhand, possibly by Johnson's mother, "a sad but true article of Death March Keith was part of."

The number of casualties during the death march is impossible to know with any certitude, but all estimates agree that it was horrifyingly high. Gavan Daws, who devoted a decade to studying the plight of prisoners of the Japanese, phrased his conclusion in stark terms: "a body every ten or fifteen paces, and every death a Japanese atrocity" (*Prisoners of the Japanese: POWs of World War II in the Pacific* [New York: William Morrow, 1994], p. 80).

General Homma, commander of Japanese forces in the Philippines and thus responsible for the fate of these prisoners, did not fare well. Removed from command in June 1942, he "returned in virtual disgrace to Japan," spending the remainder of the war in "an insignificant assignment in the reserves" (Olson, *O'Donnell,* p. 175).

When the war was over, Homma was returned to the Philippines to be tried as a war criminal. Convicted, he was executed at Los Banos on 3 April 1946, "four years to the day that he had opened his Good Friday offensive" (Newcomb, *Seattle Times*).

12. Daws, *Prisoners of the Japanese*, p. 84.

13. Olson, *O'Donnell*, pp. 41–42.

14. Ibid., p. 50.

15. Ibid., pp. 93–96.

16. Foreword to *South to Bataan, North to Mukden: The Prison Diary of Brigadier General W. E. Brougher*, ed. D. Clayton James (Athens: University of Georgia Press, 1971), p. xiii.

17. Olson, *O'Donnell*, p. 108.

18. Ibid., pp. 53–54.

19. Ibid., p. 167.

20. Ibid., p. 65.

21. Ibid., p. 119.

22. Johnson, "Col. Johnson Tells about Death March."

23. Lt. Gen. Harris W. Hollis, "Giants among Men: An Anecdotal Capsule of the Leadership Traits of Generals Johnson and Abrams," unpublished typescript, p. 2.

24. Olson, *O'Donnell*, p. 55.

25. The Japanese character also came into play among Japanese soldiers taken prisoner by the Americans. "Japanese prisoners had to deal with their depression at having broken with comrades who had died in battle or committed suicide," wrote Shohei Ooka, captured by American troops as they liberated the Philippines in January 1945. "Captivity was bewildering because Japanese military indoctrination prevented the prisoners from accepting the Americans' warmheartedness with simple gratitude. Whereas they saw themselves as dishonorable captives, the Americans treated them as human beings, and this . . . confounded them completely." But over time, "corrupted by American largess" and "growing fat on 2,700 calories a day," the Japanese learned to accept their circumstance, in later years recalling it as a "paradise" and speaking of the time they spent there as "the best year of their lives." As quoted by John Glenn in his review of *Taken Captive: A Japanese POW's Story*, *New York Times Book Review*, 1 September 1996, p. 17.

26. Foreword to *South to Bataan*, p. xiii.

27. Olson, *O'Donnell*, p. 1.

28. The estimate of 1,800 deaths, equating to nearly a 20 percent loss rate, is contained in Johnson's MHI Oral History. Olson states that the total number of Americans who entered O'Donnell was 9,180, and that after the war the bodies of 1,547 were disinterred, which would reflect a loss rate of just under 17 percent (see Olson, *O'Donnell*, p. 156). Whatever the statistical reality, Olson expressed the essence of the O'Donnell experience very simply: "Without any embellishment, it was tragic and horrible" (*O'Donnell*, p. 3).

7. Cabanatuan

1. Col. John E. Olson, "USMA in the Philippines 1941–42," *Assembly* (July 1993): 25.

2. *Time,* 10 December 1965, p. 32.

3. After the war, Johnson wrote a moving and detailed account of the humanitarian assistance rendered the prisoners by civilians in the Philippines, singling out especially the activities led by Mr. and Mrs. Ramon Amusatique, a young woman known as Naomi Flores, and an operation known as "the Miss U group." At great risk to themselves, and with no motive of personal benefit, these people collected money, passed messages, and smuggled food and medicine to the American prisoners. Johnson's account is included in a scrapbook of family memorabilia compiled by his sister, Edna Ray Johnson Hinman, in August 1995.

Johnson personally was helped by his former servants, Ng Sen and Ah Ho, who smuggled in a note containing ten pesos and an offer of help in obtaining medicine. Later, they got to him a package containing a pair of shoes, a box of cigars, and other gifts, including five pesos. "I'm positive that I'll survive this rat race," Johnson wrote to Dorothy in the diary, "but on the off chance that I don't and this reaches you, try and do something for them."

4. "Report of Harold Keith Johnson—POW WW II 1942–1945," included in a scrapbook compiled by Edna Ray Johnson Hinman.

5. Pvt. Ernest Norquist recorded in his prison diary for 12 August 1943 the lovely rumor that "each man from Bataan is to be given a kangaroo apiece by the Australian government in token of the magnificent bravery which 'saved' Australia" (cited in "Horn Diary," *Quan* [date unrecorded], pp. 3–4).

6. "Jack" may be John G. Graham.

7. Dorothy Johnson said that it was Col. O. O. ("Zero") Wilson, a good friend, to whom Johnson paid the gambling debt.

8. Harry Stempin provided an example of such a postcard. The first blank to be filled in read "I am interned at ____." Next was a multiple-choice entry: "My health is: excellent, good, fair, poor." Then: "I am: injured, sick in hospital; under treatment; not under treatment." And: "I am: improving, not improving; better; well." Other blanks to be filled in read: "Please see that ____ is taken care of." "Please give my best regards to ____." As Stempin recalled it, the prisoners wrote the information out by hand, then someone typed it up in English.

9. Johnson spoke of this priest to Maj. Gen. Frederick R. Zierath many times after the war. Possibly the man he was referring to was Father Thomas J. Scecina, who had been with the 57th Infantry. It is known that Scecina admired Johnson greatly and saw important responsibilities ahead for him. "I remember so vividly," wrote B. T. Fitzpatrick in an 18 August 1964 letter to Johnson, "during one of my many 'chats' with Father Secina [*sic*], his almost literally predicting your future."

Another possibility is Father Anthony V. Keane, the priest who had written admiringly of Johnson after accompanying him on the prewar basketball tour. "There was a priest in prison that he admired very much," Dorothy recalled. "Johnny had met him before the war when he was on tour with a soldier basketball team."

According to "P.O.W. Chaplains," a paper by Stan Sommers contained in the Olson Papers at MHI, Chaplain John K. Borneman named thirty-one of the thirty-seven chaplains referred to by him in his April 1946 "From Bataan through Cabanatuan." Colonel Olson annotated the list with one additional name, making thirty-two. Scecina is on that list, whereas Keane is not, perhaps indicating that Scecina was more likely the man who inspired Johnson. Whoever he was, his example was powerful. Dorothy said that the admiration her husband had for this priest was so great that "he almost became a Catholic."

8. Hell Ships

1. This account is based on an article Johnson prepared for a local newspaper soon after his repatriation: "Col. Harold Johnson Tells of 'Death Trip' from Manila to Korea," *Walsh County Record* (Grafton, N.D.), 15 November 1945. An abridged version was also published in a South Dakota newspaper where Dorothy was living and where Johnson went to recuperate after repatriation. The 9 November 1945 edition of the *Aberdeen American-News* noted that while Johnson was undergoing this ordeal, "many of the Jap prisoners of war in this country 'languished' at the palatial hotel at Hershey, Pa., while they sweated out the war."

2. Volckmann later told the story of his guerrilla exploits in a book pointedly entitled *We Remained.*

3. There were five vessels carrying POWs that came to be known as "hell ships," and Johnson was on three of them: the *Oryoku Maru,* which was bombed in Subic Bay on 15 December 1944, killing about half the 1,800 men on board; the *Enoura Maru,* which was bombed in the harbor of Takao, Formosa, on 9 January 1945; and the *Brazil Maru,* which reached Japan with survivors of the other two ships. Besides those killed in the bombings and those who later died of wounds, many other prisoners on these ships died of malnutrition, dehydration, disease, exposure, and even suffocation. *1996 Register of Graduates and Former Cadets* (West Point, N.Y.: Association of Graduates, 1996), p. 61.

As a result of war crimes trials, two Japanese officers were hanged for the bombing of the *Oryoku Maru.* The commandant of Cabanatuan also received a death sentence, and the commandant of Camp O'Donnell was sentenced to life imprisonment. Gavan Daws, *Prisoners of the Japanese: POWs of World War II in the Pacific* (New York: William Morrow, 1994), pp. 369–70.

4. Roy L. Bodine, *No Place for Kindness: The Prisoner of War Diary of Roy L. Bodine* (Fort Sam Houston, Tex.: Fort Sam Houston Museum, 1983), p. 11. Bodine's entry for 27 January 1945: "Father Cummings died."

5. After the war, Johnson signed an affidavit stating that among the "known dead" was Maj. Elbridge R. Fendall, killed 15 December 1944 while en route to Japan.

6. Fred Quarles, "1000 GIs Who Rode a Death Ship," *Quan* (April 1990): 3. Estimates vary widely as to how far it was to shore. Johnson recalled it as 500 yards, Quarles indicates 200 yards, and others give different distances.

7. Other sources put the sailing on 28 December 1944. See, for example, the *1996 Register of Graduates and Former Cadets,* p. 61.

8. Takao was subsequently renamed Kaohsiung.

9. Johnson was not alone in the effect these experiences had on his religious convictions. Lt. Gen. John M. Wright, Jr., recalled that from the time he was confirmed while a cadet, he "took much more seriously than I ever had my obligation, my duty to God, and I felt that that was an important part of a soldier's life. As a result of my experience [as a POW] and, particularly, as a result of the situation on the

316 *Honorable Warrior*

Oryoku Maru, I believe that more strongly today than I did thirty or forty years ago. I tried the rest of my career to make that an important part and a visible part of my service, particularly when in command positions, because I felt that there was a very important place for deep religious convictions in the lives of soldiers." Wright was one of a handful of former prisoners of the Japanese who overcame the experience, regained professional competitiveness, and rose to senior levels, along with Lt. Gen. Alva R. Fitch, Lt. Gen. Thomas J. H. Trapnell, and of course Gen. Harold K. Johnson.

10. Brian Kelly, *Washington Star,* 18 July 1966. Dr. Kostecki's daughter, Helen Kostecki Hannett, is the source of the information about her father's Japanese schoolmate.

11. That officer was Col. Clinton S. Maupin.

12. In various accounts, Johnson gives the date of their release as 7 or 8 September, but in the official affidavit he executed during repatriation processing, he stated it as 7 September 1945. Apparently, 7th Division elements arrived on 7 September, and the prisoners were taken out the following day.

By the date of his release, Johnson weighed 136 pounds, a huge improvement over the 92 pounds of late February, but still a long way from his customary 165 or so.

Gavan Daws estimated that "on the clinical evidence, three and a half years in a Japanese prison camp aged a man physically ten to fifteen years. A POW coming up to his seventieth birthday was eighty or eighty-five years old in his body" (*Prisoners of the Japanese,* p. 388).

13. Daws, *Prisoners of the Japanese,* p. 18. According to Timothy Benford, of the fourteen U.S. military cemeteries overseas in which American armed services personnel killed in World War II are buried, the largest is near Manila, where there are 17,208 graves and commemoration of an additional 36,279 persons recorded as missing in action (*The World War II Quiz & Fact Book* [New York: Harper and Row, 1984], p. 208). Precise figures are not available, but according to one account, "of the 38,000 men captured by the Japanese early in 1942, only 3,800 survived to return to the United States" (William Anderson, *Chicago Tribune,* 6 December 1964). Fred Quarles estimates that of the original 1,619 prisoners put aboard the *Oryoku Maru* in December 1944, only about 300 survived to the time of the Japanese surrender. "1000 GIs Who Rode a Death Ship" (*Quan* [April 1990], p. 14).

14. A copy is included in the scrapbook of family memorabilia put together by Edna Ray Johnson Hinman. The cable was dated 14 September 1945.

9. Adrift

1. USMA Class of 1933, *Golden Anniversary Book* (n.p.: privately printed, 1983), p. 52.

2. Gavan Daws, *Prisoners of the Japanese: POWs of World War II in the Pacific* (New York: William Morrow, 1994), p. 344.

3. Earlier, Johnson had been assigned to the Army and Army Group Committee, responsible for instruction on operations by those high-level organizations.

4. HKJ speech, USAC&GSC, Fort Leavenworth, Kans., 23 March 1965, HKJP.

10. Korea

1. Association of the United States Army, *The U.S. Army Between World War II and the Korean War* (Arlington, Va.: AUSA, March 1992), pp. 3–8.

2. Despite the "cavalry" designation, a holdover from the days of the horse cavalry, the regiment and the division were now infantry formations.

3. Gen. Dennis J. Reimer, Association of the United States Army annual meeting luncheon, Washington, D.C., 17 October 1995.

4. J. Lawton Collins, *War in Peacetime: The History and Lessons of Korea* (Boston: Houghton Mifflin, 1969), pp. 92–94.

5. Later Johnson wrote to his mother to tell her that he had been awarded the Distinguished Service Cross. "Actually I didn't do any more than I should have done under the circumstances," he said, "but I'm awfully proud of the fact that my own men thought enough of the action to make the recommendation for the award. At least this wasn't a case of a high commander visiting command posts and handing out the medals."

6. Lt. Col. George Allen, quoted in *Time,* 10 December 1965, p. 33.

7. Roy E. Appleman, *South to the Naktong, North to the Yalu* (Washington, D.C.: Office of the Chief of Military History, Department of the Army, 1961), pp. 430–31.

8. Kenneth Ward Miller had joined Johnson's battalion in the midst of all this, a young lieutenant assigned as a platoon leader in K Company. His understrength unit had only thirty-two men when he took it over, all—like him—green soldiers except for a couple of experienced sergeants. Within two weeks, Miller had only fifteen men left. Then he was shot in the abdomen and evacuated. Later, his platoon sergeant wrote to tell him that after that firefight the platoon had just seven men left. Other small units were also being decimated as Johnson's battalion stood up to some tough, bloody battles (Miller, letter to author, 2 April 1997).

9. Gen. Matthew B. Ridgway, *The Korean War* (Garden City, N.Y.: Doubleday, 1967), p. 31. Speaking at the Army War College on 23 June 1994, Prof. Russell Weigley said this: "General Walker's defense of the Pusan perimeter is a campaign which, in the tactical and operational aspects, deserves a great deal more study than it has ever received. And General Walker deserves more credit for his achievements than he has ever received." During that battle, acknowledged an Army historical publication, the 1st Cavalry Division fought "outnumbered, outtanked, and outgunned" (Department of the Army, *Korea—1950* [Washington, D.C.: Office of the Chief of Military History, 1952], p. 20).

10. D. Clayton James with Anne Sharp Wells, *Refighting the Last War: Command and Crisis in Korea, 1950–1953* (New York: Free Press, 1993), photo caption, n.p.

11. Collins, *War in Peacetime,* pp. 186–87.

12. Appleman, *South to the Naktong,* pp. 704–7.

13. Collins, *War in Peacetime,* pp. 187–88.

14. This is apparently the way it looked to Johnson in the field. Reviewing this manuscript, Lt. Gen. Sidney B. Berry offered an alternative explanation: "Logistical difficulties caused by MacArthur's giving priority to shifting X Corps from western Korea to eastern Korea were the principal cause of the lack of winter clothing and equipment."

15. Capt. Norman Allen, I Company, 5th Cavalry, 4 November 1950, in Donald Knox, *The Korean War: Pusan to Chosin, an Oral History* (New York: Harcourt Brace Jovanovich, 1989), p. 440.

16. Pfc. James Cardinal, I Company, 5th Cavalry, in Knox, p. 414.

17. Ridgway, *Korean War*, p. 59.

18. Joseph R. Cerami, "Battle Focus: Ridgway Seizes the Initiative," *Assembly* (November 1994): 9.

19. Ibid.

20. Ibid., p. 11. During the Vietnam War, when Lyndon Johnson was briefed on an operation known as Masher, he complained that that sounded too bloodthirsty. The operation was renamed White Wing, but then, to avoid confusion, it was referred to as Masher/White Wing, beautifully illustrating LBJ's predicament during the whole war.

21. Ibid.

22. Maj. James R. Huey, letter to the editor, *Army* (October 1968): 8.

11. Moving Up

1. Greene went to Mannheim and took command of the 510th Tank Battalion, which had not only a drum and bugle corps, but also a live buffalo mascot. Every morning at reveille, the drums and bugles, accompanied by the buffalo, paraded in the battalion area. The record does not reflect what kind of an example Johnson considered this to be.

2. Quoted in Martin Blumenson, "A Most Remarkable Man," *Army* (August 1968): 19.

3. Johnson's frugality extended to himself as well. While serving at Fort Leavenworth, he wrote to a friend in Europe that he had bought a uniform from the well-known Baltimore firm A. Jacobs & Sons but that, since they charged thirty-four dollars more for gold braid than for nylon, he had used some gold braid brought back from Europe (which cost only fourteen or fifteen dollars). Now he wanted more gold braid for a mess uniform and asked his friend to buy it for him in the PX in Germany.

12. Fort Leavenworth

1. "After the military service I believe the teaching profession does more for people and has a greater influence on the character of our country than any other profession," Johnson wrote.

2. Johnson was strongly persuaded that, among other things, it was an officer's duty to keep his uniforms in top condition. To make this point, he put one of his own service caps on display in a glass case in the foyer of Bell Hall, the main academic building. Alongside it was a card reading: "If your cap doesn't look better than this, replace it immediately."

3. Upon his departure, McGarr left behind an article entitled "Some Thoughts

on Leadership" for publication in the College's quarterly journal *Military Review*. The piece was referred to Johnson, who wrote to McGarr as follows: "I believe that it is in the best interests of the College at this point to avoid publication of material prepared by you that is strongly flavored by your recent position here. Consequently, I have disapproved the publication of your article."

4. Talbott Barnard, comp., *The History of Fort Leavenworth, 1952–1963* (Fort Leavenworth, Kans.: USAC&GSC, 1964), p. 21.

5. Gen. Harold K. Johnson, "Land Power!" *Army Information Digest* (August 1964): 13.

6. Boyd L. Dastrup, *The US Army Command and General Staff College: A Centennial History* (Manhattan, Kans.: Sunflower University Press, 1982), pp. 108, 110.

7. The recollection of Carol Wilson Alexander, Colonel Wilson's daughter, is that it was her mother who erected the sign. It so happened that one of the dogs was named Jo, the same as the affronted neighbor, and the other was known as Sis. In her version of the story, the sign read "Sis and this Jo are not vicious bitches."

8. Not until 1974, six years after Johnson retired from the Army, did authorization for a Master of Military Arts and Sciences degree come through, in large part due to Johnson's efforts while he was Chief of Staff.

9. *Leavenworth Times,* 26 September 1985.

10. Adam Yarmolinsky, "How the Pentagon Works," in *Readings in American Government,* 5th ed., ed. Shelley Schmidt (Belmont, Calif.: Wadsworth, 1993), p. 669.

11. This study was designated Project 23.

12. Peter Wyden, *Wall: The Inside Story of Divided Berlin* (New York: Simon and Schuster, 1989), p. 67. Wyden states that only Adam Yarmolinsky and Daniel Ellsberg were present when these statements were made.

13. Dastrup, *US Army Command,* p. 110.

14. HKJ letter to the Class of 1963, *The Bell* (1963), CARL.

13. DCSOPS

1. During Johnson's previous Pentagon assignment, he served in what was then known as the Office of the Assistant Chief of Staff G-3. By the time he rejoined, it had been redesignated Office of the Deputy Chief of Staff for Military Operations, or DCSOPS for short (pronounced "des-ops"), but it was the same staff element.

2. Typescript, "Salient Times—General Howze," c. 14 May 1963, HKJP.

3. These events transpired 12–13 May 1963, and in discussing them, Johnson always characterized them as occurring on his first day as Acting DCSOPS. Other apparently authoritative sources show that he assumed those duties on 6 May 1963, and in correspondence with his family Johnson also uses that date, so his memories of the turbulent events of his first days in the job may have run together.

General Wheeler had maintained that the Army did not need an Army Operations Center because the Army didn't have any forces to operate directly, arguing that deployed Army forces would come under one of the unified commands for operations. When it came to civil disturbances, that did not turn out to be the case. As

DCSOPS, Johnson initiated a case for the JCS to make the Army the executive agent for civil disturbance operations, which was done in May 1963.

4. Martin Blumenson, *Reorganization of the Army, 1962* (Washington, D.C.: Department of the Army, [1965]), p. 117.

5. Douglas Kinnard, *The Secretary of Defense* (Lexington: University Press of Kentucky, 1980), p. 79.

6. There was apparently no end to the diversity of matters coming before the Joint Chiefs or their operations deputies. On one occasion, for example, Johnson's notes indicate that the ops deps had on their agenda this item: "VI . . . Who ordered the Army Library *not* to buy the new book on JFK" (HKJ Notes, Ops Deps Meeting, 1000 hours, 10 September 1963, HKJP).

7. General Taylor maintained that "the Secretary of Defense has never by-passed the Joint Chiefs of Staff on any matter that I know about. If anything," he said, "we have been swamped with requests for advice and comment to the point that it has been very hard to keep up with the procession. The Joint Staff must work nights and weekends to produce answers to the many questions of the Secretary of Defense and his [the word "inquiring" is scratched out here in the delivery copy] staff. As an example of the increase in the tempo of the work, we find that in the calendar year 1958 the JCS acted on 4,785 papers and processed about 189,000 messages. Four years later in 1962, the JCS acted on 11,401 papers and processed over 369,000 messages. Thus, for all practical purposes, the workload of the JCS has more than doubled since 1958" (Gen. Maxwell D. Taylor, address, U.S. Army War College, 12 June 1963, Taylor Papers).

8. Andrew F. Krepinevich, Jr., *The Army and Vietnam* (Baltimore: Johns Hopkins University Press, 1986), p. 133.

9. *The Pentagon Papers: The Defense Department History of United States Decisionmaking on Vietnam*, Senator Gravel ed., 5 vols. (Boston: Beacon Press, 1971), p. 3:17, citing a 2 October 1963 White House statement of "U.S. Policy on Vietnam" (hereafter, *PP*).

10. HKJ Memo for ASD(SA), 27 September 1963, HKJP. In his notes regarding "Ground Forces Paper" from an 18 October 1963 JCS meeting, Johnson wrote: "Enthoven given a mission of deflating the threat—this is it. Secy apparently has same charge from President" (HKJ Notes, JCS Meeting, 1400 hours, 18 October 1963, HKJP).

11. HKJ Notes, JCS Meeting, 1400 hours, 29 October 1963, HKJP.

12. Quoted in William Conrad Gibbons, *The U.S. Government and the Vietnam War: Executive and Legislative Roles and Relationships*, pt. 3, *January–July 1965* (Washington, D.C.: U.S. Government Printing Office, 1988), pp. 2–3.

13. Robert S. McNamara, *In Retrospect: The Tragedy and Lessons of Vietnam* (New York: Times Books, 1995), p. 102.

14. McNamara, p. 108. The text of NSAM 273 belies McNamara's denial that the President had staked out victory as the goal, and his introduction of any calculus regarding the cost in lives is fanciful. NSAM 273 stated the U.S. purpose in Vietnam clearly and unequivocally as being "to assist the people and Government of that country to win their contest against the externally directed and supported Communist conspiracy" (*PP* 2:276).

15. JCS Memorandum for the Secretary of Defense, JCSM-46-64, 22 January 1964, cited in Gibbons, *U.S. Government,* 3:497–99.

16. Richard N. Goodwin, *Remembering America: A Voice from the Sixties* (Boston: Little, Brown, 1988), p. 271.

17. Summary of a conversation between Commandant of the Marine Corps and Military Aide, 27 March 1964, Greene Papers.

18. Talking paper, 27 March 1964, National Security File, Files of C. V. Clifton, Box 2, LBJ Library. The President had met with the JCS earlier that month, but spent the time asking each Chief to give him a report on progress in cost consciousness rather than discussing the war (C. V. Clifton Memo for Bundy, 19 March 1964, same file).

19. Wendy Wilson Sticht, telephone interview, 9 January 1996. Mrs. Sticht is Colonel Wilson's daughter. The Khanh-led coup toppled Minh on 30 January 1964. In the wake of President Diem's earlier overthrow and assassination—brought about with American acquiescence, if not connivance—Robert Shaplen made a telling observation: "The admission must be made that we had no more of a post-coup plan than the Vietnamese had" (*The Lost Revolution: The Story of Twenty Years of Neglected Opportunities in Vietnam and of America's Failure to Foster Democracy There* [New York: Harper and Row, 1969], p. 214).

Capt. Dave R. Palmer was in Vietnam when Khanh staged his coup, serving as aide-de-camp to General Westmoreland, who had only recently arrived. Palmer sat in on a meeting his boss had with Ambassador Lodge, accompanied by *his* aide, a young Foreign Service officer named Tony Lake, as they drafted a cable reporting the situation to Washington. Harkins was not present and apparently had not been contacted. "It was clear," reflected Palmer, "that Khanh's American advisor, Colonel Jasper Wilson, had known the coup was coming and had so informed the American leadership, which had not interfered" (Lt. Gen. Dave R. Palmer, interview, 13 November 1995).

A day or two later, Lt. Col. Brad Schoomaker, who had worked closely with Johnson and Wilson at Fort Leavenworth, wrote to Johnson that he had seen Wilson the previous evening: "He is, with good reason, proud of his achievements. I don't pretend to know all of the details, altho I know J. J. figured in on the coup rather prominently" (Lt. Col. F. B. Schoomaker, letter to HKJ, 2 February 1964, HKJP).

20. HKJ letter to Col. J. J. Wilson, 18 May 1963, HKJP.

21. Col. Jasper J. Wilson, letter to HKJ, 7 January 1964, Col. Jasper J. Wilson Papers, MHI.

14. Vietnam Trip

1. Just as Johnson departed Honolulu, flying west, he heard over the radio that the Army Vice Chief of Staff, Gen. Barksdale Hamlett, had suffered a severe heart attack. Johnson got in touch with General Wheeler and asked if he should return to Washington, but Wheeler advised Johnson to go ahead with his Vietnam visit.

2. Wilson later told Johnson that, "on instructions from competent authority, I personally persuaded Khanh to give up gracefully his position as Commander in Chief—a

thing which may or may not have been inevitable—and to depart Vietnam—a thing which was necessary only from the U.S. point of view" (Col. Jasper J. Wilson, memorandum for General Johnson, 25 January 1966, Wilson Papers, MHI).

Nine more changes of power took place between August 1964 and June 1965, when Gen. Nguyen Van Thieu became chief of state and Air Vice Marshal Nguyen Cao Ky the premier.

3. Gen. Donn A. Starry, interview, 31 May 1995. General Harkins's stepdaughter married Starry's West Point classmate Leslie D. Carter, Jr., and Starry had known Harkins since cadet days.

4. Mark Perry, *Four Stars* (Boston: Houghton Mifflin, 1989), pp. 128–29.

5. Samuel Zaffiri, *Westmoreland: A Biography of General William C. Westmoreland* (New York: Morrow, 1994), p. 102. In his book *In Retrospect* (New York: Times Books, 1995), McNamara says about Harkins, "I did not then and do not now believe that he or other officers consciously misled me" (p. 47).

6. David Halberstam, "The Story We Never Saw in Vietnam," *Washington Post*, 14 May 1995. Harkins, wrote Halberstam, "did what Taylor and McNamara wanted, which was to suppress negative reporting and to try and make the progress of the policy look better than was justified" (p. C3).

7. John Mecklin, *Mission in Torment: An Intimate Account of the U.S. Role in Vietnam* (Garden City, N.Y.: Doubleday, 1965), p. 18. Mecklin quotes a ditty of the time, sung to the tune of "Twinkle, Twinkle, Little Star": "We are winning, this I know, General Harkins told me so. If you doubt me, who are you? McNamara says so, too" (p. 117).

8. Arthur Schlesinger, Jr., "Review of John M. Newman, *JFK and Vietnam,*" *New York Times Book Review*, 29 March 1992, p. 3.

9. Gen. William B. Rosson, "Four Periods of American Involvement in Vietnam," unpublished doctoral dissertation, copy in MHI Archives, pp. 136, 155, 179.

10. Gen. Bruce Palmer, Jr., "US Intelligence and Vietnam," in *Studies in Intelligence* (Special Issue) (Washington, D.C.: Central Intelligence Agency, 1984), p. 35. In both cases, the Station transmitted unexpurgated versions of the assessments to CIA Headquarters.

11. Henry F. Graff, *The Tuesday Cabinet: Deliberation and Decision on Peace and War under Lyndon B. Johnson* (Englewood Cliffs, N.J.: Prentice-Hall, 1970), p. 36.

12. In a White House meeting with Generals Wheeler and Abrams, Lyndon Johnson said: "I like Westmoreland. He was one of four recommended to me. The other three were: General Abrams, General Palmer and General Johnson. Westmoreland has played on the team to help me" (Tom Johnson, "Notes of President's Meeting with General Earle Wheeler, JCS and General Creighton Abrams, March 26, 1968, Family Dining Room," LBJ Library).

At the time Westmoreland was sent to Vietnam to be deputy to Harkins, Gen. Earle G. Wheeler, then Army Chief of Staff, made this observation during a Joint Chiefs of Staff discussion on reporting from Vietnam: "[The] war can be lost in Washington if Congress loses faith" (HKJ Notes, JCS Meeting, 1400 hours, 17 January 1964, HKJP).

13. Shelby L. Stanton, *The Rise and Fall of an American Army: U.S. Ground Forces in Vietnam, 1965–1973* (New York: Dell, 1985), p. 11.

14. Special Forces were also brought to Johnson's attention by Air Force Chief of

Staff Gen. J. P. McConnell, who sent him a clipping describing a Saigon scam in which some Special Forces types had hired an elderly Vietnamese woman to manufacture Viet Cong flags. They'd take the finished products, stomp them in mud and sprinkle them with chicken blood, then sell them to souvenir-hungry Air Force pilots. The scheme went awry when Vietnamese police arrested the seamstress as a Viet Cong, and it took two days for her Special Forces customers to explain and get her released. McConnell's accompanying note read: "Johnny—Your guys should be thoroughly ashamed taking advantage of my poor country boy airmen."

15. CIDG was the Vietnamese element manning the camps advised by U.S. Special Forces.

16. Lt. Gen. Dave R. Palmer, LBJ Library Conference, Austin, Texas, 16 October 1993.

17. *The Pentagon Papers: The Defense Department History of United States Decisionmaking on Vietnam,* Senator Gravel ed., 5 vols. (Boston: Beacon Press, 1971), 3:3–4.

18. Ibid., 3:64–65.

19. John H. Cushman, "The Military Owes the President(s) More," Naval Institute *Proceedings* (July 1995): 10.

15. Aviation

1. Talking paper, "Army and Air Force Responsibilities Regarding the Use of Aerial Vehicles," 16 October 1963, HKJP.

2. Air assault meant helicopter-borne attacks, accompanied by helicopter-borne fire support, by units specially configured for the purpose. The lead unit of this type was the 1st Cavalry Division (Airmobile), deployed to Vietnam in July 1965.

3. This account is based primarily on the Oral History Interviews of Gen. Hamilton H. Howze, Lt. Gen. George P. Seneff, Lt. Gen. John J. Tolson III, Lt. Gen. Robert R. Williams, Maj. Gen. Delk Oden, and Col. Delbert Bristol, in The History of Army Aviation Collection, MHI; Lt. Gen. John J. Tolson's *Airmobility 1961–1971* (Washington, D.C.: Department of the Army, 1989); and Lt. Gen. Edward L. Rowny's *Engineer Memoirs* (Alexandria, Va.: Office of History, U.S. Army Corps of Engineers, 1995).

4. Tolson, *Airmobility,* pp. 14–15.

5. Ibid., p. 18.

6. Oden Oral History Interview.

7. Seneff Oral History Interview.

8. In his Oral History Interview, Williams acknowledges having drafted the memo, saying that Secretary McNamara signed it "almost exactly" as he wrote it.

9. Oden Oral History Interview. General Williams agreed: "Although the Howze Board concepts were based on war in Europe, it did devote a chapter to counterinsurgency operations" (Williams Oral History Interview).

10. Howze Oral History Interview.

11. Report, *Army Air Mobility Concept,* Headquarters, Department of the Army, December 1963, HKJP.

12. Lt. Gen. Edward L. Rowny, interview, 18 January 1990. In his later *Engineer*

Memoirs, General Rowny displayed a different outlook, saying that "the DCSOPS, General Johnson, and the chief of staff, General Wheeler, were not favorably disposed toward the concept of tactical air mobility. The situation only got worse when Harold K. Johnson became the chief of staff of the Army and General Earle Wheeler moved up to become the chairman of the Joint Chiefs of Staff" (*Memoirs,* p. 91). Other senior officers centrally involved in these matters do not agree. Lt. Gen. Robert R. Williams, for example, recalled how "Mr. McNamara was pushing the Army very hard to get with it and . . . without the backing of General Wheeler and General Abrams, it would have been absolutely impossible." Abrams was Johnson's Vice Chief of Staff and could not have adopted a course of action contrary to what his Chief wanted done. Nor does Rowny explain how it was that the 1st Cavalry Division (Airmobile) was formed and deployed to Vietnam on Johnson's watch, along with many other aviation and airmobility assets.

13. Rowny, *Engineer Memoirs,* pp. 75–76.

16. Chief of Staff

1. Robert S. McNamara, *In Retrospect: The Tragedy and Lessons of Vietnam* (New York: Times Books, 1995), p. 176.

2. Wrote Lawrence J. Korb, "the Army's Harold Johnson is the only post–World War II chief to rise to the top without having held at least one major command as a flag officer." *The Joint Chiefs of Staff: The First Twenty-five Years* (Bloomington: Indiana University Press, 1976), pp. 88–89.

3. General Howze seems to have been a more logical choice to become Chief of Staff. A member of the West Point Class of 1930, he had extensive command experience in World War II, winning a Silver Star while leading a tank battalion, and then an armored regiment, in the Mediterranean and leading a combat command of the 1st Armored Division in Italy. After the war, he was assistant division commander of the 2d Armored Division in Germany and then commanding general of the 82d Airborne Division, the XVIII Airborne Corps at Fort Bragg, and finally the Eighth Army in Korea, where he was serving when Johnson was appointed Chief of Staff. Howze had thus commanded at every level and in just about every major theater to which U.S. forces were deployed during his thirty-five years of service. Other attractive candidates would have been Gen. Hugh P. Harris, the CONARC (Continental Army Command) commander, who was sitting in for the disabled Barksdale Hamlett as Acting Vice Chief of Staff; and Gen. Paul L. Freeman, commanding U.S. Army, Europe.

Johnson himself attributed his selection to "a lot of different conditions just sort of coming together at one time." One was that Gen. Barksdale Hamlett, the Vice Chief of Staff, had had a heart attack and elected to retire. Then Gen. Maxwell D. Taylor, Chairman of the Joint Chiefs of Staff, was sent to Vietnam to replace Henry Cabot Lodge as U.S. Ambassador. Gen. Earle G. Wheeler, the Army Chief of Staff, replaced Taylor as Chairman. Johnson, having been Wheeler's DCSOPS, had been in close daily contact with him for the past year and was familiar with the key issues confronting the Army and the other services. "Under the ordinary course of events my credentials for that job, in terms of being a student of history and so on, would not have equipped me, and don't equip me, to occupy the position that I had the good fortune, the misfortune, to occupy," said Johnson.

Maj. Gen. Charles E. Brown, Jr., then the Army's Chief of Chaplains. was an amateur clock maker. One afternoon he went to the home of Secretary of the Army Stephen Ailes to fix a clock for him. Afterward, the two men were sitting on the back stoop having a beer when Ailes asked Brown what he thought of Johnny Johnson. "Stephen," Brown replied, "he's the strongest spiritual strength in the Army today." Two or three weeks later, it was announced that Johnson was being appointed Chief of Staff.

George Blanchard, who served as executive officer to Ailes, thought that his boss had helped Johnson get the appointment. In Blanchard's view, Ailes "was the last Secretary of the Army who has really been good for the Army, and who has really understood the whole process, and has really contributed to it and really loved it. Some of them did each of those, some of his successors, but he put it all together." Added Blanchard, "Mr. Ailes was the one who believed that General Johnson was the right kind of guy for Chief of Staff and had recommended him to the SECDEF."

4. *Los Angeles Times,* 12 July 1964.

5. U.S. Congress, Senate Committee on Armed Services, Hearing, *Nomination of Lt. Gen. Harold K. Johnson to Be Chief of Staff, U.S. Army,* 2 July 1964, p. 4. Some members of the committee were apparently a little vague on the lineage of previous Army Chiefs of Staff. Sen. J. Glenn Beall of Maryland observed that "this is something a little unusual, to recognize the Infantry as the all-round soldier. It is a little unusual. Something new, I think." Sen. Daniel K. Inouye also commented that he was "extremely pleased, personally, to see an Infantry officer become the Chief of Staff." Gen. Johnson listened to all that, then volunteered: "I would remind the committee, if it is not presumptuous, that General Wheeler is also an Infantry officer. He has spent a good deal of time on high-level staff work, but in addition he has commanded every unit from a platoon to a corps and has been a deputy theater commander." Johnson didn't mention that George C. Marshall, Dwight D. Eisenhower, Omar N. Bradley, J. Lawton Collins, and Matthew B. Ridgway were also Infantry officers.

6. These remarks were delivered at a second swearing-in conducted publicly on 6 July 1964. The earlier, private oath on 3 July was administered to ensure continuity of authority over the Fourth of July holiday.

7. Quoted in Martin Blumenson, *Reorganization of the Army, 1962* (Washington, D.C.: Department of the Army, [1965]), p. 52.

8. Quoted in ibid., p. 69.

9. Ibid., p. 80. Other significant aspects of the wide-ranging reorganization included establishment of an Army Materiel Command and a Combat Developments Command.

10. Gen. Harold K. Johnson, *Challenge: Compendium of Army Accomplishment: A Report by the Chief of Staff: July 1964–April 1968* (Washington, D.C.: Department of the Army, 1 July 1968), p. vi. By August 1965, Special Forces had, under White House pressure, expanded elevenfold. McNamara statement before the Defense Subcommittee of the Senate Appropriations Committee, 4 August 1965.

11. Memorandum, 22 June 1964, Subject: The Army's Unit Readiness Reporting System, as quoted in the Chief of Staff's *Weekly Summary,* 30 June 1964, p. 2, CMH.

12. *Journal of the Armed Forces,* 6 July 1968, p. 9.

13. *Time,* 3 July 1964, p. 16. According to Lt. Gen. Dennis P. McAuliffe, "on an early trip to Europe somebody gave him [Wheeler] a set of ribbons to wear, because he didn't have many of his own. He wore them. The idea was to make him seem more important in his meetings with the Europeans" (Interview, 12 June 1995).

14. Lt. Gen. John B. McPherson, interview, 19 May 1995. "Wheeler had a proclivity towards high-level planning," he added. "He was definitely very competent. But there's a difference between those types and guys like Johnny Johnson. Wheeler was content to have a broad perspective. He liked to think in big terms all the time. Guys that get the job done, like Johnny Johnson, have a different outlook."

15. B. Karpovich, *Sketches for Portraits: American Generals and Aggression in Vietnam* (Moscow: Pravda Publishing House, 1967), pp. 13, 17.

16. CBS Television News Special, "LBJ: Lyndon Johnson Talks Politics," 27 January 1972, Oral History Collection, LBJ Library. LBJ never quite grasped that Wheeler's nickname was "Bus," short for "Buster," consistently calling him "Buzz."

17. Maj. Gen. H. W. Buse, Jr., "MFR: Special JCS Meeting at 1000 on Monday, 27 July 1964," 28 July 1964, Greene Papers, MCHC.

18. *Army Information Digest* (August 1964): 10.

19. Ibid., p. 14.

20. SIGMA II-64 Summary, Earle G. Wheeler Papers, Records Group 218, p. D-17, NA.

21. Ibid., p. D-14.

22. Ibid., p. D-18.

23. The key staff officer in developing the program was Lt. Col. Marie Baird, Women's Army Corps.

24. After General LeMay retired, he wrote his memoirs, stating in the foreword his philosophy: "I have indeed bombed a number of specific targets. They were military targets on which the attack was, in my opinion, justified morally. I've tried to stay away from hospitals, prison camps, orphan asylums, nunneries and dog kennels. I have sought to slaughter as few civilians as possible" (*Mission with LeMay: My Story* [Garden City, N.Y.: Doubleday, 1965], p. viii).

25. As characterized by Gen. Bruce Palmer, Jr., "US Intelligence and Vietnam," *Studies in Intelligence,* Special Issue (Washington, D.C.: Central Intelligence Agency, 1984), p. 34.

26. *Washington Star,* 13 May 1965.

27. LBJ, cable to Amb. Taylor, CAP 64375, 30 December 1964, in William Conrad Gibbons, *The U.S. Government and the Vietnam War,* pt. 4, *July 1965–January 1968* (Washington, D.C.: U.S. Government Printing Office, 1994), p. 13.

28. Quoted in Gibbons, *U.S. Government,* 4:13.

17. March 1965

1. Quoted in William Conrad Gibbons, *The U.S. Government and the Vietnam War,* pt. 3, *January–July 1965* (Washington, D.C.: U.S. Government Printing Office, 1988), pp. 149–50.

2. Quoted in ibid., 3:153.

3. Those present included HKJ, Lt. Gen. K. K. Compton, Maj. Gen. J. B. McPherson, and Rear Adm. R. W. Mehle. At the meeting, HKJ handed out copies of McNaughton's paper setting out the twenty-eight points.

4. *The Pentagon Papers: The Defense Department History of United States Decisionmaking on Vietnam,* Senator Gravel ed., 5 vols. (Boston: Beacon Press, 1971), 3:94. Hereafter, *PP.*

5. Maj. Gen. Delk Oden, Oral History Interview, HAAC.

6. During their meeting, Ky pulled a check for 9 million piasters from a pocket of his flying suit. That was, he told Johnson, the residue of the junta's slush fund, given to him by General Khanh when he left the country. Ky said that he wasn't going to use the money for personal purposes, but would put it in the airmen's relief fund. "So I had him checked out," said Johnson. "And in one year he had had a divorce which cost him more than his annual salary. And he had had a remarriage, and the wedding reception and so on had cost him more than his annual salary. And so I came to the conclusion that he probably was a principal beneficiary of the airmen's relief fund, but he didn't think there was anything unusual about this. After all, he was an airman. He was the number one airman" (HKJ CMH Oral History Interview).

7. HKJ cover letter to the Secretary of Defense et al., "Report on Survey of the Military Situation in Vietnam," 14 March 1965, National Security File, Country File, Vietnam, Box 191, LBJ Library (hereafter, Trip Report).

8. HKJ memorandum for ASD(ISA), "Survey of the Military Situation in Vietnam," 25 March 1965, HKJP.

9. Gibbons, *U.S. Government,* 3:152.

10. Trip Report, p. 2.

11. U.S. Congress, Senate, Committee on Armed Services, Preparedness Investigating Subcommittee, *Hearings: Air War against North Vietnam,* August 1967, p. 420.

12. Trip Report, p. 3.

13. Ibid., p. 5.

14. Ibid., pp. 11–12.

15. Secretary of the Army Stephen Ailes later said that "certainly by January 1965 we knew a major buildup for Vietnam was going to take place. Resor came in as Under Secretary when Ignatius went to be ASD(I&L). Resor was given the task of overseeing the buildup" (Interview, 8 February 1994). HKJ's calendar shows lunch with new Under Secretary Resor on 2 April 1965. On 7 July 1965 Resor moved up to be Secretary of the Army.

16. Edward C. Janicik, *Southeast Asia Force Deployments Buildup,* pt. 1, *1965* (Washington, D.C.: Institute for Defense Analyses, March 1968), pp. 47–48.

17. Trip Report, p. 12.

18. As quoted in Mark Perry, *Four Stars* (Boston: Houghton Mifflin, 1989), p. 150.

19. Robert S. McNamara, *In Retrospect: The Tragedy and Lessons of Vietnam* (New York: Times Books, 1995), p. 177.

20. LBJ's immediate decisions on the HKJ recommendations were promulgated in NSAM 328 dated 6 April 1965. Cutting the Ho Chi Minh Trail with ground forces was not approved.

21. *PP,* 3:429.
22. Gen. Wallace M. Greene, Jr., USMC, Memorandum for Record, Conference with the President, 081530-1740 APR 65, Greene Papers, MCHC.
23. Perry, *Four Stars,* p. 152. Meyer later became Army Chief of Staff.
24. Janicik, *Southeast Asia,* p. 75.
25. Gen. William B. Rosson, perhaps the American military officer with the most extensive and varied service in Vietnam, said that from his point of view the forty-four-battalion decision "meant American assumption of responsibility for the war. And it made the war an American war" ("Nine Steps into the Maelstrom," *Army* [August 1984]: 54).
26. Janicik, *Southeast Asia,* p. 107. These conclusions were stated in "Report of Ad Hoc Study Group to CJCS," 14 July 1965, JCS 2343/630.
27. *PP,* 4:290–91; emphasis in original.
28. Janicik, *Southeast Asia,* p. 106.
29. Gen. Harold K. Johnson, *Challenge: Compendium of Army Accomplishment: A Report by the Chief of Staff: July 1964–April 1968* (Washington, D.C.: Department of the Army, 1 July 1968), p. 223.
30. LBJ, "Remarks at a Military Reception on the White House Lawn," 26 May 1965, *Public Papers of the Presidents of the United States: Lyndon B. Johnson, 1965, Book 1* (Washington, D.C.: U.S. Government Printing Office, 1966), pp. 584–85.
31. Gibbons, *U.S. Government,* 3:381ff.

18. July 1965

1. *The Pentagon Papers: The Defense Department History of United States Decisionmaking on Vietnam,* Senator Gravel ed., 5 vols. (Boston: Beacon Press, 1971), 2:363 (hereafter, *PP*).
2. William Conrad Gibbons, *The U.S. Government and the Vietnam War: Executive and Legislative Roles and Relationships,* pt. 3, *January–July 1965,* pt. 4, *July 1965–January 1968* (Washington, D.C.: Government Printing Office, 1988, 1994), 3:330–31.
3. Ibid., 3:369.
4. Ibid., 3:476.
5. Organization of the Joint Chiefs of Staff, "Intensification of the Military Operations in Vietnam: Concept and Appraisal," Report of the Ad Hoc Study Group, 14 July 1965, pp. iv, C-7; copy lent to the author by General Goodpaster.
6. Robert S. McNamara, *In Retrospect: The Tragedy and Lessons of Vietnam* (New York: Times Books, 1995), p. 201.
7. *PP,* 3:416.
8. Gibbons, *U.S. Government,* 3:381. Under the statutes then pertaining, the President could declare a national emergency and thereby gain authority to call as many as a million reserve forces to active duty for two years; alternatively, he could ask Congress for authority to call such forces.
9. Ibid., 3:395–96.
10. Ibid., 3:398.

11. Gen. Wallace M. Greene, Jr., MFR, 22 July 1965, Greene Papers, MCHC.

12. Gibbons, *U.S. Government*, 3:399–400.

13. McNamara, *In Retrospect*, p. 204.

14. Gen. Wallace M. Greene, Jr., MFR, 22 July 1965, Greene Papers, MCHC.

15. Gibbons, *U.S. Government*, 3:409. President Johnson expressed fear that the Chinese would enter the war, a concern that he often raised. Whether that fear was genuine or an excuse to delay actions he was reluctant to take for other reasons is not clear. Pertinent to the validity of such a fear, however, was the fact that when China did go against Vietnam after North Vietnam had conquered the South, the Vietnamese dealt roughly with the Chinese, leading to the conclusion that the United States and South Vietnam could have done likewise had the need arisen.

16. Papers of LBJ (1963–1969), Meeting Notes Files, Box 1, 22 July 1965, Cabinet Room, Noon, LBJ Meeting with JCS and Others, LBJ Library.

17. Gibbons, *U.S. Government*, 3:408.

18. Ibid., 4:19.

19. Ibid., 3:399.

20. Ibid., 3:414–15.

21. Gen. Wallace M. Greene, Jr., MFR, 24 July 1965, Greene Papers, MCHC.

22. Gen. Johnson apparently did not have advance notice, as his Marine colleague General Greene did, that LBJ had decided against calling the reserves.

23. Gen. Wallace M. Greene, Jr., MFR, 24 July 1965, Greene Papers, MCHC.

24. HKJ comments on Draft Manuscript on Vietnam Buildup, CMH, n.d. Johnson added, "I was unable to find the note prior to retirement, which is regrettable."

25. Gibbons, *U.S. Government*, 3:418.

26. George McT. Kahin, *Intervention: How America Became Involved in Vietnam* (New York: Knopf, 1986), p. 390. Kahin cites a 13 May 1985 letter to him from Goldberg regarding Goldberg's threat to withdraw his resignation from the Court.

27. Gibbons, *U.S. Government*, 4:17.

28. "Final Report of SIGMA II-65 Political-Military Game," 20 August 1965, Wheeler Papers, NA.

29. Papers of LBJ (1963–1969), Meeting Notes File, Box 1, NSC Meeting, 5:45 PM, 27 July 1965, LBJ Library.

30. Gibbons, *U.S. Government*, 3:427–29.

31. The Dirksen-McNamara exchange is quoted in Kahin, p. 396; emphasis in original.

32. Gibbons, *U.S. Government*, 4:16.

33. Larry Berman, *Planning a Tragedy: The Americanization of the War in Vietnam* (New York: Norton, 1982), p. 104n.

34. Robert S. McNamara, telephone interview, 16 February 1994.

35. Brig. Gen. Harold W. Nelson, Society for Military History 1992 annual conference, Fredericksburg, Va., 10 April 1992.

36. Gen. William C. Westmoreland, interview, 10 February 1986.

37. Gibbons, *U.S. Government*, 3:419.

38. Edward C. Janicik, *Southeast Asia Force Deployments Buildup*, pt. 1, *1965* (Washington, D.C.: Institute for Defense Analyses, 1968), p. 123.

39. Gibbons, *U.S. Government*, 4:45, quoting JCS Memorandum for the Secretary of Defense, "Concept for Vietnam," 27 August 1965.

40. Gibbons, *U.S. Government*, 4:47.

41. Ibid., 4:48.

42. Janicik, *Southeast Asia*, pp. 127–28.

43. Gen. Bruce Palmer, Jr., "Commentary," in *The Second Indochina War: Proceedings of a Symposium Held at Airlie, Virginia, 7–9 November 1984,* ed. John Schlight (Washington, D.C.: CMH, 1986), p. 155.

44. Maj. Gen. John K. Singlaub, *Hazardous Duty: An American Soldier in the Twentieth Century* (New York: Summit Books, 1991), p. 279.

45. Mark Perry, *Four Stars* (Boston: Houghton Mifflin, 1989), p. 149.

46. Lt. Gen. Harry W. O. Kinnard, Oral History Interview, MHI. President Johnson made the decision to deploy the 1st Cavalry Division to Vietnam during an 18 June 1965 White House meeting with Rusk, McNamara, and McGeorge Bundy (Gibbons, *U.S. Government*, 3:317).

47. Lt. Gen. Harold G. Moore and Joseph L. Galloway, *We Were Soldiers Once . . . and Young: Ia Drang: The Battle that Changed the War in Vietnam* (New York: Random House, 1992), p. 25.

48. Department of the Army, *Command Comment* (Washington, D.C.: U.S. Army Command Information Unit, 19 October 1966).

49. Maj. Gen. Ellis W. Williamson, unpublished memoir; copy lent to the author by General Williamson.

50. Commander's Combat Note Number 73, Headquarters, 173d Airborne Brigade (Separate), 5 August 1965; copy provided to the author by General Williamson.

51. Joint Chiefs of Staff, *The History of the Joint Chiefs of Staff* (Washington, D.C.: Historical Division, Joint Secretariat, Joint Chiefs of Staff, 1 July 1970), II:22-13. En route to Vietnam, the division, with its 365 helicopters, "staged out of Mobile, Alabama, and Jacksonville, Florida, on the USS *Boxer* and three Military Sea Transportation Service ships." Lt. Gen. John J. Tolson, *Airmobility 1961–1971* (Washington, D.C.: Department of the Army, 1989), p. 62.

52. McNamara, *In Retrospect*, p. 213.

53. Ibid., p. 192.

54. *Washington Post*, 28 October 1965.

55. McNamara on direct examination, *Westmoreland v. CBS* libel trial, in *Vietnam: A Documentary Collection* (New York: Clearwater Publishing, 1985), pp. 4907–11.

56. McNamara, *In Retrospect*, p. 221.

57. As quoted in Brig. Gen. C. J. Quilter, USMC, MFR, JCS Meeting, 24 November 1965, Greene Papers, MCHC.

58. Gibbons, *U.S. Government*, 4:180, 611.

59. Daniel Ellsberg, *Papers on the War* (New York: Simon and Schuster, 1972), p. 221.

60. Henry F. Graff, *The Tuesday Cabinet: Deliberation and Decision on Peace and War under Lyndon B. Johnson* (Englewood Cliffs, N.J.: Prentice-Hall, 1970), p. 50.

61. Rowland Evans and Robert Novak, *Lyndon B. Johnson: The Exercise of Power* (New York: New American Library, 1966), p. 539.

62. Gen. James K. Woolnough, Oral History Interview, MHI.

63. Lt. Gen. Harry Lemley, Oral History Interview, MHI.

64. Ibid.

65. There are some apparent problems with this date. Lyndon Johnson had gall-bladder surgery on 8 October 1965 and spent most of the rest of the year recuperating at his ranch in Texas—"his long, frustrating, sometimes self-pitying convalescence," Joe Califano called it (Joseph A. Califano, Jr., *The Triumph and Tragedy of Lyndon Johnson: The White House Years* [New York: Simon and Schuster, 1991], p. 120). Records at the LBJ Library show no meetings of the JCS with the President at the White House during the last quarter of 1965, nor do the calendars in the Harold K. Johnson Papers at MHI reflect any such meeting. General Johnson's own tabulation of meetings with the President has nothing for this period either. Lieutenant General Cooper, however, is fairly certain that the meeting took place in early November, since it was after his return from a trip to Vietnam at the end of September 1965 and before he was promoted to lieutenant colonel on 1 December 1965. General Greene confirmed to the author that the event took place as Cooper stated and estimated that it was sometime in November 1965. Admiral McDonald similarly corroborated the substance of the Cooper account in correspondence with the author. Admiral McDonald, upon being informed by his press officer that LBJ had displayed the scar from his operation to photographers, shot back without missing a beat, "Damn good thing he didn't have a circumcision."

In regard to dating the event, on 10 November the Joint Chiefs of Staff had forwarded JCSM-810-65 proposing "a systematic air attack on the NVN POL storage and distribution system," which could have precipitated their request to go to the President directly (*PP*, 4:2). Only three days earlier, McNamara had discussed with the President a draft memo that recommended a bombing halt and suggested that more aggressive action was unlikely to achieve anything other than "stagnation at a higher level" (*PP*, 4:303).

66. This account is drawn from Lt. Gen. Charles G. Cooper, "The Day It Became the Longest War," *Naval Institute Proceedings* (May 1996): 77–80, and Cooper interview, 4 February 1997, and telephone interview, 2 April 1996.

67. Meanwhile, said Adm. Elmo R. Zumwalt, Jr., "McNamara had met with the President in advance, had disagreed with the Chiefs' position, and had urged the President to disapprove it." Vietnam War Symposium, Texas Tech University, Lubbock, 18 April 1996.

68. Quoted in Douglas Brinkley, *Dean Acheson: The Cold War Years, 1953–1971* (New Haven, Conn.: Yale University Press, 1992), p. 270.

69. *Time,* 10 December 1965.

70. Extract of letter provided to the author by Lieutenant General Berry.

71. Boyd L. Dastrup, *The US Army Command and General Staff College: A Centennial History* (Manhattan, Kans.: Sunflower University Press, 1982), p. 112. At the Command & General Staff College, wrote Dastrup, during Johnson's tenure as Commandant the "leaders argued that military methods to defeat the insurgency were insufficient."

72. Transcription of CMC debrief, 23 August 1967, Greene Papers, MCHC.

73. Hanson W. Baldwin, *Strategy for Tomorrow,* as quoted in Harry G. Summers, Jr., *On Strategy: The Vietnam War in Context* (Carlisle Barracks, Pa.: Strategic Studies Institute, U.S. Army War College, [1981]). pp. 30–31.

19. PROVN

1. As quoted in William Conrad Gibbons, *The U.S. Government and the Vietnam War: Executive and Legislative Roles and Relationships*, pt. 3, *January–July 1965* (Washington, D.C.: U.S. Government Printing Office, 1988), 3:170.

2. Brig. Richard L. Clutterbuck, *The Long, Long War: Counterinsurgency in Malaya and Vietnam* (New York: Praeger, 1966), p. 176.

3. Ibid., p. 51.

4. Ibid., p. 73.

5. Later both Warner and Brown became four-star generals.

6. HKJ memorandum for Col. J. J. Wilson, 3 May 1965, and CSM 65-283, "Study—A Program for the Pacification and Long Term Development of Vietnam," 21 June 1965, both in Marshall Papers, Indochina Archive, University of California at Berkeley.

7. Department of the Army, Office of the Deputy Chief of Staff for Military Operations, *A Program for the Pacification and Long-Term Development of Vietnam* (Washington, D.C.: Department of the Army, 1 March 1966), p. G-8.

8. Quoted in Mark Perry, *Four Stars* (Boston: Houghton Mifflin, 1989), p. 157.

9. As his parting contribution, Heck worked up a "PROVN Coloring Book" satirizing each member of the team.

10. Here PROVN relied on NSAM 288, which had established that as the objective. In the course of their research, the team found that there were desk officers in the State Department who were ignorant of that directive, or who ignored it, denying that a noncommunist South Vietnam was a U.S. objective.

11. Free World forces (more commonly called FWMAF for Free World Military Assistance Forces) were those troops contributed by nations other than South Vietnam or the United States, principally those of the Republic of Korea, Australia and New Zealand, and Thailand.

12. Lt. Gen. C. H. Bonesteel III memorandum for Lt. Gen. V. P. Mock, 19 April 1966; copy provided to the author by Colonel Hanifen.

13. Lt. Col. Donald S. Marshall, PROVN briefing for the Joint Chiefs of Staff, 1966; copy provided to the author by Colonel Marshall.

14. Blue indicated areas under friendly control, orange indicated contested areas, and red indicated those areas controlled by the enemy.

15. As quoted in Robert Gallucci, *Neither Peace nor Honor: The Politics of American Military Policy in Vietnam* (Baltimore: Johns Hopkins University Press, 1975), pp. 38–39.

16. PROVN was briefed at CINCPAC 17 May 1966 and at MACV on 21 May. *The Pentagon Papers: The Defense Department History of United States Decisionmaking on Vietnam*, Senator Gravel ed., 5 vols. (Boston: Beacon Press, 1971), 2:379 (hereafter, *PP*).

17. Thomas W. Scoville, citing the MACV Command History, in R. W. Komer, *Organization and Management of the New Model Pacification Program, 1966–1969* (Santa Monica, Calif.: Rand Corporation, 7 May 1970), p. 32.

18. Phillip B. Davidson, *Vietnam at War: The History: 1946–1975* (Novato, Calif.: Presidio Press, 1988), p. 411.

19. By about this time, General Mock had come around in a big way, calling PROVN "beautifully done" and writing to Hanifen with an enthusiastic, if wildly inaccurate, report of how it was faring. "Suffice it to say that it has exceeded all expectations and has been received most favorably by the Joint Chiefs of Staff, CINCPAC and the staff in Hawaii, Westmoreland and staff in Saigon, and General Maxwell Taylor. It is scheduled for Mr. McNamara at a staff meeting next week, and I honestly believe that before too long it will be given to State, AID [Agency for International Development], and other governmental agencies which are concerned with it. In fact, some of the senior people concerned have suggested that the NSC [National Security Council] be assembled as a body to hear it, but we don't know yet whether that will eventuate. On balance, it is a masterpiece of understatement to say that the study exceeded everybody's expectations, and you left us a legacy that will not be forgotten." Lt. Gen. Vernon P. Mock, letter to Col. Thomas J. Hanifen, 11 June 1966; copy provided to the author by Colonel Hanifen.

20. The Systems Analysis work referred to is described in Alain C. Enthoven and K. Wayne Smith, *How Much Is Enough? Shaping the Defense Program, 1961–1969* (New York: Harper and Row, 1971), passim. Enthoven confirmed that McNamara had been made aware of the results of that research in annotations of a letter to him from the author dated 10 February 1996.

21. *PP,* 4:369, quoting McNamara, 17 November 1966 Draft Presidential Memorandum.

22. Ibid., 4:369.

23. Ibid., 4:371.

24. Ibid., 4:374.

25. Ibid., 4:376.

26. Ibid.

27. Krulak paper, "A Strategic Appraisal, Vietnam," quoted in Gibbons, *U.S. Government,* 4:198.

28. Lt. Gen. Krulak, message to CG FMFPAC/I MAC FWD and CG FIRST MARDIV, 270218 OCT 1965, Greene Papers, MCHC.

29. Komer, *Organization and Management,* p. 32.

30. *PP,* 2:571. Komer's outlook on all matters having to do with pacification owes much to the insights and experience of Col. (later Brig. Gen.) Robert M. Montague, Jr., who served in the delta in Vietnam, developed the "oil spot" plan for the 21st ARVN Division, and served under Ambassador Maxwell Taylor in the embassy in Saigon, altogether spending five years in Vietnam. Subsequently, Montague was assigned to Komer's White House staff, where, observed one admirer, "Komer never signed anything that was worth a damn that wasn't written for him by Montague."

20. Troubles

1. Issue dated 7 January 1966.

2. Gen. William C. Westmoreland, Oral History Interview (Draft), MHI.

3. Ibid.

4. Lt. Gen. Phillip B. Davidson, *Secrets of the Vietnam War* (Novato, Calif.: Presidio Press, 1990), p. 9.

5. Alain C. Enthoven and K. Wayne Smith, *How Much Is Enough? Shaping the Defense Program, 1961–1969* (New York: Harper and Row, 1971), p. 302.

6. Joint Chiefs of Staff, *The History of the Joint Chiefs of Staff* (Washington, D.C.: Historical Division, Joint Secretariat, Joint Chiefs of Staff, 1 July 1970), p. 29-10.

7. *The Pentagon Papers: The Defense Department History of United States Decisionmaking on Vietnam,* Senator Gravel ed., 5 vols. (Boston: Beacon Press, 1971), 2:548 (hereafter, *PP*).

8. Ibid., 2:554.

9. Gen. Harold K. Johnson, foreword to *The U.S. Infantry: Queen of Battle,* ed. Col. Richard J. Stillman (New York: Franklin Watts, [1965]), p. I.

10. HKJ lecture, Command and General Staff College, Fort Leavenworth, 28 November 1961, CARL.

11. Gen. James K. Woolnough, interview, 15 February 1994.

12. Brig. Gen. Archelaus L. Hamblen, Jr., telephone interview, 2 January 1995.

13. Gen. Donald V. Bennett, interview, 23 August 1994.

14. Col. Thomas G. Irwin, telephone interview, 11 October 1995.

15. Gen. Donald V. Bennett, interview, 23 August 1994.

16. Robert J. Johnson, interview, 27 September 1994. "I said I had not" apparently indicated that Bobby had not committed an offense himself, but rather had failed to report someone else who had, a violation of the nontoleration clause.

17. Ibid.

18. Gen. Nguyen Khanh, letter to Wilson, 5 July 1966, Col. Jasper J. Wilson Papers, MHI; emphasis in original.

19. This account is based on an undated Jasper J. Wilson handwritten Memorandum for the Record, HKJP.

20. Lt. Gen. Nguyen Khanh, interview, 1 April 1995. Khanh confirmed the substance of Colonel Wilson's memo concerning their New York City meeting.

21. *PP,* 4:353.

22. Ibid., 4:489.

23. Truong Nhu Tang with David Chanoff and Doan Van Toai, *A Vietcong Memoir* (New York: Harcourt Brace Jovanovich, 1985), p. 66.

24. Johnson personnel records, NPRC.

25. Attributed to "one of the Joint Chiefs" in Douglas Kinnard, *The War Managers* (Hanover, N.H.: University Press of New England, 1977), p. 56. In a 16 April 1996 telephone conversation with the author, Kinnard identified Johnson as the source.

26. Loikow himself was an impressive soldier, remembered Lt. Col. John Wickham, the assistant executive officer to Johnson. "I got a lot of sage advice from Loikow—about the Army and about life," said Wickham, who later reached four-star rank and was Chief of Staff in his own right.

27. SMA William O. Wooldridge, letter to author, 12 July 1995.

28. Wooldridge letter and telephone interview, 22 July 1995.

29. Col. Eugene R. Cocke, interview, 1 November 1996.

30. Lieutenant General Berry annotation of draft manuscript.

31. MACJ 341 Fact Sheet, "Summation of Progress," 16 August 1967, USMACV Fact Book #25, August 1967, MHI. MACV reported achieving 64 percent of the attrition goal.

32. "Westmoreland on Vietnam," CBS News report, CBS television network, 27 December 1966. The interview with Westmoreland by correspondents Charles Collingwood and Morley Safer was filmed 20 December 1966 at MACV headquarters in Saigon. In later years, including during the *Westmoreland v. CBS* libel trial, Westmoreland claimed that he had never used the phrase "light at the end of the tunnel," but they had him on videotape doing so.

21. *Slogging*

1. HKJ address, Fort Ord, Calif., 15 January 1965. On this same trip to California, HKJ made headlines when he said during a press conference at Los Angeles International Airport that "the war in Viet Nam could last as long as ten years before a victory is won for the free world."

2. There were, though, many who were willing to help. General Johnson wrote to one gentleman in Florida to say, "I should like to express the Army's thanks for volunteering your loft of racing pigeons . . . for duty in Vietnam," but he explained that at present there was no requirement for them.

3. HKJ obituary, *Army* (November 1983): 11. During the Vietnam era, some 27 million Americans were of draft age. About a third, or 9 million, served in the U.S. armed forces during that time; of those, nearly a third, or 2.9 million, served in Vietnam (William T. Bennett, Texas Tech Vietnam Conflict Conference, Lubbock, Texas, 1 April 1995).

4. Secretary of the Army Stanley R. Resor, Comments, Army Policy Council, 30 March 1966, as reported in *Weekly Summary,* 3 May 1966, CMH.

5. *Weekly Summary,* 17 August 1965 and 18 January 1966, CMH.

6. Lt. Gen. Joseph M. Heiser, Jr., *Logistic Support* (Washington, D.C.: Department of the Army, 1974), p. 251.

7. *Weekly Summary,* 21 September 1965, CMH.

8. Those counseling against calling up reserve forces often stressed how disruptive it would be to the lives of those mobilized, without acknowledging how disruptive it was for those who were drafted to fill the slots instead. They also failed to remark on the fact that reservists had signed up to serve, whereas draftees were simply requisitioned.

9. Gen. Ferdinand J. Chesarek, interview, 22 June 1989.

10. *Weekly Summary,* 12 April 1966, CMH.

11. As quoted in Benjamin Schemmer, "Review of *How Much Is Enough?*" *Armed Forces Journal,* 1 February 1971, p. 40.

12. *Weekly Summary,* 28 February 1967, CMH.

13. HKJ letter to Gen. William C. Westmoreland, 31 July 1968, HKJP. This letter may not have been sent, as what appears to be the original is in the file.

14. Gen. Ferdinand J. Chesarek, "Historical Background Surrounding the Position of the Assistant Vice Chief of Staff," unpublished essay; copy made available to the author by General Chesarek.

15. *New York Times*, 9 January 1967, and attached materials, HKJP.

16. Gen. Maxwell D. Taylor, letter to President Johnson, 6 February 1967, National Security File, Files of Robert Komer, Box 6, LBJ Library.

17. Gen. Bruce Palmer, Jr., *The 25-Year War: America's Military Role in Vietnam* (Lexington: University Press of Kentucky, 1984), p. 49.

18. *The Pentagon Papers: The Defense Department History of United States Decisionmaking on Vietnam*, Senator Gravel ed., 5 vols. (Boston: Beacon Press, 1971), 4:460.

19. Ibid., 4:467.

20. Ibid., 4:466.

21. Ibid., 4:482.

22. John S. Bowman, ed., *The Vietnam War: An Almanac* (New York: World Almanac Publications, 1985), p. 174.

23. Tom Johnson's notes of meetings, Box 1, meeting of 13 July 1967, LBJ Library.

24. Jack Anderson, *Washington Post,* 20 July 1967.

25. Tom Johnson's notes of meetings, Box 1, meeting of 13 July 1967, LBJ Library.

26. Tom Johnson's Notes of Meetings, Box 1, Tuesday Luncheon Group, 12 July 1967, LBJ Library.

27. LBJ News Conference, Exhibit 409A, *Westmoreland v. CBS* libel trial, in *Vietnam, A Documentary Collection* (New York: Clearwater Publishing, 1985), p. 22211.

28. Springfield, Mass., *Sunday Republican,* 22 October 1967.

29. Chester L. Cooper, *The Lost Crusade: America in Vietnam* (New York: Dodd, Mead, 1970), pp. 416–17.

30. Remarks of 10 October 1967 as quoted in Martin Blumenson, "A Most Remarkable Man," *Army* (August 1968): 21.

22. Airpower

1. Robert S. McNamara, *In Retrospect: The Tragedy and Lessons of Vietnam* (New York: Times Books, 1995), pp. 152–53.

2. Ibid., p. 153.

3. John Schlight, "Response to Letter to the Editor," *Journal of Military History* (Fall 1994): 200–201.

4. Doris Kearns, *Lyndon Johnson and the American Dream* (New York: Harper and Row, 1976), p. 270. Kearns likened LBJ to the Wizard of Oz, "an ordinary man concealed behind a giant screen, pulling strings, pointing at targets, playing with the illusion of power" (p. 275).

5. McNamara deposition, *Westmoreland v. CBS*, p. 388. McNamara got important help from the State Department in restraining the bombing campaign. An example found in the JCS history is instructive: State objected to hitting a thermal power plant and a POL installation at Nam Dinh on the grounds that they were too close to Haiphong, to SAM Site #1, and to Phuc Yen Airfield. The targets measured

27 miles from the SAM site and 51 miles from the airfield (Joint Chiefs of Staff, *The History of the Joint Chiefs of Staff* [Washington, D.C.: Historical Division, Joint Secretariat, Joint Chiefs of Staff, 1 July 1970], p. 25-12; hereafter, *JCS History*).

6. Carl Bernstein interview of McNamara, *Time*, 11 February 1991, pp. 70–72.

7. Stated at 11 July 1966 news conference.

8. *JCS History*, p. 25-2. Also HKJ in 28 August 1967 Hearings, p. 409.

9. Prof. George C. Herring, LBJ Library Conference, 16 October 1993.

10. Memorandum, "The Vietnamese Communists' Will to Persist," Directorate of Intelligence, CIA, 26 August 1966, Joint Exhibit 217, *Westmoreland v. CBS*, p. I-9.

11. According to Gen. Bruce Palmer, Jr., who made a detailed study of CIA reporting on Vietnam: "When President Johnson saw the study, he put a close hold on it, telling McNamara and CIA Director Helms not to show it to anyone. Thus the Chiefs were not aware of this study at the time. . . . And so the JCS naturally perceived that McNamara had lied to them when, in his defense, he was abiding by the President's orders" (Letter to author with enclosure, "The JCS, SecDef McNamara, and Congressional Hearings on Vietnam in August 1967," 14 September 1995). Despite his decision to deny the document to the JCS, President Johnson directed that three senators be briefed on its findings (Gen. Bruce Palmer, Jr., "US Intelligence and Vietnam," in *Studies in Intelligence,* Special Issue [Washington, D.C.: Central Intelligence Agency, 1984], p. 47).

12. That course of action also entailed enormous human costs, with the U.S. Air Force alone losing 2,257 aircraft during the years 1962–1975 (Earl H. Tilford, Jr., "Letter to the Editor," *Journal of Military History* [Fall 1994]: 198).

13. *JCS History*, pt. 3, p. 36-24.

14. CIA, "The Role of Air Strikes in Attaining Objectives in North Vietnam," March 1966, in William Conrad Gibbons, *The U.S. Government and the Vietnam War*, pt. 4, *July 1965–January 1968* (Washington, D.C.: U.S. Government Printing Office, 1994), 4:362.

15. Gen. Paul D. Adams, Oral History Interview, MHI. Adams was present when LeMay made this statement.

16. Lt. Gen. John J. Tolson, *Airmobility 1961–1971* (Washington, D.C.: Department of the Army, 1989), pp. 104, 106.

17. Johnson later cited another reason for his decision to give up the Caribou: "We were not getting anywhere in getting replacement aircraft for them anyway from OSD. The Air Force had a surplus of the C-130's in terms of the number of aircraft that were authorized them, and it was viewed by the analysts in OSD as being a suitable and proper substitute for the Caribou. When we went in for authorization for replacement aircraft, we simply weren't getting it. Our fleet was attriting, and in order to . . . salvage something from this, why the agreement with the Air Force seemed to be a desirable agreement" (HKJ, Oral History Interview, MHI).

18. Tolson, *Airmobility,* p. 105.

19. Ibid., p. 106.

20. Williamson commanded the 173d Airborne Brigade on Okinawa, then took it to Vietnam in the spring of 1965.

Completion date for transfer of the Caribous to the Air Force was established as 1 January 1967. An Army study made after the Air Force had been operating the Caribou fleet in Vietnam for a full year "showed a 12.4 percent increase in hours flown and an 11.4 percent increase in Caribou cargo tonnage" (Tolson, *Airmobility,* p. 107).

21. Williams noted that the issue was fogged by controversy over "the Cheyenne, which the Air Force would not agree was a helicopter because it had stub wings."

22. HKJ, Oral History Interview, MHI.

23. See Lt. Gen. Edward L. Rowny, *Engineer Memoirs* (Alexandria, Va.: Office of History, U.S. Army Corps of Engineers, 1995), p. 110 and passim. Johnson was punctilious in treating Rowny fairly. When Gen. Paul D. Adams requested Rowny's assignment to India as chief of a military mission, Johnson declined, noting that if he made such an assignment, it "would be promptly interpreted as my device for burying him, regardless of my actual motives and regardless of anything that might be said. I fully appreciate that if I want to send Rowny to Timbuctoo, I can; however, I would prefer not to take this action. Rowny very badly needs the tempering influence that division command will give him and I intend to move him to a division as soon as an opening occurs" (HKJ letter to Gen. Paul D. Adams, 25 July 1964, HKJP). Rowny was given command of the 24th Infantry Division sometime the following year.

24. Johnson was also concerned that concentration of the Army's aviation assets in additional airmobile divisions would further aggravate a situation that already disturbed him. On a trip to Vietnam, he had seen 434 helicopters in the one division; meanwhile, the senior advisor to ARVN forces in that corps area had two helicopters for their support. "That aspect troubled him, too," said Gen. Edward C. Meyer.

25. Quoted in Tolson, *Airmobility,* p. 58.

26. Even though it was McNamara's memorandum that had stimulated much of the Army's aviation and airmobility activity, when it came time to field what had been developed, OSD put numerous obstacles in the way. Just before Christmas 1964, wrote Benjamin Schemmer, it was learned that "McNamara had just 'canceled' Army aviation in a budget decision that denied any funds for new helicopters, spare parts, and pilot training until the Army produced a study justifying every single plane in its force structure." Six months later, after a visit to Vietnam, "McNamara ordered massive, impossible, overnight increases in helicopter production and the immediate deployment of new aviation units that, in fact, would take months, even years, to form" ("Review of *Thunderbolt,*" *Strategic Review* [Spring 1993]: 65–66).

27. Tolson, *Airmobility,* p. 89.

28. Ibid., p. 109.

29. Ibid. The Army was so hard-pressed for pilots that it mailed individual letters to nearly 2,000 aviators in the reserve forces asking for volunteers for active duty. Only sixty applications were received.

30. In retirement, General LeMay wrote his autobiography, *Mission with LeMay.* It is a remarkable document. Vietnam does not appear in the index, and the only mention of General Wheeler is of his having been one of the 1,400 present at LeMay's retirement ceremony.

31. *Time,* 5 February 1965.

32. Martin Blumenson, "A Most Remarkable Man," *Army* (August 1968): 26.

33. U.S. Congress, Senate, Committee on Armed Services, Preparedness Investi-

gating Subcommittee, *Hearings on the Air War against North Vietnam,* August 1967, pt. 2, p. 126 (hereafter, Stennis Hearings).

34. Ibid., pt. 4, p. 279. Perhaps McNamara's state of mind going into the hearings is reflected by a requirement passed to General Johnson the day before McNamara was scheduled to testify: get me a paper written by a "pacifistic" colonel as to what would happen "if we tried to get it all over quickly" (HKJ Calendar, 24 August 1967, HKJP).

35. Stennis Hearings, pt. 4, p. 298.

36. Ibid., p. 281.

37. Ibid., p. 347.

38. Ibid., p. 368.

39. Ibid., p. 327.

40. Ibid., p. 334.

41. Townsend Hoopes, *The Limits of Intervention* (New York: David McKay, 1969), p. 90.

42. Prof. George C. Herring, comment on draft manuscript.

43. Lester A. Sobel, ed., *South Vietnam: U.S.-Communist Confrontation in Southeast Asia,* vol. 2, 1966–67 (New York: Facts on File, 1969), p. 420.

44. Joint Exhibit 249, Minutes of 18 August 1967 Meeting in White House Cabinet Room, *Westmoreland v. CBS* libel trial, in *Vietnam, A Documentary Collection* (New York: Clearwater Publishing, 1985).

45. McNamara deposition, in *Vietnam: A Documentary Collection,* p. 113.

46. McNamara on cross-examination, in *Vietnam: A Documentary Collection,* p. 4958.

47. McNamara, *In Retrospect,* p. 284.

48. Mark Perry, *Four Stars* (Boston: Houghton Mifflin, 1989), pp. 162–66. Perry later indicated that he had been given details of the story by Gens. John Vessey, Bruce Palmer, and Edward C. Meyer. Also, said Perry: "General Greene wasn't present at the meeting with General Wheeler. General Bruce Palmer told me Greene was never there because they knew which way he would go." General Greene said in an interview, regarding published assertions that at one point the JCS considered mass resignation, "That's not true. I'm absolutely sure that they never considered resignation. And I do not think individual members considered resigning, either." There is, as documented elsewhere in this manuscript, abundant evidence that General Johnson, for one, considered resignation on many occasions. Lt. Gen. Charles G. Cooper, who as a major was Marine aide to Adm. David L. McDonald when he was Chief of Naval Operations, stated that "Admiral McDonald seriously considered resigning, but he thought it would be ineffective. He'd [meaning LBJ] "just reach down and get somebody else."

49. Quoted in Mark Perry, "Just for the Record," *Veteran* (December 1985): 11.

50. Lt. Gen. Dennis P. McAuliffe, interview, 12 June 1995.

51. Lt. Gen. John B. McPherson, interview, 19 May 1995.

52. Gen. Bruce Palmer, Jr., letter to author with enclosure, "The JCS, SecDef McNamara, and Congressional Hearings on Vietnam in August 1967," 14 September 1995. General Palmer also stated in a questionnaire for the LBJ Library that "the JCS came very close to resigning en masse over the mobilization issue and was par-

ticularly unhappy with Secretary McNamara's testimony" (Ted Gittenger, ed., *The Johnson Years: A Vietnam Roundtable* [Austin, Tex.: LBJ Library, 1993], p. 160).

53. Betty Wheeler Besson, interview, 17 May 1995.

54. Dr. Gilmore S. Wheeler, interview, 24 May 1995.

55. Chester L. Cooper, *The Lost Crusade: America in Vietnam* (New York: Dodd, Mead, 1970), p. 414.

56. Quoted in Gibbons, *U.S. Government*, 3:156n73. According to Lt. Gen. Harry Lemley, General Wheeler "used to complain that [at the Tuesday Lunch] they always had liver, and it was tough liver" (Oral History Interview, MHI).

23. Explosions

1. Quoted in Chester Cooper, *The Lost Crusade: America in Vietnam* (New York: Dodd, Mead, 1970), p. 506.

2. *The Pentagon Papers: The Defense Department History of United States Decisionmaking on Vietnam,* Senator Gravel ed., 5 vols. (Boston: Beacon Press, 1971), 2:403.

3. Robert S. McNamara, *In Retrospect: The Tragedy and Lessons of Vietnam,* p. 283.

4. Message, Johnson to Abrams, WDC 15663, 221857Z November 1967, CMH Files.

5. Gen. William C. Westmoreland, *A Soldier Reports* (Garden City, N.Y.: Doubleday, 1976), p. 276.

6. Quoted in Larry Berman, *Lyndon Johnson's War: The Road to Stalemate in Vietnam* (New York: Norton, 1989), pp. 57–58.

7. Gen. Bruce Palmer, Jr., *The 25-Year War: America's Military Role in Vietnam* (Lexington: University Press of Kentucky, 1984), p. 75.

8. HKJ, Oral History Interview, MHI.

9. McNamara's memoirs display his disdain for the military leadership, for the South Vietnamese, indeed almost across the board for people of all stripes. And his perfect arrogance is on display throughout. At one point, for example, having catalogued at some length the errors of omission and commission perpetrated by himself and his colleagues, McNamara maintains that the civilian leadership he assembled in the Department of Defense was "the most outstanding group ever to serve in a cabinet department." Given a history that includes cabinet departments headed by the likes of Thomas Jefferson and Alexander Hamilton, McNamara's self-congratulatory assessment is, in the kindest terms, simply ludicrous (see *In Retrospect,* p. 17).

10. Gen. Andrew J. Goodpaster, Oral History Interview, MHI.

11. CBS television news special, "The Decision to Halt the Bombing," 6 February 1970, Oral History Collection, LBJ Library.

12. It is now widely recognized that Gen. Earle G. Wheeler, Chairman of the Joint Chiefs of Staff, elicited this request from Westmoreland by dangling before him the prospect of a revised strategy that would remove many of the constraints on offensive action that LBJ and McNamara had imposed to that point. Wheeler then represented that request in Washington as one necessitated by the enemy threat. See Her-

bert Y. Schandler, *The Unmaking of a President: Lyndon Johnson and Vietnam* (Princeton, N.J.: Princeton University Press, 1977), pp. 99–101.

13. William L. Hauser, *America's Army in Crisis: A Study in Civil-Military Relations* (Baltimore: Johns Hopkins University Press, 1973), p. 172.

14. HKJ handwritten note to SMA William O. Wooldridge, 25 February 1967, HKJP.

15. Even after Johnson learned of Wooldridge's dishonesty, he did not cut himself off from the man. When Wooldridge wrote to Johnson to tell him that he had gone back to school and finished his education, Johnson responded with encouragement free of condemnation.

16. Hauser, *America's Army in Crisis*, pp. 170–72.

17. HKJ remarks, John Carroll University, Cleveland, Ohio, 29 April 1968, as quoted in Martin Blumenson, "A Most Remarkable Man," *Army* (August 1968): 25.

24. *Compline*

1. Quoted in Lt. Gen. Harris W. Hollis, "Giants among Men," unpublished transcript of remarks, Fort Jackson, S.C., 20 August 1985, p. 11.

2. Martin Blumenson, "A Most Remarkable Man," *Army* (August 1968): 23.

3. Gen. Earle G. Wheeler, Oral History Interview, LBJ Library.

4. Lt. Gen. J. L. Richardson, memorandum to HKJ, 17 December 1964, Johnson personnel records, NPRC.

5. Lt. Gen. Harry Lemley, Oral History Interview, MHI.

6. SFC Frank X. Kaiser, letter to author, 31 January 1995. Examination of General Johnson's calendar suggests that this conversation probably took place following a 1 February 1968 White House luncheon honoring Gen. Matthew Ridgway.

7. Joint Chiefs of Staff, *The History of the Joint Chiefs of Staff* (Washington, D.C.: Historical Division, Joint Secretariat, Joint Chiefs of Staff, 1 July 1970), p. 52-1.

8. Bobby subsequently served in Vietnam with the 101st Airborne Division until a knee injury suffered while playing basketball in a rear area forced his medical evacuation and eventually his departure from the Army. He is now a respected and successful college basketball coach.

9. HKJ departing remarks to the staff, 2 July 1968, HKJP. Johnson also calculated the attendance records of all the members of the JCS. Johnson's tabulation shows that during four years as Chief of Staff he attended 460 JCS meetings, amounting to 80.4 percent of the 572 meetings held. That put him in first place in attendance, followed by the Chairman (76.4 percent), Navy Chief (72.7 percent), Air Force Chief (69.9 percent), and Marine Commandant (63.9 percent). Many of Johnson's absences were attributable to his frequent trips to Vietnam.

Epilogue

1. "The Boy Scout motto, oath and laws, taken together," Johnson once told a Scouting audience, "define our individual purpose, provide a specific constructive

goal, and give to each of us attainable heights to which we can aspire." These constitute "the finest possible" statement "of what America stands for" (HKJ address, Kaw Council, Fort Leavenworth, Kans., 21 November 1961, CARL). To a friend he wrote: "I know you are especially proud of the fact that your three sons are now all Eagle Scouts. One of the regrets of my life is that my two boys are not" (HKJ letter to Lt. Col. W. L. Albright, 3 June 1967, HKJP).

2. Brig. Gen. Albion W. Knight, Jr., interview, 1 February 1997, and telephone interview, 16 June 1995. Also, Knight letter to Col. Harry G. Summers, Jr., 4 August 1984; copy provided to the author by Colonel Summers. General Johnson made similar statements to or in the presence of several other officers, including Colonel Summers, Colonel Harold Birch, and General Bruce Palmer, Jr.

SELECTED BIBLIOGRAPHY

Books

Adams, Sam. *War of Numbers: An Intelligence Memoir.* South Royalton, Vt.: Steerforth Press, 1994.

Appleman, Roy E. *South to the Naktong, North to the Yalu.* Washington, D.C.: Office of the Chief of Military History, Department of the Army, 1961.

Barrett, David M. *Uncertain Warriors: Lyndon Johnson and His Vietnam Advisers.* Lawrence: University Press of Kansas, 1993.

Bergerson, Frederic A. *The Army Gets an Air Force: Tactics of Insurgent Bureaucratic Politics.* Baltimore: Johns Hopkins University Press, 1980.

Berman, Larry. *Lyndon Johnson's War: The Road to Stalemate in Vietnam.* New York: Norton, 1989.

———. *Planning a Tragedy: The Americanization of the War in Vietnam.* New York: Norton, 1982.

Bowman, John S., ed. *The Vietnam War: An Almanac.* New York: World Almanac Publications, 1985.

Brewin, Bob, and Sydney Shaw. *Vietnam on Trial: Westmoreland vs. CBS.* New York: Atheneum, 1987.

Bunker, Ellsworth. *The Bunker Papers: Reports to the President from Vietnam, 1967–1973.* Ed. Douglas Pike. 3 vols. Berkeley: Institute of Asian Studies, University of California, 1990.

Buzzanco, Robert. *Masters of War: Military Dissent and Politics in the Vietnam Era.* New York: Cambridge University Press, 1996.

Cable, Larry. *Conflict of Myths: The Development of U.S. Counter-insurgency Doctrine and the Vietnam War.* New York: NYU Press, 1986.

———. *Unholy Grail: The U.S. and the Wars in Vietnam, 1965–68.* New York: Routledge, 1991.

Califano, Joseph A., Jr. *The Triumph and Tragedy of Lyndon Johnson: The White House Years.* New York: Simon and Schuster, 1991.

Chanoff, David, and Doan Van Toai. *Portrait of the Enemy.* New York: Random House, 1987.

Charlton, Michael, and Anthony Moncrieff. *Many Reasons Why: The American Involvement in Vietnam.* London: Scolar Press, 1978.

Clark, Gen. Mark W. *From the Danube to the Yalu.* New York: Harper, 1954.

Clutterbuck, Brig. Richard L. *The Long, Long War: Counterinsurgency in Malaya and Vietnam.* New York: Praeger, 1966.

Collins, J. Lawton. *War in Peacetime: The History and Lessons of Korea.* Boston: Houghton Mifflin, 1969.

Cooper, Chester L. *The Lost Crusade: America in Vietnam.* New York: Dodd, Mead, 1970.

Dastrup, Boyd L. *The US Army Command and General Staff College: A Centennial History.* Manhattan, Kans.: Sunflower University Press, 1982.

Davidson, Lt. Gen. Phillip B. *Secrets of the Vietnam War.* Novato, Calif.: Presidio Press, 1990.

Daws, Gavan. *Prisoners of the Japanese: POWs of World War II in the Pacific.* New York: William Morrow, 1994.

Duiker, William J. *The Communist Road to Power in Vietnam.* Boulder, Colo.: Westview Press, 1981.

Enthoven, Alain C., and K. Wayne Smith. *How Much Is Enough? Shaping the Defense Program, 1961–1969.* New York: Harper and Row, 1971.

Gallup, George H. *The Gallup Poll: Public Opinion 1935–1971.* Vol. 3, *1959–1971.* New York: Random House, 1972.

Gibbons, William Conrad. *The U.S. Government and the Vietnam War: Executive and Legislative Roles and Relationships.* Pt. 3, *January–July 1965,* and pt. 4, *July 1965–January 1968.* Washington, D.C.: U.S. Government Printing Office, 1988, 1994.

Graff, Henry F. *The Tuesday Cabinet: Deliberation and Decision on Peace and War under Lyndon B. Johnson.* Englewood Cliffs, N.J.: Prentice-Hall, 1970.

Halberstam, David. *The Best and the Brightest.* Greenwich, Conn.: Fawcett, 1969.

Herring, George C. *America's Longest War: The United States and Vietnam 1950–1975.* 2d ed. New York: Knopf, 1986.

———. *LBJ and Vietnam: A Different Kind of War.* Austin: University of Texas Press, 1994.

Hoopes, Townsend. *The Limits of Intervention.* New York: David McKay, 1969.

Hunt, Richard A. *Pacification: The American Struggle for Vietnam's Hearts and Minds.* Boulder, Colo.: Westview Press, 1995.

James, D. Clayton, ed. *South to Bataan, North to Mukden: The Prison Diary of Brigadier General W. E. Brougher.* Athens: University of Georgia Press, 1971.

Joes, Anthony James. *Modern Guerrilla Insurgency.* Westport, Conn.: Praeger, 1992.

———. *The War for South Viet Nam, 1954–1975.* Westport, Conn.: Praeger, 1989.

Johnson, Lyndon Baines. *The Vantage Point: Perspectives of the Presidency, 1963–1969.* New York: Holt, Rinehart and Winston, 1971.

Joint Chiefs of Staff. *The History of the Joint Chiefs of Staff: The Joint Chiefs of Staff and the War in Vietnam, 1960–1968.* Washington, D.C.: Historical Division, Joint Secretariat, Joint Chiefs of Staff, 1 July 1970.

Kahin, George McT. *Intervention: How America Became Involved in Vietnam.* New York: Knopf, 1986.

Kearns, Doris. *Lyndon Johnson and the American Dream.* New York: Harper and Row, 1976.

Kinnard, Douglas. *The War Managers.* Hanover, N.H.: University Press of New England, 1977.

Knox, Donald. *Death March: The Survivors of Bataan.* New York: Harcourt Brace Jovanovich, 1981.

Korb, Lawrence J. *The Joint Chiefs of Staff: The First Twenty-five Years.* Bloomington: Indiana University Press, 1976.

Krepinevich, Andrew F., Jr. *The Army and Vietnam.* Baltimore: Johns Hopkins University Press, 1986.

Lanning, Michael Lee, and Dan Cragg. *Inside the VC and the NVA: The Real Story of North Vietnam's Armed Forces*. New York: Ivy Books, 1992.

LeMay, Curtis E., with MacKinlay Kantor. *Mission with LeMay: My Story.* Garden City, N.Y.: Doubleday, 1965.

McMaster, H. R. *Dereliction of Duty: Lyndon Johnson, Robert McNamara, the Joint Chiefs of Staff, and the Lies that Led to Vietnam*. New York: HarperCollins, 1997.

McNamara, Robert S. *In Retrospect: The Tragedy and Lessons of Vietnam*. New York: Times Books, 1995.

Morton, Louis. *The Fall of the Philippines*. Washington, D.C.: Office of the Chief of Military History, Department of the Army, 1953.

Olson, James, ed. *Dictionary of the Vietnam War*. New York: Peter Bedrick Books, 1988.

Olson, John E. *Anywhere–Anytime: The History of the Fifty-seventh Infantry (PS)*. N.p.: Privately printed, 1991.

———. *O'Donnell: Andersonville of the Pacific*. N.p.: Privately printed, 1985.

Palmer, Gen. Bruce, Jr. *The 25-Year War: America's Military Role in Vietnam*. Lexington: University Press of Kentucky, 1984.

Palmer, Dave Richard. *Summons of the Trumpet: A History of the Vietnam War from a Military Man's Viewpoint*. New York: Ballantine Books, 1978.

The Pentagon Papers: The Defense Department History of United States Decision-making on Vietnam. Senator Gravel ed. 5 vols. Boston: Beacon Press, 1971.

Perry, Mark. *Four Stars*. Boston: Houghton Mifflin, 1989.

Pike, Douglas. *PAVN: People's Army of Vietnam*. Novato, Calif.: Presidio Press, 1986.

Prados, John. *The Hidden History of the Vietnam War*. Chicago: Ivan R. Dee, 1995.

Ridgway, Matthew B. *The Korean War*. Garden City, N.Y.: Doubleday, 1967.

Schandler, Herbert Y. *The Unmaking of a President: Lyndon Johnson and Vietnam*. Princeton, N.J.: Princeton University Press, 1977.

Schlight, John. *The War in South Vietnam: The Years of the Offensive, 1965–1968*. The United States Air Force in Southeast Asia. Washington, D.C.: Office of Air Force History, U.S. Air Force, 1988.

Shackley, Theodore. *The Third Option: An American View of Counterinsurgency Operations*. New York: Dell, 1981.

Shapley, Deborah. *Promise and Power: The Life and Times of Robert McNamara*. Boston: Little, Brown, 1993.

Sharp, Adm. U.S. Grant. *Strategy for Defeat: Vietnam in Retrospect*. San Rafael, Calif.: Presidio Press, 1978.

Shulimson, Jack. *U.S. Marines in Vietnam, 1968*. Washington, D.C.: Marine Corps Historical Center, 1995 ("For Comment" draft).

Sorley, Lewis. *Thunderbolt: General Creighton Abrams and the Army of His Times*. New York: Simon and Schuster, 1992.

Stanton, Shelby L. *The Rise and Fall of an American Army: U.S. Ground Forces in Vietnam, 1965-1973*. New York: Dell, 1985.

Summers, Harry G., Jr. *Historical Atlas of the Vietnam War*. Boston: Houghton Mifflin, 1995.

———. *On Strategy: The Vietnam War in Context.* Carlisle Barracks, Pa.: Strategic Studies Institute, U.S. Army War College [1981].

U.S. Corps of Cadets. *1933 Howitzer.* West Point, N.Y.: USCC, 1933.

Westmoreland, Gen. William C. *A Soldier Reports.* Garden City, N.Y.: Doubleday, 1976.

Whitman, John W. *Bataan: Our Last Ditch.* New York: Hippocrene, 1990.

Zaffiri, Samuel. *Westmoreland: A Biography of General William C. Westmoreland.* New York: Morrow, 1994.

Articles and Chapters

Birch, Harold. "Vietnam and the Gulf War: Comparing Decision-Making in America's Longest and Shortest Wars." In *The Presidency and the Persian Gulf War,* edited by Marcia Lynn Whicker, James P. Pfiffner, and Raymond A. Moore. Westport, Conn.: Praeger, 1993.

Blumenson, Martin. "A Most Remarkable Man." *Army* (August 1968): 18–26.

Borneman, Chaplain John K. "From Bataan through Cabanatuan." *Army and Navy Chaplain* (April–May 1946): 1–10. Reprint.

Bui Diem. "Reflections on the Vietnam War: The Views of a Vietnamese on Vietnamese-American Misconceptions." In *Looking Back on the Vietnam War,* edited by William Head and Lawrence E. Grinter. Westport, Conn.: Praeger, 1993.

Connor, Maj. Arthur W., Jr. "Breakout and Pursuit: The Drive from the Pusan Perimeter by the 1st Cavalry Division and Task Force Lynch." *Armor* (July–August 1993): 26–31.

Cushman, John H. "The Military Owes the President(s) More." Naval Institute *Proceedings* (July 1995): 8, 10.

Davis, Gen. Raymond G., USMC. "Politics and War: Twelve Fatal Decisions that Rendered Defeat in Vietnam." *Marine Corps Gazette* (August 1989): 75–78.

Johnson, Col. Harold. "Col. Harold Johnson Tells of 'Death Trip' from Manila to Korea." *Walsh Country Record* (Grafton, N.Dak.), 15 November 1945.

———. "Col. Johnson Tells about Death March, Atrocities in Jap Prisons." *Aberdeen American-News,* 9 November 1945.

Johnson, Lt. Col. H. K. "Defense along the Abucay Line." *Military Review* (February 1949): 43–52.

Johnson, Lt. Gen. Harold K. "Opportunities Unlimited." *Army* (June 1964): 28–32.

Johnson, Gen. Harold K. "The Enclave Concept: A 'License to Hunt.' " *Army* (April 1968): 16–17.

———. Foreword to *The U.S. Infantry: Queen of Battle,* ed. Col. Richard J. Stillman. New York: Franklin Watts [1965].

———. "Land Power!" *Army Information Digest* (August 1964): 8–15.

Meixsel, Richard B. "Major General George Grunert, WPO-3, and the Philippine Army, 1940-1941." *Journal of Military History* (April 1995): 303–24.

Olson, Col. John E. "USMA in the Philippines 1941-42." *Assembly* (July 1993): 10–25.

Perry, Mark. "Just for the Record." *Veteran* (December 1985): 10–11.
"Renaissance in the Ranks." *Time,* 10 December 1965, pp. 30–34.
Young, Stephen. "How North Vietnam Won the War." *Wall Street Journal,* 3
    August 1995.

Studies and Reports

Association of the United States Army. *The Early Stages of World War II.* AUSA
    Background Brief No. 39. Arlington, Va.: AUSA, March 1992.
——. *Korean War: The First Days of the Ground War.* AUSA Background Brief
    No. 41. Arlington, Va.: AUSA, March 1992.
——. *The U.S. Army Between World Wars I and II.* AUSA Background Brief
    No. 38. Arlington, Va.: AUSA, March 1992.
Bailey, Jennifer L. *Philippine Islands: The U.S. Army Campaigns of World War II.*
    CMH Publication 72-3. Washington, D.C.: U.S. Government Printing Office,
    1992.
Barnard, Talbott, comp. *The History of Fort Leavenworth, 1952–1963.* Fort
    Leavenworth, Kans.: U.S. Army Command and General Staff College, 1964.
Blumenson, Martin. *Reorganization of the Army, 1962.* Washington, D.C.: Depart-
    ment of the Army [1965].
Cass, Early Millard. *Ada Ball Cass: A Descendant of Captain Myles Standish.*
    New Castle, Pa.: Privately printed, 1949.
Department of the Army. *Korea—1950.* Washington, D.C.: Office of the Chief of
    Military History, Department of the Army, 1952.
——. *A Program for the Pacification and Long-Term Development of Vietnam
    (PROVN).* Washington, D.C.: Department of the Army, 1 March 1966.
Dobrinic, Maj. Matt P. "The Struggle for the Philippines, 7 Dec 1941–10 May
    1942." Fort Benning, Ga.: Military History Committee, The Infantry School,
    Advanced Officers Course 1946–1947.
Eckhardt, Maj. Gen. George S. *Command and Control, 1950–1969.* Vietnam
    Studies. Washington, D.C.: Department of the Army, 1974.
Gittenger, Ted, ed. *The Johnson Years: A Vietnam Roundtable.* Austin, Tex.: Lyn-
    don Baines Johnson Library, 1993.
Karpovich, B. *Sketches for Portraits: American Generals and Aggression in Viet-
    nam.* Znamya (Banner) No. 1, 1967. Moscow: Pravda Publishing House, Janu-
    ary 1967. Translation No. J-1737, Office of the Assistant Chief of Staff for
    Intelligence, Department of the Army, Washington, D.C., 20 February 1967.
Komer, R. W. *Organization and Management of the New Model Pacification Pro-
    gram, 1966–1969.* Santa Monica, Calif.: Rand Corporation, 7 May 1970.
Lung, Col. Hoang Ngoc. *Strategy and Tactics.* Indochina Monograph. Washing-
    ton, D.C.: U.S. Army Center of Military History, 1980.
Palmer, Gen. Bruce, Jr. "US Intelligence and Vietnam." *Studies in Intelligence*
    (Special Issue). Washington, D.C.: Central Intelligence Agency, 1984.
Rosson, Gen. W. B. *Assessment of Influence Exerted on Military Operations by
    Other than Military Considerations.* Headquarters, U.S. Army Pacific, 1970.
    Republished, Washington, D.C.: U.S. Army Center of Military History, 1993.

Rowny, Lt. Gen. Edward L. *Engineer Memoirs*. Alexandria, Va.: Office of History, U.S. Army Corps of Engineers, 1995.

Sparrow, Herbert G. *The Times of Our Lives: Story of a West Point Class*. N.p.: Privately printed, 1983.

Tolson, Lt. Gen. John J. *Airmobility 1961-1971*. Washington, D.C.: Department of the Army, 1989. Reprint of 1973 publication.

Documents

Abrams Papers, Creighton. U.S. Army Military History Institute, Carlisle Barracks, Pa.

Association of Graduates, United States Military Academy. *Register of Graduates and Former Cadets*. West Point, N.Y.: AOG, various years.

Bodine, Roy L. *No Place for Kindness: The Prisoner of War Diary of Roy L. Bodine*. Fort Sam Houston, Tex.: Fort Sam Houston Museum, 1983.

Bunker, Ambassador Ellsworth. Oral History (unpublished transcript). Interview by Stephen Young.

Johnson, Lt. Col. Harold K. "Defense of the Philippine Islands, Anyasen and Silaiim Points, Bataan: Personal Experience of a Regimental S-3, 57th Infantry (PS)." Typescript report. Fort Leavenworth, Kans.: School of Combined Arms Regular Course 1946-1947, Command and Staff College.

Johnson, Maj. Gen. Harold K. *Addresses*. Fort Leavenworth, Kans.: Combined Arms Research Library, n.d.

Johnson, Gen. Harold K. *Challenge: Compendium of Army Accomplishment: A Report by the Chief of Staff: July 1964-April 1968*. Washington, D.C.: Department of the Army, 1 July 1968.

————. Personnel records. National Personnel Record Center, St. Louis, Mo.

U.S. Congress. Senate. Committee on Armed Services, Preparedness Investigating Subcommittee. "Air War against North Vietnam," Hearings, 90th Cong., 1st sess., August 1967. Washington, D.C.: U.S. Government Printing Office, 1967.

————. Committee on Armed Services. "Nomination of Lt. Gen. Harold K. Johnson to be Chief of Staff, Army," Hearing, 88th Cong., 2d sess., 2 July 1964. Washington, D.C.: U.S. Government Printing Office, 1964.

Vietnam: A Documentary Collection: Westmoreland vs. CBS. New York: Clearwater Publishing, 1985. Microform.

Other Sources

INTERVIEWS CONDUCTED

Julia Harvey Abrams, Stephen Ailes, Carol Wilson Alexander, Lieutenant General Elmer H. Almquist, Jr., Colonel Francis R. Baker, Brigadier General Raymond E. Bell, Jr., General Donald V. Bennett, Betty Wheeler Besson, Vice Admiral Thomas J. Bigley, Brigadier General Donald D. Blackburn, Charles V. Boykin, Brigadier General Zeb B. Bradford, Jr., General Arthur E. Brown, Jr., Major General Charles E. Brown, Jr., Lieutenant General Frederic J. Brown, Colonel John Wilson Calloway, Brigadier

General Thomas J. Camp, Jr., Major General George A. Carver, Colonel George Chase, Lieutenant Colonel Roger Cirillo, Major General Richard L. Clutterbuck (British Army), Colonel Charles H. Coates, Jr., Colonel Eugene R. Cocke, Lieutenant General Charles G. Cooper (USMC), Lieutenant General Charles A. Corcoran, Colonel Maury S. Cralle, Lieutenant General John H. Cushman, Major General Chester A. Dahlen, Lieutenant General Phillip B. Davidson, Jr., General Michael S. Davison, Colonel Earle L. Denton, Colonel Melville A. Drisko, Jr., Lieutenant General John H. Elder, Jr., Command Sergeant Major Anthony Ferrelli, Lieutenant General Harvey H. Fischer, Brigadier General Roy K. Flint, Lieutenant Colonel John R. Flynn, Brigadier General Stephen O. Fuqua, Jr., Colonel Robert J. Gerard, Major General George A. Godding, General Andrew J. Goodpaster, Brigadier General Michael J. L. Greene, General Wallace M. Greene, Jr. (USMC), Colonel David Hackworth, General Ralph E. Haines, Jr., Brigadier General Archelaus L. Hamblen, Jr., Colonel William A. Hamilton, Colonel Thomas J. Hanifen, Helen Kostecki Hannett, Colonel William S. Hathaway, Dr. William L. Helkie, Colonel Morris J. Herbert, Sergeant First Class Harvey C. Hill, Edna Ray Johnson Hinman, Brigadier General Elizabeth P. Hoisington, Lieutenant General Oren E. Hurlbut, Colonel Thomas G. Irwin, Major General Bruce Jacobs, Brigadier General John H. Johns, Major General Chester L. Johnson, Dorothy Rennix Johnson, Harold K. Johnson, Jr., Herbert T. Johnson, Robert J. Johnson, William L. Jones, Sergeant First Class Frank X. Kaiser, Colonel John B. Keeley, Ellen Kay Johnson Kern, James C. Kern, Lieutenant General Nguyen Khanh (ARVN), Admiral Isaac C. Kidd, Jr., Brigadier General Joseph C. Kiefe, Jr., Brigadier General Albion W. Knight, Jr., General William A. Knowlton, Clarence K. Larson, Major General Richard M. Lee, Colonel William E. LeGro, Janet Johnson Levy, Lieutenant General Lawrence J. Lincoln, Major William W. Little, Sergeant Major George E. Loikow, Colonel Andrew J. Mansinne, Colonel Donald S. Marshall, Colonel Orville W. Martin, Jr., Lieutenant General Dennis P. McAuliffe, David E. McGiffert, Robert S. McNamara, Lieutenant General John B. McPherson (USAF), General Edward C. Meyer, Brigadier General Robert M. Montague, Jr., Admiral Thomas H. Moorer, Colonel Murl D. Munger, Colonel John W. Myers, Mona K. Nason, Brigadier General John W. Nicholson, Lieutenant General William E. Odom, Colonel John E. Olson, General Bruce Palmer, Jr., Lieutenant General Dave R. Palmer, Mark Perry, Brigadier General Paul D. Phillips, John Pickering, Brigadier General James Piner, Jr., Lieutenant General William E. Potts, Lieutenant General William W. Quinn, Major General Lloyd Ramsey, Colonel Raymond Renola, Brigadier General Royal Reynolds, Jr., General Bernard W. Rogers, General William B. Rosson, Lieutenant General Edward L. Rowny, Anthony J. Savello, Colonel Herbert Y. Schandler, Colonel Fred B. Schoomaker, Colonel Edson Schull, Colonel Frederic J. Schweiger, Brigadier General Richard P. Scott, James B. T. Sebolka, Colonel Robert Segal, General Robert W. Sennewald, Dr. Harry J. Shaw, John J. Shay, Eleanor Sibley, Colonel John D. Sitterson, Jr., Colonel John F. Sloan, Lieutenant General DeWitt C. Smith, Jr., Meredith L. Smith, Major General Herbert G. Sparrow, Major General Charles E. Spragins, General Donn A. Starry, Colonel Harry J. Stempin, Wendy Wilson Sticht, Major General Adrian St. John, General Maxwell R. Thurman, Lieutenant General Thomas J. H. Trapnell, Colonel Albert F. Turner, Colonel John H. VonDerBruegge, Major General Clifton F. von Kann, Colonel Neil M. Wallace, General Volney F. Warner, Brigadier General Charles West, Lieutenant

General Richard L. West, Dr. Gilmore S. Wheeler, Colonel William M. Whitesel, General John A. Wickham, Jr., Nils F. Wikner, Major General Ellis W. Williamson, Charles E. Wilson, Sergeant Major of the Army William O. Wooldridge, General James K. Woolnough, Lieutenant General William P. Yarborough, Colonel Frederick J. Yeager, Brigadier General Kenneth F. Zitzman.

MHI ORAL HISTORY INTERVIEWS CONSULTED

General Paul D. Adams, General Dwight E. Beach, General Donald V. Bennett, General Frank S. Besson, Jr., Lieutenant General Austin W. Betts, General George S. Blanchard, Colonel Delbert Bristol, Major General Charles E. Brown, Jr., Lieutenant General Robert E. Coffin, Lieutenant General Alva R. Fitch, Lieutenant General Hobart R. Gay, General Ralph E. Haines, Jr., General Hamilton H. Howze, General Harold K. Johnson, Lieutenant General H. W. O. Kinnard, General William A. Knowlton, Lieutenant General Harry Lemley, Major General Delk Oden, General William B. Rosson, Lieutenant General George P. Seneff, General John L. Throckmorton, Lieutenant General John J. Tolson III, Lieutenant General Walter F. Ulmer, Jr., General Volney F. Warner, Lieutenant General Robert R. Williams, General James K. Woolnough, Lieutenant General John M. Wright, Jr.

OTHER ORAL HISTORY INTERVIEWS CONSULTED

Ambassador Ellsworth Bunker, LBJ Library; General Leonard F. Chapman, USMC, MCHC; General Harold Keith Johnson, CMH; General Harold K. Johnson, Freedoms Foundation at Valley Forge (copy in MHI); General Walter T. Kerwin, Jr., LBJ Library; Ambassador Robert Komer, LBJ Library; General John P. McConnell, USAF, LBJ Library; Stanley R. Resor, LBJ Library; General Earle G. Wheeler, LBJ Library; Lieutenant General Samuel T. Williams, LBJ Library.

ACKNOWLEDGMENTS

During the course of earlier research for a biography of General Creighton Abrams, I learned a great deal about General Harold K. Johnson, especially in the three years when Johnson was the Army's Chief of Staff and Abrams his Vice Chief. The two could not have been more different in personality, yet—according to both men and all who saw them operate—they established a famous friendship and gave the Army a superb leadership team.

As a lieutenant colonel assigned to the Office of the Chief of Staff just at the end of General Johnson's tenure, I had a brief glimpse of him in action, and during my years as a soldier, I had several occasions to see what Abrams was like. As I thought about the basis for their close relationship, it became clear that it was a congruence of outlook, shared values and shared commitment, that brought them together. These included personal qualities of selflessness, modesty, devotion to duty, loyalty, and competence, expressed in love of the soldier, the Army, the country, and family, all fiercely felt, all faithfully served. As I neared completion of the work on Abrams, I determined that a book on Harold K. Johnson would be next.

There was a complication, however. A professor at the small college in southern Virginia where the Johnsons' son Bobby was the basketball coach had become interested in General Johnson and was in fact at work on his story. I did not feel that I could horn in there, nor did I want to compete with another scholar to undertake the project. Thus I spun my wheels for a year or two on a couple of other projects, but in my head I kept thinking about Harold K. Johnson. When the professor was offered, and accepted, the presidency of an Illinois college, leaving him no time to pursue the research, the way was cleared and I thankfully began work on the Johnson story.

In the intervening four years, I have been back to many familiar places, for the span of the professional careers of Johnson and Abrams was very similar, both men having their first significant battle experiences in World War II, both rising to prominence in the difficult era of the Vietnam War. Once again, then, I made repeated visits to the Lyndon Baines Johnson Library in Austin, a wonderful place for a researcher to work. The staff there again helped me in many ways, from access to documents, papers, and oral histories to selections from their robust collection of photographs, as well as invitations to attend pertinent conferences sponsored by the library. I thank particularly Director Harry Middleton, Ted Gittenger, Regina Greenwell, Linda Hanson, Michael Parrish, John Wilson, and Philip Scott.

Again of particular importance were the superb holdings of the U.S. Army Military History Institute at Carlisle Barracks, Pennsylvania. There, with the scholarly hospitality and expert help of Dr. Richard Sommers, Chief Archivist, and his associates David Keough and Pam Cheney, I worked with the extensive collection of oral histories and—centrally important to this study—the papers of General Johnson, all 149 boxes of them. The most candid and honest of men, General Johnson even included his personal income tax returns for his years as Chief of Staff in the papers on deposit. Making my way through this treasure trove took most of a year, during which I also benefited from the professional assistance of many other members of the MHI staff, including Colonel Stephen L. Bowman, then Director of the Institute; Library Director John Slonaker, Louise Arnold-Friend, Kathleen Gildersleeve, Michelle Stalnecker, Dennis Vetock, and other members of his staff; Michael Winey and Randy Hackenburg, who preside over the audiovisual collection, which includes valuable recordings of talks by General Johnson; and especially Randy Rakers, the energetic and able security manager. Also at Carlisle Barracks, the U.S. Army War College Library proved a valuable resource, thanks to the friendly and expert assistance of Jane Gibish and Lydia Gole.

The U.S. Army Center of Military History assisted at several points during the research, and I thank Brigadier General John W. Mountcastle, the Army's Chief of Military History; Dr. Jeffrey J. Clarke, Chief Historian; and Drs. John M. Carland, Richard A. Hunt, and William M. Hammond for their help.

General Wallace M. Greene, Jr., former Commandant of the Marine Corps, generously allowed me the use of his papers on deposit at the Marine Corps Historical Center. I am also grateful for the assistance of Brigadier General Edwin H. Simmons, Dr. Jack Shulimson, Fred Graboske, and other members of the staff.

I consulted at several points with Brigadier General David A. Armstrong, Chief of the Joint Chiefs of Staff Historical Office, and with Dr. Walter S. Poole of his staff. My thanks to them, and to Commander Moira Wuertzel of the Joint Staff, who helped me gain access to the recently declassified Joint Chiefs of Staff History covering the period of my interest.

The Combined Arms Research Library at Fort Leavenworth, Kansas, made available unique materials relating to General Johnson's tenure as Commandant of the U.S. Army Command & General Staff College, for which I thank Karla C. Norman, Archives Librarian, and Elaine McConnell.

At West Point I found valuable material in the U.S. Military Academy Library's Special Collections, presided over by Alan Aimone with help from Judith Sibley; in the USMA Archives, where Suzanne Christoff and Alicia Mauldin assisted me; and in the Office of the Registrar, USMA, where Lieutenant Colonel James H. McEliece and Joanne Rera were very helpful. Colonel Seth F. Hudgins, Jr., President of West Point's Association of Graduates, also provided valuable materials. My friend Colonel Morris J. Herbert, a venerable member of the Association's staff, helped in innumerable ways throughout the project. Colonel Julian M. Olejniczak, Editor-in-Chief of *Assembly*, West Point's alumni magazine, was also very supportive.

My particular thanks to William Seibert, a superb archivist at the National Personnel Records Center in St. Louis. He made an invaluable find during my earlier research on General Creighton Abrams and again assisted me greatly during my research on General Johnson's career.

The Old Guard Museum at Fort Myer, Virginia, current home of Johnson's first outfit, the 3d Infantry, provided copies of orders pertaining to his assignment to the regiment, for which I thank Curator Robert C. Alley and Alan Bogan. Thanks also to Richard M. Barone, Reference Librarian at the Donovan Technical Library of the U.S. Army Infantry School at Fort Benning, Georgia; Mikki C. Lott at the Pentagon Phone Center; Sergeant Major Michael Lowery of the Army Staff, British Embassy, Washington; George Ehling at the Association of the United States Army; and Sergeant Temple Ferrell of the Army's General Officer Management Office in the Pentagon.

Through the courtesy of Lieutenant General Paul G. Cerjan, former President of the National Defense University, I was able to use the outstanding facilities of the NDU Library. Thanks to Lieutenant Colonel David Robinson for administrative help, and to Susan Lemke of Special Collections and other members of the staff for their good counsel.

No scholar working in the period of the Vietnam War can fail to acknowledge the superb volumes prepared by Professor William Conrad Gibbons, valuable for making accessible so much documentation on the war and for insightful commentary, logical structure, and catholicity of sources.

I am grateful for the loan of personal papers and unpublished manuscripts by Brigadier General Zeb B. Bradford, Jr., the late General Ferdinand J. Chesarek, Lieutenant General John H. Cushman, Dr. Donald S. Marshall, Lieutenant General Harris W. Hollis, Major H. R. McMaster, Dr. Harry J. Shaw, and Major General Ellis W. Williamson, and for the use of Dr. William A. Hamilton's dissertation. Of particular importance was the unpublished oral history transcript of interviews with Ambassador Ellsworth Bunker generously made available by Stephen B. Young. I appreciate Dr. Gilmore S. Wheeler's lending me a fascinating Soviet document, B. Karpovich's *Sketches for Portraits,* containing analyses of several American general officers. The Johnson family also made available selected letters of General Johnson. Eunice Biggar Anders and Marion Presler lent splendid photographs from the collection of the late Lieutenant Colonel Franklin O. Anders.

Some 150 people provided invaluable assistance by allowing me to interview them, often on multiple occasions, and I express my deepest thanks to them all. Their recollections and insights have enriched the account delightfully.

Once again, Albert D. McJoynt assisted me by preparing excellent maps. Many people helped by responding to queries, including Colonel James H. Aarestad, Colonel Dale E. Buchanan, Maxine Clark, Colonel Charles H. Coates, Jr., Patricia Coates, Lieutenant General Robert E. Coffin, Colonel Maury S. Cralle, Colonel Maury S. Cralle, Jr., Colonel Wesley J. Curtis, the late Lieutenant General Phillip B. Davidson, Jr., Colonel William B. DeGraf, Sergeant First Class George H. DeLapp, Colonel Louis R. Delmonico, Pauline McDonald Dolph, John Eddleman, Rhonda Evans, Major General George A. Godding, Brigadier General Samuel McC. Goodwin, Major General John S. Guthrie, Colonel Thomas J. Hanifen, the late Colonel William S. Hathaway, Colonel Richard L. Hunt, Colonel Thomas G. Irwin, Major General Chester L. Johnson, William L. Jones, Sergeant First Class Frank X. Kaiser, Brigadier General Joseph C. Kiefe, Jr., Brigadier General Douglas Kinnard, Clarence K. Larson, Sergeant Major George E. Loikow, Major General William J. Maddox, Jr., Dr. Donald S. Marshall, Kenneth Ward Miller, Mona K. Nason, Brigadier General John W. Nicholson, John A. Patterson, Mark Perry, Brigadier General Paul D. Phillips, Dr. Douglas Pike, Brigadier General James Piner, Jr., Major General Louis W. Prentiss, Jr., General William B. Rosson, Lieutenant Colonel Robert F. Sawallesh, Colonel Fred B. Schoomaker, Brigadier General Richard P. Scott, Elinor J. Sibley, Brigadier General Wilfred K. G. Smith, Colonel John C. Snodgrass, Wendy Wilson Sticht, Major General John C. F. Tillson III, Lieutenant General William F. Train, Colonel Albert F. Turner, Major General Clifton F. von Kann, Sergeant Major of the Army William O. Wooldridge, Major General Frederick R. Zierath, and Brigadier General Kenneth F. Zitzman.

Lieutenant General Dave R. Palmer, a valued friend since cadet days, provided wise counsel and encouragement all along the way. Lieutenant

General Frederic J. Brown III, also a close friend since West Point, helped me get up and running with a computer setup I could handle, then served cheerfully as a knowledgeable guru. Colonel David D. Farnham, longtime friend and colleague, has been with me all the way. Colonel John E. Olson was particularly helpful with the Philippine period, to which he has devoted many years of study. Edna Ray Hinman, General Johnson's sister, functions as the family historian and provided much useful information, as did Major General Herbert G. Sparrow, Scribe of the West Point Class of 1933. Major H. R. McMaster, a brilliant young scholar and superb soldier, was very generous in sharing pertinent research materials, becoming in the process a valued friend. I have also benefited from the support of John A. Baird, Martin Blumenson, Dr. Robert Buzzanco, Douglas A. S. Chalmers, Judith Sorley Chalmers, Colonel Paul W. Child, Jr., the late Ambassador William E. Colby, Major General Eugene Fox, General John R. Galvin, General Andrew J. Goodpaster, Richard Halloran, the late Major General Frank B. Horton III (USAF), Elizabeth Sorley Lyon, Colonel John J. Madigan III, Colonel O. W. Martin, Jr., Colonel Lloyd J. Matthews, Colonel Paul L. Miles, Jr., the late Colonel Roger H. Nye, Rudy L. Ruggles, Jr., Captain Richard U. Scott (USN), Lieutenant General DeWitt C. Smith, Jr., Colonel Harry G. Summers, Jr., Lieutenant General Herbert R. Temple, Jr., Lieutenant General Walter F. Ulmer, and Charles E. Wilson.

In a special category is General Bruce Palmer, Jr., an officer whose example and friendship have been very important to me over the years and who provided invaluable insight into the many complex issues that confronted General Johnson.

Of particular importance, too, was the help of three officers who carefully reviewed the manuscript in draft form and provided many helpful comments and suggestions. My sincere thanks to General Volney F. Warner, General John A. Wickham, Jr., and Lieutenant General Sidney B. Berry, Jr. Subsequently, Professor George C. Herring and Colonel Harry G. Summers, Jr., read the completed manuscript and made many useful suggestions. Michael Briggs, Editor-in-Chief at the University Press of Kansas, was the very model of an efficient, considerate, and supportive editor.

I want to close by saying that, again and always, my gratitude to my wife, Virginia Mezey Sorley, is beyond words.

INDEX